Treating Traumatized Childı ⌐..

While recent years have seen a vast increase in the literature on adult trauma, interest in childhood trauma has only recently started to gain momentum, encouraging new research and evidence-based interventions.

Here the editors have brought together an international list of contributors to look at both innovative and established treatments of trauma in a range of contexts, and provide up-to-date coverage of what is on offer in prevention, assessment, treatment, and research.

Main topics discussed in the three parts of the book are:

- risk and protective factors for the development of posttraumatic disorders
- conceptualizations of resilience and suggestions for making them operational
- evidence-based treatment models for traumatized children.

Treating Traumatized Children provides professionals with an up-to-date international perspective on the subject, as well as helping professionals and researchers develop future treatments based on current evidence.

Danny Brom is a Clinical Psychologist and founding Director of the Israel Center for the Treatment of Psychotrauma at Herzog Hospital in Jerusalem and lecturer at the School of Social Work of the Hebrew University. His main interest and experience are in the prevention and treatment of, and research on the consequences of traumatic stress.

Ruth Pat-Horenczyk is a Clinical Psychologist and Director of the Child and Adolescent Clinical Services at the Israel Center for the Treatment of Psychotrauma at Herzog Hospital in Jerusalem. She is also a lecturer at the School of Social Work of the Hebrew University.

Julian D. Ford is a Clinical Psychologist and Associate Professor in the Department of Psychiatry at the University of Connecticut School of Medicine and Health Center. He is also the founding Director of the Center for Trauma Response, Recovery and Preparedn

Treating Traumatized Children

Risk, resilience, and recovery

Edited by Danny Brom,
Ruth Pat-Horenczyk, and
Julian D. Ford

Routledge
Taylor & Francis Group

LONDON AND NEW YORK

First published 2009
by Routledge
27 Church Road, Hove, East Sussex BN3 2FA

Simultaneously published in the USA and Canada
by Routledge
711 Third Ave, New York, NY 10017

Routledge is an imprint of the Taylor & Francis Group, an Informa business

Typeset in Times by RefineCatch Limited, Bungay, Suffolk
Paperback cover design by Andy Ward

British Library Cataloguing in Publication Data
A catalogue record for this book is available from the British Library

Library of Congress Cataloging-in-Publication Data
Treating traumatized children: risk, resilience, and recovery/edited
by Danny Brom, Ruth Pat-Horenczyk, and Julian Ford.
    p. cm.
    Includes bibliographical references.
    ISBN 978–0–415–42636–7 (hardback)—ISBN 978–0–415–47150–3
(pbk.)
    1. Post-traumatic stress disorder in children—Treatment.
    2. Psychic trauma in children—Treatment. 3. Resilience
(Personality trait) in children. I. Brom, D. II. Pat-Horenczyk, Ruth.
III. Ford, Julian D.
    RJ506.P55T75 2008
    618.92′8521—dc22   2008003888

ISBN: 978-0-415-42636-7 (hbk)
ISBN: 978-0-415-47150-3 (pbk)

For our parents

Golda and Mordechai Brom
Hanna and Akiva Pat
Anne and Jim Ford

our models for resilience and care for children

Contents

Notes on the editors
and contributors

Danny Brom is a Clinical Psychologist and founding Director of the Israel
Center for the Treatment of Psychotrauma at Herzog Hospital in Jerusa-
lem, Israel. His main interest and experience are the prevention and
treatment of, and research on the consequences of traumatic stress.
Dr. Brom has worked in the field of traumatic stress since 1979 in the
Netherlands and was the Director of the Dutch Institute of Psychotrauma
from 1985 until 1988. In 1989 he was appointed Director of the Latner
Institute for Research in Social Psychiatry and Psychotherapy at Herzog
Hospital in Jerusalem. In addition, he was Director of Research at
Amcha, the Israeli National Center for Psychosocial Support of Survivors
of the Holocaust and the Second Generation from 1994 until 2000. Since
1997 he has been the Chairman of the Committee of Appeal of the Dutch
Holocaust Reparation Authority in Israel. Dr. Brom has taught at the
Hebrew University since 1998 at the Department of Clinical Psychology
and the Department of Social Work. In 1990 he received, together with
Dr. Rolf Kleber, the Award of the Dutch Academy of Sciences for the
best summary article in the Social Sciences. He has published numerous
articles and chapters. His books include *The trauma of terrorism: Sharing
knowledge and shared care – An international handbook*, co-edited by
Yael Danieli and Joe Sills (Haworth 2005), and *Coping with trauma: Consequences, prevention and treatment*, co-authored with Rolf Kleber (Taylor
and Francis 1992). He has been active in training mental health professionals in different countries. Since 1999 he has been Director of the Israel
Center for the Treatment of Psychotrauma in Jerusalem, which seeks to
raise the level of trauma-related services in Israel. He is co-founder of the
Israel Trauma Coalition, which he initiated together with UJA-Federation
of New York.

Ruth Pat-Horenczyk is a Clinical Psychologist, Director of the Child and
Adolescent Clinical Services at the Israel Center for the Treatment of
Psychotrauma of Herzog Hospital in Jerusalem, Israel and a lecturer at
the School of Social Work of the Hebrew University. She received her PhD

in Psychology from the Hebrew University and completed her post-doctoral training at the University of California in San Diego. In previous years she was involved in clinical research and teaching work in several areas of behavioral medicine, such as sleep medicine and eating disorders. In the last few years she has been conducting a nationwide screening project aimed at posttraumatic distress among children and adolescents and providing school-based group interventions for those in need. Recently, the screening and intervention project has been applied in Palestinian schools in collaboration with mental health and educational professionals. In collaboration with child-trauma experts at Mt. Sinai School of Medicine in New York, Dr. Pat-Horenczyk initiated and directs a multi-site early childhood project aimed at building resilience in parents and toddlers exposed to ongoing terrorism and war. Additionally she is collaborating with researchers from Columbia University on the development of measures to assess flexibility and resilience. She leads an ongoing interest group for mental health professionals on the treatment of traumatized children and adolescents. She has published a variety of articles and chapters in the field of child trauma and presented clinical material and research at numerous international conferences.

Julian D. Ford is a Clinical Psychologist and Associate Professor in the Department of Psychiatry at the University of Connecticut School of Medicine and Health Center. Dr. Ford is the founding Director of the Center for Trauma Response, Recovery and Preparedness, which provides public and professional resources and technical assistance to mental health, health care, education, and faith-based responders serving survivors and family members in the wake of disaster, terrorism, and family and community violence (www.ctrp.org). He serves as a Senior Academic Fellow for the Child Health and Development Institute and the Center for Effective Practice in Child Behavioral Health. Dr. Ford has developed and is working with colleagues in Connecticut, nationally, and internationally on the evaluation and dissemination of the Trauma Affect Regulation: Guide for Education and Therapy (TARGET: www.advancedtrauma.com) model for enhancing self-regulation as a method of prevention and treatment of posttraumatic and developmental traumatic stress disorders with adults, children, and families. Relevant recent publications include "Altered attachment, affect regulation, and information processing as the core biopsychosocial sequelae of child maltreatment: Review and implications for psychiatric treatment," *Psychiatric Annals* (May 2005) and "Treatment of complex posttraumatic self-dysregulation," *Journal of Traumatic Stress* (October 2005).

David B. Albert is a licensed Clinical Psychologist and Assistant Professor of Psychiatry at the University of Connecticut Health Center (UCHC). Dr. Albert is Director of Child and Adolescent Ambulatory Psychiatry at UCHC. Dr. Albert's research interests have focused on the epidemiology of PTSD and severe mental disorders, and more recently on the impact of chronic maltreatment on child development. Prior to joining the Department of Psychiatry at the UCHC, Dr. Albert was responsible for the design and implementation of an agency-wide Trauma Initiative at the Connecticut Department of Children and Families (DCF).

Thomas Babayan served as a lecturer for the Department of English at University of California, Irvine (UCI) before earning his MS in Counseling from California State University, Long Beach. He currently heads the SPIRIT Program at UCI, an academic outreach initiative helping young people in underserved communities, and works as a Marriage and Family Therapist Intern in Long Beach, CA.

William R. Beardslee is the George P. Gardner and Olga E. Monks Professor of Child Psychiatry at Harvard Medical School and Academic Chairman of the Department of Psychiatry at the Children's Hospital. His primary interests are in the prevention of depression in families and in how to enhance resilience in those undergoing adverse circumstances, about which he has published extensively.

Callie J. Beck is currently an undergraduate student at Brigham Young University. She plans to pursue a doctoral degree in clinical psychology.

Antonia Bifulco is a psychology professor, heading the Lifespan Research Group at Royal Holloway, University of London, researching social causes of psychological disorders over the lifespan and intergenerationally. This includes adversity and trauma as well as attachment style, self-esteem and support. She is engaged in "knowledge exchange" to extend research dissemination to community and professional groups of psychologists and social workers.

Esther Cohen (Michigan State University, 1973) is a faculty member and the former head of the Child-Clinical Psychology Program at the Hebrew University of Jerusalem, Israel. She is a clinical psychologist and family therapist with thirty years of experience in treating traumatized children. Her main publications focus on the parenthood experience and on the effects of exposure to terrorism on children and families.

Ruth DeRosa is a Consultant to North Shore University Hospital on trauma treatment grants in Manhasset, NY. She is also Co-Director of Cognitive Behavioral Associates, LLP, a center specializing in Dialectical Behavior Therapy for adults, adolescents, and their families. In addition to publishing on traumatic stress, she has conducted multidisciplinary trainings around the country with agencies adopting trauma-focused evidence-based treatments.

B. Heidi Ellis is a licensed Clinical Psychologist and Instructor of Psychiatry at Children's Hospital Boston, Harvard Medical School, Boston, MA. Dr. Ellis' primary focus is on the development and dissemination of interventions for refugee children and their families. She has also conducted research with the Somali community on issues of stigma, mental health, and service utilization.

Paul Geltman works in clinical, policy, and public health settings with refugee populations. His publications have investigated poverty and child health, refugee and immigrant health epidemiology, and community-based oral health prevention projects, and the prevention of iron deficiency anemia among low-income infants. Dr. Geltman published the most extensive report on lead poisoning among refugee children and was principal investigator of a nationwide study of health outcomes in Sudanese unaccompanied refugee minors.

Wanda Grant-Knight is a Clinical Psychologist whose publications and clinical activities investigate the impact of trauma in diverse child and adolescent populations, including immigrants and refugees, and currently, children adjusting to traumatic injury and disability. In her refugee work, Dr. Grant-Knight developed and coordinated the Refugee Trauma Program at Boston Medical Center, which was part of the National Child Traumatic Stress Network.

Josephine Hawke is Assistant Professor in the Department of Psychiatry at the University of Connecticut Health Center. Dr. Hawke's work focuses on the effects of trauma, violence and childhood abuse on drug use and mental health outcomes, and currently on clinical research into evidence-based services for adolescents.

Stevan E. Hobfoll is Distinguished Professor of Psychology and Director of the Summa-KSU Center for the Treatment and Study of Traumatic Stress and the Applied Psychology Center at Kent State University. He is the author of *The ecology of stress and stress culture and community: The psychology and philosophy of stress* (Hemisphere 1988). His Conservation of Resources (COR) theory is one of the most cited theories in stress, ranging from burnout at work to severe trauma.

Patricia Van Horn is Associate Clinical Professor in the Department of Psychiatry, University of California San Francisco (UCSF), and Associate Director of the Child Trauma Research Project, located at San Francisco General Hospital.

Katie J. Horsey is a graduate student in the Clinical Psychology Doctoral Program at Kent State University. She completed her undergraduate work at Portland State University and is pursuing her PhD with a specific interest in stress and trauma research and interventions.

Joop de Jong is Professor of Mental Health and Culture at the Vrije University in Amsterdam and Adjunct Professor of Psychiatry at Boston University Medical School. He is Medical Director of the Municipal Health Services of Amsterdam. In the past, he was the founding Director of the Transcultural Psychosocial Organization, a non-governmental organization that developed psychosocial and mental health programs in Africa, Asia, Europe and Latin America. Professor Jong publishes in the fields of cultural psychiatry and psychotherapy, public mental health, medical anthropology and epidemiology.

Mark D. Jordans holds a degree in Developmental Psychology from Leiden University. He works as a technical advisor for HealthNet TPO and is a PhD candidate at the Vrije University, Amsterdam. His work has concentrated on the development of long-term training courses in psychosocial interventions and on the development, adaptation and implementation of comprehensive psychosocial care systems from a transcultural perspective.

Richard Kagan is the author and co-author of six books and over twenty articles on child and family services, trauma therapy, foster care, and adoption, including *Rebuilding attachments with traumatized children* (Haworth 2004), *Real life heroes: A life storybook for children* (Haworth 2004) and *Real life heroes: Practitioner's manual* (Haworth 2007). Dr. Kagan's presentations, articles, and books highlight practical and innovative approaches that practitioners can utilize to help traumatized children and families.

Miri Keren is a lecturer, head of Early Childhood Psychiatry Course, continuing education school, Sackler Medical School, Tel Aviv University, and President of the Israeli Affiliate of the World Association for Infant Mental Health.

Rolf Kleber is Professor of Clinical and Health Psychology at the University of Utrecht, the Netherlands. He was among the founders of the Dutch Institute for Psychotrauma. He leads a variety of studies into the consequences of disaster and war, the prediction of posttraumatic problems, and the efficacy of intervention and counseling programs.

Brittain E. Lamoureux is a student in the Clinical Psychology Doctoral Program at Kent State University. She completed her undergraduate work in anthropology and women's studies at the University of Georgia and received her master's degree in psychology from New York University in 2005. She is particularly interested in the impact of trauma on interpersonal relationships.

Christopher M. Layne is currently Director of Treatment and Intervention Development at the UCLA National Center for Child Traumatic Stress.

His research interests include clinical assessment, test construction, research design, and the treatment of adolescents exposed to traumatic stress and bereavement.

Patricia Lester is a board-certified child and adolescent psychiatrist, and the Medical Director of the UCLA Child and Family Trauma Psychiatry Service. Dr. Lester has extensive experience in developing, implementing, and evaluating clinical interventions for high-risk families, such as an ongoing family-based intervention replication trial for mothers with HIV and their children, which was evaluated in a randomized controlled trial.

Alicia F. Lieberman holds the Irving B. Harris Endowed Chair in Infant Mental Health at the UCSF Department of Psychiatry, where she is Professor, Vice-Chair for Academic Affairs, and Director of the Child Trauma Research Project at San Francisco General Hospital. Her research involves treatment outcome studies with infants, toddlers, and preschoolers from low-income and under-represented minority groups.

Donald Meichenbaum is Distinguished Professor Emeritus, University of Waterloo, Waterloo, Ontario, Canada, and Research Director of the Melissa Institute for Violence Prevention and Treatment of Victims of Violence, Miami, Florida.

Marko A. Moreno received his undergraduate degree from Brigham Young University in 2007. He is a student in the Clinical Psychology Doctoral Program at the University of Buffalo, State University of New York (SUNY), where he plans to conduct research relating to traumatic stress.

David Pelcovitz holds the Gwendolyn and Joseph Straus Chair in Psychology and Education at Yeshiva University. Before assuming his position on the faculty of Yeshiva University, Dr. Pelcovitz was Director of Psychology at North Shore University Hospital-NYU School of Medicine. He has published and lectured extensively on a variety of topics involving PTSD in children and adults.

Robert S. Pynoos is Professor of Psychiatry in Residence and Director of the Trauma Psychiatry Program at the Jane and Terry Semel Institute of Neuroscience and Human Behavior at UCLA. Dr. Pynoos leads and coordinates a nationwide network of academic and community-based centers dedicated to raising the standard of care and improving access to services for traumatized children, families, and communities throughout the United States.

Renee G. Rabinowitz is a psychologist and a lawyer. She received her PhD from the University of Chicago and her law degree from Notre Dame University. She taught Psychology at Indiana University and later served as Legal Counsel at Colorado College. She currently lives in Jerusalem and is a professional volunteer at the Israel Center for the Treatment of Psychotrauma.

Ria Reis is Associate Professor in Medical Anthropology at the University of Amsterdam and Director of the Amsterdam Master's in Medical Anthropology (AMMA). Her earlier research focused on neuro-psychiatric disorders and traditional healing in Africa. Presently, she chairs a qualitative research program on child health and child agency at the Amsterdam School for Social Science Research (ASSR).

Aya Rice completed her master's degree in clinical psychology at the Hebrew University in Jerusalem. She currently works at the Israel Center for the Treatment of Psychotrauma in various projects relating to traumatic grief.

Holland Rimmasch received her undergraduate degree in psychology from Brigham Young University in 2006. She is currently an autism teacher aide with Wasatch Mental Health in Orem, Utah.

William R. Saltzman is a nationally recognized expert on the treatment of childhood and family trauma and bereavement. Dr. Saltzman is a faculty and staff member at the UCLA Trauma Psychiatry Program and the National Center for Child Traumatic Stress. He is co-developer of a family-based trauma program that is being used across the United States in military, medical, and post-disaster settings.

Jason Southwick received his undergraduate degree in psychology from Brigham Young University in 2006. He is currently enrolled in the Clinical Psychology Doctoral Program at Brigham Young University, with research interests in psychotherapy process and outcome.

Wietse A. Tol received a master's degree in Clinical and Health Psychology from Leiden University. He is a PhD candidate at the Vrije University Medical Center, doing research with HealthNet TPO. His clinical and research interests involve the design, implementation, and evaluation of psychosocial projects for populations exposed to organized violence and other complex emergencies in low-income settings.

Arlene Tucker-Levin received a PhD in psychology from the University of Chicago. She was a Professor at Rutgers University (Newark Division) and was Director of their Graduate Program in Child Clinical Psychology. She practiced as a child clinical psychologist in New York and was the founder and director of an early intervention program for very young children with developmental challenges.

Sam Tyano is a previous president of the National Council on Psychiatry, vice-president of the International Association of Child and Adolescent

Psychiatry, member of the EC of the World Psychiatric Association, and author of four books and two hundred publications in international journals. He is Director of the National Project on Outpatient Centers for Infant Psychiatry.

Acknowledgements

It has been a pleasure to work on this book with so many clinicians and researchers who have volunteered their wisdom and efforts and who were willing to engage in this international ongoing discourse on children, trauma, and resilience. We thank all of the authors for their creativity and innovative contributions geared for implementation in the field of building resilience in children. It is humbling to work with so many highly committed clinicians and scientists who lead the translation of theory into practice, and their insights from their experience into knowledge. Through these efforts we hope to make a difference in the lives of children facing the pain of trauma.

Special appreciation goes to Professor Arlene Tucker-Levin and Dr. Renee Rabinovitz, for their enthusiastic involvement in editing chapters of this book and their willingness to share their enormous knowledge and experience. We also thank Dr. Naomi Goldblum for her careful and critical language editing of the book, and Atoosa Khodabakhsh for her outstanding dedication in getting the manuscript formatted. We are grateful to all of our colleagues at the Temmy and Albert Latner Israel Center for the Treatment of Psychotrauma, the University of Connecticut School of Medicine Department of Psychiatry, and the National Child Traumatic Stress Network for their support and tolerance throughout the process of creating this collaborative work.

We appreciate the opportunity that Routledge has provided us to be part of its prestigious publications and to Sarah Gibson for her continuing guidance.

We have been blessed with partners and families who have supported our work on this book and tolerated our long hours of absence. We are grateful and happy for their resilience and shared enthusiasm.

Chapter I

Introduction

Julian D. Ford, Ruth Pat-Horenczyk, and Danny Brom

Children speak to the heart, and mothers, fathers and other caregivers speak of their children from the heart. Yet, in the literature on psychological trauma, children and their adult caregivers occupy a disproportionately small place. This paradox reflects the pervasive tendency toward denial, and skepticism regarding the mere existence of severe effects of psychological trauma in childhood, resulting in the lack of proper care for many children in need of it. The purpose of this book is to present the state of the art on children's vulnerability and resilience in the wake of psychological trauma, and contribute to the developing systems of care for traumatized children.

Psychological trauma is common in the lives of children. Millions of children are exposed to psychological trauma every year, including life-threatening accidents, disasters, or violence in their families, communities, or nations, as well as physical, sexual, or emotional abuse or neglect. Although research on children shows convincingly that psychological trauma has an enormously damaging effect on their development and mental and physical health, there is little systematic information about the ways they actually cope with trauma or possible avenues for helping them. The need for this information is felt throughout the world and has led, for example, to the founding of the National Child Traumatic Stress Initiative (www.NCTSNet.org) in the United States and the Child Trauma Treatment Interest Group of the Israel Trauma Coalition in Israel.

In the world situation post 9/11, trauma and terrorism have become a focus of international attention for both professionals and the general public (Danieli et al. 2005). General interest in the traumatic stress field has burgeoned, but studies of how children cope with and recover from psychological trauma have lagged behind. The development of specific interventions for traumatized children has not received the major attention it deserves. The emphasis has been on extrapolating from clinical experience and research on adults exposed to psychological trauma. Systematic research is needed to elucidate how children not only cope but grow and thrive after exposure to psychological trauma.

Fortunately, scientific and clinical studies of the long-term impact of traumatic experiences on the developmental trajectories of children and adolescents are beginning to appear more often. Clinicians and scientists are exploring the interplay of possible protective factors in coping, adaptation, resilience, and recovery from trauma, with sensitivity to the developmental phase of the child. The major thrust of this book is to provide clinicians, educators, and researchers with updated and innovative theoretical, developmental, and clinical conceptualizations and research on risk and resilience among traumatized children and youth. In addition, the book highlights innovative and promising evidence-based treatments developed in various international contexts to address these risk and resilience factors in the prevention and treatment of posttraumatic distress in children and youth.

When children are exposed to psychological traumas they may develop a variety of transient or chronic emotional, behavioral, or physical health problems that may include posttraumatic stress disorder (PTSD). A community sample study in the United States (Copeland et al. 2007) showed that more than two out of three children had experienced at least one traumatic event, with 13.4 percent of the exposed children developing some posttraumatic stress symptoms. These numbers are drawn from a Western society. Obviously data from other cultures and less privileged circumstances will reflect harsher states of affairs.

Children exposed to trauma have almost twice the rate of psychiatric disorders as those not exposed, particularly anxiety and depressive disorders. Although the prognosis is generally favorable after a single childhood trauma, this is not true for children experiencing multiple traumatic events (Copeland et al. 2007). An overview of epidemiological studies (Gabbay et al. 2004) points to the differential rates of posttraumatic distress after different types of traumatic experiences, such as maltreatment, traffic accidents, medical illness, disaster, war, and violence.

Children take many different paths to recover from the shock of psychological trauma and to resist or recover from posttraumatic problems such as persistent anxiety, depression, anger, dissociation, alienation, and impulsivity. Some children are adversely affected but show remarkable resilience in overcoming their initial stress reactions and regaining good adjustment. Some seem to alternate between periods of resilient recovery and periods of recurrent distress and dysfunction. Still other children never seem to fully overcome the impact of psychological trauma, and instead develop chronic psychological, behavioral, and medical problems that may persist for the rest of their lives, possibly becoming progressively more extensive and severe over time. Yet others seem almost impervious to posttraumatic stress and might even be able to grow stronger in the face of psychological trauma.

In this book, a number of expert clinicians and researchers address several critical questions raised by these variations in the course or trajectory of children's lives in the wake of trauma. One question is how we diagnose and identify PTSD in childhood with sensitivity to age-specific phenomenology.

The new diagnosis of posttraumatic stress disorder was officially introduced in the 1980 version of the *Diagnostic and statistical manual of mental disorders* (DSM-III) (American Psychiatric Association 1980); the realization that children's reactions to traumatic events may well differ from adult PTSD had to wait another seven years. In the 1987 publication of the DSM-III-R (American Psychiatric Association 1987) features of PTSD specific to children were added, to account for the unique characteristics of the clinical picture in childhood and developmental differences. For example, although adults diagnosed with PTSD must either be aware of troubling memories of past psychological traumas or react to fairly clear reminders of traumatic past experiences with emotional or physical distress, children with PTSD may not have (or disclose) actual memories but may instead enact past traumatic experiences repetitively in play or artwork. Children or adolescents with PTSD also may regress developmentally in reaction to reminders of past traumatic experiences; for example, a school-age child may start bedwetting or become clingy when exposed to family or community events that are reminiscent of early abuse experiences.

Prior to the classification of PTSD in the DSM-III-R there was a considerable amount of professional skepticism regarding the development of PTSD-type symptoms in previously healthy children who had been subjected to extreme stressors (Sack et al. 1986). The general opinion was that normal infants and young children were not seriously harmed in the long term by emotional or physical trauma (Cohen 1998). The rationalization was that children were too young, or too psychologically and emotionally immature, to recall traumatic events they had undergone or experience their repercussions (Benedek 1985).

Even now, the definition of what type of event can be traumatic for a child, and the developmental stage at which experiencing psychological trauma is most critical, remains controversial. In an effort to reconcile the differences and establish a working definition for trauma in children, a group of child psychologists and psychiatrists from the National Child Traumatic Stress Network (NCTSN) are in the process of defining a set of additional factors to accompany the diagnosis of PTSD in children. When this process is completed, NCTSN intends to propose its findings for inclusion in DSM-V, which is scheduled for publication in 2011.

This diagnosis, termed "developmental trauma disorder" (DTD), is an attempt to capture the unique qualities of children's reactions to trauma. The new diagnosis better reflects the fact that children are most often traumatized within relationships (DeAngelis 2007). Children exposed to such trauma are likely to develop unique symptoms that are markedly different from adult PTSD. Additionally, the diagnosis takes into consideration that interpersonal trauma may have a differential impact depending on the child's stage of development (Ford 2005). For example, diagnosing a child's sense of a fore-shortened future must be made in comparison with the way non-traumatized children at a similar developmental stage perceive the future, an issue about which we have limited knowledge (Salmon and Bryant 2002).

The second question is whether there are indeed distinct and predictable pathways for posttraumatic change in childhood that can help us determine the likely outcome for each traumatized child. Layne and colleagues (Chapter 2) identify seven specific trajectories of functioning that may occur following a child's exposure to psychological trauma. Resistance (i.e. continued positive functioning), resilience (i.e. initial disturbance followed by rapid full recovery), posttraumatic growth (i.e. initial distress followed by an acceleration in positive development and functioning), and protracted recovery are trajectories that lead to relatively good outcomes. Severe persisting distress, decline (i.e. initial stress-resistance followed by deterioration), and stable maladaptive functioning are unhealthy trajectories. With these trajectories as templates, clinicians and researchers can develop models to predict the course of change for individual traumatized children to whom they are providing services, or cohorts of children whose change over time they are assessing, to empirically test and refine the theoretical trajectories of posttraumatic adjustment and functioning.

The third question involves the search for risk and protective factors for posttraumatic distress, particularly to identify and assist children who are likely to experience negative posttraumatic trajectories. Pat-Horenczyk et al. (Chapter 3) open Part I by surveying the existing research on children's responses to a variety of traumatic experiences, with special focus on risk and protective factors that affect young children. They also outline promising new directions in the field specifically, the notion that childhood PTSD must be viewed within a developmental framework and that the identification of risk and protective factors needs to be accompanied by an understanding of underlying processes. In addition, possible implications and future avenues for intervention in the field of childhood PTSD are discussed.

A related question is the converse one: are there factors associated with positive trajectories of children's posttraumatic adjustment and functioning, and, if so, what are they? Why are some children able not only to avoid developing posttraumatic disorders, but also to flourish in the wake of psychological trauma: to grow, learn, play, be physically healthy, and get along with people as well as, if not better than, prior to the trauma exposure? Most children who experience psychological trauma do *not* develop PTSD or other persistent psychological or behavioral problems, and many resume or even experience an acceleration in positive psychological development (i.e. posttraumatic growth). All the chapters in Part I: Risk and Protective Factors, are concerned with the challenge of identifying such factors for childhood PTSD and resilience.

The fourth issue is the centrality of the role of parents, in early childhood (Chapter 4), throughout childhood and in adolescence (Chapter 7). Cohen's chapter (Chapter 4) emphasizes the particularly crucial role of parents and caregivers for young children's development and for their posttraumatic resistance, resilience, and recovery. We might then ask: do parents play an essential role in influencing the posttraumatic paths taken by children of every age? Paralleling the maxim stated by the psychoanalyst Frieda Fromm-Reichman, the parent's anxiety is the child's anxiety. Strong evidence exists that children are at particular risk for posttraumatic persisting distress or decline if their parent(s) experience unresolved distress, decline, or maladaptive functioning (e.g. untreated psychiatric or substance use disorders). In contrast, when parents are able to respond resiliently – not implacably resistant, but instead experiencing some very understandable distress and transforming these reactions into confident and empathic support for their child's recovery and growth – this is a sufficiently potent, robust, durable, and facilitative protective factor (Layne et al. Chapter 2). It serves to overcome many of the adverse effects of risk factors (e.g. the child's emotional distress, family or community conflict) across a wide range of potentially severe psychological traumas (including sexual abuse, war, family violence, and disasters).

The fifth issue involves the specific challenges in identifying PTSD in early childhood. Some studies have shown that even pre-verbal children may develop posttraumatic symptoms, although detecting the presence of these symptoms is more difficult than in older children and adults (Terr 1988, 1991; see also Scheeringa et al. 1995, 2006). Eight of the official PTSD symptoms require *verbal* descriptions of internal affective states and memories, a task which is likely to be difficult for preschool children (Scheeringa et al. 1995). Very young children rarely present symptoms that are classified as symptoms of PTSD. Instead, they may present more behavioral and developmental problems, such as fears, separation anxiety, sleep disturbances, and posttraumatic play in which they repeat themes of the trauma. Toddlers may fail to develop age-appropriate skills or even lose a previously acquired developmental skill such as toilet training (Scheeringa et al. 2006). Keren and Tyano (Chapter 5) focus on infant (age 0–3) psychiatry by examining the clinical and research literatures on the impact of, and recovery from, psychological trauma. As these authors note, infants are remarkably resilient, and therefore may appear to be unaffected by life-threatening or abusive experiences that are profoundly shocking, terrifying, or horrifying to most older children and adults. However, infants also are largely dependent upon their caregivers not only for their physical survival but also for learning how to manage bodily and affective reactions to sustain the extremely rapid biological and psychosocial development that is the hallmark of this early phase of life. Infants learn and remember more than they can consciously know, because brain development is still creating the building blocks for conscious verbal and visuospatial thought and memory. Therefore, infants are paradoxically both highly protected against and extremely vulnerable to adverse developmental outcomes as a result of psychological trauma. Understanding the risk and protective factors, and potential posttraumatic trajectories, that are specifically relevant to infancy is a continuing critical challenge for trauma (and developmental psychology) researchers and clinicians.

A sixth issue involves growing up under continuing severe adverse circumstances, i.e. complex traumatic environments. Although some children are more vulnerable than others to experiencing unfavorable developmental and psychosocial trajectories in the wake of psychological trauma, even very hardy, resilient children may develop PTSD or other forms of persistent posttraumatic distress or impairment. This may occur if the trauma they have experienced is severe or prolonged enough to overwhelm the buffering effects of the protective factors in their lives. How do children survive, and in some cases thrive, when exposed to devastating traumas that tear the very fabric of their own and their family's and community's existence? Two chapters rounding out the Risk and Protective Factors part address this question with different populations and settings. Grant-Knight and colleagues (Chapter 6) describe the multiple stressors experienced by Sudanese youth who immigrated to the United States after spending much of their childhood amidst almost perpetual violence, profound physical, emotional, and educational neglect, and separation from or loss of their families. Bifulco (Chapter 7) describes the intergenerational dilemma of living on the streets in a massive urban environment (London), including coping with violence, neglect, separation and loss, substance abuse, and a culture infused with the adverse effects of impoverishment and crime. Both chapters highlight not only the severe and prolonged exposures to multiple psychological traumas experienced by these children, but also their remarkable resilience and the importance of protective factors such as religious faith, supportive peer relationships, and an adult confidant (as well as the sense of connection to people and to community that these provide even when children are separated from or lose their family or their entire community). The impact that psychological trauma (along with physical hardship) may have upon children's physical as well as mental health and upon children's ability to form secure internal beliefs ("working models") about relationships ("attachment") is also highlighted in these chapters. Many survivors of childhood psychological trauma, especially when it is prolonged and pervasive, experience lifelong problems with physical illness and conflict in or isolation from relationships, even though they may have coped and recovered resiliently from PTSD or other mental health symptoms.

The remarkable resilience of many chronically traumatized children therefore should not lead us to disregard or discount the psychological and biological cost that these children pay to resist or recover from traumatization. A related question, therefore, is how this costly and effortful achievement of resilience in the wake of psychological trauma is actually achieved. How do risk and protective factors interact with each other, and with different types and amounts of trauma over time, to create a trajectory of posttraumatic adaptation which parallels (and potentially influences) the child's psychological development and maturation? As an example, in Chapter 7 Bifulco describes the results of a longitudinal study of children whose mothers were at high risk due to childhood abuse or neglect, ongoing family conflict, or social isolation, and identifies a trajectory consistent with Layne and colleagues' "resistant" or "resilient" posttraumatic course of adjustment. More specifically, having had a close relationship with one's mother in early childhood was predictive of positive academic and peer experiences in the latency period, which in turn predicted self-acceptance and having a trusted confidant as a teen – each of which was associated with testing in the psychologically healthy range as a teen. Thus, both a trajectory of resistance/resilience and its opposite (a trajectory of distress/decline) were delineated for youths who were raised by high-risk single-parent mothers (and who experienced domestic violence while growing up). Bifulco's repeated assessment of potential risk and protective factors in childhood and psychological outcomes in late adolescence provides a sample of the valuable empirical findings that can inform the development of clinical models of posttraumatic trajectories of development and functioning in childhood and adolescence. Further follow-up of the participants in that study as adults may yield additional insights into posttraumatic trajectories beginning in childhood and extending across the lifespan.

The seventh question is how resilience can be operationalized to be promoted by prevention specialists and interventionists. In Chapter 8, the opening chapter of Part II, Brom and Kleber sharpen the focus on *posttraumatic resilience* by looking at the capacity for cognitive processing. They conceptualize coping with trauma from the information-processing perspective. Healthy or successful coping thus is seen as the ability to integrate the traumatic experience and its meaning into existing cognitive schemas. The challenge for the individual is to minimize the need for systemic change of schemas, which makes it possible to regain a flexible relationship with one's environment.

Another perspective on resilience that addresses traumatized children's need to draw upon inner and outer resources is presented by Hobfoll and colleagues (Chapter 9). They catalogue the domains of physical, interpersonal, informational, technological, and cultural resources that children must acquire and conserve in order not only to survive but also to continue to grow and develop in the wake of psychological trauma. Tol and colleagues (Chapter 10) provide a complementary taxonomy of the ecological systems that are necessary to support posttraumatic resilience in traumatized children – from the microsystem of the immediate physical environment and the home and family, to the mesosystem of relationships beyond the family, to the exosystem of environments and networks beyond the child's immediate participation, and on to the macrosystem of politics, culture, and technology that are the largely invisible infrastructure of each person's life. Resilience therefore depends upon the accessibility, potency, and robustness (Layne et al. Chapter 2) of the child's inner biological and psychological resources (i.e. strengths, knowledge, tools, and capabilities), as well as those external to the child in her or his family, peer group, school, community, and society. Most theoretical and clinical analyses and scientific studies of the impact of psychological trauma on children focus on the child's inner resources and those of her or his family. As vital as those inner resources are, Chapters 9 and 10 by Hobfoll and Tol and their colleagues remind us that the full array of resources across multiple systems must be considered when investigating or seeking to enhance children's posttraumatic resilience. Part II: Resilience is concluded by Meichenbaum (Chapter 11), who summarizes the lessons learned from thirty years of active clinical and research work, approached from an international perspective.

The eighth question moves from theory to practice: how can traumatic stress practitioners best help traumatized children achieve resilience or recovery? It is easy to describe and indicate where vital resources such as self-confidence, mental agility and acuity, social support, sources of physical energy, and technological tools and equipment can be found. However, having the presence of mind to think of and draw upon these resources when in the midst of terrifying or horrifying experiences is a much greater challenge. As one boy put it, "I can use my anger management skills anytime . . . except when I'm angry." In Part III, Ford and colleagues (Chapter 12) provide a bridge from the theory and description of resilience to the actual promotion of posttraumatic resilience in prevention and treatment, by focusing on the core competence of self-regulation. In their view, self-regulation involves:

- secure attachment (seeking connectedness, receptiveness to nurtance, intimacy, and partnering, managing the stress of separations and reunions, developing inner values and beliefs that support healthy relationships – "working models")
- emotion regulation (body awareness, detecting threats, seeking rewards, emotion labeling, using emotions as a guide)
- mental regulation (focusing and sustaining attention, developing an inner conversation with one's own thoughts, observing and shaping one's own thoughts, choosing what to remember and what to forget, and creating a personal life story – "autobiographical memory").

Each self-regulatory capability develops its foundation in early childhood. Persistent survival coping (as a result of continuing trauma, or due to the emergence of PTSD despite no further trauma) interferes with the development of self-regulatory capabilities. Self-regulation is a process of thinking first (to gather information from the body, emotions, perceptions, and mind), and then thinking while acting (to make critical "course corrections" based on new learning). Therefore, prevention and treatment for children who have survived psychological trauma can be understood as enhancing resilience by promoting self-regulation as an alternative to the survival coping characteristic of PTSD.

Based on this conceptual model, the remaining chapters in the book describe models of psychotherapy for traumatized children and their families that systematically address emotion regulation and attachment security. We chose to focus on emerging models in order to provide readers with a fresh perspective and a sampling of innovations in the rapidly growing field of clinical research on the psychosocial treatment of traumatized children. We recommend that readers consult other recent publications for descriptions of the most extensively researched and widely disseminated approaches to psychotherapy for traumatized children – notably Trauma-Focused Cognitive Behavior Therapy (TF-CBT; Cohen et al. 2006), as well as other cognitive behavioral approaches such as Eye Movement Desensitization and Reprocessing (EMDR; Greenwald 2006) and Skills Training for Affective and Interpersonal Regulation/Narrative Story Telling (STAIR/NST; Cloitre et al. 2006). In addition, readers are encouraged to consult publications describing several promising approaches to multi-systemic treatment for traumatized children which have been developed recently, including Trauma Systems Therapy (TST; Saxe et al. 2007) and the Attachment, self-Regulation, and Competency framework (ARC; Kinniburgh et al. 2005).

Leading off the exposition of innovative approaches to enhancing emotion regulation and attachment security in traumatized children and their families, Van Horn and Lieberman (Chapter 13) describe their evidence-based Child Parent Psychotherapy (CPP) model, in which the caregiver and the very young traumatized child can repair the emotional injury of psychological trauma by reinstating the core process of co-regulation and together move toward mutually supported self-regulation. In addition to CPP, they highlight other evidence-informed approaches to dyadic psychotherapy with traumatized infants and toddlers and their primary caregivers, showing that this can be achieved either through either a relational attachment-based approach or a behavioral parent-management approach. When children feel safe and calm enough to explore the environment and enjoy activities and relationships, they are able to focus on their immediate needs and interests – and not only to grow but also develop the capacity to self-regulate. This is because they do not have to rely upon the automatic stress response reactions that are a hallmark of posttraumatic stress even in the first years of life. As the caregiver and child resume their bonding and exploration of life together, their mutual reinstatement of self-regulation provides a positive cycle of resilience and renewal.

As children become more autonomous in the elementary school years and early adolescence, posttraumatic self-regulation depends upon several conditions that form the basis for the SPARCS model of education and treatment described by DeRosa and Pelcovitz (Chapter 14). The first step in helping children recover from PTSD is to create an environment, that is truly safe for the child, that is, where the child has consistent supportive relationships and is not threatened with physical, emotional, or mental harm. The second step goes hand in hand with the first – enabling the child to have experiences that build and strengthen three fundamental self-regulation skills:

* balancing excitement and enthusiasm with careful planning and frequent course corrections
* thinking in advance about her or his core goals and values, and basing choices on the likelihood of achieving these goals and fulfilling these values rather than simply doing what is most expedient, provocative, or compliant
* choosing to be with people who respectfully and appreciatively listen to, learn from, and build on the strengths that each brings to the relationship.

In middle childhood and adolescence, the entire family is profoundly affected when a child is traumatized. It is thus essential not only to bring to bear the resources of the family to support and protect the traumatized child, but also to replenish and enhance the family's often fragmented and frayed emotional and psychological resources when the whole family is experiencing traumatic shock. Saltzman and colleagues (Chapter 15) provide a map to assist families in moving from this state of shock and horror to regaining the capacity to self-regulate – both as individual persons, using the cognitive behavioral skills that this family therapy model teaches, and as a family system. When the family is able to face and manage the intense distress and challenges to their core beliefs and values that occur when trauma strikes a child, resilience and even growth become achievable.

While no single model can encompass all facets of posttraumatic resilience, Kagan (Chapter 16) identifies a focal theme that is archetypal in childhood: the hero. As Kagan describes it, a hero is a person who faces adversity with courage (as well as fear), and transforms it by acting according to noble principles and achieving outcomes that increase not only her or his own well-being but also that of other persons (especially those who depend upon the hero and share the bonds of friendship or love with the hero). A "real-life hero" is therefore an ideal to which children (and their adult caregivers) can aspire and a model that they can apply and realize in their own lives. With this perspective, children and adults can understand and practice in their ordinary lives the inner resources that are a basis for resilience, as well as accessing and utilizing the external resources (e.g. friendship, mentorship, information, practical tools) that a hero needs to overcome adversity and win the day even in the face of fear, sorrow, helplessness, and defeat (to be resilient in the aftermath of psychological trauma). The metaphor of the hero thus can illuminate and bring to life the concept of posttraumatic resilience for children.

Although psychological trauma in childhood poses many painful and challenging questions, when clinicians seek to enhance recovery and resilience through psychotherapy, prevention specialists teach skills to enhance safety and resilience, and researchers seek better ways of understanding post-traumatic risk, resilience, and recovery, their common goal is to transform these questions into healing, health, and knowledge. In this book, clinicians, educators, and researchers describe innovative ways of both asking and answering the questions that must be addressed when psychological trauma strikes the life of a child. By exploring the nature and meaning of risk, resilience, and recovery, the authors in this book have provided trauma professionals with new perspectives to inform their vital work on behalf of the millions of children whose lives are profoundly affected by psychological trauma.

References

American Psychiatric Association (APA) (1980). *Diagnostic and statistical manual of mental disorders*, 3rd edition. Washington, DC: APA.

American Psychiatric Association (1987). *Diagnostic and statistical manual of mental disorders*, 3rd edition revised. Washington, DC: APA.

Benedek, E.P. (1985). *Children and psychic trauma: A brief review of contemporary thinking*. Washington, DC: American Psychiatric Press.

Cloitre, M., Cohen, L., and Koenen, K. (2006). *Treating survivors of childhood abuse: Psychotherapy for the interrupted life*. New York: Guilford.

Cohen, J.A. (1998). Practice parameters for the assessment and treatment of children and adolescents with posttraumatic stress disorder. *Journal of the American Academy of Child and Adolescent Psychiatry, 37*(10, suppl.), 4S–26S.

Cohen, J.A., Mannarino, A.P., and Deblinger, E. (2006). *Treating trauma and traumatic grief in children and adolescents*. New York: Guilford.

Copeland, W.E., Keeler, G., Angold, A., and Costella, E.J. (2007). Traumatic events and posttraumatic stress in childhood. *Archives of General Psychiatry, 64*, 577–584.

Danieli, Y., Brom, D., and Sills, J. (2005). *The trauma of terrorism: Sharing knowledge and shared care. An international handbook*. New York: Haworth.

DeAngelis, T. (2007). A new diagnosis for childhood trama? *Monitor on Psychology, 38*(3), 32–34.

Ford, J.D. (2005). Treatment implications of altered neurobiology, affect regulation and information processing following child maltreatment. *Psychiatric Annals, 35*, 410–419.

Gabbay, V., Oatis, M.D., Silva, R.R., and Hirsch, G.S. (2004). Epidemiological aspects of PTSD in children and adolescents. In R.R. Silva (ed.), *Posttraumatic stress disorders in children and adolescents* (pp. 1–17). New York: Norton.

Greenwald, R. (2006). Eye movement desensitization and reprocessing with traumatized youth. In N.B. Webb (ed.), *Working with traumatized youth in child welfare* (pp. 246–264). New York: Guilford.

Kinniburgh, K., Blaustein, M., Spinazzola, J., and van der Kolk, B. (2005). Attachment, self-regulation and competency. *Psychiatric Annals, 35*, 424–430.

Sack, W.H., Angell, R.H., Kinzie, J.D., and Rath, B. (1986). The psychiatric effects of massive trauma on Cambodian children: II. The family, the home, and the school. *Journal of the American Academy of Child and Adolescent Psychiatry, 34*, 1160–1166.

Salmon, K., and Bryant, R.A. (2002). Posttraumatic stress disorder in children: The influence of developmental factors. *Clinical Psychology Review, 22*, 163–188.

Saxe, G., Ellis, H., and Kaplow, J. (2007). *Psychological approaches for children with PTSD*. New York: Guilford.

Scheeringa, M.S., Wright, M., Hunt, J., and Zeanah, C.H. (2006). Factors affecting the diagnosis and prediction of PTSD symptomatology in children and adolescents. *American Journal of Psychiatry, 163*, 644–651.

Scheeringa, M.S., Zeanah, C.H., Drell, M.J., and Larrieu, J.A. (1995). Two approaches to the diagnosis of posttraumatic stress disorder in infancy and early childhood. *Journal of the American Academy of Child and Adolescent Psychiatry, 34*, 191–200.

Terr, L. (1988). What happens to early memories of trauma? A study of twenty children under age five at the time of documented traumatic events. *Journal of the American Academy of Child and Adolescent Psychiatry, 27*, 96–104.

Terr, L. (1991). Childhood traumas: An outline and overview. *American Journal of Psychiatry, 148*, 10–20.

Chapter 2

Promoting "resilient" posttraumatic adjustment in childhood and beyond

"Unpacking" life events, adjustment trajectories, resources, and interventions

Christopher M. Layne, Callie J. Beck, Holland Rimmasch, Jason S. Southwick, Marko A. Moreno, and Stevan E. Hobfoll

In an authoritative review, Friedman et al. (2007) observed that "it is a very hopeful sign that the trauma field has shifted from an exclusive interest in diagnosis and treatment of chronic PTSD [posttraumatic stress disorder] to an interest in resilience and prevention" (Friedman et al. 2007, pp. 554–555). The authors advocated the adoption of a *wellness orientation* combined with a *public health approach* to intervention following mass casualties and disasters that is directed towards two primary goals. First, where possible, to prepare the population at large before it is exposed to traumatic events by both enhancing naturally occurring resilience processes and supplementing additional resources that support adaptive coping with the traumatic stressors to which the population is most likely to be exposed. Second, to identify subgroups deficient in resilience-promoting resources who are most likely to benefit from focused interventions that compensate for these deficiencies, thereby reducing their vulnerability. Consistent with public health principles, this approach would incorporate risk screening and monitoring procedures; an emphasis on early prevention, early intervention, and community-based strategies; and the selective use of traditional therapeutic approaches for severely affected individuals. Consistent with wellness principles, this approach would emphasize "resilience"-building through the provision of adaptive coping resources to resilient and vulnerable individuals alike.

These aims are consistent with developmental psychopathology-based principles for promoting mental health in children and adolescents at risk for exposure to various forms of trauma (Pynoos and Steinberg 2006). Specifically, a wellness-oriented public health approach can be applied not only to disasters and mass casualty events, but also to prevention efforts, circumscribed acute traumatic events, and the recurrent, all too commonplace violent events to which children and adolescents are exposed worldwide. Given the magnitude of this challenge and the early stage of our understanding of resilience in trauma-related contexts, we must recognize that our prospects for mounting successful wellness-oriented public health interventions depends heavily on the success with which we accumulate knowledge in two key areas. These are, first, the causal pathways through which traumatic stress may lead to persisting severe posttraumatic distress, dysfunction, and developmental derailment, and second, the causal pathways through which adaptive (i.e. resistant and resilient) trajectories of posttraumatic adjustment are promoted and sustained. It is thus crucial that we shift from a superficial focus on assembling shopping lists of attributes *associated with* "resilient" versus "non-resilient" adaptation that may or may not *cause* resilience (Layne et al. 2007; Silva and Kessler 2004), to a more penetrating focus that seeks to explicate the dynamic, multilevel biopsychosocial mechanisms, processes, and pathways of influence that give rise to, mediate, and moderate resilient adaptation (Masten 2007). Given this shift in emphasis from risk markers to causal pathways, it is appropriate that we critically evaluate the stress diathesis model as it applies to trauma-exposed populations. This conceptual framework has heavily influenced our research and intervention efforts up to the present, often serving, both explicitly and implicitly, as the anchoring reference point for the widely (and loosely) used terms *risk factor*, *protective factor*, and *vulnerability factor*.

How can we unpack stressful and beneficial life events and adjustment processes into components and configurations that are theoretically and clinically useful? Deconstructing beneficial and adverse life events – and the processes through which individuals and groups adjust to them – into their "molecular" configurations and interconnections will potentiate two major advances in our ability to design effective wellness-oriented public health interventions with populations at elevated risk for trauma exposure. First, this deconstruction will deepen our understanding of the causal pathways that influence whether trauma-exposed individuals enter into resilient versus non-resilient posttraumatic adjustment trajectories. Second, it will increase the empirical and theoretical knowledge base we need to address questions relating to which specific prevention and intervention procedures are indicated, with whom, why they are needed, and where, how, and when to undertake them (Layne et al. 2007). Major advances have thus far been made in identifying links between adverse life events and a range of adverse outcomes, including eating disorders, somatic problems, conduct disorder, depression, anxiety, suicidal behavior, and physical illness (e.g. Dohrenwend 2006). Of particular note are advances in mapping out the causal pathways through which adversities may influence physical and mental health. These include Harris et al.'s (1986) finding that a lack of adequate parental care following the loss of a mother in childhood mediates the link between the loss and psychiatric disorder in adulthood, and Brown's (2000) identification of links between perceptions of the meaning of stressful life events and circumstances – including appraisals of humiliation, entrapment, loss, and danger – and psychiatric disorder.

Drawing on this seminal work, researchers have sought to understand the nature and effects of traumatic stressors and the causal pathways through which they exert their influences. In particular, Brown and Harris (1978), Dohrenwend et al. (1993), and Hobfoll (1988, 1998) have each made key contributions in delineating the need to move beyond treating life events as fundamental, atomic units. These life stress researchers have each advocated the practice of "unpacking" life events and circumstances, such as by evaluating the nature and impact of a traumatic event according to its magnitude, scope, unpredictability, duration, secondary adversities, demands on coping resources, available coping resources, and appraisal processes. Also key are Hobfoll's assertions that risk and beneficial (i.e. promotive or protective) factors aggregate and travel in "caravans" across time, often exerting their influences through resource gain and loss cycles. In particular, because people's risk factors and coping resources seldom operate or travel in isolation, the practice of examining risk and beneficial factors one at a time both decontextualizes the object of study and misses the broader point.

The trauma field must build on these advances to progress efficiently in its wellness mandate. Specifically, we must develop theories and methods that are capable of describing a range of adaptive and maladaptive posttraumatic adjustment trajectories, predicting which subgroups are at risk for moving into specific adjustment trajectories, explaining the configurations and causal pathways through which beneficial and adverse causal factors intersect to influence the course of posttraumatic adjustment; and guiding wellness-oriented interventions to maximize the proportion of trauma-exposed groups that enter adaptive posttraumatic adjustment trajectories. Accordingly, this chapter will address four basic questions:

- What *configurations* are adverse and beneficial life events and circumstances likely to form as they intersect and combine to influence wellness-related outcomes in populations at risk for various forms of trauma exposure?
- What common adaptive and maladaptive *posttraumatic adjustment trajectories* may trauma-exposed individuals enter as the joint consequence of their trauma exposure and the adverse (e.g. vulnerability) and beneficial (e.g. protective) factors that make up their surrounding ecological contexts?
- What specific *attributes of beneficial resources* may influence the degree to which they help individuals to cope with specific types of trauma or other major adversities?
- What *constellations* of beneficial and adverse causal factors make up the

life caravans of individuals who exhibit similar posttraumatic adjustment trajectories?

In responding to these questions, we first unpack five content domains relevant to designing wellness-oriented public health interventions, and then integrate these strands in clinically and theoretically informative ways. Specifically, we will

- examine a range of configurations that adverse and beneficial life events may form as they intersect and combine to influence posttraumatic adjustment
- describe a range of adaptive and maladaptive trajectories of post-traumatic adjustment
- propose ten attributes of coping resources that may influence their "degree of fit" in contending with specific stressor demands
- propose a method for unpacking individuals who share similar trajectories of posttraumatic adjustment based on the compositions of their risk and resource caravans
- review public health-based intervention procedures commonly undertaken in disasters.

We then draw on Conservation of Resources (COR) theory (Hobfoll 1988, 1998) to illustrate the implications that interweaving these five elements holds for designing and implementing wellness-oriented interventions. Our aim is to assist in laying the groundwork for a general wellness-oriented public health approach to intervention across a diverse range of trauma types and severe hardships, an approach that places high priority on prevention, the accurate identification of at-risk subgroups, and effective early intervention with subgroups deemed at high risk. We hope that this framework will serve as a heuristic tool that stimulates further research and intervention-related applications.

Avenue 1: Unpacking stressful and beneficial life events and circumstances

Strengths of the stress-diathesis model

The stress-diathesis model has heavily influenced the search for determinants of chronic PTSD (Harvey and Yehuda 1999). As originally formulated in the mid-1970s (Zubin and Spring 1977), the model was an attempt to integrate and revitalize a scattered schizophrenia literature that could not account for the clinical course of schizophrenia in a great majority of diagnosed patients, proposing that psychopathological episodes resulted from the interaction between challenging life events and individual diatheses (i.e. vulnerabilities).

Liberman and Corrigan (1992, 1993) elaborated on the model by incorporating protective factors as integral elements. Among the stress-diathesis model's many strengths are the ability to account for a broad set of trauma-related concepts, including *causal risk factors, strain,* and *adjustment processes* (i.e. coping efforts to remove, contend with, or contain the source of strain); *vulnerability factors,* both inborn (e.g. genetic and neurophysiologic) and acquired (e.g. diseases, perinatal complications, adverse life experiences); and *protective factors,* both inborn (e.g. intelligence, genetic constitution) and acquired (e.g. social skills). The model also distinguishes between *adjustment trajectories: stress resistance* results from the use of effective coping resources that allow the individual to function within normal limits during and after exposure to stress, whereas *failures in adaptation* result when inadequate coping efforts lead to a breach in the stress-resistance threshold. Resulting *maladjustment* is transient in *resilient* individuals, who experience a "bad day" or "rough week" and then quickly recover; and prolonged in *vulnerable* individuals, who experience persisting dysfunction and increased risk for psychiatric disorder. The model also accounts for the *phasic nature* of psychiatric disorder by positing that when stress abates and sinks below the threshold, the episode ends and the individual returns to pre-episode levels of adaptation; and for the possibility of *growth* through processes of *accommodation.*

Weaknesses of the stress-diathesis model

The major weaknesses of the stress-diathesis model as applied to traumatic stress stem from the simple fact that *"true" protective and vulnerability factors are moderator variables whose effects are manifest only in the presence of the risk variable* (Kraemer et al. 1997, 2001; Rutter 1987). Protective and vulnerability factors respectively protect against, and increase vulnerability to, developing a psychopathological episode following exposure to a given risk factor, but *neither exerts a direct causal effect on the outcome variable.*[1] Researchers and clinicians who adopt the stress-diathesis model as a conceptual framework thus implicitly adopt a *pathology-oriented, risk-factor-centric, moderator-bound approach to explaining the processes through which individuals adjust to stressful circumstances.* This greatly restricts the explanatory power of the model, permitting it to account for only the first three of the twenty-one models in Table 2.1 and opening it to four major criticisms. These include:

- The model accounts for beneficial agents only in the form of protective factors – that is, moderator variables that buffer the adverse effects of risk factors. *Conspicuously missing is a beneficial counterpart to the risk factor* (termed a *promotive factor*) that contributes to well-being through direct effects, not interactive effects.

Table 2.1 Unpacking adverse and beneficial factors: twenty-one possible relationships between three variables

Name of relationship	Description of pathway of influence[a, b, c]	Modeled pathway of influence (where C is an adverse outcome variable)[d]	Modeled effects on well-being (where C is an adverse outcome variable)
1 Single risk factor	Risk factor A exerts a direct adverse effect on C. B's influence is inert in the model: it neither moderates the effect of A on C, nor exerts a direct effect on C. Example: Traumatic bereavement (A) increases depression (C). Political orientation (liberal vs. conservative; B) has no effect on this relationship.	A → + → C B	
2 Risk and vulnerability factors (interactive relationship)	Risk factor A exerts a direct adverse effect on C. Vulnerability factor B is a moderator variable that interacts with A, such that B exacerbates the adverse effect of A on C. Example: Traumatic bereavement in childhood via the death of one's father (A) increases depression (C). The magnitude of the adverse effect of traumatic bereavement on depression increases as current life adversities (B) increase.	A → + → C + B	
3 Risk and protective factors (interactive relationship)	Risk factor A exerts a direct adverse effect on C. Protective factor B is a moderator variable that interacts with A, such that B buffers (i.e. mitigates or weakens) the adverse effect of A on C. Example: Traumatic bereavement (A) increases depression (C). The magnitude of the adverse effect of traumatic bereavement on depression decreases as social support (B) increases.	A → + → C − B	

4 Independent risk factors (additive relationship)

Risk factors A and B each exerts an adverse effect on C. A's effect on C, and B's effect on C, are independent of one another.
Example: Traumatic bereavement (A) and life adversities (B) each increases depression (C). The magnitude of effect of each risk factor is not influenced by the presence or magnitude of the other factor.

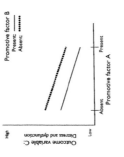

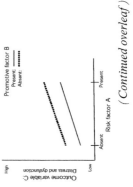

5 Independent promotive factors (additive relationship)

Promotive factors A and B each exerts a beneficial causal effect on C. A's effect on C, and B's effect on C, are independent of one another.
Example: Perceived social support (A) and perceived self-efficacy (B) each decreases depression (C). The magnitude of effect of each promotive factor is not influenced by the presence or level of the other factor.

6 Independent risk and promotive factors (additive relationship)

Risk factor A exerts an adverse effect on C. Promotive factor B exerts a beneficial effect on C. A's and B's effect on C are independent of one another.
Example: Traumatic bereavement (A) increases depression (C), whereas perceived social support (B) decreases depression (C). The magnitude of effect of each factor is not influenced by the presence or level of the other.

(Continued overleaf)

Table 2.1 Continued

Name of relationship	Description of pathway of influence[a,b,c]	Modeled pathway of influence (where C is an adverse outcome variable)[d]	Modeled effects on well-being (where C is an adverse outcome variable)
7 Promotive and facilitative factors (interactive relationship)	Promotive factor A exerts a direct beneficial effect on C. B is a "pure" facilitative factor that moderates (only) the effect of A on C. *Example:* Perceived social support (A) decreases depression (C). The magnitude of the beneficial effect of social support on depression increases when individuals possess effective social support recruitment skills (B).	A [−] C, B [+]	Outcome variable C: Distress and dysfunction (Low–High); Promotive factor A (Absent–Present); Facilitative factor B: Present / Absent
8 Promotive and inhibitory factors (interactive relationship)	Promotive factor A exerts a direct beneficial effect on C. B is an inhibitory factor that inhibits the beneficial effect of A on C. *Example:* A program that teaches social support recruiting skills (A) directly reduces depression symptoms (C). The magnitude of the beneficial effect of the program decreases as pessimistic attitudes towards help-seeking increase (B).	A [−] C, B [−]	Outcome variable C: Distress and dysfunction (Low–High); Promotive factor A (Absent–Present); Inhibitory factor B: Present / Absent
9 Risk factor and weak or selectively promotive factor (interactive relationship)	Risk factor A both exerts an adverse effect on C and suppresses the beneficial effect of B on C, such that B has an effect only when A is absent. When A is present, B's beneficial effect on C disappears. *Example:* Traumatic bereavement (A)	B [−] C, A [+] [−]	Outcome variable C: Distress and dysfunction (Low–High); Risk factor A (Absent–Present); (selectively) Promotive factor B: Present / Absent

increases aggression (C). A conflict resolution skills program (B) reduces aggression in non-traumatically bereaved students, but is ineffective in reducing aggression in traumatically bereaved students.

10 Risk and synergistic risk/vulnerability factors (interactive relationship)

Risk factor A exerts an adverse effect on C. B is a synergistic factor that both exerts an adverse effect on C (acting as a risk factor) and exacerbates the effect of A on C (acting as a vulnerability factor).

Example: Both traumatic bereavement (A) and life adversities (B) increase depression (C). The magnitude of the adverse effect of traumatic bereavement on depression increases as life adversities increase.

11 Promotive and synergistic promotive/facilitative factors (interactive relationship)

Promotive factor A exerts a direct beneficial effect on C. B is a synergistic factor that both exerts a promotive effect on C and facilitates the beneficial effect of A on C.

Example: Perceived social support (A) and perceived self-efficacy (B) each reduces depression symptoms (C). The magnitude of the beneficial effect of social support in reducing depression increases as self-efficacy increases.

Table 2.1 Continued

Name of relationship	Description of pathway of influence[a, b, c]	Modeled pathway of influence (where C is an adverse outcome variable)[d]	Modeled effects on well-being (where C is an adverse outcome variable)
12 Risk and synergistic promotive/protective factors (interactive relationship)	Risk factor A exerts an adverse causal effect on C. B is a synergistic factor that both exerts a direct *promotive* effect on C, and *buffers* (acting as a protective factor) the adverse effect of A on C. *Example:* Traumatic bereavement (A) increases depression (C). Social support (B) directly reduces depression, and buffers the adverse effect of bereavement on depression.		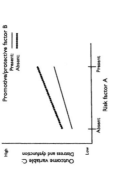
13 Equifinality (additive relationship)	Outcome variable C may be the causal product of either risk factor A or risk factor B, or both A and B. *Example:* Depression (C) may be the effect of traumatic bereavement (A), stressful life events (B), or the joint product of both.	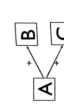	(see independent risk mechanisms or independent promotive mechanisms models, above)
14 Multifinality	Risk factor A may causally produce either outcome variable B, outcome variable C, or both B and C. *Example:* Traumatic bereavement (A) may increase depression symptoms (B), PTSD symptoms (C), or both.		(many different effects are possible)

15	Inter-risk factor causation (additive relationship)	Risk factors A and B are causes of one another, and are joint causes of outcome variable C. A and B each partially mediates the effect of the other on C. *Example:* Trauma exposure (A) increases life adversities (B), life adversities increase trauma exposure, and both increase depression (C).	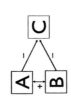	(many different effects are possible)
16	Inter-promotive factor causation (additive relationship)	Promotive factors A and B are causes of one another, and are joint causes of C. A and B each partially mediates the effect of the other on C. *Example:* Perceived social support (A) increases self-efficacy (B), self-efficacy increases social support, and both decrease depression (C).		(many different effects are possible)
17	Fully mediated relationship	Variable B fully mediates (transmits) the causal effect (either adverse or beneficial) of A on C. A's influence in C is *indirect*, where A is a *distal* cause, and B a *proximal* cause, of C. *Example:* The adverse effect of traumatic bereavement in childhood (A) on depression in adolescence (C) is fully transmitted via its effect in increasing life adversities (B).		(many different effects are possible)

(*Continued overleaf*)

Table 2.1 Continued

Name of relationship	Description of pathway of influence [a, b, c]	Modeled pathway of influence (where C is an adverse outcome variable) [d]	Modeled effects on well-being (where C is an adverse outcome variable)
18 Partially mediated relationship	A exerts a direct causal effect on C. A also exerts an indirect effect on C as mediated through B. A's influence in C is indirect, where A is a distal cause, and B a proximal cause, of C. Example: Traumatic bereavement (A) exerts a direct effect on depression in adolescence (C), and an indirect effect by increasing life adversities (B).	A → C; A → B → C	(many different effects are possible)
19 Mutual causation	Variables A, B, and C are each causes and effects of one another. Each variable may exert either an adverse or a beneficial effect on the others. Example: Depression (A) decreases social support (B) and self-efficacy (C), social support increases self-efficacy and decreases depression, and self-efficacy increases social support and decreases depression.	C ↔ A, A ↔ B, C ↔ B	(many different effects are possible)
20 Combined mediation and moderation (mediated synergistic risk/ vulnerability mechanisms) (interactive relationship)	Risk factor A exerts a direct adverse effect on both C and B. B functions as both a mediator and a moderator: it partially mediates the link between A and C, and acts as a synergistic factor that both exerts an adverse direct effect on C and exacerbates the effect of A on C. Example: Traumatic bereavement (A)	A →(+) C; A →(+) B; B →(+) C	

(Continued overleaf)

increases depression (C) and generates secondary adversities (B). These adversities both increase depression and exacerbate the effect of bereavement on depression.

| 21 | Combined mediation and moderation (mediated synergistic promotive/facilitative mechanisms) (interactive relationship) | Promotive factor A exerts a direct beneficial effect on both C and B. B functions as both a mediator and a moderator: it partially mediates the link between A and C, and acts as a synergistic factor that both exerts a beneficial effect on C and facilitates the effect of A on C.

Example: Social support (A) reduces depression (C) and increases optimism (B). Optimism both decreases depression and augments the effect of social support on depression. |
 |

Notes:

a When depicting a relationship between two variables, "+" denotes a direct causal effect, and "−" denotes an inverse causal effect.

b When depicting a moderated (interactive) relationship (e.g. B moderates the effect of A on C), "+" denotes that increases in B *increase* the effect of A on C, and "−" denotes that increases in B *decrease* the effect of A on C.

c "Factor" refers to a causal mechanism that produces the outcome.

d All relationships are presumed to be linear.

- *The model is heavily biased towards explaining vulnerability, psychopathology, and dysfunction, rather than wellness.* This orientation downplays at least three strength-based literatures, including positive psychology (Seligman 2002; Watson et al. 2006); resilience (Masten 2001; Masten and Obradović 2007); and positive youth development (Benson et al. 2006; Bernat and Resnick 2006), which emphasize that preparing all youth for successful adulthood must go far beyond reducing the prevalence of significant pathology, vulnerability, and high-risk behaviors. The fundamental unit of currency for these approaches is the promotive factor, as manifested in their strong emphasis on providing positive interpersonal relationships, successful experiences, nourishing resources, and stimulating opportunities to *all* youths.
- *Moderator-based models do not support causal inference.* A moderator variable and the variable it moderates are statistically interchangeable – B can moderate the effect of A on C (Table 2.1, Models 2–3), or A can moderate the effect of B on C (Model 9; Baron and Kenny 1986). The ambiguity in causal roles inherent in moderated designs often cannot be clarified unless the design meets the four conditions generally required for causal inference, including covariation, temporal precedence, ruling out reasonable alternative explanations, and embedding the variables of interest in a coherent theoretical framework that proposes a causal mechanism (Haynes 1992).[2]
- Last, the model has *limited scope* and *flexibility.* It does not readily accommodate multiple risk or promotive factors (Table 2.1, Models 4–6), synergistic factors (Models 10–12; see Cooke 1985), causal factors that influence one another (Models 15–21), risk factors that eventuate in multiple outcomes (Model 13), outcomes produced by multiple causes (Model 14), or the domain-specific nature of many adjustment processes.

As applied to traumatic stress, the stress-diathesis model cannot adequately explain the causal processes through which vulnerability is increased before and after trauma exposure through the depletion of beneficial resources (Hobfoll 1998). More important, it cannot explain how individuals and groups build up beneficial resources *before*, and healthy recovery *after*, exposure to stress, and how beneficial resources promote positive adaptation *irrespective* of the presence or absence of risk and vulnerability factors, thereby exerting "promotive factor main effects" rather than "protective factor moderated effects". Thus, although it has served as a valuable workhorse in supporting our early preoccupation with chronic PTSD, the stress-diathesis model (and its meager conceptual and methodological "toolkit" of risk, vulnerability, and protective factors) is a woefully inadequate vehicle to guide our wellness-oriented mandate, especially our preventive efforts.

What about the stress-diathesis model remains relevant to traumatic stress? The stress-diathesis model is not irrelevant to studying and treating the effects of trauma; it is insufficient. Consistent with Albert Einstein's maxim that "Everything should be made as simple as possible, but not one bit simpler", the many meaningfully distinct configurations that trauma-related variables can form requires that our conceptual and methodological palettes contain more than three colors if we are to clearly depict and differentiate between the specific processes that lead to adaptive versus maladaptive posttraumatic adaptation. Figure 2.1 illustrates many relevant components of the model. The stress resistance threshold is placed under dynamic tension in the model, such that outcomes reflect the current cumulative effects of risk, vulnerability, and countervailing protective factors. The model proposes that negative, neutral, or positive outcomes may varyingly eventuate, depending on the specific composition of risk, vulnerability, and protective factors and their cumulative influences over time. The model also distinguishes between *causal factors*, *outcomes*, and *markers*. In their role as predictors or indicators, markers may consist of actual causal factors or outcomes (if these can be readily and accurately measured), but may also consist of proxy variables (e.g. correlates or byproducts of unmeasured causal processes). Markers also serve as heuristic tools by encouraging a search for potential common causes.

Beyond risk, vulnerability, and protective factors: expanding on the stress-diathesis model

We now suggest the incorporation of six supplemental conceptual and methodological tools for systematically unpacking adverse and beneficial life events and circumstances in order to increase the breadth and precision with which we understand, explain, and therapeutically address trauma-related adjustment processes. Our aim is to promote the integration and vitalization of a scattered traumatic stress literature that cannot, at present, account for the clinical course of "resilient" adaptation exhibited by a great majority of trauma-exposed individuals. In combination with the stress-diathesis model and other recommendations (Layne et al. 2007), these tools may expand researchers' and practitioners' conceptual and methodological repertoires, allowing them to account for all the models presented in Table 2.1.[3]

Incorporate positive outcomes

Placing greater emphasis on positive outcomes in conceptual models of adaptation to traumatic stress (e.g. action-focused posttraumatic growth; Hobfoll et al. 2007) carries at least three major benefits. First, it will enhance the capacity of the traumatic stress field to cross-pollinate with the fields of positive psychology, positive youth development, and resilience, described earlier. Second, this shift will encourage a more balanced approach to the

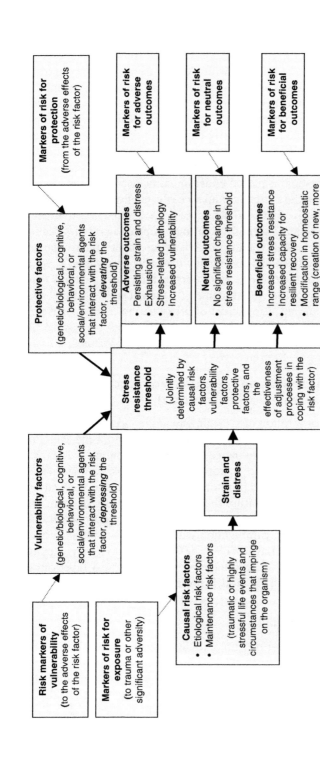

Key:
Causal pathway of influence:
Predictive relationship:

Note: The term *risk* is used in a probabilistic sense only. A *risk marker* is a variable whose presence or magnitude signals a substantial statistical likelihood that the event or circumstance (whether favorable or unfavorable) is present or will occur.

Figure 2.1 Unpacking stressful and beneficial life events: an application of the stress-diathesis model to traumatic stress.

Source: Adapted from Steinberg and Ritzman (1990).

study of stress adjustment processes. Specifically, it will reflect a recognition that risk and vulnerability factors *are* adverse not simply because they increase the risk for psychopathology, functional impairment, and risky behavior, but because they decrease the likelihood of attaining positive outcomes, such as developing successful romantic attachments (Bernat and Resnick 2006). A third major benefit will be a marked increase in the explanatory power of our conceptual models. In particular, all the models in Table 2.1, although almost exclusively illustrated by maladaptive outcomes (particularly depression), *can each be referenced to a positive outcome as the dependent variable(s)* (e.g. self-efficacy, optimism, prosocial behavior, happiness) *while retaining its integrity and meaning.* These relationships can be re-plotted by reversing the poles of the Y-axis (so that high values are desirable), reversing the signs (+ vs. −) in the model pathways, and flipping the image of the plotted lines upside down. This creates forty-two possible relationships out of twenty-one models – a doubling in explanatory power.[4]

Incorporate positive mechanisms in the form of promotive and facilitative factors

As discussed earlier, promotive factors (see Table 2.1, Model 5) are critically needed to permit the traumatic stress field to progress beyond the ability to merely account for the risk-buffering effects of protective factors (Model 3). A strong benefit of including promotive factors is an enhanced capacity to elucidate the pathways of influence through which beneficial resources are built up before stress exposure occurs (thereby promoting stress resistance), or replenished during and following stress exposure (thereby maintaining stress resistance, or facilitating recovery following "failures in adaptation" that result in maladjustment; Hobfoll 1988, 1998; Layne et al. 2007). By extension, a *facilitative factor* is to a promotive factor what a vulnerability factor is to a causal risk factor: as a vulnerability factor interacts with a risk factor to exacerbate its adverse effects on the outcome variable, a facilitative factor interacts with a promotive factor to increase its beneficial effects. Facilitative factors are thus beneficial *catalysts* that enhance the potency, robustness, durability, accessibility, or other desirable effects of promotive factors (Model 7). The incorporation of promotive factors also necessitates the inclusion of *inhibitory factors* (Model 8). An inhibitory factor is to a promotive factor what a protective factor is to a causal risk factor: as a protective factor interacts with a risk factor to diminish its adverse effects on the outcome variable, an inhibitory factor interacts with a promotive factor to diminish its beneficial effects. Taken together, incorporating promotive, facilitative, and inhibitory factors will permit a more balanced and comprehensive approach to the study of adjustment (both adaptive and maladaptive) under stressful conditions.

Incorporate synergistic factors

Studying vulnerability and facilitative factors in relation to risk factors and promotive factors will also permit the study of *synergistic factors* (also termed *potentiating factors*; Foy et al. 1992). The defining feature of synergistic factors is that they exert both direct and interactive effects; accordingly, they constitute some of the most potentially influential elements in our conceptual and methodological armamentarium. *Synergistic risk/vulnerability factors* (see Table 2.1, Model 10) exert both a direct adverse effect and increase vulnerability to the adverse effect of other modeled risk factors. In contrast, *synergistic promotive/facilitative factors* (Model 11) both exert a beneficial direct effect and interact with the other promotive factors, enhancing their beneficial effect. Last, *synergistic promotive/protective factors* (Model 12) both exert a direct beneficial effect and buffer the adverse effects of the risk factors on the outcome variable.

Incorporate both moderators and mediators

The explanatory power and clinical utility of trauma theories will be further enhanced by incorporating moderating and mediating elements. In contrast to moderated models, which can legitimately be studied in cross-sectional designs (Baron and Kenny 1986), true mediated models require causal inference and thus must meet the rigorous requirements for causal inference, including the use of a longitudinal design (Haynes 1992). By definition, mediators are links in pathways of influence that either fully transmit (Table 2.1, Model 17) or partially transmit (Model 18) the effects of causally antecedent variables to consequent variables. Because adjustment to stress may well involve both moderation and mediation (Models 20–21), conceptual and statistical approaches that integrate both (e.g. Edwards and Lambert 2007) may be best suited for explaining the processes through which individuals prepare for, and adjust to, trauma and other major stressors. Indeed, integrated mediated/moderated designs may prove to be powerful tools for explicating the pathways through which resource loss and gain cycles may form and accelerate over time. Their use may thus facilitate empirical testing of Hobfoll's (1998) propositions that, first, resource loss induces further loss, whereas resource gain induces further gain; second, subsequent loss exacerbates the effects of prior losses by interfering with recovery processes, whereas subsequent gain consolidates and enhances the beneficial effects of previous gains; and third, resource buildup buttresses stress resistance and the capacity for resilient recovery, whereas resource depletion increases vulnerability. These tools will thus help the field to move beyond simply identifying risk, vulnerability, protective, and promotive factors; to explaining the mechanisms, processes, and pathways of influence through which they operate over time.

Incorporate equifinality, multifinality, and domain-specific trajectories of adaptation

Criticisms of the stress-diathesis model's lack of flexibility may be addressed by incorporating the principles of equifinality and multifinality (Table 2.1, Models 18–19), and the possibility of multiple trajectories of adaptation within the same individual across multiple life domains. Specifically, *equifinality* is typified by circumstances wherein a given outcome may be the consequence of multiple risk factors operating through different pathways of influence. Conversely, *multifinality* is exemplified in circumstances wherein the same risk factor may produce multiple outcomes (Holmbeck et al. 2006). Moreover, studies of resilient groups indicate that resistance, resilience, and other trajectories of adaptation may be domain-specific (Luthar 2006). For example, stress-exposed individuals may manifest stress resistance in one life domain (e.g. school performance), resilient recovery in other domains (e.g. family and peer relationships), and protracted recovery in other domains (e.g. romantic relationships) (Layne et al. 2007). We discuss these trajectories in the next section.

Distinguish between causal factors, risk markers, and outcomes

Last, in light of Vogt et al.'s (2007) sobering caution that the majority of "risk factors" as discussed in the PTSD literature do not actually constitute risk factors, we propose that it is crucial that the trauma field maintain a clear distinction between causal factors, outcomes, and markers, as defined earlier (see Figure 2.1). Accordingly, protective factors should not be defined as "individual or environmental characteristics that *predict or are correlated* with positive outcomes" nor should risk factors be defined as "factors that *predict or are correlated* positively with negative outcomes" (Harris et al. 2006, pp. 316–317). Given that correlation alone does not signify causation (but does qualify a variable to serve as a marker for an often unmeasured causal mechanism), the use of such definitions blurs critically important distinctions between causes, consequences, and their respective "proxy" correlate markers. As applied to our framework described earlier, the above definition of *protective factor* may refer to protective factors, promotive factors, facilitative factors, or positive outcomes, or their respective markers (eight potential referents); whereas the above definition of *risk factor* may refer to causal risk factors, vulnerability factors, inhibitory factors, or adverse outcomes, or their respective markers (eight potential referents; see Figure 2.1).

Avenue 2: Unpacking trajectories of adjustment – stress resistance and resilient recovery

Trajectories of adjustment

A second fruitful application of an unpacking-oriented approach centers on distinguishing between various possible trajectories of posttraumatic adjustment. Drawing on the developmental psychopathology literature and general systems theory (see Steinberg and Ritzmann 1990), Layne et al. (2007) delineated four possible trajectories of posttraumatic adjustment, including *stress resistance, resilience, protracted recovery*, and *severe persisting distress* (see Figure 2.2). As defined by the authors, *stress resistance* occurs when a system, upon exposure to stress, uses effective adjustment processes to maintain homeostatic balance and thereby maintains a generally stable level of adaptive functioning during and after exposure to stress (Path 1).[5] The attribute of resistance is thus similar to a bar made of metal, whose resistance can be gauged by the amount of stress it can tolerate without becoming bent or broken. In contrast, *resilience* occurs when a system implements effective early adjustment processes to alleviate strain imposed by stress, and thus efficiently *restores* homeostatic balance or adaptive functioning following a temporary "failure in adaptation" and consequent disruption therein. Accordingly, resilient adaptation is best characterized as a trajectory of *expeditious recovery* following a brief but marked decrease in functioning, and can thus be distinguished by an adjustment trajectory that has a pronounced "V" shape (Path 2). The attribute of resilience is similar to a spring hung from a hook, the resilience of which can be gauged by the amount of weight it can suspend while quickly "springing back" to its former state after the weight is removed without becoming bent out of shape. *Protracted recovery* occurs when a system's efforts to implement effective adjustment processes to alleviate the strain imposed by exposure to stress are inadequate, so that restoration to healthy functioning progresses slowly (Path 3). The distinction between resilient recovery and protracted recovery is thus a relative one, gauged via the time required to restore healthy system functioning following stress exposure in an individual or other system in comparison to other similarly exposed individuals. Last, *severe persisting distress* occurs when a system's efforts to implement effective adjustment processes to alleviate strain imposed by stress are inadequate, resulting in a lack of restoration to homeostatic balance and adaptive functioning over an extended period (Path 5).

We now expand on this framework by proposing three additional trajectories of posttraumatic adjustment, including *decline, stable maladaptive functioning*, and *posttraumatic growth*, and six causal pathways that may lead to them, while recognizing that other trajectories are possible (Masten and Obradović 2007). This line of research, which facilitates both cross-trajectory

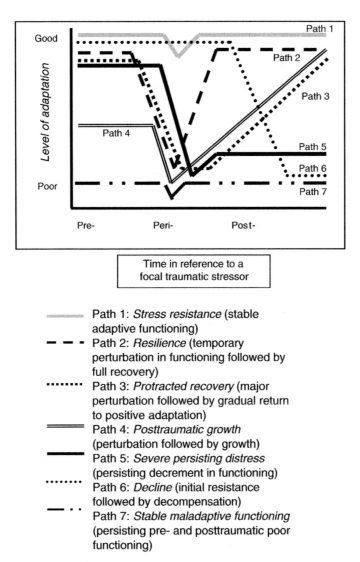

Figure 2.2 Unpacking adjustment trajectories: seven possible courses of posttraumatic adjustment.

Source: Adapted from Layne et al. 2007.

and within-trajectory analyses, may intersect in fruitful ways with approaches that rely on cross-risk group and within-risk group analyses (Luthar et al. 2006). *Decline* occurs when a system, upon exposure to stress, is able to successfully maintain adaptive functioning for a limited period during, and perhaps soon after, exposure to stress. However, the adjustment processes used become exhausted or otherwise inadequate over time, resulting in a downward spiral in functioning over time (see Path 6). *Stable maladaptive functioning* is characterized by a relatively stable trajectory of poor functioning before and after exposure to a focal stressor (see Path 7). Last, *posttraumatic growth* occurs when a system is able to implement effective adjustment processes that not only *restore* homeostatic balance and adaptive functioning over time, but also increase its level of functioning and associated capacities to levels that are higher than those found prior to trauma exposure.

Pathways of influence that may produce poor posttraumatic adjustment trajectories

Drawing on general systems theory, Steinberg and Ritzmann (1990) proposed a typology of pathways to poor adjustment following exposure to stress that may help to explain the marked initial decreases in functioning that characterize *resilience*, *protracted recovery*, *severe persisting distress*, and *decline* (see Figure 2.2). The authors theorize that a decrease in a given system's functioning (whether at the level of individuals, groups, communities, organizations, or societies) is the consequence of one or more deleterious processes that compromise adaptive adjustment processes. These deleterious processes include *a lack of access* to appropriate adjustment processes that, if available, would be effective in contending with the stressor, the *exhaustion* of an appropriate adjustment process due to unreplenished energy expenditure, and *interference* in the initiation or maintenance of appropriate adjustment processes. Other deleterious processes constitute various forms of *maladjustment*. These include *inefficiency*, characterized by the selection of an adjustment process that, though alleviating strain and distress, requires greater energy expenditure than another available adjustment process, *partial ineffectiveness*, characterized by the selection of an adjustment process that only partially alleviates stress and strain when more effective processes are available, and *complete ineffectiveness*, characterized by the selection of an adjustment process that has a negligible effect in alleviating stress and strain. Lack of access to effective adjustment processes, exhaustion, interference, inefficiency, and ineffectiveness constitute forms of vulnerability that decrease the system's stress-resistance threshold, rendering it more susceptible to stress. Clearly, a theory is needed that can describe, explain, predict, and guide interventions to address the complex ways in which these six potential pathways may lead to poor posttraumatic adjustment.

Avenue 3: Unpacking resources according to their "goodness of fit" properties

A third dimension of unpacking involves categorizing resources according to attributes that may substantially influence their "goodness of fit" for coping with specific types of stressors. Hobfoll (1998) has proposed four basic categories of beneficial resources, including *object resources* (e.g. a vehicle, home, furniture), *condition resources* (e.g. a good marriage, job seniority, social status), *personal resources* (e.g. self-esteem, self-efficacy, useful knowledge), and *energy resources* (e.g. money, credit). We build upon this typology by suggesting ten theoretically derived, interrelated dimensions of resource attributes. Figure 2.3 illustrates two coping resources (emotional regulation skills and self-efficacy) theorized to differ along these dimensions in reference to a given stressful event.

- *Pre-event level* refers to the "starting point" quantity and general quality of the resource that exists at the commencement of a focal event or circumstance. Resources are generally presumed to be in constant flux over time, changing in their quantities and quality as the net products of the particular constellation of factors that influence them (including risk, vulnerability, protective, promotive, inhibitory, and facilitative factors).
- *Shelf life* refers to the capacity of a resource, once obtained, to remain usable over time, including the additional resources that must be invested to maintain it. Resources with a long shelf life include the ability to read and emotional regulation skills. In contrast, many professional skills require regular intensive upgrading to avoid becoming obsolete.
- *Potency* refers to the degree to which a resource is effective in contending with the demands imposed by a given stressor, thereby reducing strain and distress and promoting positive adjustment. Potency is gauged via the *specific match* between the particular demands of the stressor and the

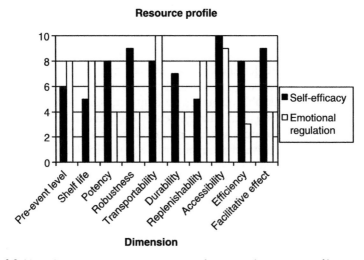

Figure 2.3 Unpacking coping resources: two ten-dimensional resource profiles.

specific beneficial properties of the resource. Perceived social support has emerged as a potent resource under many stressful circumstances (Hobfoll 1998).

- *Robustness* refers to the range of potency of a given coping resource across a spectrum of diverse stressful circumstances. Examples of highly robust resources include perceived social support and self-esteem (Brown 2000). Self-efficacy is less robust, in that its potency is limited to settings over which the individual exercises some control (Hobfoll 1998). Resources with low robustness may be potent in relation to circumscribed stressors with which they have "good fit" (i.e. a financial counselor friend in times of financial strain). Resource transportability and accessibility enhance robustness.
- *Transportability* refers to the degree to which a resource can be transported from one physical location or social sphere to another. For example, emotional regulation skills are a highly transportable resource that can be implemented in a broad variety of stressful circumstances. In contrast, object resources such as homes, and condition resources such as high social status within a specific community, often have very limited transportability and may be threatened or lost if one leaves the setting in which they are located.
- *Durability* refers to the capacity of a resource to maintain its utility under sustained use. A carbide-tipped saw blade is a potent and durable resource in the aftermath of a hurricane, withstanding heavy use in cleanup and reconstruction without becoming dull. Self-efficacy, self-esteem, and spirituality may also be durable resources, sustaining victims under prolonged stress when other resources become exhausted or wear out (Crawford et al. 2006). In contrast, social support, although a potent and robust resource, may become exhausted under sustained use, especially if timely replenishment of support providers does not take place (Hobfoll 1998).
- *Replenishability* refers to the ease and efficiency with which depleted resources can be replenished, recharged, reconstructed, or replaced. For example, battery packs on power tools (assuming electricity is accessible) are highly replenishable resources. In contrast, such potent and durable personal resources as self-efficacy, self-esteem, and religious faith, and such condition resources as a strong marriage or a fulfilling job, may be very resource-intensive or even impossible to replenish once they become exhausted, damaged, or lost.
- *Accessibility* refers to the degree to which resources can be obtained and utilized as needed to contend with specific stressors. Personal resources such as self-esteem are highly accessible. Although resources with low transportability may be less accessible across contexts, accessibility involves more than transportability and physical proximity. Gasoline stored in hurricane-stricken regions becomes inaccessible if a power

outage renders the pumps inoperable, and farmers cannot utilize their seed corn as food without endangering their ability to plant a new crop.

- *Efficiency* refers to the resources that must be expended to ensure that a given coping resource, when engaged, adequately meets the demands imposed by a specific stressor. For example, climbing a tree is a much more efficient method of staying alive during a flood than treading water. Resources that are ineffective in relation to a stressor cannot be efficient.
- *Facilitative effect* refers to the degree to which a resource functions as a facilitative factor in relation to beneficial factors (see Table 2.1). Variables with a high facilitative effect are resource catalysts, enhancing the beneficial effects of other resources.

Accordingly, just as Charney (2004) suggests a general resilience-promoting neurobiological profile (which may have limited or no capacity for therapeutic enhancement), it may be possible to delineate one or more "optimal" resource profiles for a given stressor (which may be much more amenable to therapeutic enhancement; see Luthar et al. 2006). This profile would be formed by aggregating the individual profiles (see Figure 2.3) of the resources that comprise one's resource caravan. The specific configuration of an *optimal* resource profile will likely vary across stressors as a function of, first, its severity, breadth, duration, and the specific demands it places on coping resources; second, specific resource attributes that enhance adaptive coping in relation to the stressor; third, appraisal processes; and fourth, the cumulative effects of other risk, vulnerability, protective, and promotive factors that make up the surrounding ecological context. Multiple resource configurations are possible to the extent that resources (e.g. self-esteem and social support) are functionally interchangeable and can thus compensate for deficits in the other.

Avenue 4: Unpacking people and caravans within adjustment trajectories

A fourth promising direction for an unpacking approach involves the use of recently developed research tools that integrate both person-centered and variable-centered approaches (e.g. Muthén and Muthén 2000) as well as qualitative methods (e.g. Maxwell 2004). Primary research aims include identifying adverse and beneficial factors that are salient (i.e. prevalent) within focal life contexts, are amenable to intervention, exert relatively enduring effects over youths' lives, and facilitate the beneficial effects of other factors, thereby promoting resource gain cycles (Luthar et al. 2006). We suggest a five-pronged approach:

1   Empirically differentiate, describe, and label specific trajectories of

posttraumatic adjustment exhibited within specific life domains in focal trauma-exposed populations (Avenue 2).

2   Identify the specific individuals nested within each trajectory within the life domains of interest (e.g. school performance, school behavior, peer relationships).
3   Unpack the risk and resource caravans of individuals nested within each trajectory within each life domain of interest by identifying the specific beneficial and adverse elements, respectively, that predict trajectory membership or otherwise form a significant part of group members' ecologies.
4   Unpack each significant coping resource found in the resource caravans of each nested group by examining the causal processes through which beneficial resources promote positive adaptation by applying the framework proposed in Avenue 3, and by examining the causal processes through which beneficial resources are adversely acted upon by the pathways proposed by Steinberg and Ritzmann (1990).
5   Evaluate the specific configurations and processes through which "resource-growing" beneficial life events intersect with "resource-depleting" adverse life events to influence adjustment within the life domains of interest, using the framework proposed in Avenue 1.

It is fruitful to identify the specific posttraumatic adjustment trajectories that emerge within a given life domain in specific populations, and to unpack the risk and resource caravans of each subgroup. Notably, specific trajectories of adaptation may have unique sets of correlates (and by extension, potentially unique sets of markers and causal mechanisms; Wiesner and Capaldi 2003). This approach may particularly benefit risk screening: since the elements that make up risk caravans often co-occur *within people* (e.g. low socioeconomic status, poverty, impaired parenting), such a person-centered approach as the one laid out in Avenues 2 to 4 may be a more efficient method for identifying "at risk" individuals in acute need of intervention than the variable-centered approach laid out in Avenue 1 (Q. Zhou, personal communication, August 2007).

We should, however, be even more keenly interested in *the processes through which group members' resources are managed, acted upon, and function in ways that contribute to their trajectory membership as an outcome*. This is because the most clinically and theoretically informative difference between trajectories may not be in members' overall *level* of, for example, social support; but in how this resource is recruited, maintained, employed in coping efforts, and acted upon for good or ill. For example, we theorize that *stress resistance* may eventuate from the effective buildup, utilization, and sustaining of good-fitting coping resources before, during, and following trauma exposure (see Figure 2.2). In contrast, *resilient recovery* may reflect either the depletion of well-fitting resources faster than they can be replenished (a common occurrence when stressors are severe, prolonged, or repeated); the utilization of resources that lack the durability or shelf life necessary to sustain stress resistance; or the use of inefficient or partially effective coping strategies. Regardless of how resources are depleted, resilient recovery involves efficient post-exposure resource replenishment and consequent recovery. Further, the slow recovery trajectory characteristic of *protracted recovery* may signify the depletion of resources that have limited replenishability, the influence of ongoing loss cycles, barriers to resource replenishment, or some combination thereof. *Posttraumatic growth* may reflect the gradual buildup of resources through gain cycles (cf. Hobfoll et al. 2007). *Severe persisting distress* may reflect the massive depletion of resources that cannot be replenished, or that induce or accelerate loss cycles from which the individual does not recover. *Decline* may reflect the initial use of well-fitting resources without access to replenishment; or alternatively, the use of resources that lack replenishability, durability, or shelf life, and consequently become exhausted, worn out, or obsolete over time. Last, *stable maladaptive functioning* may reflect the impact of massive, high-momentum loss cycles from which the individual cannot escape without the infusion of external aid.

Avenue 5: Unpacking interventions to promote wellness-oriented public health goals

A fifth promising application of an unpacking-oriented approach involves delineating the procedures that are employed in public health-oriented interventions for trauma-exposed populations and articulating the implications of the four unpacking-based approaches described earlier hold at each stage. Figure 2.4 presents eleven procedures that are often conducted in a progressive sequence, returning to previous steps or iterating the cycle as needed. These steps are described in detail elsewhere in this volume (Ford, Albert, and Hawke, Chapter 12; Van Horn and Lieberman, Chapter 13; Saltzman et al., Chapter 15).

Assembling the components to guide interventions: an illustration using COR theory

We now further develop the theme described in Avenue 5 by illustrating ways in which unpacked stages of intervention can be assembled to guide wellness-oriented public health interventions following trauma exposure. We chose COR theory (Hobfoll et al. 1988, 1998) on the basis of its ecological perspective, its emphasis on prevention and early intervention, and its capacity to address both traumatic and less severe stressors, and because of its capacity to account for the ways in which adverse and beneficial life events may intersect to influence the clinical course of posttraumatic adjustment.

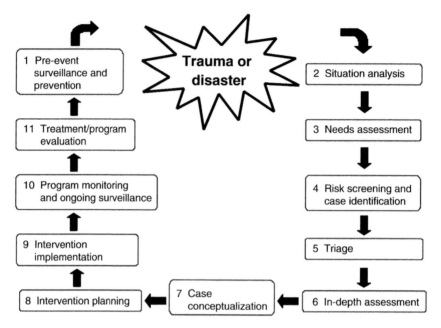

Figure 2.4 Unpacking public health-oriented, trauma-focused interventions into their constituent steps.

Pre-event surveillance and prevention

Based on the COR principles that loss is more salient than gain, and that gain cycles proceed more slowly than loss cycles, the pre-event period is a critically important window of opportunity in which to carry out wellness-oriented preventive activities. These include:

- identify populations at risk for exposure to the traumatic stressor
- where possible, reduce the risk for exposure to the stressor
- anticipate the demands that the stressor will likely impose on those exposed
- identify configurations of coping resources that will provide a good 'fit' for the stressor
- implement programs where possible to build up these resources in developmentally and culturally appropriate ways (Layne et al. 2007).

Stopping or slowing resource loss cycles is also a high priority. Accordingly, the optimal elements from which such preventive efforts should be built are *promotive* and *beneficial synergistic factors*. Because these resources exert a beneficial effect regardless of whether the focal risk factor(s) is present, programs that enhance these resources are a good investment for promoting general wellness and positive youth development. Also desirable are *robust resources*, which are potent in relation to a range of different stressors, and *facilitative factors*. Collectively, these beneficial agents may serve as the nucleus around which constellations of resources can aggregate through gain cycles, creating *stress-inoculating resource caravans* that accompany youths through critical developmental periods and beyond. Extra care is needed during developmental transitions to ensure that resource caravans maintain their continuity and momentum while being appropriately reconfigured to accommodate emerging developmental tasks, challenges, and competencies (Masten et al. 2004).

Moreover, in accordance with the public health principle that disproportionately more resources should be allocated to subgroups with greater needs, additional preventive goals include:

- identify subgroups that are vulnerable to the stressor(s)
- where possible, reduce vulnerability to the stressor(s).

By definition, the resource profiles of vulnerable subgroups match up poorly with the anticipated demands of the stressor. Their resources may lack potency, durability, transportability, accessibility, or a mechanism for replenishment; may have an insufficient shelf life given the anticipated duration of the stressor and access to replenishment; may inefficiently consume scarce resources; or may consist of an insufficient amount of well-fitting resources. Accordingly, in addition to promotive factors described above (which benefit 'resilient' and 'non-resilient' groups alike), the primary elements from which vulnerability-reducing interventions should draw are *promotive/protective synergistic* and *protective factors*. Because synergistic factors, when found, are "powerhouse" resources that exert both a direct promotive effect and an incremental protective effect in the presence of the risk factor(s), they are generally more desirable vulnerability-reducing tools than protective factors, which yield their benefits only under stressful circumstances.

Situation analysis and needs assessment

Once a given traumatic event has occurred, wellness-oriented public health interventions should seek to evaluate the nature and effects of the event with respect to its breadth, duration, the levels of the ecology that have been impacted, and the types and amounts of resource loss that have occurred. Also important are an evaluation of the types of resource loss cycles set in motion or accelerated by the event, as well as barriers to gain cycles. Of equal importance is the need to appraise the specific demands that the event and its aftermath will likely place on exposed individuals, families, and communities, and the types of well-fitting coping resources that intervention programs should seek to deliver or support.

Risk screening, case identification, and triage

Efforts to identify and appropriately triage victims should place highest priority on identifying individuals at risk for severe persisting distress, dysfunction, and developmental derailment. Markers of high risk include:

- massive resource loss induced by exposure to trauma-related risk factors, as these factors interact with vulnerability factors
- insufficient amounts of well-fitting coping resources
- the exhaustion of well-fitting coping resources
- interference in the capacity to access or replenish well-fitting coping resources
- the use of inefficient coping resources
- the use of ineffective coping resources
- the presence of significant resource loss cycles
- barriers to orchestrating gain cycles, including insufficient resources or opportunities for resource investment, or the adoption of defensive resource-conserving strategies that inhibit investment (Hobfoll et al., Chapter 9 in this volume; Steinberg and Ritzmann 1990).

In-depth assessment, case conceptualization, and intervention planning

The overarching aim of wellness-oriented public health interventions is to channel as many trauma-exposed survivors *into* adaptive posttraumatic adjustment trajectories in as many developmentally salient life domains; and to channel as many survivors *away from* less desirable posttraumatic adjustment trajectories in as many developmentally salient life domains, as possible under the circumstances. Key intervention objectives include promoting stress resistance and resilient recovery through such activities as facilitating the use of maximally potent and efficient coping resources and strategies; enhancing accessibility; and enhancing resource replenishment. Enhancing effective coping *strategies* may be equally as important as enhancing the use of coping *resources* – for example, potent resources that lack durability (e.g. money) may nevertheless be managed to function like durable resources when paired with access to replenishment (e.g. a regular income). Just as a hemorrhaging medical patient requires procedures that both staunch the loss of blood and replace lost blood, resource-based interventions should target both halting or slowing loss cycles and, as soon as possible, initiating and accelerating gain cycles. Because highly impacted groups possess comparatively fewer resources and will tend to employ defensive resource-conserving strategies (Hobfoll et al., Chapter 9), assisting these groups will often require undertaking specialized, resource-intensive, multi-tiered interventions. These interventions will likely target both the enhancement of naturally existing coping resources (e.g. support-seeking and parenting skills), and the inculcation of specialized skills shown to be potent in coping with the stressor (e.g. teaching skills for coping with trauma reminders). In addition, multi-tiered interventions within the individual, family, and broader community will set the stage for beneficial "trickle-down" and "trickle-up" effects across levels of the ecology.

Implementation of the intervention, program monitoring, and surveillance

As intervention progresses, efforts should be directed towards reducing the risk for exposure to subsequent trauma and secondary adversities, and in seeking opportunities to halt or slow loss cycles and to initiate or accelerate gain cycles.

Conclusion

As readers have been cautioned concerning the overuse of the term "risk factor" (Vogt et al. 2007), we also caution that many "protective" and "vulnerability" factors may be mislabeled in the literature. Such looseness in our conceptual and methodological terminology unfortunately blurs distinctions between classes of variables that vary in important ways in their implications for intervention planning and implementation. This looseness in how we think and communicate will also slow the rate at which we accumulate scientific knowledge about various forms of posttraumatic adjustment (Layne et al. 2007). Until we are better able to accurately describe, explain, and predict how adverse and beneficial causal factors intersect and causally influence posttraumatic adjustment, it is possible that our greatest single advances in undertaking wellness-oriented interventions will be made in refining our risk screening technology: we will get better and better at identifying those *in need* of intervention, but we will still lack crucial knowledge about *how to best help them* – knowledge that only a well-grounded understanding of how their difficulties and strengths are caused, maintained, and influence one another can bring. Until that time, our interventions may rely as much on borrowing from other fields (as evidence-informed practices), clinical lore, and educated assumptions, as on the solid footings of our own rigorously tested theories and empirical evidence. We hope that the unpacked, integrative framework we have proposed will promote further discovery of the processes through which beneficial resources are built up, utilized, depleted, and replenished over time. These advances will, in turn, promote the development of evidence-based, theoretically grounded, wellness-oriented public health interventions that strategically build up stress resistance before traumatic events occur and, when needed, promote resilient recovery afterwards.

Acknowledgements

Support for this work was provided by research grants to the first author from the Family Studies Center and the Kennedy International Studies Center, both of Brigham Young University; and the UCLA Trauma Psychiatry Bing Fund. The authors are grateful for the assistance of members of the BYU Developmental Psychopathology Research Lab, including Anthony Albano, Jacob Tanner, Jonathan Zabriskie, and Paul Hanson; and for the administrative support of Preston Finley. The authors wish to thank Drs. Qing Zhou, Joseph Olsen, and Susan Ko for their helpful suggestions on an earlier draft of this chapter.

Notes

1 Kaufman et al. (2004) found evidence of genetic vulnerability to develop childhood depression when childhood maltreatment is present: homozygosity of the short allele of the 5-HT transporter gene appears to increase the likelihood of childhood depression only in children with histories of maltreatment.
2 The correlational nature of non-experimental longitudinal research makes causal inference pertaining to "risk" and "protective" factors a probabilistic enterprise. Intervention research (especially randomized controlled trials) may provide more definitive evidence of causal links between risk factors and outcomes (Masten 2007).
3 The role a given variable may play (e.g. risk vs. vulnerability vs. synergistic factor) may vary across studies, and within the same study, as a function of the type of disaster, other variables in the model, guiding theory, and analytic strategy. Replication is thus essential for identifying consistently influential variables and their "behavioral" tendencies across studies and contexts.
4 In contrast to "unipolar" variables, "bipolar" variables (see Masten 2001) may exhibit not only inhibitory and facilitative moderating effects at opposing ends of their continua in relation to a given *promotive* factor, but also protective and vulnerability-enhancing moderating effects in relation to a given *risk* factor. Such variables should be termed *facilitative/inhibitory factors* and *protective/vulnerability factors* respectively; each can be represented in a single model. Bipolar *promotive/ risk factors* may be found in circumstances where direct beneficial versus adverse effects are found at opposing ends of the variable's continuum.
5 Not all agents that enhance stress resistance are socially desirable, and not all agents that increase vulnerability are socially undesirable (e.g. empathic distress vs. indifference in a child who witnesses a classmate's victimization).

References

Baron, R.M., and Kenny, D.A. (1986). The moderator-mediator variable distinction in social psychological research: Conceptual, strategic, and statistical considerations. *Journal of Personality and Social Psychology, 51*, 1173–1182.
Benson, P.L., Scales, P.C., Hamilton, S.F., and Sesma, A. (2006). Positive youth development: Theory, research, and applications. In W. Damon and R.M. Lerner (eds.), *Handbook of child psychology* (pp. 894–941). Hoboken, NJ: Wiley.

Bernat, D.H., and Resnick, M.D. (2006). Healthy youth development: Science and strategies. *Journal of Public Health Management and Practice* (suppl.), S10–S16.

Brown, G.W. (2000). Emotion and clinical depression: An environmental view. In M. Lewis and J.M. Haviland-Jones (eds.), *Handbook of emotions* (pp. 75–90). New York: Guilford.

Brown, G.W., and Harris, T.O. (1978). *The social origins of depression: A study of psychiatric disorder in women.* London: Tavistock.

Charney, D.S. (2004). Psychobiological mechanisms of resilience and vulnerability: Implications for successful adaptation to extreme stress. *American Journal of Psychiatry, 161*, 195–216.

Cooke, D.J. (1985). Psychosocial vulnerability to life events during the climacteric. *British Journal of Psychiatry, 147*, 71–75.

Crawford, E., Wright, M.O., and Masten, A.S. (2006). Resilience and spirituality in youth. In E.C. Roehlkepartain, P.E. King, L. Wagener, and P.L. Benson (eds.), *The handbook of spiritual development in childhood and adolescence* (pp. 355–370). Thousand Oaks, CA: Sage.

Dohrenwend, B.P. (2006). Inventorying stressful life events as risk factors for psychopathology: Toward resolution of the problem of intracategory variability. *Psychological Bulletin, 132*, 477–495.

Dohrenwend, B.P., Raphael, K.G., Schwartz, S., Stueve, A., and Skodol, A.E. (1993). The structured event probe and narrative rating method (SEPRATE) for measuring stressful life events. In L. Goldberger and S. Breznitz (eds.), *Handbook of stress: Theoretical and clinical aspects*, 2nd edition (pp. 174–199). New York: Free Press.

Edwards, J.R., and Lambert, L.S. (2007). Methods for integrating moderation and mediation: A general analytical framework using moderated pathway analysis. *Psychological Methods, 12*, 1–22.

Foy, D.W., Osato, S.S., Bouskamp, B.M., and Neumann, D.A. (1992). Etiology of posttraumatic stress disorder. In P.A. Saigh (ed.), *Posttraumatic stress disorder: A behavioral approach to assessment and treatment*. New York: Macmillan.

Friedman, M.J., Resick, P.A., and Keane, T.M. (2007). Key questions and an agenda for future research. In M.J. Friedman, T.M. Keane, and P.A. Resick (eds.), *Handbook of PTSD: Science and practice* (pp. 540–561). New York: Guilford.

Harris, T.O., Brown, G.W., and Bifulco, A. (1986). Loss of parent in childhood and adult psychiatric disorder: The role of lack of adequate parental care. *Psychological Medicine, 16*, 641–659.

Harris, W.H., Putnam, F.W., and Fairbank, J.A. (2006). Mobilizing trauma resources for children. In A.F. Lieberman and R. DeMartino (eds.), *Interventions for children exposed to violence*. Johnson and Johnson Pediatric Institute. Retrieved June 1, 2007 from www.jjpi.com

Harvey, P.D., and Yehuda, R. (1999). Strategies to study risk for the development of PTSD. In R. Yehuda (ed.), *Risk factors for posttraumatic stress disorder* (pp. 1–22). Washington, DC: American Psychiatric Press.

Haynes, S.N. (1992). *Models of causality in psychopathology: Toward synthetic, dynamic and nonlinear models of causality in psychopathology*. Des Moines, IA: Allyn and Bacon.

Hobfoll, S.E. (1988). *The ecology of stress*. New York: Hemisphere.

Hobfoll, S.E. (1998). *Stress, culture, and community: The psychology and philosophy of stress*. New York: Plenum.

Hobfoll, S.E., Hall, B.J., Canetti-Nisim, D., Galea, S., Johnson, R.J., and Palmieri, P.A. (2007). Refining our understanding of traumatic growth in the face of terrorism: Moving from meaning cognitions to doing what is meaningful. *Applied Psychology: An International Review, 56*, 345–366.

Holmbeck, G.N., Friedman, D., and Abad, M. (2006). Development and psychopathology in adolescence. In D.A. Wolfe and E.J. Mash (eds.), *Behavioral and emotional disorders in adolescents: Nature, assessment, and treatment* (pp. 21–55). New York: Guilford.

Kaufman, J., Yang, B.-Z., Douglas-Palumberi, H., Houshyar, S., Lipschitz, D., Krystal, J.H., et al. (2004). Social supports and serotonin transporter gene moderate depression in maltreated children. *Proceedings of the National Academy of Sciences USA, 101*, 17316–17321.

Kraemer, H.C., Kazdin, A.E., Offord, D.R., Kessler, R.C., Jensen, P.S., and Kupfer, D.J. (1997). Coming to terms with the terms of risk. *Archives of General Psychiatry, 54*, 337–343.

Kraemer, H.C., Stice, E., Kazdin, A., Offor, D., and Kupfer, D. (2001). How do risk factors work together? Mediators, moderators, and independent, overlapping, and proxy risk factors. *American Journal of Psychiatry, 158*, 848–856.

Layne, C.M., Warren, J., Watson, P., and Shalev, A. (2007). Risk, vulnerability, resistance, and resilience: Towards an integrative conceptualization of posttraumatic adaptation. In M.J. Friedman, T.M. Keane, and P.A. Resick (eds.), *Handbook of PTSD: Science and Practice.* (pp. 497–520). New York: Guilford.

Liberman, R.P., and Corrigan, P.W. (1992). Is schizophrenia a neurological disorder? *Journal of Neuropsychiatry, 4*(2), 119–124.

Liberman, R.P., and Corrigan, P.W. (1993). Designing new psychosocial treatments for schizophrenia. *Psychiatry, 56*, 238–249.

Luthar, S.S. (2006). Resilience in development: A synthesis of research across five decades. In D. Cicchetti and D.J. Cohen (eds.), *Developmental psychopathology, Volume 3: Risk, disorder, and adaptation*, 2nd edition (pp. 739–795). Hoboken, NJ: Wiley.

Luthar, S.S., Sawyer, J.A., and Brown, P.J. (2006). Conceptual issues in studies of resilience: Past, present, and future research. *Annals of the New York Academy of Science, 1094*, 105–115.

Masten, A.S. (2001). Ordinary magic: Resilience processes in development. *American Psychologist, 56*, 227–238.

Masten, A.S. (2007). Resilience in developing systems: Progress and promise as the fourth wave rises. *Development and Psychopathology, 19*, 921–930.

Masten, A.S., and Obradović, J. (2007). Disaster preparation and recovery: Lessons from research on resilience in human development. *Ecology and Society, 13*(1), 9.

Masten, A.S., Burt, K.B., Roisman, G.I., Obradović, J., Long, J.D., and Tellegen, A. (2004). Resources and resilience in the transition to adulthood: Continuity and change. *Development and Psychopathology, 16*, 1071–1094.

Maxwell, J.A. (2004). Using qualitative methods for causal explanation. *Field Methods, 16*, 243–264.

Muthén, B.O., and Muthén, L.K. (2000). Integrating person-centered and variable-centered analyses: Growth mixture modeling with latent trajectory classes. *Alcoholism: Clinical and Experimental Research, 24*, 882–891.

Pynoos, R.S., and Steinberg, A.M. (2006). Recovery of children and adolescents after exposure to violence: Developmental ecological framework. In A.F. Lieberman and R. DeMartino (eds.), *Interventions for children exposed to violence* (pp. 17–43). New Brunswick, NJ: Johnson and Johnson Pediatric Institute.

Rutter, M. (1987). Psychosocial resilience and protective mechanisms. *American Journal of Orthopsychiatry, 57*, 316–331.

Seligman, M.E. (2002). Positive psychology, positive prevention, and positive therapy. In C.R. Snyder and S.J. Lopez (eds.), *Handbook of positive psychology* (pp. 3–9). New York: Oxford University Press.

Silva, R.R., and Kessler, L. (2004). Resiliency and vulnerability factors in childhood PTSD. In R.R. Silva (ed.), *Posttraumatic stress disorders in children and adolescents* (pp.18–37). New York: Norton.

Steinberg, A., and Ritzmann, R.F. (1990). A living systems approach to understanding the concept of stress. *Behavioral Science, 35*, 138–146.

Vogt, D.S., King, D.W., and King, L.A. (2007). Risk pathways for PTSD: Making sense of the literature. In M.J. Friedman, T.M. Keane, and P.A. Resick (eds.), *Handbook of PTSD: Science and Practice* (pp. 99–115). New York: Guilford.

Watson, P.J., Ritchie, E.C., Demer, J., Bartone, P., and Pfefferbaum, B.J. (2006). Improving resilience trajectories following mass violence and disaster. In E.C. Ritchie, P.J. Watson, and M.J. Friedman (eds.), *Interventions following mass violence and disasters: Strategies for mental health practice* (pp. 37–53). New York: Guilford.

Wiesner, M., and Capaldi, D.M. (2003). Relations of childhood and adolescent factors to offending trajectories of young men. *Journal of Research in Crime and Delinquency, 40*, 231–262.

Zubin, J., and Spring, B. (1977). Vulnerability: A new view of schizophrenia. *Journal of Abnormal Psychology, 86*, 103–126.

Part I

Risk and protective factors

Chapter 3

The search for risk and protective factors in childhood PTSD

From variables to processes

Ruth Pat-Horenczyk, Renee G. Rabinowitz, Aya Rice, and Arlene Tucker-Levin

This chapter presents a bird's-eye view of the burgeoning literature on risk and protective factors associated with posttraumatic distress in children and adolescents. We summarize the existing research on the responses of children to a variety of traumatic experiences, with a special focus on risk and protective factors that affect young children. We also outline promising new directions in the field, specifically, the notion that childhood PTSD must be viewed within a developmental framework and that the identification of risk and protective factors needs to be accompanied by an understanding of underlying processes. Finally, we discuss possible implications and future avenues for intervention in the field of childhood PTSD.

Evidence on risk and protective factors

Individuals exposed to trauma respond in a unique fashion, based on complex combinations of risk and protective factors. We divide risk and protective factors into two groups:

- environmental and contextual factors, with special emphasis on the role of parents
- individual determinants, particularly biological factors and their corre-lates.

Environmental and contextual factors

The nature of the traumatic event

There are many types of stressors with the potential for triggering PTSD including human-made events such as war and civilian violence and natural disasters such as tsunamis and earthquakes. Some events are stronger than others in precipitating PTSD. Norris et al. (2002) found that mass vio-lence and human-made disasters (e.g. terrorism, shooting sprees) were more influential than natural or technological ones. Furthermore, Van der Kolk et al. (2005) indicated that childhood interpersonal trauma was more likely to be associated with complex PTSD than accidents, disasters, or adult onset trauma.

It is not only the type of traumatic event that is associated with the development of PTSD, but also the physical proximity of the child to it (Pine et al. 2005). Children who were close to the site of the September 11 attacks in New York reported more symptoms congruent with and related to PTSD than those located further away (Duggal et al. 2002). Proximity to and severity of Scuds missile attacks in Israel during the first Gulf War were directly linked to the development of PTSD among young children (Laor et al. 1996). Another Israeli study, in the context of ongoing terrorism, showed that adolescents personally exposed (e.g. having been present at a terrorist attack or knowing someone who was wounded or killed in the attack) and those with a "near miss experience" (e.g. having planned to be at the site of a terrorist attack) reported significantly more severe posttraumatic stress symptoms than those not directly involved in any terrorist attack (Pat-Horenczyk et al. 2007a).

Another issue related to indirect exposure to traumatic events is the effect of media exposure on posttraumatic symptoms. There is concern for all ages for the potential exacerbation of posttraumatic reactions through media coverage, but children present a special case due to their immature cognitive capacities (Pine et al. 2005). For direct victims, media coverage which includes graphic images of the attack may be retraumatizing. A study by Ahern et al. (2002) found that television viewing of some images was associated with measures of PTSD and depression in those with direct event experiences but not in those without. In terms of direct exposure, a dose–response relationship with risk for psychopathology emerges in children as in adults. The results reported by Pfefferbaum et al. (2003) showed that among indirectly exposed children, reactions were more severe among those with a history of previous trauma, suggesting the impact of individual vulnerability. At the same time, in a study of children exposed to the 9/11 World Trade Center disaster, even those who were only indirectly exposed through media coverage, exhibited psychiatric disorders that were two to three times as severe in New York City than in nearby urban and suburban school students tested a year earlier (Hoven et al. 2003). Thus, there seems to be insufficient evidence for claiming that media coverage generates posttraumatic symptoms and related negative emotional responses (Pfefferbaum et al. 2002). More research is needed on the characteristics of children that make them more or less susceptible to the influence of the media, the role of various media modalities, and the specific and problematic aspects of media coverage. In addition there is a need to look at the range of both negative and positive outcomes of media coverage, and to examine the impact of the media on a broader scope of children's reactions, beyond PTSD, such as fear, anxiety, attitudes and behavior (Pfefferbaum et al. 2002). Meanwhile, as Pine et al. (2005) suggested:

While American society values not concealing things from children and providing opportunities for them to express their fears and anxieties, there is strong evidence that younger children, at least, do better if provided with some protection from the full intensity and repeated coverage by media of trauma and disaster.

(Pine et al. 2005, p. 1786)

Culture and ethnicity

Research in this area is hampered by a lack of uniformity in the definition of race and ethnicity and by the confounding effect of such variables as socio-economic status. In addition, ethnic and cultural differences in beliefs about how to handle emotional disturbances may influence access to care and the manner in which individuals present symptoms to clinicians (Pfefferbaum 1997). For example, in a study involving Palestinian youth exposed to political violence, extremely high rates of somatic complaints were found (Pat-Horenczyk et al. 2007c). One explanation offered was that this is a socially acceptable way to express emotional distress within that community. Studies of the levels of PTSD among Hispanic and Black children have resulted in different findings, with LaGreca et al. (1996) reporting higher levels among Hispanic and Black children, and Shannon et al. (1994) and Garrison et al. (1993) finding no differences. In a review of the few available studies on the role of cultural and ethnic differences in disaster-related research, Rabalais et al. (2002) concluded that culture may serve as either a risk or a protective factor.

Social support

The presence of social support has been found to be a very important protective factor while the lack of it is a risk factor for the development of adult PTSD. Pine and Cohen (2002) in fact suggest that social support is the single strongest protective factor. Brewin et al. (2000), in their meta-analysis of risk factors, found that the absence of social support and the presence of contextual life stress were risk factors with a greater effect on the development of PTSD, than the more traditional risk or moderator variables, including intelligence, a history of child abuse and even the magnitude of the trauma exposure.

Considering adolescents, Schiff et al. (2007) found that among Israeli adolescents exposed to terrorist attacks, lack of social support was a significant predictor for posttraumatic and depressive symptoms. However, social support was not found to play a buffering role and the researchers concluded instead that it had a positive compensatory effect on the youths' mental health irrespective of the type and level of experienced stressors. These findings are consistent with other studies showing social support to be a largely protective mediator (Jackson et al. 2007) or moderator (Kaufman et al. 2004) of children's posttraumatic problems in coping with traumatic stressors, including accidents, violence, and maltreatment. The current paucity of studies of the role of social support among traumatized adolescents and children indicates a need for more work in this important area.

Parents

ATTACHMENT

It is quite clear that the parent–child relationship is the most crucial risk or protective factor for children exposed to traumatic events. Attachment serves as the mechanism through which parents affect their children's sense of "felt security" when they feel threatened, vulnerable, or distressed. Proximity to a caregiver is an innate means for affect regulation that calms the nervous system (Schore 1994). Johnson (2005) expressed this as follows:

> If a child or adult experiences fear, but has confidence that another will be present and responsive, there will be an expectation of relief and support. Fear and the need to escape and protect the self are, then, not so overwhelming, and fear cues will be dealt with effectively. Thus, secure emotional connections with significant others may offer a powerful antidote to traumatic experience.
>
> (Johnson 2005, p. 49)

It is through the attachment relationship with a primary caregiver (usually the mother) that children learn to organize and regulate their emotional experiences, an ability shown to be an important factor in healthy psychological development. Of great help in this process is the mother's skill in reflecting the infant's emotions and representing them symbolically, as in her verbal interactions with the infant (Fonagy 1999). Many researchers, such as Stafford et al. (2003), believe that the attachment relationship is so important that its role should be explicitly incorporated into conceptualizations of PTSD in young children. For a more extensive discussion of self-regulation, see Chapter 12 by Ford, Albert, and Hawke in this volume.

The power of parental attachment and bonding may be seen in the role these factors play in strengthening resilience and countering the negative effects of a problematic family and community in children from high-risk backgrounds. Specifically, it has been suggested that a warm, nurturing, and supportive relationship with at least one parent may protect against, or mitigate, the effects of family adversity (Herrenkohl et al. 1994; Seifer et al. 1992; Werner 1989). Results of a longitudinal study on adolescents in London conducted by Bifulco (see Chapter 7 in this volume) provides information on the protective factors in high-risk families. More specifically, a child's close relationship with the mother in early childhood was predictive of positive academic and peer experiences in the latency period. This in turn predicted self-acceptance and a relationship with a trusted confidant as a teen, each of which was associated with testing in the psychologically healthy range as an adolescent.

It is not only parents who are a possible protective resource. Research on first responders, such as police officers, firefighters, emergency management teams, and other significant adults such as childcare providers, has shown how effective they may be as adult attachment figures. These first responders, who reach out to young children in distress, may take on the role of "angels", providing an alternative response to that of an ineffective parent. They may help children internalize a positive working model of the self, perhaps building a sense that there may be other people in their lives whom they can trust to be available at difficult times. Another possible explanation for the effectiveness of first responders is offered by Lieberman et al. (2005). Encounters with first responders may bring to mind the more positive experiences young children have had with primary attachment figures earlier in their lives. In essence, all the studies concur that the most important protective resource is a strong relationship with a competent, caring, positive adult, who is most often a parent but can also be another trusted person. For a comprehensive review of the mechanisms of parental influence on children's coping with trauma, see Chapter 4 by Cohen in this volume.

PARENTAL PSYCHOPATHOLOGY

Mental illness in parents has been found to be highly correlated with various developmental problems in their children (Seifer and Dickstein 2000). One possible explanation for this is found in the work of Fonagy (1999), in which he states that parental psychopathology is likely to endanger the quality of the parent–child attachment. Parents' disorganized attachment strategies during a child's infancy have consistently been shown to be risk factors for later psychopathology in preschool, middle childhood, and adolescence (Lyons-Ruth and Jacobvitz 1999). In support of this, and specifically with regard to PTSD, Schuengel et al. (1999) note that it has been rather well established that maternal PTSD symptoms have a significant effect on infants' behavior and their ability to develop secure attachments. Furthermore, in a study of Cambodian refugees living in the United States, it was shown that parental PTSD predicted higher rates of child PTSD for older children. A gradient effect was found such that when neither parent had PTSD, 12.9 percent of the children had PTSD; when one parent had PTSD, 23.3 percent of the children had PTSD; and, when both parents had PTSD, the percentage of children with PTSD jumped to 41.2 percent. Various environmental factors, such as reported war trauma, personal loss, living arrangements, and socioeconomic status, were not associated with the findings (Sack et al. 1995).

A possible mediating factor for the harmful effect of parental PTSD on children is that parents with PTSD are less able to react sensitively to their children (Samper et al. 2004). Conversely, parental social competence is thought to be an important protective factor for children, buffering them from stressors and helping to prevent serious emotional and behavioral problems in the children's later life (Garmezy 1991). Children whose parents are supportive, emotionally available and teach their children effective emotional regulation strategies and coping skills are more likely to be socially competent and less prone to experience negative emotions and behaviors with peers (Denham et al. 1997).

Of special interest are studies in which parents and their children were exposed to the same traumatic event. Laor et al. (1996, 1997) studied 3 to 5-year-old children and their mothers, who were exposed to rocket attacks in Israel during the Gulf War. They found significant correlations between the intrusive thoughts and avoidance symptoms of the mothers and the severity of PTSD in the 3–4 year olds. However, this association did not persist among the 5 year olds. These studies suggest that younger children are more vulnerable to PTSD because they are more dependent on parental protective factors than are school-aged children and adolescents. Older children may be less vulnerable because of their more advanced ability to process events cognitively and regulate affect independently of their parents.

Scheeringa and Zeanah (2001) have suggested a number of models for understanding the connections between PTSD in children under the age of 4 years and their relations with their parents. Keren and Tyano (see Chapter 5 in this volume) present a more in-depth review of current knowledge and developing ideas in our understanding of trauma in infants. Other studies of concurrent exposure of parents and children to a traumatic event have found a significant correlation between the severity of the parent's distress and symptoms on the one hand, and the severity of the child's distress and symptoms, on the other (Koplewicz et al. 2002; Sack et al. 1995; Scheeringa and Zeanah 2001). Another finding, reported by Ajdukovic (1998), was a connection between the child's perception of the parent's anxiety and the severity of PTSD symptoms in the child.

An important question that arises is whether the child's symptoms are the result of the parent's PTSD or mainly due to the fact that the parent was exposed to danger. There has been research supporting both views, with some showing that parental PTSD is the significant factor in predicting detrimental effects on their children (Caselli and Motta 1995; Yehuda et al. 2001), while other researchers have found that the mere exposure of their parents to danger predicted children's symptoms (Dansby and Marinelli 1999; Rosenheck and Fontana 1998). Scheeringa and Zeanah (1995) have demonstrated that the strongest predictor of whether or not traumatized infants develop PTSD is whether the child's caregiver was also threatened by the event or circumstance. This factor was even more powerful than whether or not the infant was physically injured.

TRANSGENERATIONAL TRANSMISSION OF TRAUMA

Much of our knowledge of the "intergenerational transmission of trauma" (Lieberman et al. 2005) is taken from clinical reports and research on families of Holocaust survivors and Vietnam veterans. A discrepancy developed between clinical findings, which reported a wide range of emotional difficulties, such as high levels of anxiety, depression, maladaptive behavior, and personality disorders (Barocas and Barocas 1979; Danieli 1982), and empirical research that did not confirm these results in controlled studies (Schwartz et al. 1994). The research, although clearly refuting the existence of specific psychopathology, did confirm some differences between children of Holocaust survivors and peers whose parents had not had this experience. The two groups differed in their interaction patterns with their environment (Brom et al. 2001). Moreover, the children of survivors showed an increased vulnerability to the development of PTSD when faced with a traumatic experience (Yehuda et al. 2001). A significant relationship also was found between PTSD among Vietnam veterans and behavior problems such as aggressiveness, hyperactivity, and delinquency in their children (Parsons et al. 1990). Fathers who served in Vietnam and developed PTSD were more likely to treat their children in a controlling, aggressive, demanding, and overprotective manner and at times found it difficult to differentiate between their children's age-appropriate aggressiveness and the violence they had experienced during the war (Galovski and Lyons 2004).

Ancharoff et al. (1998) noted a few possible mechanisms by which trauma is transmitted to the next generation. One mechanism, which they call *the silent mechanism*, is when the child senses the parent's vulnerability and makes every effort to avoid providing any stimulus that will hurt the parent or remind them of the trauma. This silence thus becomes a barrier between the parent and child and prevents the child from seeking help or consolation from the parent. A second mechanism is *when parents reveal too much*, describing their experiences to their children in detail, so that the children become traumatized by their inability to handle the information. A third mechanism is called *identification*, when the children are repeatedly exposed to their parents' posttraumatic behavior, identify with the parental role as victim, and mimic the parents' behavior.

Individual determinants

Clearly, a child may be at increased risk or may be further protected due to individual characteristics and previous experiences.

Exposure history

Extensive research has identified an individual's trauma history as an important determinant of his or her response to trauma. Contrary to the common belief that experiencing traumatic events may "strengthen" or "inoculate" the survivor, the evidence shows that those previously exposed to a significant stressor may have a greater propensity to develop PTSD upon subsequent exposure to trauma (Silva 2004). Cortina and Kubiak (2006) found that a history of sexual victimization during childhood was a significant determinant of women's increased risk of PTSD. The total number of traumas experienced by children also was found to be the strongest predictor of PTSD severity in a study of Palestinian children (Thabet and Vostanis 1999). At the same time, Grant-Knight, Geltman, and Ellis (Chapter 6 in this volume) present a study of Sudanese adolescents who emigrated to the United States after spending much of their childhood surrounded by almost perpetual violence, profound physical, emotional and educational neglect, and separation from and loss of their families. Despite their extreme exposure to trauma, these youths displayed fairly low rates of PTSD. The authors explain these findings by attributing possible protective mechanisms to the supportive social networks, the meaning ascribed to their experiences by their culture, and the resettlement program which may have promoted mental health among these youths.

Age

Although the manifestations of PTSD are age-dependent, the existing literature yields inconsistent data on age as a risk factor for PTSD. Some studies imply that adolescents are at greater risk, while others indicate that younger children are (Saigh et al. 1999). Fletcher (as cited in Salmon and Bryant 2002) conducted a meta-analysis of thirty-four samples of traumatized children, and concluded that the rate of diagnosed PTSD did not change significantly across developmental levels, in a comparison of preschoolers, school-aged children, and teenagers. In general, it appears that age is not an independent risk factor, but may interact with other factors, such as familial variables and the type of trauma.

Gender

Although several studies have found that women have a greater propensity to develop PTSD (Breslau et al. 1997), this seemingly greater vulnerability may be connected with other aspects that are differentially associated with gender, such as coping style (Pfefferbaum 1997). Among children, research has shown that gender affects symptom development. Following a natural disaster (Shannon et al. 1994), and following sexual and physical abuse

(Ackerman et al. 1998), girls tend to manifest more symptoms related to a form of emotional processing known as *internalization*. Boys, on the other hand, experience symptoms of a cognitive or behavioral nature, known as *externalizing* symptoms. Similarily, Pat-Horenczyk et al. (2007a) reported that in a situation of ongoing terrorism adolescent girls tend to report more posttraumatic symptoms while boys exhibit more functional impairment, mainly in family interaction and social relationships.

Cognitive ability

Tiet et al. (1998) found that higher IQ among youths bolstered their adjustment process. Similarly Silva et al. (2000) found verbal IQ to be the strongest resiliency measure providing protection against the development of PTSD. However, other conditions that may account for both lower IQ and PTSD vulnerability, such as brain damage caused by childhood abuse or early maternal deprivation, cannot be ruled out.

Self-efficacy

Perceived self-efficacy, the belief in one's abilities to deal effectively with specific situations, including threat (Bandura 1997), has been shown to be one of the major protective factors in resilience. Adolescents with PTSD have significantly lower than average self-efficacy ratings on most of the subtests of Bandura's Multidimensional Scales of Perceived Self-Efficacy (1997). Diehl and Prout (2002) further maintain that self-efficacy beliefs impact the course and treatment of PTSD because perceived self-efficacy mediates the ability to cope with trauma. In this view, competence in dealing with stress-related emotions can be learned and provides a basis for treating PTSD. However, there is clearly a need for prospective evidence-based studies to substantiate this hypothesis.

Biological determinants

Advances in technology, including neuroimaging techniques such as fMRI (functional magnetic resonance imaging), have produced a wealth of research on the psychobiology of stress and PTSD since the late 1990s. Excellent reviews of this literature are available (Charney 2004; Gunnar and Quevedo 2007), which highlight the roles of two interrelated systems – the hypothalamic pituitary adrenal axis (HPA) and the sympathetic adrenal medullary (SAM). In addition, the hippocampus, amygdala and prefrontal cortex are brain structures implicated in the biological underpinnings of stress and PTSD. The interest of this short review is limited to some biological findings related to risk/vulnerability and resistance/resilience.

RISK/VULNERABILITY

A current conceptualization of PTSD by Yehuda (2006) regards it not as a simple stress-related reaction to a perceived traumatic event, but rather as the interaction of that experience with a particular phenotype having difficulty coping with stress. These difficulties are manifested on both the psychological and the biological level, and genetic, epigenetic, and experiential factors are all thought to contribute to vulnerability. With regard to experiential factors, research supports the view that stressful events may shape brain chemistry and structure through an increase in stress hormone activity. Adversity, particularly interpersonal traumatic stress, during windows of brain plasticity (early childhood and adolescence) may lead to altered development of stress systems, including but not limited to, structural changes in the brain in which neurons involved in learning and memory are reduced while the firing activity of neurons involved in fear and anxiety is increased (Ford 2005; McEwen 2001, 2007). This biological mechanism may be a mediating factor in the finding that prior trauma history increases the probability of PTSD in children.

Focusing on specific brain structures that might be involved in vulnerability, Stern et al. (2007) and Yehuda (2004) both suggest that reduced hippocampal volume may be a risk factor for PTSD. De Bellis (2001) found reduced corpus callosum volume in maltreated children. Teicher et al. (2002) in a study of 18–22 year olds with childhood sexual abuse, also implicated a smaller hippocampal volume (in addition to reduced development of the corpus callosum, left neocortex and amygdala) as a morphological change in the brain induced by early severe stress. They point out that these changes occur after some delay, and are not found at or near the time of abuse. Atrophy in the hippocampus and the prefrontal cortex were found by McEwen (2001, 2007) in adults with PTSD. To address the question of whether the reduced hippocampal size predated the traumatic exposure or was concurrent with the trauma, Pitman (2006) studied twin Vietnam veterans and found that the smaller hippocampal volume was a pre-existing condition.

Charney (2004) published an extensive review of neurochemical, neuropeptide, and hormonal factors that might be involved in vulnerability and resilience. Among these, he noted that levels of the adrenal steroid cortisol increased with exposure to many forms of psychological stress and contributed to immediate adaptive behavior. However, he also pointed out that if cortisol levels were not ultimately restrained by a negative feedback system involving the HPA axis, the long-term effects would be physiologically deleterious. This has implications for PTSD based on Bremner's (1999) finding that long-term stress-induced high levels of cortisol are associated with hippocampal damage, which (as discussed above) could increase vulnerability to PTSD.

Frewen and Lanius (2006) argue that PTSD is a disorder of affect-arousal regulation, so any factors that impact negatively on biological structures underpinning this system would increase vulnerability to PTSD. The amygdala is a brain region critical for emotional response, particularly fear (Shin et al. 2006). The prefrontal cortex and anterior cingulate cortex exert control over the amygdala; if their inhibitory capacities are impaired (as may be the case with PTSD; Lanius et al. 2007) then this may be a biological basis for persistent and severe anxiety. McEwen (2001) has found atrophy in the prefrontal cortex in chronically stressed adults but this has not been clearly established in infants and children.

RESISTANCE/RESILIENCE

It has been suggested that behavioral flexibility and effective emotional regulation are psychological markers of resilience (Ford et al., Chapter 12 in this volume; Greenberg 2006; Lewis et al. 2006). The biological correlates of flexibility involve the cortex, particularly the orbital frontal cortex, the anterior cingulate cortex, and the dorsolateral prefrontal cortex (Lewis et al. 2006). Expressed another way, the prefrontal cortex governs self-regulation, while the more primitive subcortical systems involving the amygdala and hypothalamus are involved in rapid, unthinking adaptive responses. In a study at the School of Medicine at Stanford University (2007) severely traumatized children with PTSD symptoms showed less activity in the left middle frontal cortex than their non-traumatized peers. This brain area is known to be involved in response inhibition.

In support of this, Charney (2004) points out that people who function well after experiencing high levels of fear may have very effective inhibition of amygdala responses by the medial prefrontal cortex. Some very interesting work by Mayes (2006) and Arnsten (2000) shows that at low levels of stress stimulation prefrontal cortex systems are engaged, but as stress intensifies, the posterior cortex or the more primitive subcortical systems become more engaged. This switch results in diminished executive function, but enhanced vigilance. Mayes (2006) and Arnsten (2000) suggest that abused children's increased sensitivity to stress might be correlated with this switch. That is, abused children may make the switch at a lower level of stress than non-abused children. Liberzon and Martis (2006) caution against a too simplified view of the cortical subregions. Their work shows that the cingulate cortex and the medial prefrontal cortex, in addition to keeping a brake on the amygdala, also modulate and evaluate emotional responses. This is done by amplifying or reducing cortical responses.

New conceptual frameworks: processes and underlying mechanisms

It seems that the era of the search for individual isolated risk factors for childhood PTSD has indeed ended. The central objective of current research on posttraumatic distress and resilience has moved away from delineating lists of variables toward understanding the mechanisms or processes whereby children may be protected from the adverse effects of exposure to trauma (Layne et al. 2007). As indicated by Luthar (2006), if studies are to help us design appropriate interventions, they must move beyond the identification of variables linked with competence toward understanding specific underlying processes. An example of such research is the work of Criss et al. (2002), who describe the processes by which peer acceptance may confer advantages for children who have experienced disturbed family functioning. These researchers suggest that good peer relationships may provide alternative ways to meet children's need for connectedness; they may also serve to modify inappropriate behaviors that distressed parents cannot adequately address. In addition, good peer relationships may facilitate bonding with teachers and other school personnel.

From a developmental perspective, researchers have begun to focus on the methodological and theoretical frameworks within which resilience is conceptualized and operationalized in order to better understand the positive trajectories that lead to adaptive development despite adverse circumstances (see Layne, Beck, Rimmasch, Southwick, Moreno, and Hobfoll, Chapter 2 in this volume). There is general consensus that developmental transitions are based on reorganization in multiple systems in response to changes within the organism and the environment and interactions between the two. Brain development and physical maturation trigger some of these transitions; however, experiences may also set off a multitude of internal changes, including brain reorganization. Nonetheless, most current conceptualizations of childhood PTSD are some distance away from a genuinely developmental approach (Cicchetti and Lynch 1995; Salmon and Bryant 2002).

A conceptual framework proposed by Sroufe (1979) is one of the notable exceptions. Sroufe argues that consistent supportive care fosters early competence, which in turn plays a crucial role in later adaptation. Understood in this manner, early experiences are essential for understanding later adaptive or maladaptive behaviors. Competence during one developmental period provides children with a foundation that enables them to meet subsequent challenges. Conversely, maladaptation at an earlier stage of development is likely to endanger success in meeting the tasks posed by later developmental periods. "In this way, developmental patterns are magnified . . . by virtue of the coherence with which . . . maladaptive and adaptive behaviors are organized" (Yates et al. 2003, p. 247).

Applied to the study of risk and resilience, the model allows the examination of adaptive outcomes at any given stage of development in the context of current situational and developmental demands. "Adaptive outcomes at given stages of development derive from transactional exchanges between the child and his or her current environment, as well as from the developmental history that the child brings to these exchanges" (Yates et al. 2003, p. 249).

In this view resilience is an ongoing process of gathering resources that enables children to deal with current issues adaptively and provides a foundation for dealing with later challenges. According to these researchers, "resilience reflects the developmental process by which children acquire the ability to use both internal and external resources to achieve positive adaptation despite prior or concomitant adversity" (Yates et al. 2003, p. 250).

Data from the Minnesota Longitudinal Study of Parents and Children, a twenty-five-year study of impoverished mothers and their first-born children, support Sroufe's (1979) model and suggest that an early history of consistent and supportive care is a major contributor to positive adaptation in the face of continuing adversity. Moreover, an early foundation of support engenders positive adaptation at later times despite intervening maladaptation. For example, Sroufe et al. (1999) found that early secure attachment in infancy and generally supportive care in the first two years provided a group of high-risk elementary school children with greater ability to rebound successfully from a period of poor adaptation during the preschool years. These researchers also found that children who were able to progress from behavior problems in middle childhood to competence in adolescence were able to draw on a foundation of early support and positive adaptation. Their interpretation of these data is "that the process of resilience is manifest in the entire developmental trajectory" (Sroufe et al. 1999, p. 251). The alternative interpretation, where resilience is posited as an underlying trait, would require them to assume that "some of these children were resilient, then were not, and then were again" (Sroufe et al. 1999, p. 251), a supposition that is clearly less persuasive than a developmental perspective.

As evidenced by the Minnesota Longitudinal Study, longitudinal research is crucial from a developmental perspective. This is true for experimental studies of intervention as well as studies of naturally occurring pathways in development. Another illustration is brought by Masten (2004). As part of a prospective study of adolescent antisocial behavior in Seattle, the investigators included an experimental intervention with a group of children in the study, all residents of neighborhoods known to foster antisocial behavior. The treatment effects were clear at age 13, a year after the treatment had ended, but then disappeared for several years, only to reappear in late adolescence. According to Masten (2004), "it is intriguing to consider the possibility that the treatment effects were temporarily swamped by the noise of developmental change during the early teen years" (pp. 313–314). The point is that such longitudinal studies are essential for a clear picture of change over the course of children's development. As Garmezy (1991) has emphasized, longitudinal research on resilience provides important opportunities to study changes in developmental trajectories, including the emergence of new strengths and vulnerabilities at each stage of development.

Implications for intervention

Sroufe et al. (1999) suggested that prevention and intervention programs for high-risk populations should be "aimed at developing strong, supportive, responsive, and successful early parent–child relationships" (p. 258). This is based on their findings that early transactions between children and their caretakers provide the scaffold that facilitates the development of children's capacities for adaptive emotional regulation, social engagement, and positive expectations from themselves and their social environment.

Scheeringa and Zeanah (2001) emphasized the importance of first attending to the caregiver's symptoms and only afterwards to those of the child. There are several reasons for doing this. First, the most powerful potential changing agent for young children's development and symptoms is their relationship with their primary caregiver (Lyons-Ruth and Jacobvitz 1999). Second, a sustained change in the parents' symptoms is likely to make them better able to respond sensitively to their children's needs. Third, since young children and their caregivers are often together when traumatizing events occur, they may both be affected profoundly by these events. If parents become symptomatic, particularly if they avoid reminders of the trauma, they may find it difficult to be present when their young child reenacts the experience in play. Lastly, primary caregivers are uniquely important as a central aspect of the young child's experience of traumatic events due to the importance of the parent–child relationship for current and subsequent adaptation.

From a resilience perspective, efforts aimed at empowering parents' abilities for emotional co-regulation, enhancing their dyadic attunement to their children's needs, and increasing their ability for reflective functioning will enhance their strengths, and may lead to building resilience in both parents and children. Indeed, dyadic treatment (see Van Horn and Lieberman, Chapter 13 in this volume) focuses on assisting the parent to become sufficiently emotionally regulated to both enable the child to co-regulate and then self-regulate emotionally as well as to think clearly enough (see Lewis et al. 2006) to be able to autonomously self-regulate emotions as well as solve problems and achieve external goals. One example is a community and clinical project for building resilience in young children and parents under continual threat of Kassam missiles. This work was carried out in Sderot, Israel from 2003 to 2007. The focus has been on increasing parental awareness of the impact of terrorism on parents and toddlers, while acquiring skills in the co-regulation of anxiety and fears, increasing parental attunement, and learning to create a safe place for the dyad that fosters the ability for parent–child play (Chemtob and Abramovitz 2007; Pat-Horenczyk et al. 2007b). This is consistent with the view (Ford, Albert, and Hawke, Chapter 12 in this volume) that interventions for traumatized children must focus not on the child's (or parent's) present state, but on helping the parent help the child resume the trajectory of learning, functioning, and growth that has been interrupted or disrupted by traumatic stressors.

Concluding comments

Our understanding of posttraumatic stress disorder is constantly expanding, as is evident in the adaptation of the disorder to account for its relevance to children in the 1987 DSM-III-R edition. However, empirical development in the field has not ended there, and the conceptual framework for understanding the disorder has also evolved. In an effort to reconcile the differences and establish a working definition of trauma in children, a group of child psychologists and psychiatrists are in the process of compiling a set of additional factors to accompany a PTSD diagnosis in children, which they intend to propose for inclusion in the DSM-V. This diagnosis, termed "developmental trauma disorder" (DTD), is an attempt to capture the unique qualities of children's reactions to trauma. Its proponents believe that the diagnosis should better reflect the fact that children are most often traumatized within relationships (DeAngelis 2007). The diagnosis takes into consideration the fact that interpersonal trauma may have a differential impact depending on the child's stage of development (Ford 2005).

Based on the state of the field nowadays, we propose adopting a new integrative perspective, the concept of "interconnectedness" as our vision for a future approach to childhood PTSD, applying a developmental perspective. Interconnectedness operates on two levels. The first is the level of connecting the various risk and protective factors into a more integrated perspective on the mechanisms and trajectories that underlie the effect of these factors on individual children. We are also now able to better understand the relationships among biological, emotional, and behavioral factors, and how they interconnect. The second level, perhaps the most salient aspect of the notion of interconnectedness, involves the parent–child relationship, in which childhood PTSD must be viewed. The interconnectedness approach has implications for research, diagnosis and intervention. There is a need for more longitudinal studies to better assess the mechanisms by which risk and protective factors operate. The parental relationship is increasingly seen as a necessary consideration in diagnosis, and hence in therapeutic intervention as well.

The systematic search for risk and protective factors for childhood posttraumatic distress is an essential component for training trauma-informed clinicians and educators. This body of knowledge forms the basis for early identification of children at high risk for severe chronic PTSD. Screening for posttraumatic symptoms is the first stage in developing a continuity of services, including prevention and intervention modules for both vulnerable and resilient children. The challenge is to develop longitudinal models and to evaluate their effectiveness prospectively.

References

Ackerman, P.T., Newton, J.E.O., McPherson, W.B., Jones, J.G., and Dykman, R.A. (1998). Prevalence of posttraumatic stress disorder and other psychiatric diagnoses in three groups of abused children (sexual, physical, and both). *Child Abuse and Neglect, 22*(8), 759–774.

Ahern, J., Galea, S., Resnick, H., Kilpatrick, D., Bucuvalas, M., Gold, J., et al. (2002). Television images and psychological symptoms after the September 11 terrorist attacks. *Psychiatry, 65*, 289–300.

Ajdukovic, M. (1998). Displaced adolescents in Croatia: Sources of stress and post-traumatic stress reaction. *Adolescence, 33*, 209–217.

Ancharoff, M.R., Munroe, J.F., and Fisher, L.M. (1998). The legacy of combat trauma: Clinical implications of intergenerational transmission. In Y. Danieli (ed.), *International handbook of multigenerational legacies of trauma* (pp. 257–276). New York: Plenum.

Arnsten, A.F.T. (2000). Through the looking glass: Differential noradrenergic modulation of prefrontal cortical function. *Neural Plasticity, 7*, 133–146.

Bandura, A. (1997). *Self-efficacy: The exercise of control.* New York: Freeman/Times/Holt.

Barocas, H., and Barocas, C. (1979). Wounds of the fathers: The next generation of Holocaust victims. *International Review of Psychoanalysis, 5*, 331–341.

Bremner, J.D. (1999). Does stress damage the brain? *Biological Psychiatry, 45*(7), 797–805.

Breslau, N., Davis, G.C., Andreski, P., Peterson, E.L., and Schultz, L.R. (1997). Sex differences in posttraumatic stress disorder. *Archives of General Psychiatry, 54*(11), 1044–1048.

Brewin, C., Andrews, B., and Valentine, J. (2000). Meta-analysis of risk factors for posttraumatic stress disorder in trauma-exposed adults. *Journal of Consulting and Clinical Psychology, 68*, 748–766.

Brom, D., Kfir, R., and Dasberg, H. (2001). A controlled double-blind study on children of Holocaust survivors. *Israel Journal of Psychiatry and Related Sciences, 38*, 47–57.

Caselli, L.T., and Motta, R.W. (1995). The effect of PTSD and combat level on Vietnam veterans' perceptions of child behavior and marital adjustment. *Journal of Clinical Psychology, 51*(1), 4–12.

Charney, K.D.S. (2004). Psychobiological mechanisms of resilience and vulnerability for successful adaptation to extreme stress. *American Journal of Psychiatry, 161*, 195–216.

Chemtob, C.M., and Abramovitz, R.A. (2007) Protocol for dyadic treatment in the context of trauma and disaster. Unpublished Manuscript.

Cicchetti, D., and Lynch, M. (1995). Failures in the expectable environment and their impact on individual development: The case of child maltreatment. In D. Cicchetti and D.J. Cohen (eds.), *Developmental psychopathology: Risk, disorder, and adaptation*, Volume 2 (pp. 32–71). Oxford: Wiley.

Cortina, L.M., and Kubiak, S.P. (2006). Gender and posttraumatic stress: Sexual violence as an explanation for women's increased risk. *Journal of Abnormal Psychology, 115*(4), 753–759.

Criss, M.M., Pettit, G.S., Bates, J.E., Dodge, K.A., and Lapp, A.L. (2002). Family adversity, positive peer relationships, and children's externalizing behavior: A longitudinal perspective on risk and resilience. *Child Development, 73*, 1220–1237.

Danieli, Y. (1982). Families of survivors of the Nazi Holocaust: Some short and long term effects. In C.D. Speilberger, I.G. Sarason, and N.A. Milgram (eds.), *Stress and anxiety*, Volume 8 (pp. 405–421). New York: Hemisphere.

Dansby, V.S., and Marinelli, R.P. (1999). Adolescent children of Vietnam combat veteran fathers: A population at risk. *Journal of Adolescence, 22*(3), 329–340.

DeAngelis, T. (2007). A new diagnosis for childhood trauma? *Monitor on Psychology, 38*(3), 32–34.

De Bellis, M. (2001). Developmental traumatology. *Psychoneuroendocrinology, 27*, 155–170.

Denham, S.A., Mitchell-Copeland, J., Strandberg, K., Auerbach, S., and Blair, K. (1997). Parental contributions to preschoolers' emotional competence: Direct and indirect effects. *Motivation and Emotion, 21*(1), 65–86.

Diehl, A.S., and Prout, M.F. (2002). Effects of posttraumatic stress disorder and child sexual abuse on self-efficacy development. *American Journal of Orthopsychiatry, 72*(2), 262–265.

Duggal, H.S., Gennady, B., and Vineeth, J. (2002). PTSD and TV viewing of World Trade Center. *Journal of the American Academy of Child and Adolescent Psychiatry, 41*(5), 494–495.

Fonagy, P. (1999). Transgenerational consistencies of attachment: A new theory. Paper presented at the Developmental and Psychoanalytic Discussion Group, American Psychoanalytic Association, Washington, DC, May 13, 1999. Available www.dspp.com/papers/fonagy2.htm, accessed November 8, 2007.

Ford, J. (2005). Treatment implications of altered affect regulation and information processing following child maltreatment. *Psychiatric Annals, 35*(5), 410–420.

Frewen, P.A., and Lanius, R.A. (2006). Toward a psychobiology of posttraumatic self-dysregulation: Reexperiencing, hyperarousal, dissociation, and emotional numbing. *Annals of the New York Academy of Sciences, 1071*, 110–124.

Galovski, T., and Lyons, J.A. (2004). Psychological sequelae of combat violence: A review of the impact of PTSD on the veteran's family and possible interventions. *Aggression and Violent Behavior, 9*, 477–501.

Garmezy, N. (1991). Resilience and vulnerability to adverse developmental outcomes associated with poverty. *American Behavioral Scientist, 34*(4), 416–430.

Garrison, C.Z., Weinrich, M.W., Hardin, S.B., Weinrich, S., and Wang, L. (1993). Post traumatic stress disorder in adolescents after a hurricane. *American Journal of Epidemiology, 138*, 522–530.

Greenberg, M.T. (2006). Promoting resilience in children and youth: Preventive interventions and their interface with neuroscience. *Annals of the New York Academy of Sciences, 1094*, 139–150.

Gunnar, M., and Quevedo, K. (2007). The neurobiology of stress and development. *Annual Review of Psychology, 58*, 145–173.

Herrenkohl, E.C., Herrenkohl, R.C., and Egolf, B. (1994). Resilient early school-age children from maltreating homes: Outcomes in late adolescence. *American Journal of Orthopsychiatry, 64*(2), 301–309.

Hoven, C., Duarte, C., and Mandell, D. (2003). Children's mental health after disasters: The impact of the World Trade Center attack. *Current Psychiatry Reports, 5*, 101–107.

Jackson, Y., Kim, K.L., and Delap, C. (2007). Mediators of control beliefs, stressful life events, and adaptive behavior in school age children: The role of appraisal and social support. *Journal of Traumatic Stress, 20*(2), 147–160.

Johnson, S.M. (2005). *Developing interventions to reduce risk, enhance resilience, and support growth in children in the wake of psychologicalt trauma.* New York: Guilford.

Kaufman, C.E., Beals, J., Mitchell, C.M., Lemaster, P., and Fickenscher, A. (2004). Stress, trauma, and risky sexual behaviour among American Indians in young adulthood. *Culture, Health, and Sexuality, 6*(4), 301–318.

Koplewicz, H.S., Vogel, J.M., Salonto, M.V., Morrissey, R.G., Alanso, C.M., Gallangher, R., and Novick, R.M. (2002). Child and parent response to the 1993 World Trade Center bombing. *Journal of Traumatic Stress, 15*(1), 77–85.

LaGreca, A.M., Silverman, W.K., Verberg, E.M., and Prinstein, M.J. (1996). Symptoms of posttraumatic stress in children after Hurricane Andrew: A prospective study. *Journal of Counseling and Clinical Psychology, 64*, 712–723.

Lanius, R., Frewen, P., Girotti, M., Neufeld, R.W.J., Stevens, T.K., and Densmoree, K. (2007). Neural correlates of trauma script-imagery in posttraumatic stress disorder with and without comorbid major depression: A functional MRI investigation. *Psychiatry Research: Neuroimaging, 155*(1), 45–56.

Laor, N., Wolmer, L., Mayes, L.C., Golomb, A., Silberberg, D.S., Weizman, R., et al. (1996). Israeli preschoolers under Scud missile attacks. *Archives of General Psychiatry, 53*, 416–442.

Laor, N., Wolmer, L., and Mayes, L. (1997). Israeli preschoolers under Scuds: A 30-month follow-up. *Journal of the American Academy of Child and Adolescent Psychiatry, 36*, 349–356.

Layne, C.M., Warren, J., Shalev, A., and Watson, P. (2007). Risk, vulnerability, resistance, and resilience: Towards an integrative conceptualization of posttraumatic adaptation. In M.J. Friedman, T.M. Keane, and P.A. Resick (eds.), *Handbook of PTSD: Science and Practice.* New York: Guilford.

Layne, C.M., Beck, C.J., Rimmasch, H., Southwick, J.S., Moreno, M.A., and Hobfoll, S.E. (2008). Promoting "resilient" posttraumatic adjustment in childhood and beyond: "Unpacking" life events, adjustment trajectories, resources, and interventions. In D. Brom, R. Pat-Horenczyk, and J. Ford (eds.), *Treating traumatized children: Risk, resilience, and recovery.* New York: Routledge.

Lewis, M., Granic, I., and Lamm, C. (2006). Behavioral differences in aggressive children linked with neural mechanisms of emotion regulation. *Annals of the New York Academy of Science, 1094*, 164–177.

Liberzon, I., and Martis, B. (2006). Neuroimaging studies of emotional responses in PTSD. *Annals of the New York Academy of Sciences, 1071*, 87–109.

Lieberman, A.F., Padron, E., Van Horn, P., and Harris, W.W. (2005). Angels in the nursery: The intergenerational transmission of benevolent parental influences. *Infant Mental Health Journal, 26*(6), 504–520.

Luthar, S.S. (2006). Resilience in development: A synthesis of research across five decades. In D. Cicchetti and D.J. Cohen (eds.), *Developmental psychopathology: Risk, disorder, and adaptation*, 2nd edition, volume 3 (pp. 739–785). New York: Wiley.

Lyons-Ruth, K., and Jacobvitz, D. (1999). Attachment disorganization: Unresolved loss, relational violence, and lapses in behavioral and attentional strategies. In J.

Cassidy and P.R. Shaver (eds.), *Handbook of attachment: Theory, research, and clinical applications* (pp. 520–554). New York: Guilford.

McEwen, B.S. (2001). Plasticity of the hippocampus: Adaptation to chronic stress and allostatic load. *Annals of the New York Academy of Sciences, 933*, 265–277.

McEwen, B.S. (2007). Physiology and neurobiology of stress and adaptation: Central role of the brain. *Physiological Reviews, 87*, 873–904.

Masten, A.S. (2004). Regulatory processes, risk, and resilience in adolescent development. *Annals of the New York Academy of Sciences, 1021*, 310–319.

Mayes, L.C. (2006). Arousal regulation, emotional flexibility, medial amygdala function and the impact of early experience. *Annals of the New York Academy of Sciences, 1094*, 178–192.

Norris, F.H., Friedman, M.J., Watson, P.J., Byrne, C.M., Diaz, E., and Kaniasty, K. (2002). 60,000 disaster victims speak: Part I. A review of the empirical literature, 1981–2001. *Psychiatry: Interpersonal and Biological Processes, 65*(3), 207–239.

Parsons, J., Kehele, T.J., and Owen, S.V. (1990). Incidence of behavior problems among children of Vietnam war veterans. *School Psychology International, 11*, 253–259.

Pat-Horenczyk, R., Abramovitz, R., Peled, O., Brom, D., Daie, A., and Chemtob, C.M. (2007a). Adolescent exposure to recurrent terrorism in Israel: Posttraumatic distress and functional impairment, *Journal of Orthopsychiatry, 77*(1), 76–85

Pat-Horenczyk, R., Peled, O., Achituv, M., Yosef, D., Kaplanski, N., Lahad, M., et al. (2007b). Building resilience for parents and toddlers living under continuous threat of kassam missiles. Unpublished manuscript.

Pat-Horenczyk, R., Qasrawi, R., Lesack, R., Haj-Yahia, M.M., Peled, O., Shaheen, M., et al. (2007c). Posttraumatic distress on both sides of the Israeli-Palestinian conflict: School-based screening. Manuscript submitted for publication.

Pfefferbaum, B. (1997). Posttraumatic stress disorder in children: A review of the past 10 years. *Journal of the American Academy of Child and Adolescent Psychiatry, 36*(11), 1503–1511.

Pfefferbaum, B., Nixon, S.J., Tivis, R., Doughty, D.E., Pynoos, R.S., Gurwitch, R.H., et al. (2001). Television exposure in children after a terrorist incident. *Psychiatry, 64*, 202–211.

Pfefferbaum, B., Pfefferbaum, R.L., North, C.S., and Neas, B.R. (2002). Does television viewing satisfy criteria for exposure in posttraumatic stress disorder? *Psychiatry, 65*(4), 306–309.

Pfefferbaum, B., Pfefferbaum, R., Gurwitch, R., Nagumalli, S., Brandt, E., Robertson, M., et al. (2003). Children's response to terrorism: A critical review of the literature. *Current Psychiatry Reports, 5*, 95–100.

Pine, D.S., and Cohen, J.A. (2002). Trauma in children and adolescents: Risk and treatment of psychiatric sequelae. *Biological Psychiatry, 51*(7), 519–531.

Pine, D.S., Costello, J., and Masten, A. (2005). Trauma, proximity and developmental psychopathology: The effects of war and terrorism on children. *Neuropsychopharmacology, 30*, 1781–1792.

Pitman, R.K. (2006). Combat effects on mental health: The more things change, the more they remain the same. *Archives of General Psychiatry, 63*(2), 127–128.

Rabalais, A.E., Ruggiero, K.J., and Scotti, J.R. (2002). Multicultural issues in the response of children to disasters. In A.M. LaGreca, W.K. Silverman, E.M. Verberg, and M.C. Roberts (eds.), *Helping children cope with disasters and terrorism* (pp. 73–99). Washington, DC: American Psychological Association.

Rosenheck, R., and Fontana, A. (1998). Transgenerational effects of abusive violence on the children of Vietnam combat veterans. *Journal of Traumatic Stress, 11*(4), 731–742.

Sack, W.H., Clarke, G.N., and Seeley, J. (1995). Posttraumatic stress disorder across two generations of Cambodian refugees. *Journal of the American Academy of Child and Adolescent Psychiatry, 34*, 1160–1166.

Saigh, P.A., Yasik, A.E., Sack, W.H., and Koplewicz, H.S. (1999). Child-adolescent posttraumatic stress disorder: Prevalence, risk factors and comorbidity. In P.A. Saigh and J.D. Bremner (eds.), *Posttraumatic stress disorder: A comprehensive text* (pp. 18–43). Needham Heights, MA: Allyn and Bacon.

Salmon, K., and Bryant, R.A. (2002). Posttraumatic stress disorder in children: The influence of developmental factors. *Clinical Psychology Review, 22*, 163–188.

Samper, R.E., Taft, C.T., King, D.W., and King, L.A. (2004). Posttraumatic stress disorder symptoms and parenting satisfaction among a national sample of male Vietnam veterans. *Journal of Traumatic Stress, 17*(4), 311–315.

Scheeringa, M.S., and Zeanah, C.H. (1995). Symptom differences in traumatized infants and young children. *Infant Mental Health Journal, 16*, 259–270.

Scheeringa, M.S., and Zeanah, C.H. (2001). A relationship perspective on PTSD in infancy. *Journal of Traumatic Stress, 14*, 799–815.

Schiff, M., Pat-Horenczyk, R., and Peled, O. (2007). The role of social support for Israeli adolescents continually exposed to terrorism: Protective or compensatory factors? Manuscript submitted for publication.

Schore, A.N. (1994). *Affect regulation and the origin of the self: The neurobiology of emotional development.* Hillsdale, NJ: Erlbaum.

Schuengel, C., Bakermans-Kranenburg, M.J., van IJzendoorn, M.H., and Blom, M. (1999). Unresolved loss and infant disorganization: Links to frightening maternal behavior. In J. Solomon and C. George (eds.), *Attachment disorganization* (pp. 71–94). New York: Guilford.

Schwartz, S., Dohrenwend, B.P., and Levav, I. (1994). Nongenetic familial transmission of psychiatric disorders? Evidence from children of Holocaust survivors. *Journal of Health and Social Behavior, 35*, 385–402.

Seifer, R., and Dickstein, S. (2000). Parental mental illness and infant development. In C.H. Zeanah (ed.), *Handbook of infant mental health.* New York: Guilford.

Seifer, R., Sameroff, A.J., Baldwin, C.P., and Baldwin, A.L. (1992). Child and family factors that ameliorate risk between 4 and 13 years of age. *Journal of the American Academy of Child and Adolescent Psychiatry, 31*(5), 893–903.

Shannon, M.P., Lonigan, C.J., Finch, A.J., and Taylor, C.M. (1994). Children exposed to disaster: I. Epidemiology of posttraumatic symptoms and symptom profiles. *Journal of the American Academy of Child and Adolescent Psychiatry, 33*(1), 80–93.

Shin, L.M., Rauch, S.L., and Pitman, R. (2006). Amygdala, medial prefrontal cortex and hippocampal function in PTSD. *Annals of the New York Academy of Sciences, 1071*, 67–79.

Silva, R.R. (2004). *Posttraumatic stress disorders in children and adolescents: Handbook.* New York: Norton.

Silva, R.R., Alpert, M., Munoz, D.M., Singh, S., Matzner, F., and Dummit, S. (2000). Stress and vulnerability to posttraumatic stress disorder in children and adolescents. *American Journal of Psychiatry, 157*(8), 1129–1235.

Sroufe, L.A. (1979). The coherence of individual development: Early care, attachment, and subsequent developmental issues. *American Psychologist, 34*(10), 834–841.

Sroufe, L.A., Egeland, B., and Carlson, E.A. (1999). One social world: The integrated development of parent–child and peer relationships. In W.A. Collins and B. Laursen (eds.), *Relationships as developmental contexts* (pp. 241–261). Mahwah, NJ: Erlbaum.

Stafford, B., Zeanah, C.H., and Scheeringa, M.S. (2003). Exploring psychopathology in early childhood: PTSD and attachment disorders in DC:0–3 and DSM-IV. *Infant Mental Health Journal, 24*(4), 398–409.

Stanford University, California, School of Medicine (2007). *Severe trauma affects kids' brain function, say researchers.* Retrieved July 31, 2007 from http://med.stanford.edu/news_releases/2007/march/carrion.html.

Stern, D.J., Seedat, S., Iversen, A., and Wessely, S. (2007). Posttraumatic stress disorder: Medicine and politics. *Lancet, 369*(9556), 139–144.

Teicher, M.H., Andersen, S.L., Polcari, A., Anderson, C.M., and Navalta, C.P. (2002). Developmental neurobiology of childhood stress and trauma. *Psychiatric Clinics of North America, 25*, 397–426.

Thabet, A.A.M., and Vostanis, P. (1999). Posttraumatic stress reactions in children in war. *Journal of Child Psychology and Psychiatry, 40*(3), 385–391.

Tiet, Q.Q., Bird, H.R., Davies, M., Hoven, C., Cohen, P., Jensen, P.S., et al. (1998). Adverse life events and resilience. *Journal of the American Academy of Child and Adolescent Psychiatry, 37*(11), 1191–1200.

Van der Kolk, B.A., Roth, S., Pelcovitz, D., Sunday, S., and Spinazzola, J. (2005). Disorders of extreme stress: The empirical foundation of a complex adaptation to trauma. *Journal of Traumatic Stress, 18*(5), 389–399.

Werner, E.E. (1989). High-risk children in young adulthood: A longitudinal study from birth to 32 years. *American Journal of Orthopsychiatry, 59*(1), 72–81.

Yates, T.M., Egeland, B., and Sroufe, A. (2003). Rethinking resilience: A developmental process perspective. In S.S. Luthar (ed.), *Resilience and vulnerability: Adaptation in the context of childhood adversities* (pp. 243–266). New York: Cambridge University Press.

Yehuda, R. (2004). Risk and resilience in PTSD. *Journal of Clinical Psychiatry, 65*(suppl. 1), 29–36.

Yehuda, R. (2006). Preface in the psychobiology of posttruamtic stress disorder. A decade of progress. *Annals of the New York Academy of Sciences, 1071*, xv.

Yehuda, R., Halligan, S.L., and Grossman, R. (2001). Childhood trauma and risk for PTSD: Relationship to intergenerational effects of trauma, parental PTSD, and cortisol excretion. *Development and Psychopathology, 13*(3), 733–753.

Chapter 4

Parenting in the throes of traumatic events

Risks and protection

Esther Cohen

Links between parental functioning and children's adaptation after a traumatic event

In their study of children in London in World War II during the German Blitz, Anna Freud and Dorothy Burlingham (1943) observed that children who were separated from their families in the city and sent to safe havens were much more traumatized than children who remained with their family in the bombarded city. They concluded that the disruption of family ties is more traumatic to children than the events of war. Thus they laid the foundation for conceptualizing family bonds as a protective factor for children in times of mass trauma, long before concepts of resilience and protective factors had been developed.

The recognition of the importance of human connections in coping with stress, as a protection against later trauma, and as a means of healing afterwards has since become widely accepted. However, only recently are the processes involved becoming more clearly articulated and researched. Coates (2003) suggests that trauma and human relatedness may be understood as inversely related: the greater the strength of the human bonds connecting the individual to others, and the more these bonds are accessible in times of danger, the better the individual can cope with the trauma and recover. Garbarino (2001), adopting a more somber perspective, argues that once the accumulation of risk moves beyond a low, tolerable level, there must be a major concentration of opportunity factors (including significant others and additional ecological supports) to prevent a harmful outcome.

Research evidence strongly supports the idea that parental emotional reactions to a traumatic event constitute a powerful mediator of the child's post-traumatic symptoms (American Academy of Child and Adolescent Psychiatry 1998). It appears that the impact of parental reactions may even be a better predictor of the child's posttraumatic adaptation than the traumatic event itself, explaining both resilience and psychopathology. Two comprehensive reviews of the literature yielded consistent evidence for this claim. Scheeringa and Zeanah (2001) reviewed seventeen studies that simultaneously assessed parental and child functioning following trauma, and Norris et al. (2002) summarized the research from nineteen samples regarding the influence of family factors on child outcomes following trauma. The emergent picture from both reviews shows a clear pattern of relational links between parental functioning and child functioning following disasters and traumatic events. The parental and family variables associated with the poorest child outcomes included higher rates of PTSD or posttraumatic symptoms in either parent, psychiatric problems in a parent, increased parental conflict and irritability, family chaos and inadequate family cohesion. Specific parental behaviors conspicuous for their unfavorable impact on the child's adjustment included the mother's avoidance of the trauma, parental suppression of awareness about their child's symptoms, and parental behaviors that induced guilt and anxiety in the child. These findings were further supported in the research investigating the impact of the September 11 attacks in the United States (Stuber et al. 2005).

Theoretical perspectives on the mechanisms of parental influence on children's coping with trauma

Both when a parent is directly traumatized, and also in instances where only the child is the direct victim of a traumatic event, parents vary in their ability to provide the child with the attuned, sensitive, and supportive parenting the child needs. Families vary in their ability to reorganize and adapt to new realities. The following is a discussion of various theoretical perspectives and supporting evidence explaining the mechanisms by which parents may mediate the effects of trauma on their children. These explanations are intended to complement each other rather than being mutually exclusive.

We will focus our review on the contributions of disaster mental-health theories (including crisis and trauma psychology, information-processing and cognitive behavioral theories), systemic theories, and developmental theories (including attachment theory and psychoanalytic relational theories). While the developmental theories focus mainly on understanding resilience in children, especially on pre-trauma preventive effects involving parent–child relationships, the other theories tend to focus more on the risks in the post-crisis period.

Disaster mental health

Conceptualizations in the tradition of crisis theory, trauma, or disaster mental health focus primarily on the crisis situation and its aftermath, and surmise that exposure to any traumatic situation is likely to trigger deregulation in physiological, emotional, cognitive and behavioral systems, causing distress and affecting one's level of functioning. The severity and persistence of these effects vary according to various pre-disaster personal characteristics, as well as characteristics of the traumatic event and the recovery environment. Substantial evidence (Aisenberg and Ell 2005) suggests that parents who are more distressed following a trauma are often less available emotionally to support their children. Extreme parental behavior may occur in the form of either paralysis or excessive over-protectiveness. For example, Coates et al. (2003) reported that there were parents who could not bear to have their children know about the loss a family member in the aftermath of September 11. Patterns of parental avoidance, denial and over-protection following a traumatic event have been documented by Terr (1990), Osofsky (1995) and Cohen (2005).

Similarly, Scheeringa and Zeanah (2001) observed problematic relational patterns that tended to emerge as the result of the concurrence of post-traumatic reactions in an adult caregiver and a young child. One parenting pattern involved adult withdrawal and diminished availability and responsiveness toward the child. This pattern seemed to be related to a previous trauma or loss suffered by the parent, which was reawakened by the child's trauma. A second parenting pattern involved overprotecting the child and restricting the child's actions in rigid, unwarranted ways, possibly in a defensive attempt to rectify the sense of loss of control and guilt evoked by the trauma.

The sources of these reactions are manifold, and involve both individual parental inner dynamics and role-related transactional dynamics. Many parents find it especially difficult to regulate their own affective reactions to the trauma. Claiming to be protecting the child's innocence, they may project onto the child their own need to construct an imaginary space of innocence to protect themselves from their own sense of violation (Coates et al. 2003). Additionally, the actual or imagined threat to the child's life, and the shattering of his or her belief system, may symbolize a frightening, painful, and guilt-evoking failure in their capacity to protect their child from harm. These later feelings may be fueled by the child's reactions, which appear unfamiliar to the parents, increasing their anxiety that the event has caused the child permanent psychological and developmental damage. The parent's fear of causing further harm to the child by inappropriately reacting to the child's behavior may further aggravate the parent's sense of demobilization and incapacitation.

Data from various sources underscore the potential detrimental effects to children's adjustment through this tendency of traumatized parents to ignore or belittle their children's posttraumatic difficulties, or to avoid trauma-related material (Laor et al. 1997, 2001; Pynoos et al. 1996; Stuber et al. 2005). Children need help in making sense of their traumatic experience and integrating it into their existing schemas. Salmon and Bryant (2002) documented how parents' ability to converse with their children about a traumatic experience can contribute to the children's language development and narrative production, which are necessary elements of trauma processing.

Because negative emotions are more difficult to process and more anxiety-provoking, children seem to benefit from the help of parents who actively relate to their children's negative emotions. The avoidant tendency of some traumatized parents may thus deprive the child of opportunities to reappraise the experience and correct misconceptions, as well as to regulate strong emotions.

Children's processing of information in unusual times such as war, emergency, or disaster is greatly influenced by additional, non-conversational, aspects of parental behavior. Parents' conduct and reactions appear to serve a central function in social signaling and referencing for their children. Inasmuch as children are less experienced than adults and less familiar with the complex new world created by unexpected events, they rely on the adults' appraisals of the traumatic situation. Thus, children use their parents' coping behavior to construe the meaning and significance of events and to evaluate the severity of existing or potential risks. In reality, children often seem to react more to their parents' non-verbal and verbal expressions of distress than to the distressing events per se. Younger children rely more heavily on parental stress responses as cues for interpreting traumatic events than older children do. Parental emotional expressions have been found to correlate with the children's level of distress and coping (Bat-Zion and Levy-Shiff 1993).

From the perspective of cognitive-behavioral theory, processes of parental modeling, selective shaping, and reinforcement of children's coping patterns are at work in the aftermath of trauma (Shahinfar and Fox 1997). Parents of anxious children have been found to reinforce their children's avoidant behavior more than parents of non-anxious children, who seem to encourage active coping (Salmon and Bryant 2002). Parents also structure the child's environment and often control the level of repeated exposure to traumatic information. They are important monitors of children's television viewing of a traumatic event, which involves a risk of retraumatizing the child (Pfefferbaum et al. 2001).

The widely accepted cognitive-behavioral trauma model offered by Foa and Rothbaum (1998) lends further indirect support for the important function parents may play in aiding their children's emotional processing. Through gradual exposure to corrective information about the trauma, they can weaken the link between trauma-related stimuli and conditioned emotional arousal.

Systemic theories

Risks to children in stressed and traumatized families

The study of trauma and adaptation is moving from a focus on the individual to an ecological focus on family and community (Aisenberg and Ell

2005; Garbarino 2001). Family systems theory advocates viewing individual processes within their systems in order to understand their meaning. In traumatic events that directly involve the whole family, each member is faced with the double challenge of processing his or her subjective traumatic experience, while concurrently being aware of and reacting to the experiences of the others.

A major notion of the family system approach is the "interconnectedness" of family members, implying that even in incidents exposing only a single family member to a traumatic event, the entire family system will be immediately and often dramatically affected. Members of the family tend to identify with the affected family member, and share the traumatic experience and its impact through their intimate psychological ties with that individual. Thus, siblings of children who were victims of violence or disaster are at risk for developing various emotional difficulties, including PTSD (Newman et al. 1997).

Some research, albeit limited, documents how long-term stress situations or traumatic events arising from factors external to the family, affect families and especially parenting. Stressful and crisis situations in families usually elicit emergency feelings such as anxiety, fear, anger, hate, and negativity. The investment of energy in coping with stressors over extended periods of time often depletes existing family resources, as well as prevents the family from developing new resources. Thus various aspects of family functioning are affected, including the parents' daily care for their children, which they often express as their main concern (Shamai 2002). Under extreme circumstances, parents can be pushed beyond their "stress absorption" capacity, and when that point is passed the children's development can deteriorate rapidly and markedly (Garbarino 1995).

Changes in the stressed parents' functioning may confront children with new demands and adaptations that may themselves become a source of serious stress. For example, when soldiers are deployed overseas, the remaining family members need to cope both with anxiety about the welfare of their loved one and with the added responsibilities stemming from the parent's absence in the everyday operation of the household. This combination of increased functional demands and emotional stress may also occur in families in the post-disaster stage, as in the case of war veterans suffering from PTSD returning to their families. The literature on war veterans affected by PTSD indicates that their guilt feelings, emotional withdrawal, and elevated levels of aggression make it difficult, perhaps even impossible, for the veterans to fully resume their former roles of parent, spouse, and wage earner (Galovski and Lyons 2004). Furthermore, spouses and children of these veterans revealed a high incidence of stress reactions and psychopathological symptoms, even though they were not directly exposed to the traumatizing war experiences (Arzi et al. 2000).

Additional family stressors, such as the traumatic loss of a family member, seem to have long-term consequences in impeding recovery and leading to PTSD and depression in children over time (Joshi and O'Donnell 2003). For a surviving child, the loss of a parent or sibling often becomes a multiple loss experience, depriving the child not only of the relationship with the deceased, but also of much-needed sustaining relationships with the surviving family members, who may often be psychologically unavailable due to their own distress. The severity of bereavement reactions of 2–10-year-old children, 3.5 years after the death of their father, was found to be influenced by the children's prior relationship with the father, the ability of the mother to share her grief with the child, and the availability of the extended family (Elizur and Kaffman 1983).

Traumatic injury and disability in the family also appear to constitute a serious risk factor (Cohen 2005; Garbarino et al. 2002). It seems that the disability and the chronic loss of functional abilities serve as a constant reminder of the trauma, taking a special toll on the whole family system.

Klingman and Cohen (2004) described two pathogenic relational patterns that may emerge in stressed families lacking psychosocial resources in the aftermath of traumatic events: psychological role-reversal and "scapegoating" the child. Role reversal is children's tendency to assume adult roles when traumatic circumstances do not allow parents to protect the children, forcing children "to grow up too soon" (Punamaki et al. 1997) and assume the role of caretaker. This new role is burdensome and inappropriate for the child's developmental capabilities and tasks.

"Scapegoating" is an even more problematic pattern that occurs when the child internalizes the painful, angry feelings that are communicated by a traumatized, out-of-control parent. The parent's rejecting or blaming reactions cause the child to act up, thus giving the child the role of someone "evil", who is considered responsible for the parent's frustration, anger, and sadness. Such a process of "scapegoating" may be thought of as enabling both parent and child to avoid dealing with the issues of trauma and loss, by focusing instead on their intense relational conflict. Such abusive family mechanisms have been documented in families affected by war as well as by natural disaster (Kilic et al. 2003).

A related parental pattern, associated with loneliness in traumatized parents, was described by Scheeringa and Zeanah (2001). This pattern includes adult acts of reenacting the trauma, thus endangering and frightening the young child, due to an excessive, relentless preoccupation with the trauma. In such cases, the adult's traumatic needs take precedence, and the child's needs are ignored.

It is important to keep in mind that parents' influences on children are not unidirectional. The need to adapt to numerous changes and losses may change children's behaviors, brains and development. Thus, not only may parents become insecure about their ability to protect their children, but also the traumatized child may lose faith in the parents' efficacy and power

(Pynoos et al. 1996). To defend against this frightening realization, the child may engage in developmentally inappropriate behaviors like extreme clinginess and dependency, or conversely show premature independence and self-reliance or even engage in hostile activities. Aisenberg and Ell (2005) maintain that the child's aggressive responses to traumatic exposure to community violence may diminish the parents' sense of self-esteem and self-efficacy. Parents of children living under conditions of violence and war may misinterpret behaviors of premature independence and even inadvertently support them, not realizing that "growing up too soon" may have negative psychological consequences (Punamaki et al. 1997). Punamaki et al.'s findings are of particular interest in demonstrating the complexity of the changes in relational patterns between children and parents. They reported that in Palestinian families exposed to violent events, as children experienced more traumatic events, they perceived their parents to be more punishing, rejecting, and controlling. These perceptions may have reflected both actual changes in parental behaviors as a result of their attempts to gain control, as well as feelings projected onto the parental figures by the stressed children.

Systemic resilience

Walsh (2003) organizes and extrapolates from related fields the rather limited available knowledge on family resilience in the face of trauma. She posits that family resilience pertains to three major domains of family functioning: belief systems; organizational patterns; and communication and problem-solving. Following a trauma the family needs to access its belief system to make sense of the adversity, adopt a positive outlook, and employ transcendent or spiritual resources. The family often needs to enlist organizational flexibility and connectedness, and access social and economic resources. Finally, family coping is greatly enhanced by clarity of communication and open emotional expression, as well as collaborative problem-solving. Families who have a good level of functioning prior to the trauma are likely to function better in its aftermath.

Garbarino (2001) lists some of the major helpful influences on children's ability to cope with war or community violence: social support, intact and functional families, and parents who can help their children feel protected and also model social competence. He attributes a major role to the family in providing the emotional context for the necessary emotional, cognitive and moral processing, so that children can make moral sense of their experiences. The wider social and political context in which parents function, and the extent to which it provides them with a sense of support and efficiency, have been shown to affect their own ability to support their children and to parent effectively (Aisenberg and Ell 2005; Garbarino 2001; Shamai 2005).

Developmental theories

Attachment-related risks and resilience prior to the trauma

Ever since Bowlby introduced the notion that attachment behavior is first of all a vital biological function, indispensable for both reproduction and survival, a rapidly expanding body of research has shown that disturbances of childhood attachment bonds can have long-term psychological consequences (Main 1996). Based on predictions from attachment theory, a number of studies demonstrated that children who had formed secure attachments to their parents, and those who came from more stable families, did demonstrate greater resilience following traumatic events (Wright et al. 1997). Several related mechanisms may explain these findings.

Parents with securely attached children appear to provide children with inner resources that enhance their coping ability when the children are confronted with a traumatic event. These resources, according to attachment theory, are tied to internal representations that may involve optimism, self-reliance, a sense of self-worth, trust in others, and the ability to form relationships and cooperate with others (Main 1996). Psychological and biological research has found further important developmental functions of attachment (Fonagy and Target 2003). The most important of these overlapping functions are stress regulation, the establishment of attentional mechanisms (allowing one to selectively and effectively focus attention on required demands), and the development of mentalizing capacities (the ability to reflect upon one's own and another's behavior in psychological terms). Resilience in the face of trauma is greatly diminished when these capacities are impaired. Children who have experienced sensitive caregiving develop neurological systems that function more effectively in regulating emotional arousal in times of trauma. They are also better able to effectively organize their responses in a crisis and psychologically process the traumatic material.

Fonagy and Target's (2003) work explains how secure attachment and reflective capacity become a "transgenerational acquisition". Secure, autonomous parents are three to four times more likely to have children who are securely attached to them. Reflectiveness in the parents before the child's birth powerfully predicts the child's attachment security in the second year of life. Reflective parents help the infant identify and cope with his or her own feelings and help the young child learn about the workings of the other's mind. It has been argued that these abilities may be impaired in parents who experienced massive trauma themselves, such as Holocaust survivors, or parents who suffered childhood abuse. The concept of "transgenerational transmission" of trauma was introduced to describe the effects of secondary traumatization, that is the indirect traumatic effects on the child of trauma experienced by parents years before his or her birth. It has been suggested that, paradoxically in their effort to separate their past from their present family life, the survivors created a "conspiracy of silence" (Danieli 1998) that indirectly traumatized their offspring. The scope of this phenomenon and the mechanisms of transmission have been the focus of much theoretical debate and new research using both attachment and mentalization concepts (Katz 2003), as well as biological research (Yehuda et al. 2001).

What is becoming clearer through a large variety of both human and animal studies is that early abuse, neglect, and separation may result in changes in brain development and cause far-reaching biopsychosocial effects. These include limitations in the capacity to modulate emotions, learn new coping skills, and engage in meaningful social affiliations (Schore 2001). These limitations increase the risk of further harm from additional trauma.

Attachment-related risk and resilience following a trauma

When a traumatic event disrupts the child's sense of security in, and predictability of the world and shatters the child's basic assumptions, the child's attachment system is activated, including the need to establish a secure base by reuniting with significant caretakers (Scheeringa and Zeanah 2001). The functions of the family as an important attachment system are illustrated in studies showing the harmful effects of forced separation from family members in traumatic times. Traumatized children and youth who were separated from their nuclear family, whether in Cambodia, Yugoslavia, or Israel (Klingman and Cohen 2004), exhibited greater behavioral difficulties and poorer long-term adjustment in comparison with those who were not separated from, or who quickly rejoined members of their families.

However, the mere physical presence and protection of a parent is not enough to ensure that a child will receive the needed emotional support from attachment figures during confusing, stressful times. Trauma presents a risk for the collapse of the mentalization ability, entailing a loss of awareness of the relationship between internal and external reality, for both the child and the parent (depending on their attachment histories). Fonagy and Target (2003) suggest that the "interpersonal interpretative function" of securely attached parents who accept and appreciate that the child has a mind of his or her own, is of major importance in protecting children from the deleterious effects of traumatic events. These parents can better regulate their own emotions, and are therefore better able to help their children reflect upon their traumatic experience and their current situation, thus soothing and supporting children in stressful times. Securely attached parents can also integrate memories into a coherent, meaningful narrative (Main 1996). This ability may allow them to help their children create a meaningful and coherent trauma narrative, which is important for recovery (Wirgen 1994).

Conclusions and implications

The parents' levels of adaptation and coping patterns, the parent–child relationship, and the family dynamics seem to be of paramount importance to children's adjustment in the aftermath of a traumatic event. This has important implications for intervention. Flexible family-centered interventions should be designed to empower parents at these critical times, so they can provide, at least partially, a healing setting for their children. Interventions with parents following traumatic events may thus involve a double focus: parents as affected individuals and parents as helpers. As adults affected by the trauma, and especially when traumatized themselves, parents may need help in regulating their own emotions, processing the experience and creating meaning. They may also need practical support and problem-solving help to ensure the stabilization of the family system. Additionally, they may need focused education, consultation and training in identifying their children's needs and responding to them.

The finding that the identification of children who need mental health treatment may be complicated by a decreased sensitivity of parents to their children's problems suggests that service providers have to make a special effort to locate children who have been adversely affected by a disaster. Reaching out to parents, to heighten awareness of their children's possible psychological distress, may be indicated. In addition, health workers, adult mental health professionals, and school personnel should all be attuned to the link between parental and child mental health. Consultation and therapeutic services for parents should be made easily available without stigma. In particular, it seems important to identify cases of parental PTSD and depression, as well as behaviors indicating avoidance of the trauma, withdrawal, over-protectiveness, endangerment, role-reversal, or scapegoating. Such cases call for systemic family intervention, as well as individual therapy for parents rather than child therapy.

Given the paucity of research as to the effectiveness of various models of intervention with parents, a variety of therapeutic modalities need to be developed and evaluated, including parent discussion groups (Klingman and Cohen 2004), family therapy, dyadic therapy, and filial therapy.

The literature seems clear in specifying the major parental tasks following a traumatic event, including organizing and safely structuring the child's environment; helping the child regulate emotions by soothing; providing physical proximity and psychological availability; modeling coping behavior and problem-solving and inspiring hope; communicating about and addressing confusions, fears and anxieties; and helping the child process the traumatic event, correct misconceptions and organize the event into a coherent, meaningful narrative.

Preventively, parent–child relationships which help the child develop a secure attachment, as well as self-regulating and reflective abilities prior to the trauma, should be promoted, as they contribute to the child's resilience in facing traumatic events. This is more likely to happen in families that are well organized and functioning within a supportive social system.

References

Aisenberg, E., and Ell, K. (2005). Contextualizing community violence and its effects: An ecological model of parent–child interdependent coping. *Journal of Interpersonal Violence, 20*(7), 855–871.

American Academy of Child and Adolescent Psychiatry (1998). Practice parameters for the assessment and the treatment of children and adolescents with posttraumatic stress disorder. *Journal of the American Academy of Child and Adolescent Psychiatry, 37*(suppl. 10), 4S–26S.

Arzi, N.B., Solomon, Z., and Dekel, R. (2000). Secondary traumatization among wives of PTSD and post-concussion casualties: Distress, caregiver burden and psychological separation. *Brain Injury, 14*, 725–736.

Bat-Zion, N., and Levy-Shiff, R. (1993). Children in war: Stress and coping reactions under the threat of Scud missile attacks and the effect of proximity. In L.A. Leavitt and N.A. Fox (eds.), *The psychological effects of war and violence on children* (pp. 143–161). Hillsdale, NJ: Erlbaum.

Coates, S.W. (2003). Introduction: Trauma and human bonds. In S.W. Coates, J.L. Rosenthal and D.S. Schechter (eds.), *September 11: Trauma and human bonds* (pp. 1–14). Hillsdale, NJ: Analytic Press.

Coates, S.W., Schechter, D.S., and First, E. (2003). Brief interventions with traumatized children and families after September 11. In S.W. Coates, J.L. Rosenthal, and D.S. Schechter (eds.), *September 11: Trauma and human bonds* (pp. 23–49). Hillsdale, NJ: Analytic Press.

Cohen, E. (2005). Play and adaptation in traumatized young children and their caregivers in Israel. In L. Barbanel and R. Sternberg (eds.), *Psychological interventions in times of crisis* (pp. 151–179). New York: Springer.

Danieli, Y.E. (1998). *International handbook of multigenerational legacies of trauma.* New York: Plenum.

Elizur, E., and Kaffman, M. (1983) Factors influencing the severity of childhood bereavement reactions. *American Journal of Orthopsychiatry, 53*, 668–676.

Foa, E.B., and Rothbaum, B.O. (1998). *Treating the trauma of rape.* New York: Guilford.

Fonagy, P., and Target, M. (2003). Evolution of the interpersonal interpretive function: Clues for effective preventive intervention in early childhood. In W. Coates, J.L. Rosenthal, and D.S. Schechter (eds.), *September 11: Trauma and human bonds* (pp. 99–114). Hillsdale, NJ: Analytic Press.

Freud, A. and Burlingham, D. (1943). *War and children.* New York: Medical War Books.

Galovski, T., and Lyons, J.A. (2004). Psychological sequelae of combat violence: A review of the impact of PTSD on the veteran's family and possible interventions. *Aggression and Violent Behavior, 9*, 477–501.

Garbarino, J. (1995). Growing up in a socially toxic environment: Life for children and families in the 1990s. In G.B. Melton (ed.), *The individual, the family, and social good: Personal fulfillment in times of change* (pp. 1–20). Lincoln, NE: University of Nebraska Press.

Garbarino, J. (2001). An ecological perspective on the effects of violence on children. *Journal of Community Psychology, 29*(3), 361–378.

Gabarino, J., Bradshaw, C.P., and Vorrasi, J.A. (2002). Mitigating the effects of gun violence on children and youth. *Future of Children, 12*(2), 73–85.

Joshi, P.T., and O'Donnell, D.A. (2003). Consequences of child exposure to war and terrorism. *Clinical Child and Family Psychology Review, 6*(4), 275–292.

Katz, M. (2003) Prisoners of Azkaban: Understanding intergenerational transmission of trauma due to war and state terror (with help from Harry Potter). *Journal for the Psychoanalysis of Culture and Society, 8*(2), 200–207.

Kilic, E.Z., Ozguven, H.D., and Sayil, I. (2003). The psychological effects of parental mental health on children experiencing disaster: The experience of Bolu earthquake in Turkey. *Family Process, 42*(4), 485–495.

Klingman, A., and Cohen, E. (2004). *School-based multisystemic interventions for mass trauma*. New York: Kluwer Academic/Plenum.

Laor, N., Wolmer, L., Mayes, L.C., and Gershon, A. (1997). Israeli preschool children under Scuds: A 30 months follow-up. *Journal of the American Academy of Child and Adolescent Psychiatry, 36*, 349–356.

Laor, N., Wolmer, L., and Cohen, D.J. (2001). Mothers' functioning and children's symptoms 5 years after a Scud missile attack. *Journal of Psychiatry, 158*, 1020–1026.

Main, M. (1996). Introduction to the special section on attachment and psychopathology: 2. Overview of the field of attachment. *Journal of Consulting and Clinical Psychology, 64*(2), 237–243.

Newman, M., Black, D., and Harris-Hendriks, J. (1997). Victims of disaster, war, violence, or homicide: Psychological effects on siblings. *Child Psychology and Psychiatry Review, 2*, 140–149.

Norris, F.H., Friedman, M.J., Watson, P.J., Byrne, C.M., Diaz, E., and Kaniasty, K. (2002). 60,000 disaster victims speak: Part I. An empirical review of the empirical literature, 1981–2001. *Psychiatry, 65*(3), 207–239.

Osofsky, J.D. (1995). The effects of exposure to violence on young children. *American Psychologist, 50*(9), 782–788.

Pfefferbaum, B., Nixon, S.J., Tivis, R.D., Doughty D.E., Pynoos R.S., Gurwitch, R.H., et al. (2001). Television exposure in children after a terrorist incident. *Psychiatry, 64*(3), 202–211.

Punamaki, R.L., Qouta, S., and El Sarraj, E. (1997). Models of traumatic experiences and children's psychological adjustment: The roles of perceived parenting and the children's own resources and activity. *Child Development, 64*, 718–728.

Pynoos, R.S., Steinberg, A.M., and Goenjian, A. (1996). Traumatic stress in childhood and adolescence. In B.A. van der Kolk, A.C. McFarlane, and L. Weisaeth (eds.), *Traumatic Stress* (pp. 331–358). New York: Guilford.

Salmon, K., and Bryant, R.A. (2002). Posttraumatic stress disorder in children: The influence of developmental factors. *Clinical Psychology Review, 22*, 163–188.

Scheeringa, M.S., and Zeanah, C.H. (2001). A relational perspective on PTSD in early childhood. *Journal of Traumatic Stress, 14*, 799–815.

Schore, A.N. (2001). The effects of early relational trauma on right brain development, affect regulation, and infant mental health. *Infant Mental Health Journal, 22*(1–2), 201–269.

Shahinfar, A., and Fox, N.A. (1997). The effects of trauma on children: Conceptual and methodological issues. In D. Cicchetti and S.L. Toth (eds.), *Rochester Symposium on Developmental Psychopathology: Volume 8. Developmental perspectives on trauma: Theory, research, and intervention* (pp. 115–139). Rochester, NY: University of Rochester Press.

Shamai, M. (2002). Parents' perceptions of their children in a context of shared political uncertainty: The case of Jewish settlers in the West Bank before and after the Oslo peace agreement. *Child and Adolescent Social Work Journal, 19*(1), 57–75.

Shamai, M. (2005). Personal experience in professional narratives: The role of helpers' families in their work with terror victims. *Family Process, 44*(2), 203–215.

Stuber, J., Galea, S., Pfefferbaum, B., Vandivere, S., Moore, K., and Fairbrother, G. (2005). Behavior problems in New York City's children after September 11, 2001, terrorist attack. *American Journal of Orthopsychiatry, 75*(2), 190–200.

Terr, L.C. (1990). *Too scared to cry*. New York: HarperCollins.

Walsh, F. (2003). Family resilience: A framework for clinical practice. *Family Process, 42*(1), 1–18.

Wirgen, J. (1994). Narrative completion in the treatment of trauma. *Psychotherapy, 31*(3), 415–423.

Wright, M.O'D., Masten, A.S., Northwood, A., and Hubbard, J.J. (1997). Long-term effects of massive trauma: Developmental and psychobiological perspectives. In D. Cicchetti and S.L. Toth (eds.), *Rochester Symposium on Developmental Psychopathology: Volume 8. The effects of trauma on the developmental process* (pp. 181–225). Rochester, NY: University of Rochester Press.

Yehuda, R., Halligan, S.L., and Bierer, L.M. (2001). Relationship of parental trauma exposure and PTSD to PTSD, depressive and anxiety disorders in offspring. *Journal of Psychiatric Research, 35*(5), 261–270.

Chapter 5

A developmental approach

Looking at the specificity of reactions to trauma in infants

Miri Keren and Sam Tyano

Posttraumatic stress disorder and infant psychiatry

The development of the notion of psychic pain in infants

Until quite recently the notion that infants (0–3 years) experience physical pain was ignored. Medications against pain were hardly used, and the younger the child was, the less the awareness of the infant's psychological experience of pain. Anand et al. (1987) showed the severe physiological effects of pain in medically compromised babies: pain-activated stress hormones leading to dangerous hyperglycemia. Gauvain-Piquard and Meignier (1993) reported young children's reactions to pain and medical pediatric teams' lack of attention to it. Als et al. (1994) demonstrated the positive physiological and behavioral impact of combining painful procedures regularly done on very small preterm infants into "packages".

First to point out the existence of psychic suffering in the infant was René Spitz (1946). He showed that in extreme cases psychic pain can ultimately lead to an infant's death, despite the availability of food and shelter. The fundamental significance of Spitz's observations was missed for decades, possibly because they came from extreme social situations. Stern's (1985) research, based on direct observations of babies and mothers, reinforced Dolto's (1987) concept of the infant's separate core self, and introduced the notion of "amodal" perception of external stimuli through the sensory-motor core envelope. For example, tactile stimuli may be recalled by the infant as auditory ones. As we will see later, this notion is very important in understanding how infants perceive and recall traumatic stimuli. Lebovici (1988) added the intergenerational dimension to the infant's development of self, and used his clinical observations as a basis for demonstrating the infant's ability to perceive familial pain and unconscious conflicts.

This literature, emerging from different theoretical approaches, created the necessary foundation for conceiving of psychic pain in infants. The infant's somatic symptoms began to be understood in the context of the interplay between mind and body. The establishment of the first diagnostic classification for disorders in infancy (Emde et al. 1993) signified the beginning of infant psychiatry.

Infants perceive, remember, understand, and react to traumatic events

The traditional view that infants do not remember or understand the significance of danger, and therefore cannot develop symptoms of posttraumatic stress disorder, was prominent until relatively recently. MacLean (1977) published a case of a child 48 months of age, who was evaluated after suffering a life-threatening experience. Terr's (1988) retrospective study on early memories of trauma in twenty youngsters who had suffered psychic trauma before the age of 5 years, was the first hint that at any age behavioral memories of trauma remain quite accurate and true to the events that precipitated them. Pynoos (1990) defined what constitutes a traumatic event for young children as "any direct or witnessed event that threatened his/her own and/or his/her caregiver's physical and/or emotional integrity."

Still, much was left unknown about the response of children under three to traumatic events. Gaensbauer (1982) reported a case of posttraumatic symptoms in a 3-month-old baby. Drell et al. (1993) drew two main conclusions from their pioneering review of the literature: first, infants may perceive and remember traumatic events (mostly through implicit memory) and develop many symptoms, that while developmentally distinct, are similar to those of PTSD in older children and adults; second, infants' developmental skills affect the extent to which events become traumatic and the phenomenology of their reactions. Clinical observations of PTSD-like reactions have been reported in infants and preschoolers following a car accident or witnessing a parent being murdered (Osofsky 2000; Pruett 1979), experiencing physical abuse (Gaensbauer 1982) or sexual abuse (Terr 1988), being exposed to terrorist attacks (Coates and Schechter 2004) or natural disasters (Gurwitch et al. 1998).

Developmental capacities necessary for the development of PTSD

Little is known about the lower limits of the age at which a young child can develop PTSD. The issue involves the developmental capacities needed for developing PTSD, and the earliest ages at which these capacities emerge. Scheeringa and Gaensbauer (2000) describe six relevant capacities:

- The perceptual ability necessary for awareness of traumatic events actually exists from birth. Tactile and auditory senses are about the same as in adults (Haith 1986). Vision, although myopic at birth, improves steadily until it reaches 20/20 by about 6 months of age.

- Memory is traditionally divided into two types: *nondeclarative or implicit memory* (Schacter 1987), which is essentially unconscious, and is already present in fetuses (DeCasper and Spencer 1986) and newborns (Papousek 1967); and *declarative or explicit memory* (Schacter 1987), which is conscious and expressed behaviorally or verbally. Behavioral memory has been demonstrated in 9-month-old babies (Mandler 1990). Verbal memory is rare before the age of 18 months (Sugar 1988), is intermittent for events occurring from 18 to 36 months, and becomes fully narrative after 36 months (Peterson and Bell 1996; Terr 1988).
- Affective expression, the ability to express distress, is present at birth. Sadness emerges by 3 months of age, wariness by 4 months (Sroufe 1979), anger and surprise by 6 months (Lewis 1993), and fear by 9 months. Even more relevant to PTSD in infancy is the infant's ability (already present at 5 months of age) to distinguish fear from other affects in other people (Schwartz et al. 1985).
- Behavioral expression depends on level of the infant's motor competence.
- Verbal expression, involving the production of coherent trauma narratives, has been estimated by Terr (1988) to have a lower age limit of 28–36 months.
- Sociability, often impaired with PTSD, emerges over the first 2–7 months of life, and is strongly linked to attachment security at the end of the first year.

In summary, the developmental components needed for full PTSD diagnosis, on average, do not emerge until about 9 months of age (Scheeringa and Gaensbauer 2000), and not until 2 to 3 years of age if the ability to describe an explicit memory is included.

Diagnosis

Clinical criteria

Scheeringa et al. (2003) have shown that the criteria employed for diagnosing PTSD in standard nosologies are inadequate for infants. To date the DC:0–3R classification system (Zero to Three 2005), a diagnostic system created specifically for children from birth to 3 years, requires that at least one symptom in each of the four main criteria be observed in order to diagnose a "traumatic stress disorder" (TSD) in infants or toddlers:

A. Re-experiencing

- Repetitive posttraumatic play
- Distress with reminders of the trauma
- Dissociation episodes.

B. *Numbing of responsiveness, or interference with developmental momentum*

- Social withdrawal
- Restricted affect
- Loss of skills.

C. *Increased arousal*

- Sleep disorder
- Short attention span
- Hypervigilance
- Startle response.

D. *New fears and aggression*

- Aggressive behavior
- Clinging behavior
- Fear of toileting and/or other fears.

In addition an obviously traumatic event must have occurred.

Special challenges in the assessment of PTSD in infants

Methodology

Each symptom must be characterized in terms of onset, frequency, duration, intensity and level of functional impairment. This is an especially challenging task in infants, where the majority of information must be gathered from caregivers who are themselves often traumatized, and who may over/under-endorse symptoms. Direct observation of the infant does not necessarily help since most of the symptoms occur in specific situations outside the assessment setting. From 18 to 36 months children recall more when stimulated by a context that reminds them of the past event, or when prompted by an adult (Fivush et al. 1997). Short, single traumatic events are more likely to be remembered in words than continuing traumas.

The only known instrument for assessing infants under 48 months is a semi-structured Parent Interview (Scheeringa and Zeanah 1994), supplemented by observations. In an unpublished study, Scheeringa and Zeanah performed videotaped, standardized evaluations of fifteen severely traumatized infants, using five sequences of observations. The most useful sequences for eliciting diagnostic information were free play with the caregiver and examiner-guided trauma reenactments. The least useful ones were free play with the examiner and observation of the children while the caregivers were separately interviewed about their own reactions to the trauma. Still, specific procedures for optimally diagnosing PTSD in infants have yet to be determined.

Content

Assessing the caregiver's own psychic strengths, weaknesses, and responses to the infant's traumatic experience is a particularly important aspect of the management of PTSD in infancy. Winnicott's famous dictum, "There is no such a thing as a baby, meaning of course, that whenever one finds an infant one finds maternal care, and without maternal care there would be no infant" (1960, p. 39), is very relevant in infant psychiatry in general, especially when PTSD is suspected. Co-occurrence of posttraumatic symptoms in parents and young children was noted by Drell et al. (1993) and named "PTSD à deux" or "relational PTSD". Three patterns of maternal response to a traumatic event have been described (Scheeringa and Zeanah 2001): withdrawn/unresponsive, overprotective/constrictive, and reenacting/endangering/frightening (pattern where the parent unconsciously re-exposes the infant to reminders of the traumatic event). These patterns can be detected through observation of the parent–infant interaction. As will be presented later, the prognosis of PTSD in infants is very much dependent on the parents' reactions to the traumatic event(s) (Kilic et al. 2003; Laor et al. 1997; Vila et al. 2001).

The infant's developmental status, especially the degree of developmental arrest, should be viewed as an indicator of the severity of the posttraumatic disorder.

Regarding neurophysiologic variables, two main arousal dysregulation patterns that have been observed in infancy and childhood are hyperarousal and hypoarousal. There is a continuum of hypoarousal responses from distraction to avoidance, numbing, day-dreaming, trance, and loss of consciousness. In our own experience, avoidance and falling asleep are the most common hypoarousal reactions in very young children. Sympathetic over-reactivity has been demonstrated mainly in older children (De Bellis et al. 1994; Perry 1994), but, to the best of our knowledge, no such studies have been conducted on children under 8 years old.

Differential diagnosis

Several primary axis diagnoses in the DC:0–3R diagnoses (Zero to Three 2005) need to be ruled out before making the diagnosis of PTSD in infancy:

- Disorders of affect, including anxiety disorders and depression, can be differentiated by the absence of a traumatic event and of the full list of PTSD criteria.

- Attention deficit disorder with hyperactivity is important to rule out since symptoms of restlessness and poorly focused attention are often present following trauma (Thomas 1995).
- Oppositional defiant disorder has been shown to be more strongly associated with childhood exposure to victimization trauma than ADHD or adjustment disorders (Ford et al. 2000).
- Reactive attachment disorder may occur with severe and chronic maltreatment, but is not uniquely associated with childhood trauma or maltreatment (Chaffin et al. 2006).

Epidemiology

To the best of our knowledge, no epidemiological studies of trauma exposure and PTSD using community samples have been done with infants. However, a study by Finkelhor et al. (2007) documented exposure to victimization trauma by children as young as 2 years old.

Long-term impact: neurological and psychological impact of traumatic experiences in infancy

Exposure to stressful and traumatic experience(s) at a time when the brain is undergoing rapid change may leave an indelible imprint on its structure and function (Teicher et al. 2002). Teicher et al. reviewed the cascade of neurobiological events that may significantly impact brain development and subsequent psychiatric health. These changes operate on multiple levels, such as neurohumoral (mainly the hypothalamic-pituitary-adrenal axis), structural, and functional. Structural changes due to early severe stress include reduced size of the midportions of the corpus callosum, and diminished development of the left neocortex, hippocampus, and amygdala. Functional changes include increased electrical irritability in limbic structures and reduced activity of the cerebellar vermis. These changes in neurobiological systems may result in aggravated responses to subsequent stressors experienced in childhood, rendering the child more vulnerable to the development of PTSD and related problems (Eth 2001).

This knowledge of the impact of trauma on brain development may explain the following findings. Early childhood traumatic experiences, such as abuse and maltreatment do not necessarily lead to full DSM-IV-based PTSD in childhood (Famularo et al. 1996), but may instead lead to anxiety, depression, and behavior problems in childhood, and sensitization to retraumatization and PTSD in adulthood (Yehuda et al. 2001). Adult psychiatry has taught us that early childhood traumas adversely impact the development of personality, and are especially linked to borderline and antisocial personality disorders, with representations of early childhood attachment figures and basic trust have a prominent mediating role (Fonagy et al. 1997). Traumas impinge on the psychic envelope from the outside. The infant's psychic envelope is much more vulnerable than the adult's, and is almost totally dependent on the adult's protection. Therefore domestic violence may have particularly long-term adverse posttraumatic effects on infants and young children, because the very caregivers to whom they look for security and protection are instead instigating or being victimized by violence (Scheeringa and Zeanah 1994).

Retrospective studies of survivors from childhood trauma have shown that single-incident traumas in most cases do not leave the myriad of sequelae associated with sexual and/or physical abuse or neglect (Tyano et al. 1996). Follow-up reports of infants and preschoolers with PTSD are very sparse, mainly because this diagnosis is relatively new. The main consistent finding is the correlation between the child's persistent PTSD symptoms two to three years after the traumatic event and the level of the mother's PTSD avoidant symptoms (rather than the nature of the trauma) (Laor et al. 1997; Winje and Ulvik 1998).

Scheeringa et al. (2005) reported two one-year follow-ups of traumatized children 20 months to 6 years old. They found little consistency in PTSD at the first follow-up, possibly due to additional traumas experienced by some children in the interim. Over the two-year period overall PTSD symptoms were not resolved despite treatment. PTSD re-experiencing symptoms tended to decrease, but avoidance/numbing symptoms increased (particularly for children initially diagnosed with PTSD). Twice as many children (almost 50 per cent) exhibited functional impairment as were diagnosed with PTSD, suggesting that assessment of other disorders or symptoms may be necessary in order to fully characterize the childhood sequelae of early traumatization.

Risk factors for PTSD following the infant's exposure to trauma

First, a poor early parent–child relationship is the major risk factor for childhood PTSD. Among forty-one posttraumatic children under 48 months of age, the most potent trauma variable that predicted the development of PTSD in these children was not an event directed at their own body, but whether they had witnessed a threat to their caregiver (Scheeringa and Zeanah 1994). The relational perspective of PTSD in infancy reinforces the well-known protective function of the early parent–child relationship. The caregiving relationship mediates the infant's symptoms in one of the following ways (Scheeringa and Zeanah 2001):

• the *moderating effect model*, where the extent to which the parent is able to read and to respond effectively to the child's cues and affects will either amplify or help contain the child's traumatic reaction

- the *vicarious traumatization model*, which applies when the caregiver has experienced a trauma and the child has not, but the trauma impinges on their relationship
- the *compound effect model*, wherein both caregiver and infant are traumatized, and each exacerbates the symptoms of the other.

Second, traumatic attachments are a strong risk factor for developing PTSD in childhood and adulthood. By definition, these infants have histories of neglect, abandonment, witnessing domestic violence, and/or abuse (physical and/or sexual). "Early abuse negatively impacts the developmental trajectory of the right brain, dominant for attachment, affect regulation and stress modulation, thereby setting a template for the coping deficits of both mind and body that characterize PTSD symptoms" (Schore 2002, p. 9). Consequently the younger the child is, the more at risk he or she is (Vila et al. 2001).

Third, difficult infant temperament is a constitutional risk factor for PTSD (Allen 1998).

Fourth, family factors that are risk factors for the infant to develop PTSD following exposure to trauma, include father's PTSD with externalizing and depressive symptoms (Kilic et al. 2003), traumatized mother's internal representations as a protective figure (Almqvist and Broberg 2003; Laor et al. 1997), poor general family emotional and instrumental functioning and low socioeconomic status (Gurwitch et al. 1998; Scheeringa and Gaensbauer 2000; Vila et al. 2001).

The final factor is gender: girls are more vulnerable to developing PTSD (Ohmi et al. 2002), and are at risk for a longer time. These gender-related differences may stem from the interaction of three factors:

- differences in the nature of the early traumas experienced by boys and girls
- sexually dysmorphic effects of early experience on brain development
- sex differences in brain laterality and hormonal environment (Teicher et al. 2002).

Protective factors and resilience

The main protective factors that have been identified include a positive parental relationship, as well as parental constructive coping mechanisms, physical proximity of the infant to the caregiver (Rossman et al. 1997), and social and community support (Sameroff and Fiese 2000).

Clinical case studies

The following two cases illustrate the interplay between risks and protective factors, together with the type of stressor that may determine the development of PTSD.

First case study

N., 2 years and 3 months at time of referral, presented with irritability, physical aggression toward strangers as well as familiar figures, adults and children, repeated spitting at people, intermittent refusal to go to preschool with separation anxiety, constricted play and withdrawn behavior, reduced appetite, negative mood, and difficulty in falling asleep as well as frequent awakenings with inconsolable crying.

Past history

Five months before referral, N. came back from his father's home with second-degree burns on both hands. He became very irritable, would repeat "ouch, ouch", avoid using his hands and scream whenever put in the bath. These specific behaviors disappeared within a month or so, and were replaced by the symptoms described above. The circumstances surrounding the event were unclear. The father was suspected of abuse and lost his visitation rights for an unlimited period of time. At the time of consultation, N. had no contact with him, except for sporadic phone calls.

Developmental history

N., an only child, was born after a wanted pregnancy and a normal delivery. N. was an easy baby, had no feeding or sleep problems. Psychomotor development was normal but language was delayed. N. did not have any transitional object. He stayed home with his mother until the age of 2, and started preschool two months after the burn incident.

Family background

N.'s father started to hit his wife during her pregnancy, and a month after N.'s birth he tried to strangle her. She lost consciousness and dropped the baby on the floor. N. was unconscious for a few hours. The police were involved. The mother divorced and returned to her parents' home with N. The father would take the child for visits. Arguments and shouting in his presence were the rule.

When N. was 6 months old he witnessed his father slapping his mother's face and spitting on her.

Mental status at time of referral

N., a normal-looking boy, stayed on his mother's lap and displayed no explorative behavior. Both his hands moved freely and were without scars. He looked sad and anxious, made eye contact with the examiner but refused any interaction, repeating "Don't want to" while kicking his mother's lap. Without any external trigger, N. suddenly slapped his mother's face, and she herself looked anxious and helpless. Suddenly out of the blue he started to scream, hit his mother, threw his bottle away, and repeatedly said, "Stupid, stupid". At hearing the therapist pronounce the father's name, the mother froze, and simultaneously N. fell asleep. This dissociative episode recurred following any verbal reminder of the father's existence. Severe restriction of play, social withdrawal, restricted affect, sleep and eating disorder, short attention span, hypervigilance, pervasive anger and anxiety, clingy and aggressive behavior towards the mother with lack of exploratory behavior, and dissociative spells were the infant's main clinical presenting signs across the three assessment sessions. The mother had very low self-esteem and showed signs of PTSD with a loss of self-confidence as a protective figure for her son. The type of trauma experienced by N. was Terr's Type II, a mixture of chronic witnessing of the father's physical and verbal aggression towards the mother, and acute threat to his own physical integrity (being dropped from his mother's arms while she herself was in danger, and later the burn, most probably inflicted, intentionally or not, by the father). N. was diagnosed with the following DC:0–3 diagnoses:

- Axis I: PTSD of infancy
- Axis II: Anxious/tense mother–child relationship disorder
- Axis III: Delayed language development.
- Axis IV: Domestic verbal and physical violence, maternal PTSD, loss of father's visitation rights.

Dyadic psychotherapy (see Chapter 13) was started and N.'s symptoms resolved, though his basic lack of trust remained. This partial improvement is explained by the presence of almost all the risk factors that have been described above, that is, domestic violence, physical insult inflicted by an attachment figure, traumatized mother's internal representations as a protective figure, negative parental relationship, poor maternal constructive coping mechanisms, and language delay in the child.

Second case study

F., a $2\frac{1}{2}$-year-old girl, was caught in the midst of a terrorist attack, and badly injured in her abdomen. The mother, who was pregnant, had a badly injured arm, but took the child in her arms, and they arrived together at the hospital. The child did not lose consciousness, but did not see her mother's wound or the dead and other wounded civilians.

Family background and developmental history

F. was the only child of a working father and mother, both healthy. The marital relationship was stable, in spite of some strains around F.'s education and setting limits. F. was a normally developing child, a bit "spoiled" at home, but well adapted. F's mental status at time of referral revealed signs of acute stress disorder, with arousal, avoidance, and separation anxiety symptoms, which disappeared within a month. She did not develop any PTSD symptoms but did show behaviors that were secondary to her mother's posttraumatic dysfunctioning and the birth of her sibling. This relatively good outcome was explained by several protective factors, such as the isolation of the traumatic event, the immediate maternal holding, the premorbid normal family functioning, the child's normal development, the significant community support such as special financial support for families who went through terrorist attacks, and special attention given to the pregnant mother. These positive factors had significantly greater weight than the risk factors (i.e. the mother's loss of function in her arm, and the PTSD she developed a few months after delivery).

These two cases illustrate the differential effect of chronic versus acute trauma, and domestic violence versus terrorist attack.

Treatment principles for PTSD in infancy

In the case of infants the most detrimental impact of severe trauma, especially human-made ones, is the disruption of the development of basic trust, and the ensuing aggression and anxiety. Hence, treatment needs to be aimed at restarting the disrupted process of trusting adults. In the infant's eyes, the parents have become unreliable, because they did not prevent the traumatic event(s). Therefore, very often, as illustrated in the first case, the infant's aggression is directed toward the caregiver. In turn, the parents may feel guilty, overwhelmed by the traumatic event, and powerless in the face of their infant's unusual behaviors, thus becoming even more unreliable as protective figures.

The therapist's role is to "translate" each person's behaviors into a coherent link between the traumatic event and their behaviors. The therapist is heard by the parent as well as the infant and thus may gradually change their mutual representations of one another. The basic therapeutic principles for older children, such as establishing a sense of safety, soothing techniques aimed at reducing autonomic arousal and desensitization techniques, are the same for infants. There is therefore an imperative need to involve the caregiver in the therapy sessions. The process of helping the infant re-experience the trauma in an affectively meaningful and secure way necessitates the holding presence of the child's caregiver (Lieberman et al. 2003). When the parent is traumatized, we first need to create a secure working alliance with the parent before bringing in the infant. For example, in our first case (a detailed account may be found in Keren and Tyano 2000), as long as the mother was unable to contain her own anxiety toward her ex-husband, mentioning the father's name provoked repeated dissociative spells in the infant.

The second step is to encourage and help the parent(s) play with their child in ways that re-create the challenges that occurred in the traumatic situations, while ensuring that the child's arousal state remains modulated. Arousal modulation may be achieved by modifying the nature and extent of caregiver availability and the specific challenges posed to the infant in the play scenario, and introducing alternative coping mechanisms that enable the infant and the caregiver to successfully co-regulate arousal and affect. Young children are unable to make sense of the recurring images of salient aspects of their trauma, and experience them as happening in the present (Gaensbauer 1996). The therapeutic task is therefore to educate the parents about the significance of PTSD symptomatology in their infant, so they can understand the infant's unusual behaviors and help the infant to distinguish between past and present (Terr 2003). In addition to a number of detailed treatment reports (Gaensbauer 1996; MacLean 1977; Thomas 1995; Wallick 1979), Van Horn and Lieberman (Chapter 13 in this volume) have described a dyadic psychotherapy model for traumatized young children and their caregivers that has shown evidence of efficacy in randomized trials. In our clinical experience, the treatment outcome depends very much on the interplay of risk factors in the parent, the infant, and the environment. The capacity of the parent to attribute meanings to the infant's behaviors, conceptualized as "parental reflective functioning" (Fonagy et al. 2006), is an essential factor. Attachment research has revealed a link between past parental history of traumatic attachments, poor reflective functioning, and poor parental protective function in stressful situations (Lieberman and Zeanah 1999). In that sense, the two clinical cases we described above are quite illustrative: F.'s parents had no past history of abuse, had a fair marital relationship, and good family functioning prior to the traumatic event; they displayed more (though not optimal) capacity for reflective functioning during the therapy; and F. indeed had a better outcome than N., whose mother had married a violent man, had poor self-esteem, and showed low parental reflective functioning during the therapy. We suggest using these indicators in deciding on treatment modality and length.

Is there always a need for treatment when an infant is brought to our attention after a traumatic event? In our view every case needs to be assessed not only for signs and symptoms, but also for risk and protective factors in the infant, the caregivers, and the environment, so as to identify children who are at risk for experiencing severe acute stress reactions and subsequently for PTSD.

Conclusion

In this chapter, we have tried to show how infants can become functionally impaired due to direct or indirect insult(s) to their physical and emotional integrity. We stressed the developmental and relational aspects of PTSD in infancy that must be taken into account during the assessment and treatment. Knowledge of the risks and protective factors should increase community health professionals' awareness of the need to detect, assess and treat those infants at the highest risk for developing PTSD. Well-designed studies on the short- and long-term impact of specific therapeutic modalities for PTSD in infants are still very much needed.

References

Allen, J.R. (1998). Of resilience, vulnerability, and a woman who never lived. *Child and Adolescent Psychiatric Clinics of North America, 7*(1), 53–71.

Almqvist, K., and Broberg, A.G. (2003). Young children traumatized by organized violence together with their mothers: The critical effects of damaged internal representations. *Attachment in Human Development, 5*(4), 367–380.

Als, H., Lawhon, G., Dufy, F.H., McAnulty, G.B., Gibes-Grossman, R., and Blickman, J.G. (1994). Individualized developmental care for the very-low-birth-weight preterm infant: Medical and neurofunctional effects. *Journal of the Medical Association, 272*, 853–858.

Anand, K.J., Sippell, W.G., and Ansley-Green, A. (1987). Randomized trial of fentanyl anaesthesia in preterm babies undergoing surgery: Effects on the stress response. *Lancet, 10*(1), 62–66.

Chaffin, M., Hanson, R.F., Saunders, B.E., Nichols, T., Barnett, D., Zeanah, C.H., et al. (2006). Report of the APSAC task force on attachment therapy, reactive attachment disorder, and attachment problems. *Child Maltreatment, 11*, 76–89.

Coates, S., and Schechter, D. (2004). Preschoolers' traumatic stress post-9/11: Relational and developmental perspectives. *Psychiatric Clinics of North America, 27*, 473–489.

De Bellis, M.D., Chrousos, G.P., Dorn, L.D., Burke, L., Helmers, K., Kling, M.A., et al. (1994). Hypothalamic-pituitary-adrenal axis dysregulation in sexually abused girls. *Journal of Clinical Endocrinology and Metabolism, 78*, 249–255.

DeCasper, A., and Spencer, M.J. (1986). Prenatal maternal speech influences new-borns' perceptions of speech sounds. *Infant Behavior and Development, 9*, 133–150.

Dolto, F. (1987). *Tout est language* [Everything is language]. Paris: Vertiges du Nord Carrere.

Drell, M.J., Siegel, C.H., and Gaensbauer, T.J. (1993). Posttraumatic stress disorder. In C.H. Zeanah (ed.), *Handbook of infant mental health* (pp. 291–304). New York: Guilford.

Emde, R., Bingham, D., and Harmon, J. (1993). Classification and the diagnostic process in infancy. In C.H. Zeanah (ed.), *Handbook of infant mental health* (pp. 225–235). New York: Guilford.

Eth, S. (ed.) (2001). *Review of Psychiatry Series: PTSD in children and adolescents,* Volume 20. Washington, DC: American Psychiatric Publishing.

Famularo, R., Fenton, T., Kinscherff, R., and Augustyn, M. (1996). Psychiatric comorbidity in childhood postraumatic stress disorder. *Child Abuse and Neglect, 20*, 953–961.

Finkelhor, D., Ormrod, R., and Turner, H. (2007). Poly-victimization: A neglected component in child victimization. *Child Abuse and Neglect, 31*, 7–26.

Fivush, R., Pipe, M., Murachver, T., and Reese, E. (1997). Events spoken and unspoken: Implications of language and memory development for the recovered memory debate. In M. Conway (ed.), *Recovered memories and false memories: Debates in psychology* (pp. 34–62). Oxford: Oxford University Press.

Fonagy, P., Target, M., Steele, M., and Steele, H. (1997). Morality, disruptive behavior, borderline personality disorder, crime, and their relationships to security of attachment. In L. Atkinson and K.J. Zucker, *Attachment and Psychopathology* (pp. 223–274). New York: Guilford.

Fonagy, P., Steele, M., Steele, H., Moran, G., and Higgitt, A.C. (2006). The capacity for understanding mental states: The reflective self in parent and child and its significance for security of attachment. *Infant Mental Health Journal, 12*(3), 201–218.

Ford, J.D., Racusin, R., Ellis, C., Daviss, W.B., Reiser, J., Fleischer, A., et al. (2000). Child maltreatment, other trauma exposure, and posttraumatic symptomatology among children with oppositional defiant and attention deficit hyperactivity disorders. *Child Maltreatment, 5*, 205–217.

Gaensbauer, T.J. (1982). The differentiation of discrete affects: A case report. *Psychoanalytical Study of the Child, 37*, 29–66.

Gaensbauer, T.J. (1996). Developmental and therapeutic aspects of treating infants and toddlers who have witnessed violence. *Bulletin of Zero to Three, 15*, 15–20.

Gauvain-Piquard, A., and Meignier, M. (1993). *La Douleur de l'enfant* [Pain in children]. Paris: Calmann-Levy.

Gurwitch, R.H., Sullivan, M.A., and Long, P.J. (1998). The impact of trauma and disaster on young children. *Child and Adolescent Psychiatric Clinics of North America, 7*(1), 19–32.

Haith, M.M. (1986). Sensory and perceptual processes in early infancy. *Journal of Pediatrics, 109*, 158–171.

Keren, M., and Tyano, S. (2000). A case-study of PTSD in infancy: Diagnostic, neurophysiological, developmental and therapeutic aspects. *Israel Journal of Psychiatry, 37*(3), 236–246.

Kilic, E.Z., Ozguven, H.D., and Sayil, I. (2003). The psychological effects of parental mental health on children experiencing disaster: The experience of Bolu earthquake in Turkey. *Family Process, 42*(4), 485–495.

Laor, N., Wolmer, L., and Mayes, L. (1997). Israeli preschoolers under Scuds: A 30 month follow-up. *Journal of the American Academy of Child and Adolescent Psychiatry, 36,* 349–356.

Lebovici, S. (1988). Fantasmatic interaction and intergenerational transmission. *Infant Mental Health Journal, 9,* 10–19.

Lewis, M. (1993). The emergence of human emotions. In M. Lewis and J.M. Haviland (eds.), *Handbook of emotions* (pp. 223–235). New York: Guilford.

Lieberman, A.F., and Zeanah, C.H. (1999). Contributions of attachment theory to infant parent psychotherapy and other interventions with infants and young children. In J. Cassidy and P.R. Shaver (eds.), *Handbook of attachment: Theory, research, and clinical applications* (pp. 555–574). New York: Guilford.

Lieberman, A.F., Compton, N.C., Van Horn, P., and Ippen, C.G. (2003). *Losing a parent to death in the early years: Guidelines for the treatment of traumatic bereavement in infancy and early childhood.* Washington, DC: Zero to Three Press.

MacLean, G. (1977). Psychic trauma and traumatic neurosis: Play therapy with a four-year-old boy. *Canadian Psychiatric Association Journal, 22,* 71–75.

Mandler, J.M. (1990). Recall and its verbal expression. In R. Fivush and J.A. Hudson (eds.), *Knowing and remembering in young children* (pp. 57–74). Cambridge: Cambridge University Press.

Ohmi, H., Kohima, S., Awai, Y., Kamata, S., Sasaki, K., Tanaka, Y., et al. (2002). Posttraumatic stress disorder in pre-school aged children after a gas explosion. *European Journal of Pediatrics, 161,* 643–648.

Osofsky, J.D. (2000). Infants and violence: Prevention, intervention and treatment. In J.D. Osofsky and H.E. Fitzgerald (eds.), *WAIMH handbook of infant mental health,* Volume 4 (pp. 164–196). New York: Wiley.

Papousek, H. (1967). Conditioning during early postnatal development. In Y. Brackbill and G.G. Thompson (eds.), *Behavior in infancy and early childhood* (pp. 259–274). New York: Free Press.

Perry, B.D. (1994). Neurobiological sequelae of childhood trauma: posttraumatic stress disorders in children. In M. Murberg (ed.), *Catecholamines in posttraumatic stress disorder: Emerging concepts* (pp. 253–276). Washington, DC: American Psychiatric Press.

Peterson, C., and Bell, M. (1996). Children's memory for traumatic injury. *Child Development, 67,* 3045–3070.

Pruett, K.D. (1979). Home treatment for two infants who witnessed their mother's murder. *Journal of the American Academy of Child and Adolescent Psychiatry, 18,* 647–657.

Pynoos, R.S. (1990). Posttraumatic stress disorder in children and adolescents. In B. Garfinkel, G. Carlson, and E. Weller (eds.), *Psychiatric disorders in children and adolescents* (pp. 48–63). Philadelphia, PA: W.B. Saunders.

Rossman, B.B.R., Bingham, R.D., and Emde, R.N. (1997). Symptomatology and adaptive functioning for children exposed to normative stressors, dog attack, and parental violence. *Journal of the American Academy of Child and Adolescent Psychiatry, 36,* 1089–1097.

Sameroff, A.J., and Fiese, B.H. (2000). Models of development and developmental risk. In C.H. Zeanah (ed.), *Handbook of infant mental health*, 2nd edition (pp. 3–19). New York: Guilford.

Schacter, D.L. (1987). Implicit memory: History and current status. *Journal of Experimental Psychology: Learning, Memory, and Cognition, 13*, 501–518.

Scheeringa, M.S., and Gaensbauer, T.J. (2000). Posttraumatic stress disorder. In C.H. Zeanah (ed.), *Handbook of infant mental health*, 2nd edition (pp. 225–235). New York: Guilford.

Scheeringa, M.S., and Zeanah, C.H. (1994). *Semi-structured interview and observational record for the diagnosis of PTSD in infants and young children (0–48 months)*. New Orleans, LA: Tulane University School of Medicine.

Scheeringa, M.S., and Zeanah, C.H. (2001). A relational perspective on PTSD in early childhood. *Journal of Trauma and Stress, 14*(4), 799–815.

Scheeringa, M.S., Zeanah, C.H., Myers, L., and Putnam, F.W. (2003). New findings on alternative criteria for PTSD in preschool children. *Journal of the American Academy of Child and Adolescent Psychiatry, 42*(5), 561–570.

Scheeringa, M.S., Zeanah, C.H., Myers, L., and Putnam, F.W. (2005). Predictive validity in a prospective follow-up of PTSD in preschool children. *Journal of the American Academy of Child and Adolescent Psychiatry, 44*(9), 899–906.

Schore, A.N. (2002). Dysregulation of the right brain: A fundamental mechanism of traumatic attachment and the psychogenesis of posttraumatic stress disorder. *Australian and New Zealand Journal of Psychiatry, 36*, 9–30.

Schwartz, G.M., Izard, C.E., and Ansul, S.E. (1985). The 5-month-old's ability to discriminate facial expressions of emotion. *Infant Behavior and Development, 8*, 65–77.

Spitz, R.A. (1946). Anaclitic depression. *Psychoanalytic Study of the Child, 1*, 53–74.

Sroufe, L.A. (1979). Socioemotional development. In J.D. Osofsky (ed.), *Handbook of infant development*, 1st edition (pp. 462–516). New York: Wiley.

Stern D. (1985). *The interpersonal world of the infant*. New York: Basic Books.

Sugar, M. (1988). Toddlers' traumatic memories. *Infant Mental Health Journal, 13*, 245–251.

Teicher, M.H., Andersen, S.L., Polcari, A., Anderson, C.M., and Navalta, C.P. (2002). Developmental neurobiology of childhood stress and trauma. *Psychiatric Clinics of North America, 25*, 397–426.

Terr, L.C. (1988). What happens to early memories of trauma? A study of 20 children under five at the time of documented traumatic events. *Journal of the American Academy of Child and Adolescent Psychiatry, 27*, 95–104.

Terr, L.C. (2003). Wild child: How three principles of healing organized 12 years of psychotherapy. *Journal of the American Academy of Child and Adolescent Psychiatry, 42*(12), 1401–1409.

Thomas, J.M. (1995). Traumatic stress disorder presents as hyperactivity and disruptive behavior: Case presentation, diagnoses and treatment. *Infant Mental Health Journal, 16*, 306–317.

Tyano, S., Iancu, Z., Solomon, J., Sever, I., Goldstein, Y., Touviana, Y., et al. (1996). Seven-year follow-up of child survivors of a bus-train collision. *Journal of the American Academy of Child and Adolescent Psychiatry, 35*(3), 365–373.

Vila, G., Witkowski, P., Tondini, M.C., Perez-Diaz, F., Mouren-Simeoni, M.C., and Jouvent, R. (2001). A study of posttraumatic disorders in children who experienced an industrial disaster in the Briey region. *European Child and Adolescent Psychiatry, 10*, 10–18.

Wallick, M.M. (1979). Desensitization therapy with a fearful two year-old. *American Journal of Psychiatry, 136*, 1325–1326.

Winje, D., and Ulvik, A. (1998). Long-term outcome of trauma in children: The psychological consequences of a bus accident. *Journal of Child Psychology and Psychiatry, 39*, 635–642.

Winnicott, D.W. (1960). *The child, the family, and the outside world*. Baltimore, MD: Penguin.

Yehuda, R., Spertus, I.L., and Golier, J.Q. (2001). Relationship between childhood traumatic experiences and PTSD in adults. In S. Eth (ed.), *PTSD in children and adolescents*. Review of Psychiatry Series, Volume 20(1). Washington, DC: American Psychiatric Publishing.

Zero to Three (2005). *Diagnostic classification of mental health and developmental disorders in infancy and early childhood*, revised edition. Washington, DC: Zero to Three Press.

Chapter 6

Physical and mental health functioning in Sudanese unaccompanied minors

Wanda Grant-Knight, Paul Geltman, and B. Heidi Ellis

Scope of the problem

The United Nations High Commission for Refugees (UNHCR 2005) estimates that there are approximately 11.5 million refugees who have been dislocated from their homelands because of famine, civil wars, religious persecution, or ethnic cleansing. Nearly half of these refugees are children. The term "unaccompanied minor" (UAM) refers to persons under the legal age of majority who are not being cared for by any adult. The term includes minors who are with minor siblings or in informal foster families (UNHCR 1997). Africa, which has 12 percent of the world's population, also has 28 percent of the world's refugees, the largest number of refugees in the world.

Historical context of Sudanese UAMs

Conflicts and civil wars in Africa have been largely responsible for the vast numbers of African refugees and UAMs. Among the most prolonged and destructive conflicts is the one that has raged in Sudan since 1955. The current phase of the civil war, which began in 1983, has left approximately 2 million people dead and 4.5 million uprooted from their homes.

The fighting in Sudan has targeted and exploited civilian communities and led to the separation of families. During an upsurge in fighting that began in 1987, many Sudanese youths were separated from their families. Some of these youths banded together and traveled from Sudan to Ethiopia. In 1991–1992, they were forcibly returned to Sudan and then traveled on foot to northern Kenya. During their flight, they experienced various types of additional traumatic exposure. Several accounts detailing these experiences (Duncan 2000a, 2000b, 2000c; Geltman et al. 2005; Goodman 2004) describe youths being fired upon by militia, attacked by animals, subjected to torture, as well as experiencing near-drowning, and witnessing the starvation, torture, and murder of their families and companions. Those who survived the arduous treks, approximately half of the original number, landed in a refugee camp in Kakuma, Kenya, where many spent upwards of seven years. In this camp, they maintained their formal and informal "family" groupings, and received schooling and preparation for resettlement. In the case of UAMs, the presence of friends or family meant extended, not nuclear, family members (i.e. primary caregivers/parents), although some may have had siblings.

As a first step in the resettlement of the Sudanese UAMs, the UN Commission conducted "Best Interest Assessments" to determine the course of action which would best meet their needs. Because the instability resulting from the ongoing war in the Sudan rendered repatriation impossible, resettlement was the only option. In 2000, approximately 3,600 Sudanese UAMs were resettled in the United States.

Trauma in child refugee populations

Several studies suggest that refugee youths are at risk for developing global distress-related symptoms resulting from traumatic exposure during war, flight, and resettlement. Mollica et al. (1997) assessed young refugees in a Thai-Cambodian refugee camp, using the Child Behavior Checklist (CBCL), and found that 75 percent of these youths scored in the clinical or borderline range on the CBCL as rated by others, while 40 percent self-reported symptoms that placed them in the clinical or borderline ranges for their age (Mollica et al. 1997). A study of UAMs from different countries of origin who were resettled in Finland found that nearly half were functioning within the clinical or borderline range on the CBCL (Sourander 1998). Post-traumatic stress disorder has also been noted as a significant problem among refugee youths; Khamis (2002) found that 34.1 percent of school-age Palestinian refugee children met the diagnostic criteria (from the *Diagnostic and statistical manual*, 4th edition, DSM-IV) for PTSD. Studies of Bosnian children have found PTSD rates of 28 percent among Bosnian refugees in Greece (Papageorgiu et al. 2000) and Servan-Schrieber et al. (1998) found that 11.5 percent of Tibetan refugee children met the DSM-IV criteria for PTSD.

Studies of Sudanese populations have also found significant rates of PTSD. In the "Best Interest Determination" of Sudanese UAMs (some of whom were eventually resettled in the United States), Duncan (2000a) found that among male youths, 75 percent had moderate to severe trauma symptoms, while among females, 48 percent reported severe PTSD symptoms (Duncan 2000a, 2000b, 2000c). In assessing Sudanese youths in Ugandan refugee camps, researchers using the Levonn instrument (a cartoon measure which evaluates children's psychological distress) found that 35 percent to 60 percent of the youths had PTSD symptoms (Paardekooper et al. 1999); while Peltzer (1999) found that 20 percent of Sudanese youths in Uganda suffered from chronic PTSD.

These studies indicate that PTSD is highly prevalent among young refugees. Although symptoms generally tend to decrease with time, some children continue to experience PTSD even years after resettlement. In a longitudinal study of forty Cambodian youths resettled in the United States, Kinzie and colleagues (Kinzie et al. 1986, 1989; Sack et al. 1993) found that, two years after resettlement, 50 percent of the youths had PTSD. When the same sample was reassessed three, six, and twelve years after resettlement, the rates of PTSD had decreased somewhat, but remained very significant.

UAMs may be at even greater risk than other young refugees for developing mental health problems. Several researchers have found that refugee children who either remain with or are rapidly reunited with family members show less emotional distress and better adjustment than children who survive the refugee process alone (Ressler et al. 1998). McKelvey and Webb (1995) measured psychological distress in a group of unaccompanied Vietnamese-American (Amerasian) youths who were allowed to migrate to the "land of their fathers". Those youths who migrated alone were found to have significantly more symptoms of psychological distress than their accompanied counterparts.

It should not be surprising that all children who become refugees are at increased risk for experiencing psychological distress, with those who are UAMs potentially being at greatest risk. However, few studies of unaccompanied refugee youths have assessed the precise factors which contribute to the children's distress. This was the focus of the current study.

The impact of traumatic events on children's social ecology

Bronfenbrenner (1979) set forth a model which explains how transactions between children and varying aspects of their social ecology shape their growth and functioning. The model has been elaborated to explain how children and their environments respond to traumatic events (Cicchetti and Lynch 1993). Therefore, in order to understand the impact of a traumatic event, it is necessary to study its effects across multiple systems of the child's social ecology.

Under ordinary circumstances, the environment supports the child's development of basic regulation and coping functions. Traumatic events are destabilizing and can create a sense of unpredictability and loss of control. Wars directly impact multiple circles of the child's social ecology. These effects range from making caregivers or loved ones physically unavailable or rendering them emotionally unavailable, to the disruption of other support systems, such as extended families, religious and neighborhood organizations, and schools. Cultural rituals and beliefs also may be disrupted by traumatic events. Goldson (1996) has described the impact on children of "low intensity" wars that target civilians as well as societal infrastructures. These "low intensity" wars disrupt fundamental aspects of the child's social ecology (medical, social, religious, and public services) by terrorizing the civilian population.

Social ecology of Sudanese UAMs

The civil war in the Sudan serves as a good example of a "low-intensity" war. Civilians have been the targets of military and rebel forces. As a result, many have witnessed or directly experienced personal violence, and there has been considerable breakdown in the systems supporting children, including families, schools, medical care agencies, and religious institutions. As a result, these institutions have not been available to serve their regular developmental functions for children, nor have they been available to aid children's coping with the ongoing war. In their absence, many young people have had to learn to support each other during flight, stays at refugee camps, and their subsequent resettlement in the United States. The impact of these events on their functioning is not well understood; it is therefore the target of the survey of Sudanese UAMs described in the next section.

Sudanese study

Pilot

Prior to embarking on the national survey of Sudanese UAMs, we conducted a pilot study with forty Sudanese UAMs resettled in the Boston area. The UAMs, who ranged in age from 14 to 18 years, with a mean age 16.7, were assembled for a half-day retreat and given questionnaires assessing demographic information, exposure to trauma, psychological symptoms, coping skills, and behavior. These youths had been in the United States for less than three months at the time of the pilot study and most were living in either permanent or transitional foster families at that point. Because many UAMs received schooling and instruction in English at a refugee camp in Kenya, the questionnaires were administered in English. Adult Sudanese case managers and resettlement agency staff read, translated, and addressed questions about study measures while the youths read along. The youths were then separated into focus groups of eight to ten, with two moderators, to discuss their experiences of war, flight, and resettlement. They were asked about their cultural beliefs, their understanding of mental health problems and methods, and their perceptions of what would constitute successful functioning in the Sudan and the United States. They also discussed the impact of their experiences on their current functioning and outlook and their adjustment to life in the United States. Information about participants' functioning was also gathered from resettlement agency staff and foster parents.

The pilot study provided information on key domains to be assessed in the national survey, as well as issues to consider in study design. Based on the pilot study, important background variables were included in the national study, as well as questionnaires involving coping, health, social support, trauma exposure, and symptomatology. The pilot study also highlighted methodological issues, such as the need for parsimonious use of measures (minimizing both the number and length of the measures) and replacing confusing questions and terms. It also led to the simplification of the questions and response choices to match the literacy level of the Sudanese minors. None of the youths in the pilot study expressed distress associated with answering questions about their experiences.

National survey sample

Based on the information gained in the pilot study, a larger nationwide survey was launched to systematically explore issues involving the adjustment and adaptation of Sudanese youth. Further details about the recruitment procedures, sample characteristics, and methods of this study have been published previously (Geltman et al. 2005). The study involved a sample of 476 Sudanese UAMs (boys and girls, ranging from 9 years to 25 years of age with a mean age of 17), who had arrived in the United States in late 2000 through early 2001. It should be noted that three adult staff members who had immigrated as adolescents were inadvertently included in this sample, but all other study participants were born between January 1983 and January 1986. The study was conducted from February 2001 through July 2002 and was approved and monitored by the Institutional Review Board of the Boston University Medical Center. In addition, all local resettlement programs sought and received permission from their respective state child protective services for the youths to participate. Demographic information about the sample is included in Table 6.1.

National survey methods

Participants completed questionnaires assessing background factors, traumatic experiences, traumatic reactions, health status, coping style, and health services utilization. Foster care agencies were given information about the study and measures to be assessed. They were provided with both written and

Table 6.1 Demographics

Gender	Male 85%
Age	Mean 17 years (range 9–25)
Years of formal schooling	Range 2–15 years
Lived in Kakuma camp	92%
Dinka tribal ethnicity	87%
Mean months in United States at time of study	13.6
Resettlement location	23% urban, inner-city
	28% urban
	32% suburban communities
	17% rural

videotaped instructions about how to administer the measures and address any questions or issues that arose. Youths at the various agencies completed the questionnaires either individually or in small groups in the presence of agency staff, who read the questions aloud while the youths read along. The first author (WGK), a clinical psychologist, was available by pager during the administration of the measures to provide information or address any issues that might arise. There were only three reported incidents of distress as the result of participating in the survey. One episode involved a minor already receiving psychiatric evaluation and care services. The other two episodes, which involved some emotional distress in response to questions about family loss, facilitated the identification of two minors who were subsequently deemed to be in need of psychiatric evaluation and care.

National survey measures

Background and demographics

Based on experiences reported during the pilot session and important predictive factors identified in the PTSD and other mental health literature, the research team developed an instrument to assess migration history, exposure to physically and emotionally traumatic events, current and past living conditions, and demographic information. This instrument was modeled on similar instruments used to assess and quantify traumatic experiences among refugees and victims of war.

Child Health Questionnaire (CHQ)

The CHQ (Landgraf et al. 1999) is a self-report measure that assesses the physical and psychosocial well-being of children, namely bodily pain, general health, changes in health over time, physical, behavioral, and emotional problems that affect social roles in school, self-esteem, more general mental health, family activities, and family cohesion. The CHQ includes basic demographic and medical care-seeking questions for somatic complaints (e.g. abdominal pain) and problems (e.g. injuries and enuresis) often associated with behavioral and emotional problems. The psychometric properties of this measure have been published (Geltman et al. 2005; Landgraf and Abetz 1999).

Harvard Trauma Questionnaire (HTQ)

The HTQ (Mollica et al. 1992) is a measure of trauma symptoms that yields a diagnosis of PTSD if the HTQ score is 2.5 or greater. The HTQ was selected because of its extensive use with refugees, although it has not been specifically validated with Sudanese populations.

Ways of Coping (WOC)

A shortened version of the WOC (Folkman et al. 1986) was administered to assess the thoughts and actions the youths used to cope with stressful encounters.

Utilization of health services

Questions assessing the youths' utilization of health services were derived from relevant sections of the National Health Interview Survey (www.cdc.gov/ nchs/about/major/nhis/quest_data_related_1997_forward.htm).

Analyses

The HTQ and CHQ were scored according to published criteria or cut-off values. Because a number of questions were eliminated from the WOC, no standardized scores were obtained. To analyse the WOC and the background questionnaire, multivariate stepwise logistic regression analyses were conducted to identify items from these measures that were associated with PTSD. For the CHQ, we compared mean health rating scores between youths with and without PTSD (as determined by HTQ scores). Analytic methods included Student's t-test for comparing means and chi-squared analyses for comparison of prevalence. Explanatory variables included demographics, exposure to war and violence, and aspects of the resettlement and migration process that were statistically significant in bivariate exploratory analyses. Responses to health services utilization questions were analysed with comparisons to CHQ and HTQ scores.

Results

Overall rate of PTSD symptoms

One-fifth (20 percent) of the sample met diagnostic criteria for PTSD as determined by HTQ scores.

Experience of violence

Table 6.2 presents the youths' exposure to traumatic events. The vast majority of youths reported that they were in or near their village during a time of attack, but the results suggest that being present during these attacks was not associated with later reports of PTSD symptoms. Many youths witnessed violence perpetrated against others, and many experienced personal violence or significant danger to themselves during their flight and resettlement. There were no significant associations between witnessing violence and youths'

Table 6.2 Traumatic experiences and PTSD

HTQ	PTSD (%)	No PTSD (%)	Odds ratio
Saw/heard attack	91	89	1.2 (0.39–3.8)
Saw/heard torture	62	60	1.07 (0.56–2.1)
Saw/heard injury	83	73	1.8 (0.78–4.1)
Saw/heard killing	81	75	1.4 (0.64–3.2)
Ever tortured	35	17	2.59 (1.3–5.3)
Ever injured	43	25	2.21 (1.1–4.3)
Head trauma	43	26	2.12 (1.1–4.1)

reports of PTSD symptoms. On the other hand, *direct* traumatic experiences were associated with youths' reports of PTSD symptoms. Those reporting PTSD symptoms were more than twice as likely to report that they had been tortured or injured or had experienced head trauma during their flight or resettlement.

Social support

Nearly three-quarters of the youths reported having been with family or friends during flight or resettlement. There were no significant associations between social support during flight and resettlement and youths' reports of PTSD symptoms (Table 6.3). Although social support during flight and resettlement were not associated with reports of PTSD, social support on arrival to the United States was negatively correlated with PTSD symptoms (Table 6.4). Youths reporting feeling lonely in the United States were four times more likely to report PTSD symptoms than those not reporting feelings of loneliness. Given that UAMs were placed in families or group homes upon arrival to the United States, their experiences of loneliness probably do not reflect mere lack of social support in the United States.

Table 6.3 Social support in flight, resettlement, and PTSD

HTQ	PTSD (%)	No PTSD (%)	Odds ratio
Flight	69	63	1.3 (0.7–2.6)
With family			
With friends	67	65	1.1 (0.5–2.1)
In camp	77	69	1.5 (0.7–3.2)
With family			
With friends	89	95	0.42 (0.13–1.3)

Table 6.4 Social support in United States and PTSD

HTQ	PTSD (%)	No PTSD (%)	Odds ratio
Feel lonely at home	45	16	4.14 (2.1–8.3)
Activities with United States	83	94	0.30 (0.11–0.8)
Feel safe at home	90	97	0.23 (0.06–0.8)
Feel safe at school	85	97	0.19 (0.06–0.6)

Coping styles

To investigate factors that might have contributed to resilience in these youths, we examined their reports about coping (Table 6.5). Most of the youths reported that their Christian religious faith was important in their coping: 98 percent reported that in difficult situations they often or always put their trust in God, and 97 percent reported that when bad things happened, they often or always prayed more. The next most frequently endorsed coping strategies were active ones, such as seeking help when needed (96 percent), trying to do something active when bad things happen (93 percent), and trying to improve when they are criticized (96 percent). As would be expected by the nearly universal use of these strategies, the coping styles did not demonstrate any association with PTSD symptoms. However, several other less frequently used coping strategies were associated with greater PTSD symptomatology. As shown in Table 6.5, those reporting PTSD symptoms were significantly more likely to blame themselves for bad things that happened, lacked someone they feel close to, kept problems to themselves, and wondered why bad things happen.

Table 6.5 Relation between coping styles and PTSD

WOC	PTSD (%)	No PTSD (%)	Odds ratio
Blame self	40	19	2.1 (1.3–3.3)
No close person	22	9	2.5 (1.3–5.0)
Keep problems	33	15	2.2 (1.3–3.8)
Wonder why	50	32	1.6 (1.1–2.2)

Health status

The means of all the CHQ scales were significantly lower (indicating poorer perceptions of health status) for youths reporting PTSD symptoms than the mean CHQ for those not reporting PTSD symptoms (Table 6.6). In addition, 76 percent of all minors reported seeking medical care for problems often associated with behavioral and emotional problems, such as vague somatic

Table 6.6 Health and PTSD

HTQ score	PTSD	No PTSD
Physical function	79.2	87.7**
Bodily pain	51.3	69.1**
Behavior	77.5	84.6**
Mental health	54.4	69.4**
Self-esteem	76.7	85.8**
General health	63.0	70.3*
Family activities	54.5	77.3**
Family cohesion	69.6	79.1*

Notes: * p < 0.05
** p < 0.01

complaints (e.g. stomach aches). Those reporting PTSD symptoms were also significantly more likely to report having sought medical care for such problems. The latter group also reported less satisfaction with the medical personnel providing this care.

Discussion and conclusions

The findings of this study suggest that Sudanese UAMs exhibit generally good functional outcomes despite years of deprivation, trauma, and separation from families during childhood. This observation, supported by research on coping skills among these youths (Goodman 2004), provides some assurance that efforts to provide safe and supportive environments for traumatized refugee children can be associated with good health and positive psychosocial outcomes.

Despite their adverse experiences, these Sudanese UAMs, when assessed approximately one year after resettlement, were slightly less symptomatic than many other samples of youths exposed to traumatic events (Kinzie et al. 1986; Nader et al. 1993; Sack et al. 1997; Weine et al. 1995). They also reported an overall rate of PTSD symptoms that was nearly 30 percent lower than the rate found among Cambodian youth resettled in the United States (Kinzie et al. 1986). There are several possible explanations for the lower rates of PTSD found in this study. It is possible that only those with good mental health survived the journey, that the social networks which developed in the group served as protective mechanisms, or that the resettlement programs served to promote mental health among these youths. It also is quite possible that these Sudanese youths were in some way protected by the meaning ascribed to their experiences by their culture, much as Rousseau et al. (1998) claimed for Somali UAMs. Also, the nomadic cultures from which they came could have provided a protective framework for these youths, who were culturally accustomed to separations from their parents as part of their normal development. Although the Sudanese UAMs generally displayed fewer symptoms than those reported in other studies of refugee youths, this study points to a number of factors that were associated with the increased rate of post-traumatic symptoms, including current feelings of isolation. These findings indicate the need not only to identify those exposed to direct trauma, but also to address ongoing feelings of loneliness as risk factors for continued posttraumatic distress.

The fact that 20 percent of the UAMs continued to experience symptoms consistent with a diagnosis of PTSD suggests that these youths are in need of continued mental health care despite having been resettled in supportive programs. While these symptoms might be connected with the continuing effect of their experiences in their homeland, or during flight and resettlement, they might also result from the social isolation they are experiencing in their current environments.

In terms of possible resiliency factors, we found that religious faith was significant and important to these youths. The vast majority of them reported reliance on prayer and faith in God as a significant aspect of their coping. Halcon et al. (2004), in a study of Somali and Oromo youths, found that religion was the most widely endorsed aid for combating distress associated with the refugee experience. This finding suggests that one possible means of ameliorating youths' distress might be through addressing their faith and religious beliefs. Given the limitation in the number and length of measures that we could utilize in this study, we were not able to fully assess other areas of functioning which might have provided additional information on the UAMs' coping and resilience, such as self-efficacy, self-competence, academic motivation or achievement, or peer success. Future large-scale studies of UAMs from different cultures may be able to highlight relevant protective factors for youths and possible mechanisms through which these factors could inform interventions to address any distress they may experience.

The finding in the current study of significantly poorer perceptions of health status in these UAMs is consistent with other findings in the literature regarding the medical status of refugees. While many UAMs and other refugees have health problems associated with malnutrition, exposure to disease, untreated injuries, and inadequate access to medical care, there is burgeoning evidence that some medical complaints may represent, wholly or in part, somatic embodiments of refugee-related trauma, which are called "traveling pains" among Sudanese people (Coker 2004). Coker has pointed out that it is important for caregivers to understand the connection between traumatic experiences and physical symptoms in order to fully address refugees' needs. In the current study, UAMs who reported PTSD symptoms were significantly more likely than their counterparts who did not report such symptoms to also report seeking medical care for physical symptoms. Similarly, they reported dissatisfaction with their medical care, perhaps indicating that the medical personnel failed to appreciate the emotional context in which these physical symptoms were manifested. This finding indicates the importance of both physical and mental health screening for UAMs.

As already noted, the study reported in this chapter provides some assurance that resettlement efforts for UAMs can be associated with good mental health and positive psychosocial outcomes. We believe that specific factors in the social context after the UAMs' arrival in the United States may have mediated the ultimate impact of early trauma on later functioning. This may prove important for the resettlement of children in cultural settings profoundly different from those of their origins, and may be particularly relevant for children whose race or religion sets them apart from the cultures in which they are relocated.

Limits to generalizability

This study has several limitations. We have no reason to believe that the UAMs in our study were not representative of both the other UAMs and even older Sudanese UAMs who entered through regular resettlement. However, their younger age may have made them more susceptible to trauma and deprivation than older youths while still in Africa, although their placement in the URMP was probably less traumatizing and more supportive than the resettlement experiences of the older youths once in the United States. Because this study was a national survey involving several agencies, we had to limit the scope of our questions and the length of our questionnaires. Thus, we could not assess a number of other psychological factors that might have been relevant, such as depression, anxiety, grief, or other measures of resilience. Several measures utilized had been validated with refugee populations, but not specifically for Sudanese UAMs. The survey was constructed with careful attention to cultural, linguistic, and literacy issues; nonetheless, our measures may not have fully captured the youths' experiences, either because they included culturally irrelevant questions, or because they failed to sufficiently tap culturally relevant experiences. Despite our efforts, the participants' responses may also have been adversely impacted by their lack of familiarity with the format, content, or comprehensibility of the questions. In spite of these limitations, the current study does provide important information regarding functioning in a sample of Sudanese UAMs who, while widely covered by the media, have received very little study in the scientific literature.

Implications for the state of the field

The results of this study add to the literature on the impact of refugee experiences. Unfortunately, these experiences, while seemingly extreme, are becoming more typical of children in contemporary crises in Somalia, Bosnia, Rwanda, and more recently the Darfur region of Sudan. The screening protocol used in this study made it possible to study several background variables in relation to adjustment after resettlement. The results suggest that criteria used to assess the "success" of resettlement programs should include broad measures of household or family life and emotional well-being. Similarly, particular attention should be paid to the emotional needs of minors who have directly experienced torture or injury. In this manner, the findings of this study outline not only the promise and challenges of resettling refugee children but also the important opportunities for innovative social service policies and health care interventions.

Acknowledgements

This study was funded by a grant awarded to the second author (PG) by the Joel and Barbara Alpert Endowment of Children of the City, Department of Pediatrics, Boston Medical Center, Boston, MA. The authors wish to thank staff of the Migration and Refugee Services of the US Conference of Catholic Bishops and Lutheran Immigration and Refugee Service. In particular, the authors would like to thank Julianne Duncan, Susan Schmidt, Kathy Barrett, Marla Schmidt, Bethany Christian Services (Grand Rapids, MI), Catholic Community Services (Tacoma, WA), Catholic Family Center (Rochester, NY), Catholic Social Service (Phoenix, AZ), Commonwealth Catholic Charities (Richmond, VA), Lutheran Child and Family Services of Eastern PA (Roslyn, PA), Lutheran Family Services Northwest (Seattle, WA), Lutheran Social Services of MI (Lansing, MI), Lutheran Social Services of New England (Newton, MA), and Lutheran Social Service of North Dakota (Fargo, ND).

References

Bronfenbrenner, U. (1979). *The ecology of human development: Experiments by nature and design*. Boston, MA: President and Fellows of Harvard College.

Cicchetti, D., and Lynch, M. (1993). Toward an ecological/transactional model of community violence and child maltreatment: Consequences for children's development. *Psychiatry, 56*, 96–118.

Coker, E.M. (2004). "Traveling pains": Embodied metaphors of suffering among Southern Sudanese refugees in Cairo. *Culture, Medicine and Psychiatry, 28*(1), 15–39.

Duncan, J. (2000a). Overview of mental health findings for UAM and separated children interviewed as part of UNHCR best interest determinations. Kakuma Refugee Camp, Kenya. Unpublished report.

Duncan, J. (2000b). Sudanese girls in Kakuma. Unpublished report.

Duncan, J. (2000c). Sudanese unaccompanied children best interest determination. Background information for case review. Unpublished report.

Folkman, S., Lazarus, R.S., Dunkel-Schetter, C., DeLongis, A., and Gruen, R.J. (1986). Dynamics of a stressful encounter. Cognitive appraisal, coping, and encounter outcomes. *Journal of Personality and Social Psychology, 50*, 992–1003.

Geltman, P., Grant-Knight, W., Mehta, S., Lloyd-Travigliani, C., Lustig, S., Landgraf, M., et al. (2005). The "Lost Boys" of Sudan: Functional and behavioral health of unaccompanied minors resettled in the United States. *Archives of Pediatrics and Adolescent Medicine, 159*(6), 585–591.

Goldson, E. (1996). The effect of war on children. *Child Abuse and Neglect, 20*(9), 809–819.

Goodman, J.H. (2004). Coping with trauma and hardship among unaccompanied refugee youths from Sudan. *Qualitative Health Research, 14*, 1177–1196.

Halcon, L.L., Robertson, C.L., Savik, K., Johnson, D.R., Spring, M.A., Butcher, J.N., et al. (2004). Trauma and coping in Somali and Oromo refugee youth. *Journal of Adolescent Health, 35*(1), 17–25.

Khamis, V. (2002). Posttraumatic stress disorder among school age Palestinian children. *Child Abuse and Neglect, 29*(1), 81–95.

Kinzie, J.D., Sack, W.H., Angell, R.H., Manson, S., and Rath, B. (1986). The psychiatric effects of massive trauma on Cambodian children: I. The children. *Journal of the American Academy of Child and Adolescent Psychiatry, 25*, 370–376.

Kinzie, J.D., Sack, W.H., Angell, R., Clarke, G.N., and Ben, R. (1989). A three-year follow-up of Cambodian young people traumatized as children. *Journal of the American Academy of Child and Adolescent Psychiatry, 28*, 501–504.

Landgraf, J.M., and Abetz, L.N. (1999). Functional status and well-being of children representing three cultural groups: Initial self-reports using the CHQ-CF87. *Psychology and Health, 12*, 839–854.

Landgraf, J.M., Abetz, L., and Ware, J.E. (1999). *The CHQ user's manual, 2nd edition.* Boston, MA: HealthAct.

McKelvey, R.S., and Webb, J.A. (1995). Unaccompanied status as a risk factor in Vietnamese Amerasians. *Social Science Medicine, 41*(2), 261–266.

Mollica, R.F., Caspi-Yavin, Y., Bollini, P., Truong, T., Tor, S., and Lavelle, J. (1992). The Harvard Trauma Questionnaire: Validating a cross-cultural instrument for measuring torture, trauma and posttraumatic stress disorder in Indochinese refugees. *Journal of Nervous and Mental Disorders, 180*, 111–116.

Mollica, R.F., Poole, C., Son, L., Murray, C.C., and Tor, S. (1997). Effects of war trauma on Cambodian refugee adolescents' functional health and mental health status. *Journal of the American Academy of Child and Adolescent Psychiatry, 36*, 1098–1106.

Nader, O.N., Pynoos, R., Fairbanks, L., Al-Ajeel, M., and AlAsfour, A. (1993). Preliminary study of PTSD and grief among the children of Kuwait following the Gulf Crisis. *British Journal of Clinical Psychology, 32*, 307–416.

Paardekooper, B., de Jong, J.T.V.M., and Hermanns, J.M.A. (1999). The psychological impact of war and the refugee situation on South Sudanese children in refugee camps in northern Uganda: An exploratory study. *Journal of Child Psychology and Psychiatry, 40*(4), 529–536.

Papageorgiu, V., Frangou-Garunovic, A., Iordanidou, R., Yule, W., Smith, P., and Vostanis, P. (2000). War trauma and psychopathology in Bosnian refugee children. *European Child and Adolescent Psychiatry, 9*(2), 84–90.

Peltzer, K. (1999). Trauma and mental health problems of Sudanese refugees in Uganda. *Central African Journal of Medicine, 45*(5), 110–114.

Ressler, E.M., Boothby, N., and Steinbock, D.J. (1988). *Unaccompanied children.* New York: Oxford University Press.

Rousseau, C., Said, T., Gagne M., and Bilbea, G. (1998). Resilience in unaccompanied minors from the North of Somalia. *Psychoanalytic Review, 85*(4), 615–637.

Sack, W.H., Clarke, G.N., Him, C., Dickason, D., Goff, B., Lanham, K., et al. (1993). A 6-year follow-up study of Cambodian refugee adolescents traumatized as children. *Journal of the American Academy of Child and Adolescent Psychiatry, 32*, 431–437.

Sack, W.H., Seeley, J.R., and Clarke, G.N. (1997). Does PTSD transcend cultural barriers? *Journal of the American Academy of Child and Adolescent Psychiatry, 36*, 49–54.

Servan-Schreiber, D., Lin, B.L., and Birmaher, B. (1998). Prevalence of posttraumatic stress disorder and major depressive disorder in Tibetan refugee children. *Journal of the American Academy of Child and Adolescent Psychiatry, 37*, 874–879.

Sourander, A. (1998). Behavior problems and traumatic events of unaccompanied refugee minors. *Child Abuse and Neglect, 22*, 719–727.

UNHCR (1997). *Refugee children: Guidelines on protection and care.* www.unhcr.org/cgi-bin/texis/utx/protect/opendoc.pdf?tbl=PROTECTION&id=3b84c6c67

UNHCR (2005). *Refugees by numbers, 2005.* www.unhcr.ch/cgi-bin/texis/vtx/basics/opendoc.htm?tbl=BASICS&id=3b028097c

Weine, S., Becker, D.F., McGlashan, T.H., Vojvoda, D., Hartman, S., and Robbins, J.P. (1995). Adolescent survivors of "ethnic cleansing": Observations on the first year in America. *Journal of the American Academy of Child and Adolescent Psychiatry, 34*, 1153–1159.

Chapter 7

Risk and resilience in young Londoners

Antonia Bifulco

Introduction

In spite of large-scale concern and legislation among Western countries to try to eradicate childhood neglect and abuse, many children and adolescents are still subject to maltreatment, with only a fraction obtaining relevant services (Tunstill and Aldgate 2000). Those who do reach the services and are taken away from abusive parents suffer discontinuity in care, often in multiple care arrangements throughout childhood, where the residential and fostering arrangements often lead to poor outcomes, including psychological disorders and educational problems (Chamberlain et al. 2006; Rushton 2004). Rates of psychological disorders in childhood and adolescence attributed to maltreatment are high, and these effects commonly continue into adulthood, resulting in lifetime vulnerability and disadvantages (Bifulco and Moran 1998). It is particularly important to study the protective factors that may exist among those children who suffer from maltreatment but remain in their biological families. This can serve to inform both service intervention and policy in their attempts to counteract the negative impacts of poor parenting and abuse in the family.

Childhood experiences of abuse, whether physical, sexual or psychological, constitute a form of trauma. Trauma is usually defined as something that poses "threats to life or the integrity of the self", which can be of different levels of duration or frequency, but is usually tied to particular times, occasions and events (Allen 2005). Thus abuse provides clear instances of trauma, particularly when they are of high severity, frequency or duration. The impact of abuse is great, leading to depression, anxiety, conduct disorder or substance abuse in adolescence (Bifulco and Moran 1998; Bifulco et al. 2002b). This impact is due not only to the more hostile and deprived environments of those affected, but also to the psychological vulnerability of the child. It is this interplay of risk environment and psychological state that is most predictive of disorder, but it is also likely to play a similarly complex role in the generation of resilience (Rutter 1990). As with other forms of trauma, the individual variation in the impact of abuse is substantial, with the majority of individuals surviving the experience and thus making the study of resilience possible (Bonanno 2004).

Researching resilience has necessitated a clear conceptualization of the likely mechanisms by which positive experiences may have an effect in combating negative experiences. The relevant concepts include prevention (reducing the exposure to adversity), protection (moderating the effects of adversity) and counteraction (resources used to increase the coping response). The outcomes may include the *absence* of psychopathology or maladaptive behavior *and* the presence of health or social competence (Garmezy 1985). Researchers have outlined a range of potential protective factors that are associated with better psychological outcomes in cases of adversity. These include environmental factors in various domains such as home, school and leisure (e.g. competent parenting, closeness to a parent, good support, good educational experience and organized religion), as well as individual psychological characteristics (e.g. high IQ, good coping skills, autonomy, empathy and a sense of humour) (Fonagy et al. 1994; Luthar 1991; Masten et al. 1988; Rutter 1990). The findings of resilience research are critical for both intervention and preventive action against abuse in that they locate factors in the home, the school environment, with peers or in individual coping and prosocial behavior associated with resilience. Resilience is conceptualized not only as an attribute that children are born with or acquire during development, but also as the indication of a process which characterizes a complex social system at a particular point in time (Rutter 1990). Thus it is a set of social and intrapsychic processes which combine the child's attributes with the family, social and cultural environments, with resilience best defined as normal child development despite difficult conditions.

This chapter outlines new findings from a study of a high-risk London sample of young people aimed at identifying positive experiences which promote resilience and reduce psychological disorders. The young people suffered from high levels of childhood adversity but had little past intervention from child protection services and had not been removed from the family. Therefore they had relatively stable care arrangements despite family problems. The focus is on familial abuse and the potentially protective effect of support, favorable school experiences, secure attachment style and high self-esteem against the development of psychological disorders.

The London sample

This is a naturalistic study of problem families where all the children remained living with their families (specifically their biological mothers) despite subsequent evidence of family-based adversity and high levels of abuse. Even in such circumstances over half the children suffered no psychological disorders, so that the sample provides an opportunity for exploring the naturally occurring protective factors at the critical stage of adolescence that are associated with better outcomes for adult life.

The study of high-risk young people was part of a larger investigation of intergenerational transmission of risk conducted in the 1980s and 1990s (Andrews et al. 1990; Bifulco et al. 2002b). The selection was based on questionnaire screening of women registered with health surgeries in North London to select mothers for studying vulnerability to depression. This was later extended intergenerationally to their teenage and young adult children aged 16–30. The women's response rate of around 40 percent to the initial questionnaire is comparable to those of other survey approaches, with high cooperation from the mothers for reinterview (70 percent) and just under 60 percent of the young people agreeing to be interviewed (Bifulco et al. 2002b). The final data set includes a full psychosocial history of the mothers and the children in both a typical and a vulnerable sample. The high-risk young people reported here are a subsample who were all selected because of their mother's vulnerability to depression, based on her early experience of neglect or abuse, or ongoing unfavorable family relationships and lack of social support (Bifulco et al. 2002b).

Previous studies among these high-risk young people show a fourfold higher rate of psychological disorders than in a typical sample from the same community, including depression, anxiety, conduct disorder and substance abuse. Rates of neglect or abuse in childhood were double that in the typical sample, and neglect or abuse was highly related to disorder (odds ratio of five). Other risk factors in this sample were negative experience of peer group (over one-third of the young people) and negative experience of school (over half the young people). These risks, particularly bullying by peers, predicted psychological disorders over and above neglect or abuse within the family (Bifulco et al. submitted a). The present study investigates the role of positive experiences in peer groups and school as potential protective factors against psychological disorders.

A relationship was also found between insecure and anxious attachment style, a negative evaluation of the self and internalizing disorders (depression or anxiety) in the young people. The Attachment Style Interview (Bifulco et al. 2002a), originally designed as an adult measure of support-based attachment style and administered to the mothers, was adapted for use with the young people studied. It is an assessment of secure and insecure styles, on the basis of the respondents' attitudes towards closeness/distance and anger/fear. The insecure attachment styles were common, affecting two-thirds of the adolescents, with Fearful and Enmeshed styles the most prevalent. These latter were associated with depression and anxiety, particularly at "marked" or "moderate" levels of intensity (Bifulco et al. submitted a). Enmeshed or Fearful attachment styles were related to both poor parenting from the mother (including severe neglect, physical abuse or antipathy) and negative evaluation of the self. The present analysis investigates the extreme of positive attachment style ("Clearly Secure") as a factor in resilience against disorders.

Assessments of risk and resilience

The London study utilized intensive investigator-based interviews. Such interviews have a strong tradition in UK social psychiatry in assessing social adversity and interpersonal relationships following innovative work by George Brown and Michael Rutter in the 1960s (Brown and Rutter 1966). They have become a "gold standard" for collecting contextual details of experience and narrative accounts for exploratory research, with high reliability and validity. The method is not unlike a clinical one, where full questioning about experience is continued until all the information needed to assess certain pre-existing criteria have been met. The narrative elements are used both qualitatively for hypothesis generation and to elicit the context and meaning of experiences, and quantitatively for statistical analysis. This method allows for the lifespan investigation of risk, across different developmental stages, particularly those of adolescence and mid-to-late-adulthood, as well as across generations. All researchers collecting data were fully trained in the administration of the measures, and worked with manuals detailing benchmark rating thresholds. All cases were discussed with other members blind to the outcome variables to create a team consensus to increase reliability. The Childhood Experience of Care and Abuse (CECA) interview (www.cecainterview.com) (Bifulco et al. 1994) was used to assess childhood adversity before age 17. It assesses a range of experiences, including poor care or abuse of the child, negative aspects of the family and the environment, and positive aspects of support and school environment. The measure's reliability and validity are high – for example, independently rated interviews had over 0.78 (K^w) agreement on all scales (Bifulco et al. 1994) and sisters interviewed independently had an average of 0.60 agreement (Bifulco et al. 1997). For this analysis, with its focus on trauma, emphasis was placed on abuse, including: physical, sexual or psychological abuse. Physical abuse included physical attacks on the child, such as being hit with an implement (like a belt or stick) or being punched or kicked, or repeated hitting likely to result in injuries. Sexual abuse involved sexual contact with any adult or older peer, including touching of breasts or genitals, masturbation, oral sex, and sexual intercourse. Psychological abuse involved sadistic coercive control of the child by parent figures, including incidents of humiliation or terrorizing, deprivation of basic needs or valued objects, cognitive disorientation or corruption and exploitation. The severity of all the types of abuse was determined by their intensity and frequency. A binary index of "Severe Abuse" included any one experience of the above abuses at "marked" or "moderate" levels.

Positive experiences during the teenage years

Previous analyses in adults has shown that a supportive confidant in childhood is protective against psychological disorders at later ages, and high school attainment has a positive, albeit weaker effect (Bifulco and Moran 1998). These factors were therefore examined, while the potential factors of positive peer group experiences and positive school experiences were also added to the investigation.

Good friendships during the mid-teenage years

The study assessed positive peer group experiences, such as having a group of friends over a period of time, having positive interactions in the group, being popular and accepted, and having socially acceptable group activities. In addition, the existence of a confidant was measured by asking the respondent to name a close friend who could be confided in and who would offer emotional support, when the respondent was 16 years old.

Positive school experiences during the teenage years

These were assessed by reports that school was a pleasant environment, where the young person could keep up with the workload, felt accepted by peers and teachers, and was able to study the subjects he or she enjoyed. In addition, school attainment was assessed by how well the young person performed in matriculation exams. Perceived competence as a student was assessed by the degree to which the young person felt he or she was a good student and capable of undertaking the required work, was punctual, and hard-working, and proud of her educational achievements.

Positive characteristics at the time of the interview (in late teenage/early adult years)

Secure attachment style

The Attachment Style Interview (ASI) (Bifulco et al. 2002a; see www.attachmentstyleinterview.com) assesses the quality of relationships and support, which form the basis for ratings about the individual's ability to form close relationships and attachment security. This was assessed by an interview at a time when most of the young people were past childhood (average age 20). All the raters were trained in the use of the ASI and scored the responses according to benchmark thresholds and with reference to the manual. The measure included assessments of three close support figures (including parents for those living at home). On the basis of the quality of the support and interaction across these relationships, the individual's "ability to form and maintain relationships" was assessed, forming the basis for attachment security. Questions were asked about attachment attitudes denoting anxious attachment (e.g. fear of rejection, lack of tolerance of separation, high desire for company or low self-reliance) and avoidance/distance in relationships (e.g. mistrust, constraints on closeness, high self-reliance, anger). The individual's overall attachment style was rated as Enmeshed, Fearful, Angry-Dismissive or Withdrawn, in addition to Clearly Secure. The most positive end of the attachment-style scale – the "Clearly Secure" attachment classification – was considered a potential resilience factor in this analysis. It entailed the presence of at least two close, confiding, supportive relationships and the absence of negative attitudes toward closeness (e.g. mistrust, fear of rejection, constraints on closeness, anger), as well as adaptive levels of autonomy (moderate self-reliance and desire for company, low fear of separation). The reliability of the ASI is high (for example, independent ratings of interviews reaching 0.84 (K^w) agreement on overall attachment style and has been repeated in other research studies internationally (Bifulco et al. 2004) and among adolescents (Figueirido et al. 2006).

Positive self-esteem at the time of the interview (late adolescence/early adulthood)

Detailed questionnaires on self-perceptions of both personal attributes and roles (Andrews and Brown 1991), as well as self-acceptance, were administered. In the present analysis only the results of the global scale of self-acceptance were used. This assesses the individual's degree of self-liking and self-approval. In this analysis, "marked" self-acceptance was found to be associated with good outcomes. Reliability is high, with independent ratings achieving agreement of over 0.90 (K^w).

Psychological disorders in the year before the interview

Psychological disorders in the year before the interview were assessed by the Structured Clinical Interview for DSM-IV (SCID) (First et al. 1996). It includes assessments of major depression and anxiety states (GAD, PD/Ag, Social Phobia), which were combined into an index of internalizing disorders for the past twelve months, while substance abuse/dependence and conduct disorders were combined into an index of externalizing disorders. An index of all psychological disorder in the twelve months before the interview was utilized for the main analysis.

Results

Prevalence of risk and resilience factors

Family deprivation was pervasive in this sample, with 94 percent having at least one marker of social adversity in childhood. Just over half of the young people had a single mother, one-third came from the lowest social class and one-fifth experienced domestic violence between their parents. Parental psychological disorders were also very common (75 percent), with recurrent depression in the mother accounting for just under half the sample and reports of behavior problems or psychological disorder in fathers similarly common.

One-third (32 percent) of the young people had undergone abuse at "marked" or "moderate" levels of severity, with most (28 percent) experiencing physical abuse, and a small proportion with psychological abuse (6 percent) or sexual abuse (4 percent). Just under half of the young people (42 percent) had a psychological disorder at a clinical level in the twelve months before the interview.

Table 7.1 shows the prevalence of abuse and positive experiences during the mid-teenage years and at the time of the interview, and their association with psychological disorders.

Table 7.1 Prevalence of factors and case disorder

Binary variables	Prevalence in sample total N=146 % (N)	A Case* N=66 % (N)	B Not case N=80 % (N)	A vs. B χ^2, 1 df	p<
Childhood abuse					
Abuse (physical, sexual or psychological)	32 (46)	46 (30)	20 (16)	10.85	0.001
Positive experiences at age 16					
Support from friend	56 (83)	53 (35)	60 (48)	0.71	NS
Positive peer group experience	68 (99)	58 (38)	77 (61)	6.4	0.01
Positive school experience	66 (96)	58 (38)	73 (58)	3.57	0.07
High academic attainment perceived	51 (74)	52 (34)	50 (40)	0.03	0.03
Perceived competence as a student	66 (96)	68 (45)	64 (51)	0.31	NS
Positive experiences in early adulthood					
Marked self-acceptance	14 (21)	6 (4)	21 (17)	6.77	0.01
Clearly secure attachment	30 (44)	15 (10)	43 (34)	12.84	0.0001

* Clinical levels of depression, anxiety, conduct disorder or substance abuse in the twelve months before the interview

In spite of such high levels of deprivation and harsh family experiences in the sample, there was clear evidence of favorable experiences (see also Table 7.1, col. 1). Most (80 percent) had at least one type of favorable experience, with 43 percent of the young people having *both* a supportive friend *and* a good peer group, and 40 percent experiencing all three positive school factors. At the time of the interview in early adulthood, 40 percent had a clearly secure attachment style and/or markedly high self-acceptance.

Table 7.1 shows the relationship of positive factors to disorders. It can be seen that in mid-teenage years the only positive peer group experiences and high academic attainment were significantly (and inversely) related. However, both of the most recent factors (clearly secure attachment or marked self-acceptance) were significantly related. When the dichotomized factors were entered into a binary logistic regression to look at disorder outcome, only the more recent factors (i.e. those present at interview) of clearly secure attachment (OR=0.24, Wald=10.31, p<0.001) and marked self-acceptance (OR=0.25, Wald=5.02, p<0.02) provided the best model for case disorders in the previous twelve months (goodness of fit of 69.0 percent).

The associations between positive experiences at school and with peers during the mid-teenage years were also studied. Favorable experiences in school were significantly associated with academic attainment (r=0.47, p<0.01) and perceived competence as a student (r=0.49, p<0.01). Positive peer group experiences were similarly associated with positive school experiences (r=0.36, p<0.01) and academic attainment (r=0.18, p<0.01). Table 7.2 displays the associations between positive experiences during the mid-teenage years and later positive characteristics at the time of the interview. While self-acceptance was associated with all the mid-teen experiences apart from support from a friend, a clearly secure attachment style was associated mainly with support aspects (support from a friend and a good peer group) as well as favorable school experiences. Self-acceptance and secure attachment style were correlated at 0.25 (p<0.01).

Table 7.2 Intercorrelation of positive experiences in mid-teenage years and at time of interview

Variables in mid-teenage years	In early adulthood (at interview)	
(4-point scales) (Spearman's rho)	Degree of self-acceptance	Degree of security of attachment
Support from a friend	0.04	0.23(**)
Positive peer group experience	0.17(*)	0.19(*)
Positive school experience	0.32(**)	0.19(**)
High academic attainment	0.17(*)	0.09
Perceived competence as a student	0.18(*)	0.09

* Significant at the 0.05 level (2-tailed)
** Significant at the 0.01 level (2-tailed)

Protective factors

Binary logistic regression analysis was used for both the abuse index and the positive variables (clearly secure attachment style and marked self-acceptance) in relating to disorders. The analysis, performed by the forward stepwise method, showed that a clearly secure attachment style and marked self-acceptance could be used together with the abuse index to predict psychological disorders. Each variable contributed independently to the model (all changes in -2 Log likelihood if the term is removed, $p<0.006$). Thus abuse significantly increased the chances of psychological disorders (OR=3.32, Wald=6.13, $p<0.01$), while a secure attachment style (OR=0.33, Wald=5.22, $p<0.02$) and marked self-acceptance (OR=0.17, Wald=4.00, $p<0.04$) were associated with a lower risk of such disorders (goodness of fit 66.4 percent). All three factors showed a direct effect, but no interaction effect was found among any of the variables added to the model (all p=ns).

When the results are shown graphically, the association between secure attachment style and marked self-acceptance, on the one hand, and a lower risk of psychological disorders, on the other, can be seen, with individual chi-squares significant or approaching significance (see Figures 7.1 and 7.2).

Discussion

The London sample is useful for investigating risk and resilience because of the selection procedures used. The young people were chosen because of their mothers' risk characteristics, not their own. Thus, while the families had a high degree of deprivation and problems, this did not preclude the existence of positive experiences or resilience in the young people. While nearly all of

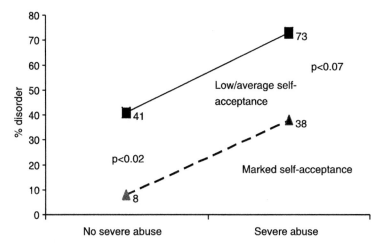

Figure 7.1 Abuse, secure attachment, and psychological disorder during previous twelve months.

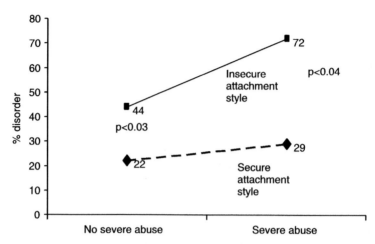

Figure 7.2 Abuse, self-acceptance and psychological disorders during the previous twelve months.

the sample had elements of adversity in terms of upbringing by a single mother, low social class, domestic violence or parental psychological disorders, all remained with their biological mothers in childhood and thus had some stability of care. Severe abuse occurred in one-third of young people, but social services were not generally notified. Most of the abuse was from parent figures, with physical abuse the most common.

Despite such negative family experiences, a surprisingly high proportion of the young people had positive experiences with peers and at school. Most (80 percent) experienced at least one such factor in their mid-teenage years, with 40 percent having both secure attachment style and high self-acceptance at the time they were seen. These factors were associated with a lower risk of psychological disorders even in the face of abuse. Although no statistical interaction was found, this does not mean that a moderating or protective effect did not occur (since statistical tests for multiplicative interaction are not always present) (Rutter 1990). This is because statistical significance is crucially dependent on the number of individuals for whom the modifying factors and risk variables occur – if the number is small, the power is reduced. This is likely in the analysis reported because of the rather small size of the sample. Also, interactive processes may rely on chains of connections over time rather than multiplicative effects at any single time. This may be true of the current analysis where the positive factors occurred at different times and not at the time of the abuse.

A UNICEF report has shown that the United Kingdom, together with the United States, has the worst level of well-being for children and young people among rich Western countries (UNICEF 2007). This report was based on data collected in the early 2000s from nationally representative school samples and household income and living conditions. High ratings for negative perception of health, school life and personal well-being were found in the UK samples, based on the responses to items such as "I feel lonely" or "How much do I like school?" or "How good is my health?" While the findings may indeed accurately reflect a lower quality of life among UK youth, the narrow range of measurement may have failed to highlight coexisting positive attitudes and experiences, which paradoxically may actively indicate a very good quality of life consistent with improved material conditions and the greater availability of educational opportunities. This may be due to polarization, with well-being very high for some young people and very low for others, with the average tending towards the lower end, but it may also reflect the complexity of modern life in metropolitan areas where good and bad experiences are often juxtaposed. Thus it may be possible to have good and bad experiences of school or home or health at various times. The results of the London study reported here suggest that such a juxtaposition does exist and that the full analysis of quality of life and well-being is a complex field of study where negative and positive experiences need to be assessed separately and not merged into average ratings, so as to reflect the true patterns of contemporary life.

There are, to be sure, some limitations to the study and analysis presented here. First, the sample was studied retrospectively and the timing of the experiences is not exact, with no retrospective psychological factors included, due to problems with accurate retrospective reporting of feeling states (Brewin et al. 1993). Security of attachment was measured at the time of the interview, and thus may have been influenced by psychological disorders rather than vice versa. However, it does have acknowledged high stability, suggesting that attachment insecurity predated the disorders (Bifulco et al. 2004). Second, there may have been bias in the retrospective reporting of childhood experience. In mitigation, the investigator-based interviews used have been shown to be robust in retrospective measurement. Third, the intensive measurement procedure is very time consuming, which led to relatively low numbers of respondents being studied, with the prevalence of positive factors among those who experienced abuse also relatively rare. This reduces the power of the analysis, which may account for the lack of interaction effects. However, positive aspects of the study include the unusual nature of the sample (high-risk families not disrupted further by child protection services) and the intensive measurement process, which allowed for exploration of experiences with a strong contextual base and systematic inclusion of both positive and negative experiences. Specifically, the use of the ASI for adolescents means that security of attachment can be assessed for this age group with a measure that is continuous with assessment for adults.

The analysis presented deals with one aspect of trauma (mainly domestically based abuse in childhood) and looks at associated common mental health problems in teenage years and early adulthood. The study did not look at

PTSD and therefore it is not clear if the findings could be generalized to aspects that might protect people against that specific disorder. Neither did it cover rarer types of trauma, such as fires, floods, violence, and terrorism. However, the findings are likely to be relevant in two ways. First, some children and young people suffering trauma associated with more public events may also have been victims of domestic trauma in the form of abuse, and therefore those with secure attachment styles and high self-esteem may be more likely to survive both. Second, these latter aspects may prove to be resilience factors against PTSD and therefore deserve further investigation.

Conclusion

Family contexts are complex, with ecological and psychological factors providing layers of influence, any one of which could have positive, negative or mixed valence for later psychological disorders. Past research has been successful in identifying the direct effects of risk factors for psychological disorders, outlining negative trajectories from childhood to adult life, with adolescence frequently a critical juncture. Integrating protective or resilience factors into such schemes has been the object of much investigation, but these effects are often harder to study, since many research samples are either representative samples where risk factors are low, or clinical samples where the negative outcome is predetermined by selection. High-risk community populations can therefore be highly advantageous for studying the overlap of risk and resilience factors, with psychological disorders and well-being clearly identifiable. This can help with locating protective factors in the natural environment, which can guide preventive interventions to enhance such elements in the community at large (Bonanno 2004).

Using contextual interviews can help not only with exploratory research study of risks and resilience, but also with the identification of key risk experiences for planned interventions. The context of experiences is usually critical in determining the meaning of the experience for the individual. Thus an abusive parent whose impact is shielded by a caring close friend, or a violent household buffered by positive school experiences, may result in a different interpretation of the experiences, forestalling future negative generalizations. This can potentially avert the generalized belief that the world is hostile, people cannot be trusted and one's self is unlovable. Such characteristics form the nexus of insecure attachment style and related low self-esteem, and are the schemata from which adult psychological disorders emerge (Beck 1967). Being able to hold on to a secure internal working model based on trust, optimism and self-acceptance can provide the basis for a more fulfilled and healthy transition from adolescence to adulthood.

Acknowledgements

This research was funded by a Medical Research Council Programme Grant. Thanks are due to the team who worked on the project (Patricia Moran, Catherine Jacobs, Bronwen Ball, Amanda Bunn, Joanna Cavagin, Helen Richards), Dr. Soumitra Pathare and Professor Tom Craig who advised on SCID ratings, and Laurence Letchford for data management. Particular thanks are due to Adriano Schimmenti and Adina Rusu for advice on statistical analyses. As ever, our appreciation is given to the young people and their mothers who engaged in the study.

References

Allen, J.G. (2005). *Coping with trauma: A guide to self-understanding*, 2nd edition. Washington, DC: American Psychiatric Press.

Andrews, B., and Brown, G.W. (1991). *The self evaluation and social support manual*. London: Royal Holloway, University of London.

Andrews, B., Brown, G.W., and Creasey, L. (1990). Intergenerational links between psychiatric disorder in mothers and daughters: The role of parenting experiences. *Journal of Child Psychology and Psychiatry, 31*, 1115–1129.

Beck, A.T. (1967). *Depression: Clinical, experimental and theoretical aspects*. New York: Hoeber.

Bifulco, A., and Moran, P. (1998). *Wednesday's child: Research into women's experience of neglect and abuse in childhood and adult depression*. London: Routledge.

Bifulco, A., Brown, G.W., and Harris, T.O. (1994). Childhood Experience of Care and Abuse (CECA): A retrospective interview measure. *Journal of Child Psychology and Psychiatry, 35*, 1419–1435 (www.cecainterview.com).

Bifulco, A., Brown, G.W., Lillie, A., and Jarvis, J. (1997). Memories of childhood neglect and abuse: Corroboration in a series of sisters. *Journal of Child Psychology and Psychiatry, 38*, 365–374.

Bifulco, A., Moran, P., Ball, C., and Bernazzani, O. (2002a). Adult attachment style. I: Its relationship to clinical depression. *Social Psychiatry and Psychiatric Epidemiology, 37*, 50–59 (www.attachmentstyleinterview.com).

Bifulco, A., Moran, P., Ball, C., Jacobs, C., Baines, R., Bunn, A., et al. (2002b). Childhood adversity, parental vulnerability and disorder: Examining inter-generational transmission of risk. *Journal of Child Psychology and Psychiatry, 43*, 1075–1086.

Bifulco, A., Figueirido, B., Guedeney, N., Gorman, L., Hayes, S., Muzik, M., et al. (2004). Maternal attachment style and depression associated with childbirth: Preliminary results from a European/US cross-cultural study. *British Journal of Psychiatry (special supplement), 184*(46), 31–37.

Bifulco, A., Moran, P., Jacobs, C., Bunn, A., and Schimmenti, A. (submitted a). Insecure attachment style, childhood experience and disorder in high-risk young people.

Bifulco, A., Rusu, A., Moran, P., Jacobs, C., and Bunn, A. (submitted b). Bullying victimisation and disorder in adolescence.

Bonanno, G.A. (2004). Loss, trauma and human resilience: Have we underestimated the human capacity to thrive after extremely aversive events? *American Psychologist, 59*(1), 20–28.

Brewin, C.R., Andrews, B., and Gotlib, I.H. (1993). Psychopathology and early experience: A reappraisal of retrospective reports. *Psychological Bulletin, 113*, 82–98.

Brown, G.W., and Rutter, M. (1966). The measurement of family activities and relationships: A methodological study. *Human Relations, 19*, 241–263.

Chamberlain, P., Price, J.M., Reid, J.B., Landsverk, J., Fisher, P.A., and Stoolmiller, M. (2006). Who disrupts from placement in foster and kinship care? *Child Abuse and Neglect, 30*(4), 409–424.

Figueirido, B., Bifulco, A., Pachecho, A., Costa, R., and Magarinho, R. (2006). Teenage pregnancy, attachment style and depression: A comparison of teenage and adult pregnant women in a Portuguese series. *Attachment and Human Development, 8*(2), 123–128.

First, M., Gibbon, M., Spitzer, R., and Williams, G. (1996). *User's guide for SCID.* New York: Biometrics Research Division.

Fonagy, P., Steele, M., Steele, H., Higgitt, A., and Target, M. (1994). The Emanuel Miller Memorial Lecture 1992: The theory and practice of resilience. *Journal of Child Psychology and Psychiatry and Allied Disciplines, 35*(2), 231–257.

Garmezy, N. (1985). *Stress resistant children: The search for protective factors.* Oxford: Pergamon.

Luthar, S.S. (1991). Vulnerability and resilience: A study of high-risk adolescents. *Child Development, 62*(3), 600–616.

Masten, A.S., Garmezy, N., Tellegen, A., Pellegrini, D.S., Larkin, K., and Larsen, A. (1988). Competence and stress in school children: The moderating effects of individual and family qualities. *Journal of Child Psychology and Psychiatry and Allied Disciplines, 29*(6), 745–764.

Rushton, A. (2004). The outcomes of late permanent placements, the adolescent years. *Adoption and Fostering, 28*(1), 49–57.

Rutter, M. (1990). Psychosocial resilience and protective mechanisms. In J.E. Rolf and A.S. Masten (eds.), *Risk and protective factors in the development of psychopathology* (pp. 181–214). New York: Cambridge University Press.

Tunstill, J., and Aldgate, J. (2000). *Services for children in need: From policy to practice.* London: The Stationery Office.

UNICEF (2007). *An overview of child well-being in rich countries. A comprehensive assessment of the lives and well-being of children and adolescents in the economically advanced nations.* Florence, Italy: UNICEF Innocenti Research Centre, Report Card 7.

Part II

Resilience

Chapter 8

Resilience as the capacity for processing traumatic experiences

Danny Brom and Rolf Kleber

Introduction

In this chapter we attempt to define the concept of resilience as the individual's capacity to process traumatic experiences. We begin by looking at how resilience has been described in the literature in various disciplines and distinguishing our approach from some of the main current concepts. We focus on the central challenge of the cognitive processing of a traumatic experience and base our view of resilience on it. To conceptualize resilience from this cognitive perspective we introduce the model of *minimal learning*, which can help define the end-state of resilient processing.

Definitions of resilience

Resilience is one of those terms that appear so easy to understand (see Layne et al., Chapter 2 in this volume, for an in-depth discussion of the definitional issue). Intuitively we know people who appear to be "resilient" and who function well even though life has dealt them difficult cards, and we also know people who appear unaffected even in the face of major disaster or who only show some minor reactions and function adequately afterwards (see Bonanno 2004). But does this really imply resilience? Is the continuation of adequate functioning or the condition of being "unaffected" the ideal reaction to disaster and violence? Are people who continue to function without disturbance the most resilient or is resilience the capacity to recover after disaster on the basis on one's own strengths and resources?

When a well-functioning adult loses his or her spouse in a motor vehicle accident, what would the natural response be? If a child experiences an earthquake and the family home is severely damaged, what immediate and longer term reactions can be expected? Are temporary disturbances in functioning "flaws in resilience"?

The concept of resilience has an interesting history in psychology and psychiatry. It began with observations of children who were functioning well despite obvious risk factors in their background. The idea came up that the relatively good functioning of these children was due to their competence. The outcome of being resilient was thought of as "a track record of effective performance in developmental tasks, which are salient for people of a given age, society or context, and historical time" (Masten and Powell 2003, p. 5).

In more complex definitions, resilience has also been described as "a dynamic process encompassing positive adaptation within a context of significant adversity" (Luthar et al. 2000, p. 543). Two critical conditions are added in this definition:

- the exposure to significant threat or severe adversity
- the achievement of positive adaptation despite major assaults on the developmental process.

The above definition leaves a lot of room for different conditions. The definition of "significant threat or severe adversity" is challenging, posing the question whether "resilience in the face of stress" is the same as "resilience in the face of trauma." In this chapter we focus on coping with traumatic experiences, leaving aside the issue of coping with stress. The definition of "positive adaptation" may be even more difficult in that context. Is the maintenance of pre-adversity levels of functioning enough to be called "positive adaptation?" We will stay close to a model of coping with trauma as information processing and will thus be able to be more specific about the definition of adaptation.

By far the most comprehensive definition of resilience, although not focused on trauma, comes from Layne et al. (2007), who wrote:

> *Resilience* refers to the capacity of a given system to implement early, effective adjustment processes to alleviate strain imposed by exposure to stress, and thus efficiently restore homeostatic balance or adaptive functioning within a given psychosocial domain following a temporary perturbation therein.
>
> (Layne et al. 2007, p. 500)

This definition makes it possible to encompass the complexities of the phenomena and provides a framework for understanding. Hobfoll and colleagues (Chapter 9 in this volume) focus on resilience as the conservation of resources, while Tol and colleagues (Chapter 10 in this volume) present the broad concept of ecological resilience. What we want to do in this chapter is narrow our focus to one of the core components of the process of coping with trauma, which is cognitive processing. This might eventually give us more focused tools for preparedness, prevention and intervention during and after traumatic events.

Resilience in other disciplines

The term "resilience" has not only been used to describe the way human beings react to adversity, but has also become a useful term in other fields as well. The first use of the term was in the field of *physics*. In the 1920s physicists were measuring the characteristics of materials to determine their maximal application. The resilience of metals was defined as "the ability of a material to absorb energy when deformed elastically and to return it when unloaded." Such resilience of material was contrasted with "toughness", in which the material totally absorbs the energy. This definition points to an interesting issue which might have relevance for the human reaction to psychological trauma.

The absorption of the energy and its reflection might have a metaphorical parallel in the human situation. Layne and colleagues (Chapter 2 in this volume) speak about stress resistance when people are almost or totally unaffected. The parallel here might have to do with the direction and severity of the energy, for instance the attack on one's self-image as an agent when one is involved in a fatal accident, and the stability of one's previous self-image as a good person who will do no harm and now has become the "victim" of this accident. The stability of one's self-image might be a parallel to the toughness of a metal. If there is a temporary change in one of the fields, such as one's self-image, and it recovers and goes back to its previous state, this might be resilience. If one's self-image does not change at all despite the blow it received, we might speak about insensitivity or toughness. What this metaphor cannot take into account is internal versus external "toughness" in humans. Does one's self-image stay untouched – that is, is it really stable? Or does it resist change – that is, are there internal changes, although at this moment there is no external change?

Another example of the use of the term is in the field of *ecology*. In 1973 Holling wrote an article entitled "Resilience and stability of ecological systems" in which he launched the use of the term resilience to describe the complex process of maintaining dynamic homeostasis in nature. Stability was the traditional term for the behavior in ecological systems, that is, how the numbers or proportions of predators and prey stay the same over time. Resilience, however, determines the persistence of relationships within a system and is a measure of the ability of these systems to absorb changes and still persist. In this usage resilience is the property of the system and the persistence or probability of extinction is the result. Resilience is the preservation of the ability to respond to environmental change and enhance the chances of survival. Stability, on the other hand, is the ability of a system to return to an equilibrium state after a temporary disturbance. The more rapidly it returns, and with the least fluctuation, the more stable it is.

Summarizing, Holling (1973) states:

The stability view emphasizes the equilibrium, the maintenance of a predictable world, and the harvesting of nature's excess production with as little fluctuation as possible. The resilience view emphasizes domains of attraction and the need for persistence. This view of resilience views adaptation to a continuously changing world as the central challenge which needs to be faced with a heterogeneous array of responses.

(Holling 1973, p. 21)

Applying this idea to psychological resilience in humans, it shows the importance of a dynamic view of psychological resilience. We are not seeking the mere ability to return to a previous state of balance, but the preservation of the ability to absorb and adapt to changes in the environment. This view is reflected in current studies of "coping flexibility" (Cheng and Cheung 2005), which has turned out to be one of the best predictors of the outcome of severe challenges to the system.

Gallopin (2006) strengthens this discussion on resilience in ecology by looking at resilience as the "capacity" of a system to respond. The capacity for response is the system's ability to adjust to a disturbance, moderate potential damage, take advantage of opportunities, and cope with the consequences of the transformation that occurs. The capacity for response is clearly an attribute of the system that exists prior to the perturbation. And here again, if we apply this view to the individual human being, it adds the possibility of not only effectively responding to change, but also utilizing the situation to create positive change.

From these two fields we can extract the following aspects of resilience and consider their relevance for human adaptation to trauma. Psychological trauma can be conceptualized as energy that enters a system; the system needs to either withstand, absorb or utilize the energy. To continue the metaphor, withstanding might parallel stress-resistance, absorption might parallel the integration of a traumatic experience, and the utilization of energy can be seen as the possibility of "posttraumatic growth" (Pat-Horenczyk and Brom 2007) or "benefit finding" (Helgeson et al. 2006).

We need to make a clear distinction between stability and resilience in human responses to trauma. This means that the goal of the integration of traumatic material into the individual's psyche should be not only a return to the previous level of functioning, but also the continued ability to respond to changes in the environment.

This distinction between stability and flexibility also shows that resilience does not necessarily mean that people are unaffected by the stressor. In his article on resiliency, Bonanno (2004) postulated four trajectories in response to trauma: chronic disturbance, restoration, resiliency, and delayed disturbance. He stated that resilient people are those who are hardly affected by violence and disaster. We disagree. Nearly all people directly confronted with these events will show posttraumatic stress reactions (intrusions, nightmares, numbness, and so on) to some extent. Findings from large epidemiological studies of disaster victims (Grievink et al. 2007; Van der Velden et al. 2006) make this clear. However, the intensity and frequency of these responses do not reach the level of disorder. These people are able to find a new equilibrium. Therefore, restoration also implies resiliency.

The above insights can be kept in mind as we consider what we see as the core of coping with trauma, that is, the ways human beings search and attribute meaning to an experience.

Coping and meaning

It has frequently been stated that assigning meaning plays a crucial role in adaptation to stressful and threatening events (Frankl 1984; Horowitz 1976; Kleber and Brom 1992). Cognitive approaches to trauma (e.g. Brewin and Holmes 2003; Creamer 1995) assume that successful processing occurs if new information is assimilated into existing structures or models. Unsuccessful processing occurs when individuals are incapable of integrating trauma-related information into existing beliefs about their self-image or worldviews. The specific meaning that individuals assign to their stressful and threatening experiences may prove to be essential in the process of adaptation. Certain beliefs about the self, others and the world are expected to be more adaptive, and may facilitate a successful integration of the threatening experience, especially if they involve inner safety and trust (Janoff-Bulman 1992).

Research findings have indicated that the processes of making sense of the extreme event and finding some benefit in the traumatic experience play independent roles in adjustment (Davis et al. 1998; Taylor 1983). The attempt to find meaning has two facets: a causal explanation that provides an answer to the question of why it happened and a rethinking of one's attitudes and priorities so as to restructure one's life along more satisfying lines, changes that are prompted by and attributed to the event. When positive meaning could be extracted from the threatening experience, Taylor (1983) found that it produced significantly better psychological adjustment among cancer patients. Davis et al. (1998) analysed the two processes of making sense of the event and finding benefit, following the loss of a family member. The results of their prospective and longitudinal study showed that making sense of the loss was associated with less distress only in the first year after the event happened, whereas benefit finding was most strongly associated with adjustment at 13 and 18 months after the loss. These findings point to two separate and independent pathways following each other in the construction of meaning as part of the psychological adjustment process to threatening experiences (Janoff-Bulman and Frantz 1997; Joseph and Linley 2005). First, one has to make sense of the event by answering the questions of what happened, how and why. Second, one has to find personal significance in the event or gain from the experience for one's present life. The empirical studies reviewed by Schok et al. (2008) clearly showed that construing positive meaning from war and peacekeeping experiences was associated with better psychological adjustment.

Most authors on psychological trauma, however, have focused on its psychopathological consequences. PTSD has become the topic of thousands of articles and studies since its formal definition was accepted in DSM-III (American Psychiatric Association (APA) 1980). Healthy coping with trauma, however, has received relatively little attention, although it has been clear from the start of modern trauma studies that only a minority of people affected by violence or disaster will develop psychopathology (e.g. Horowitz 1976; Kleber and Brom 1992). Nevertheless, starting with the writings of Pierre Janet, and throughout the history of the trauma field, several authors have attempted to conceptualize the psychological processes involved in coping with trauma. The concept of assigning meaning should be explored from a salutogenic perspective (Antonovsky and Bernstein 1986), which provides the opportunity to study the "normal" processing of stressful and threatening events. This approach broadens the scope to include normal adaptation instead of pathologizing the response to trauma. Individuals who can integrate negative experiences into existing meaning structures and successfully adapt to society may provide some answers for developing effective tools and guidelines for those who need help in coping with their experiences.

The nature of cognitive processing

The process of assigning meaning can be considered a form of cognitive coping with traumatic stress (Thompson et al. 1998). Both modern psychodynamic theorists, such as Horowitz (1976), as well as cognitive behavioral theorists, such as Ehlers and Clark (2000), and attribution theorists (e.g. Taylor 1983) have put an emphasis on the influence of traumatic experiences on the cognitive system and the need for cognitive processing in order to recover.

Horowitz (1976) conceptualizes the core process of coping with trauma as an adaptation between the cognitive representation of the traumatic experience and the individual's existing schemata. The intrusive re-experiencing of the traumatic experience and the accompanying distress is considered a sign of a mismatch between them, as well as an attempt of the organism to deal with the conflict that needs to be solved. The greater the mismatch, the more severe the symptoms and the more distress the person experiences. Coping is therefore considered a process of adaptation in the cognitive system, in which the person has to change either the way he interprets the traumatic experience or his previously held beliefs (schemata) or both. In other words, the person needs to go through a process of learning from the experience that can lead to *accommodation*, the modification of schemata to fit new information, or *assimilation*, the integration of new information within pre-existing frameworks of thought.

A second cognitive approach, which may be complementary to the above, is the "appraisal-driven" approach. This approach maintains that disorders after trauma (i.e. posttraumatic stress disorder or PTSD) develop and are maintained when negative appraisals of the event and of the person's capacity to cope prevail. Negative appraisals are conducive of feelings of threat and fear. In the words of Ehlers and Clark (2000):

> The [cognitive] model proposes that these individuals are characterized by idiosyncratic negative appraisals of the traumatic event and/or its sequelae that have the common effect of creating a sense of serious current threat. This threat can be either external (e.g. the world is a more dangerous place) or, very commonly, internal (e.g. a threat to one's view of oneself as a capable/acceptable person who will be able to achieve important life goals).
>
> (Ehlers and Clark 2000, p. 320)

This model states that a sense of threat is maintained by two processes:

- individual differences in the appraisal of the trauma and/or its sequelae
- individual differences in the nature of the memory for the event and its link to other autobiographical memories.

Cognitive and behavioral responses to current threats, according to Ehlers and Clark (2000), are aimed at preventing distress in the short term, but they often prevent the necessary cognitive changes that might bring longer term relief. Indeed, research has shown that there is a correlation between the degree to which people appraise their symptoms as negative, perceive other people's reactions as negative and believe their trauma has had a permanent negative effect on their lives on the one hand, and PTSD, on the other (Halligan et al. 2002).

A third and somewhat similar approach that sheds light on the process of coping with trauma is cognitive attribution theory (Taylor 1983; Wong and Weiner 1981). When people are confronted with a sudden drastic change they search for meaning, to answer questions such as: "Why did this happen?" "Why did this happen to me?" "What are the implications of the fact that this happened to me?" The central question that this social-cognitive perspective in psychology poses is how cognitive attributions help people regain a sense of control and sense of meaning in life.

These approaches all involve a certain part of the cognitive coping process with traumatic experiences. For the most part they have been used to understand aspects of posttraumatic stress disorder and the way the coping process is impeded in the aftermath of trauma, and much less in the attempt to define resilience. They differ in their emphasis on the coping process. The information processing approach outlined by Horowitz (1976) is a theory-driven approach that presupposes an internal cognitive/emotional process as its nucleus. The appraisal approach is a much more empirical, data-driven and correlational perspective. The fact that people who appraise the traumatic event and their own coping capacity positively cope more easily or suffer less from symptoms does not necessarily presuppose a cognitive mechanism. Finally, the attribution approach is a combination of theory-driven and data-driven approaches.

All these approaches involve the content of cognitive processing, that is the way people adapt their intake of new information into their belief system or the way their belief system is altered in order to allow the new information to be integrated. An additional aspect of the processing of traumatic material is the mode of processing. Processing traumatic material tends to be automatic and unconscious. During traumatic experiences or during posttraumatic processing, the cognitive system shifts from conscious functioning to an alarm state, or "survival mode" functioning (Chemtob et al. 1988), which includes a strong focus on the detection of danger cues in the environment, the tendency to react immediately once danger is perceived, and the loss of self-monitoring. For children, who still have not learnt the patterns of perception that reflect danger, getting out of survival mode functioning is even more difficult. Chapter 12 by Ford, Albert, and Hawke (this volume) deals with this issue in depth. People are rarely aware of the changes in their cognitive system as a result of a traumatic experience. In children the unconscious processing of traumatic material is even more common, as their cognitive system is more fluid. The younger the child the less stable the belief system (see Chapter 3 by Pat-Horenczyk, Rabinowitz, Rice, and Tucker-Levin in this volume) and the greater the chance is that the experience will actually change the child's perceptions and expectations.

From these approaches we may deduce the following conclusions which are relevant for the concept of resilience:

- From an information-processing perspective, the more drastic the changes that the traumatic experience require of the previously held belief systems, the higher the risk that the process will get stuck. The greater the discrepancy between the meaning of the event and the individual's cognitive frame, the more the adaptational system is challenged.
- Adaptive processing of traumatic experiences requires conditions such as self-regulation and stability of the cognitive schemata.
- The immediate appraisal of the event and of the person's capacity to cope with it are crucial factors in the individual's fear response.
- When people attribute what happened to them to individual, stable and specific causes – that is they think that the event happened because of their personal characteristics – they will have difficulty regaining their previous beliefs and their internal and external functioning.

- The endpoint of the active coping process is a good match between the interpretation of the event and its consequences, on the one hand, and the previously acquired beliefs and values, on the other.
- Children are more vulnerable to the effects of traumatic experiences, as their cognitive system is still being formed.

When we try to use the above approaches to help us conceptualize adaptive ways of coping, we discover that most of the research has been focused on pathology. It is not clear whether we can reverse the conclusions about pathology to draw conclusions about healthy coping. For example, if we know that negative appraisal of the event or of its impact on the individual is correlated with PTSD, it remains to be seen if a positive appraisal is necessarily correlated with healthy coping. It seems a logical conclusion, but the empirical basis remains to be established.

We propose looking at the process of coping with trauma within a model of cognitive challenges (see Figure 8.1). In this model we can look at the different phases in the process that starts with the traumatic event and ends with its full integration into memory or, in worse cases, the development of a disorder in the coping process.

The capacity to process

Modern resilience literature has become mainly data-driven and thus has very scanty theoretical underpinnings. We propose a theory-driven model based on the cognitive model of coping with trauma, and we investigate its implications for the concept of resilience. What are the conditions for an individual to cope well in the face of trauma? What constitutes the capacity to process traumatic experiences and what are the factors that contribute to this capacity?

The idea of resilience as a capacity or potential can be found in the literature. For example, it has been called "the individual's capacity for adapting successfully and functioning competently despite experiencing chronic stress or adversity, or following exposure to prolonged or severe trauma" (Cicchetti and Rogosch 1997, p. 797). Cicchetti and Rogosch stress the outcome of successful adaptation and competent functioning and are not concerned about the process.

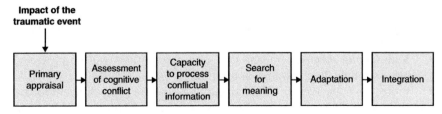

Figure 8.1 The elements of cognitive processing.

Charney (2004) conceptualizes the potential to withstand the effects of trauma within a learning theory perspective, writing, "Resilience to the effects of severe stress may be characterized by the capacity to avoid over-generalizing specific conditioned stimuli to a larger context, reversible storage of emotional memories, and facilitated extinction" (p. 205). Overgeneralization of fear stimuli and trauma-related cognitions define the status of post-traumatic stress disorder, as Janet stated in the nineteenth century (van der Hart et al. 2006) and modern cognitive behavioral therapists also believe (Ehlers et al. 2005).

The scientific literature makes it abundantly clear that even researchers such as the ones just quoted, who come up with new conceptualizations of resilience as "capacity", often base their definitions of health on the lack of pathology (e.g. "avoid overgeneralization") or on the behavioral outcome ("successful adaptation"). What we would like to do here is attempt to define the more common, healthy coping process as well as the capacity to engage in such a process.

Adaptive coping as "minimal learning"

Systems theory has maintained that there is a "resistance to change" in all systems so as to maintain a balance within the system. Within human beings and their cognitive-emotional system, the tendency for structural inertia and reluctance to change are well known. The desirable outcome of adaptation to trauma is most often described in terms of the decrease of symptoms or the maintenance or re-establishment of good functioning. The goals of cognitive processing, however, are to neutralize the immediate threat by framing the incoming information in terms of the meaning of the immediate danger or the resources for coping with the threat (primary and secondary appraisal), and to reach an integration of the experience and its implications into one's life history, with minimal change in existing cognitive frameworks and behavior patterns.

We propose a "minimal learning" model to describe the outcome of successful coping with traumatic experiences. In contrast, patients who suffer from posttraumatic stress disorder have formed overgeneralized cognitions as a result of their experience.

The model of minimal learning states that:

- People will attempt to cope with trauma while maintaining their basic assumptions or schemata intact.
- Maintaining schemata means that core assumptions will be protected more strongly than marginal assumptions.
- Protective maneuvers in minimal learning can take many different forms, such as building adaptive illusions, attributing cause and blame in rational or irrational ways, and the like.

- It is easier to change the meaning attributed to an event than to change one's deeper anchored belief system. Therefore most people will choose the former as their first coping attempt
- Minimal learning is an automatic and mostly unconscious process.

The first attempt is to minimize the "damage to the system", protecting one's cognitive framework by trying to fit the experience into one's pre-existing knowledge. By doing so, people attempt to keep their world known and predictable, so that they can lead their lives without overwhelming fear that another traumatic event will occur any moment. In other words, a traumatic experience creates the need to learn. One has to both accept the occurrence of the event and at the same time believe that such an event cannot happen again any moment. If such a belief is not attained, or if the subjective risk for reoccurrence is not diminished, fear will remain the prevailing feeling. Suddenly an individual finds him/herself in a situation of uncertainty: a life-threatening situation has occurred and the person needs to provide a meaning that will give the subjective sense that such a situation will not occur again unexpectedly and that allows the maintenance of a positive self-image.

Let us take an example:

> Jake had a traffic accident in which his car was hit by a truck from behind while he stopped for a traffic light that had turned yellow, while tending to his son who sat behind him. He and his son were slightly injured, the car was damaged and could not be repaired, but the truck driver was not injured and the truck hardly damaged.

The different options for interpreting this event will clearly have different implications. Let us review some of the options:

> Jake remembers that he was not concentrating on driving but on his son's complaints and therefore saw the traffic light at the last moment and made an emergency brake. He had not looked in his rear mirror and now blames himself for the accident.

1   Jake's narrative is that he was temporarily distracted by looking at his son, who sat behind him and although he blames himself he went back to driving almost immediately and decided that he should concentrate more on driving and less on other issues.

2   Jake's narrative is that he was always a dreamer and never could concentrate on just one activity. He feels that since the accident, he is in constant danger when driving and has developed a fear of driving during the late afternoon, which is the time the accident happened.

It is clear from these two options that each cognitive maneuver is the result of a learning process. In the first option, a good example of minimal learning, the accident is attributed to an internal unstable specific factor "I was temporarily distracted" which creates minimal dissonance with Jake's self-image as a competent individual and driver. This allows him to continue with life without adaptations. The second narrative creates a stronger challenge to his confidence in driving a car and perhaps even in broader areas of life.

Minimal learning theory would predict that the first option will be chosen unless there are circumstances that encourage the second. Such circumstances could be previous formative experiences that created a self-image of an incompetent person in tasks that require concentration. The model states that there will be an attempt to minimize changes to one's enduring view of one's self or the world.

3   Jake's son, Sam, 9 years old, sitting behind his father at the time of the accident, had angrily asked his father to go back home and not continue the trip with him. When he had become angry at his father and shouted at him, his father looked back at him and the accident occurred. Sam reacted with severe fear in the first week after the accident. He refused to get into a car and looked frightened throughout most of the day. He told his parents that the accident was his fault, that he should not have been angry. His parents spoke to him a lot about the accident and made him understand that there was no connection between his anger and the accident. They explained that Jake was to blame, because a driver should never look backwards when driving. Sam seemed to accept these explanations and started to make jokes about his father being a bad driver. After a number of weeks he managed to get into the car again while Jake was driving.

This example shows how parents can help their children avoid taking the blame for bad events and find a more soothing interpretation.

4   Jake became extremely angry at the truck driver and his anger increased when he read the police report that stated that the truck was going at 70 km/h when he was hit. His narrative of the accident is that the "criminal", as he called the truck driver, was to blame and should be punished. He also developed a cynical anger towards the judicial system after seeing that the truck driver was not held responsible. He went back to driving and for some time had a startle response whenever he saw a truck approaching in his rear mirror.

Processing the accident this way, Jake had hardly any difficulty with his own behavior or self-image. He is a competent driver who happened to become the victim of an incompetent, negligent truck driver. His attribution is external, unstable and in between specific (this driver) and general (the judicial system as well). In terms of the minimal learning model, this option necessitates some adaptation of Jake's worldview, but only a minimal change in his self-image.

5   Sam perceived the accident as a sign that Jake is incapable of protecting him from danger and he unconsciously perceived the accident as due to his father's anger. He became quite anxious and started to exhibit clinging behavior towards his mother. He became distant from his father and started to play violent games in which "the bad guys" always managed to win. He developed temper tantrums and had difficulties soothing himself.

In this option the 9-year-old boy attributes an intentional meaning to the accident, considering it a "punishment". Behavior that angered the parents became a trigger for fear and frustration, while at the same time the helplessness fed into his anger.

6   Jake was shocked at the first moment, but after regaining his senses he returned to his general pattern of thinking, which was that "bad things can happen, but I am lucky; it could have been much worse". He felt that no one really was to blame and that this is the risk of driving a car.

This option hardly requires active processing of the traffic accident, as a general cognitive frame can contain the event and his pre-existing cognitions about his self and the world, and there is no need for any change in them.

7   Jake was extremely upset by the accident and for a few weeks had a severe startle response when he tried to go to sleep. He was hypersensitive to noises and when a colleague approached him from behind unexpectedly, he jumped up so violently that he hit the colleague with one of his arms. He felt that he was losing control of his life and that he was subject to recurrent, sudden fearsome images. He started to avoid driving and being with people. His narrative was that he had no idea how this could have happened, but that now every frightening scenario had become a real possibility.

This last option shows how difficult it can be to find a meaning for the accident that can quiet down fears and to help understand why it happened and how a recurrence can be prevented. The development of PTSD in this case shows the difficulty of processing the information into pre-existing frameworks of meaning. It seems that overgeneralization has colored Jake's perception of the world and himself. A generalized cognition formed (or was strengthened) in him that gave him the feeling of being at risk for any bad event.

This example illustrates the central role of the learning process, or the process of finding meaning, in coping with trauma. Resilience exists where the need for internal change is minimized and meaning can be construed flexibly to allow the external reality to encounter internal representations and their meanings.

Implications for interventions with children

When we consider the sequence of coping with traumatic experiences, we maintain that the model of cognitive processing we described (Figure 8.1) has a variety of implications for intervention after trauma. In the first phase, which is the immediate interpretation of the event and its danger, processing might be supported by a dual approach of strengthening the child's sense of control and helping the child to realistically evaluate the actual danger. In the second phase, intervention could help the child attribute a meaning to what happened and support the child's confidence in his or her capacity to cope. The attribution of meaning should diminish the creation of conflicts in the way the child sees him/herself and the people in the child's surroundings. At the same time, during the processing phase, optimal conditions should be created for effective processing. These conditions include soothing or self-soothing, regulation of arousal and emotion, and enough subjective safety so that the experience can be reviewed. During the search for meaning, frameworks of understanding should be offered that can contain and explain the experience and produce a positive evaluation of the self and the environment.

Epilogue

This book is about children who have undergone trauma. The part of the book dealing with resilience, however, focuses on resilience in adults. The anomaly of this part reflects the problem of conceptual clarity that the chapters try to deal with. It is not true that nothing has been written on resilience in children. However, as the definition of resilience has not been dealt with sufficiently, it is still too difficult to combine the concept of resilience with the developmental dimension. As an example we can take this chapter, which focuses on the capacity for cognitive processing as a measure of resilience. The capacity for cognitive processing in children changes according to their developmental phase. In order for information to be processed, there has to be a framework that can assimilate it. If the framework is not stable enough, new information might change the framework through a process of accommodation. This might mean that the earlier the traumatic event, the greater the danger that the experience will become part of the child's experiential framework. The later the traumatization, the better the chance that the experience can be integrated in stable schemata, which hold positive views of the world and the self. The developmental axis is, for our purposes, the growth of the capacity for cognitive processing. Trauma in childhood can thus have quite distinct effects. On the one hand, it can affect the structure of perception, or, in other words, the building of the cognitive schemata, and on the other hand, it can affect the way that children cope with the conflict between the experience and its meaning and their own pre-existing schemata. These two types of effect have to be taken into account in designing interventions for children following trauma.

This might also explain the enormously important role that parents play during the development of the child as determinants of the child's resilience (Pat-Horenczyk et al., Chapter 3 in this volume). Parents represent the stability of the environment during the time that the child is growing and learning and internalizing the characteristics of the world.

We have presented the "minimal learning" concept which is a concept without empirical basis for now. It might help clarify ways in which people integrate a traumatic experience, while sustaining minimal damage to their pre-existing belief system.

The additional chapters in this book present some necessary conditions for a good capacity to process trauma. Cognitive processing can take place only when the regulatory capacities of the person are intact. The need for regulatory processes has been described extensively (Schore 2002) and is a central thesis of Chapter 12 by Ford, Albert, and Hawke. To maintain one's capacity for cognitive processing, one's state of arousal has to be kept within certain boundaries. If those boundaries are ruptured, hyperarousal or hypoarousal may interfere with the brain's ability to process information and integrate it into memory. Therefore, the most important condition for processing is the arousal regulation. Additionally, Hobfoll and colleagues (Chapter 9 in this volume) describe an innovative approach, arguing that the conservation of environmental and personal resources during and after trauma are conditions for good coping. An even broader perspective on resilience, taking sociopolitical factors into account, is described by Tol and colleagues (Chapter 10 in this volume). The integration of all of these perspectives can lead to the development of a range of interventions to create optimal conditions for children to develop and be able to cope with a world that is far from ideal.

References

American Psychiatric Association (APA) (1980). *Diagnostic and statistical manual of mental disorders*, 3rd edition (DSM-III). Washington, DC: APA.
Antonovsky, A., and Bernstein, J. (1986). Pathogenesis and salutogenesis in war and

other crises: Who studies the succesful coper? In N.A. Milgram (ed.), *Stress and coping in time of war: Generalizations from the Israeli experience* (pp. 52–65). New York: Brunner/Mazel.

Bonanno, G.A. (2004). Loss, trauma, and human resilience: Have we underestimated the human capacity to thrive after extremely aversive events? *American Psychologist, 59*, 20–28.

Brewin, C.R., and Holmes, E.A. (2003). Psychological theories of posttraumatic stress disorder. *Clinical Psychology Review, 23*(3), 339–376.

Charney, D.S. (2004). Psychobiological mechanisms of resilience and vulnerability: Implications for successful adaptation to extreme stress. *American Journal of Psychiatry, 161*(2), 195–216.

Chemtob, C.M., Roitblat, H.L., Hamada, R.S., Carlson, J.G., and Twentyman, C.T. (1988). A cognitive action theory of posttraumatic stress disorder. *Journal of Anxiety Disorders, 2*, 253–275.

Cheng, C., and Cheung, M.W.L. (2005). Cognitive processes underlying coping flexibility: Differentiation and integration. *Journal of Personality, 73*, 859–886.

Cicchetti, D., and Rogosch, F.A. (1997) The role of self-organization in the promotion of resilience in maltreated children. *Development and Psychopathology, 9*(4), 797–815.

Creamer, M. (1995). A cognitive processing formulation of posttrauma responses. In R.J. Kleber, C.R. Figley, and B.P.R. Gersons (eds.), *Beyond trauma: Cultural and societal dynamics* (pp. 55–74). New York: Plenum.

Davis, C.G., Nolen-Hoeksema, S., and Larson, J. (1998). Making sense of loss and benefiting from the experience: Two construals of meaning. *Journal of Personality and Social Psychology, 75*, 561–574.

Ehlers, A., and Clark, D.M. (2000). A cognitive model of posttraumatic stress disorder. *Behaviour Research and Therapy, 38*, 319–345.

Ehlers, A., Clark, D.M., Hackmann, A., McManus, F., and Fennell, M. (2005). Cognitive therapy for PTSD: Development and evaluation. *Behaviour Research and Therapy, 43*, 413–431.

Frankl, V.E. (1984). *Man's search for meaning: An introduction to logotherapy*, 3rd edition. New York: Touchstone.

Gallopin, G.C. (2006). Linkages between vulnerability, resilience, and adaptive capacity. *Global Environmental Change, 16*, 293–303.

Grievink, L., van der Velden, P.G., Stellato, R.K., Dusseldorp, A., Gersons, B.P.R., Kleber, R.J., et al. (2007). A longitudinal comparative study of the physical and mental health problems of affected residents of the firework disaster Enschede, the Netherlands. *Public Health, 121*(5), 367–374.

Halligan, S.L., Clark, D.M., and Ehlers, A. (2002). Cognitive processing, memory, and the development of PTSD symptoms: Two experimental analogue studies. *Journal of Behavioral Therapy and Experimental Psychiatry, 33*, 73–89.

Helgeson, V.S., Reynolds, K.A., and Tomich, P.L. (2006). A meta-analytic review of benefit finding and growth. *Journal of Consulting and Clinical Psychology, 74*(5), 797–816.

Holling, C.S. (1973). Resilience and stability of ecological systems. *Annual Review of Ecology and Systematics, 4*, 1–23.

Horowitz, M.J. (1976/1997). *Stress response syndromes*. San Francisco, CA: Jossey-Bass.

Janoff-Bulman, R. (1992). *Shattered assumptions: Towards a new psychology of trauma*. New York: The Free Press.

Janoff-Bulman, R., and Frantz, C.M. (1997). The impact of trauma on meaning: From meaningless world to meaningful live. In M. Power and C.R. Brewin (eds.), *The transformation of meaning in psychological therapies* (pp. 91–106). Chichester, UK: Wiley.

Joseph, S., and Linley, P.A. (2006). Growth following adversity: Theoretical perspectives and implications for clinical practice. *Clinical Psychology Review, 26*(8), 1041–1053.

Kleber, R.J., and Brom, D., in collaboration with Defares, P.B. (1992). *Coping with trauma: Theory, prevention and treatment*. Amsterdam: Swets and Zeitlinger International.

Layne, C.M., Warren, J., Watson, P., and Shaley, A. (2007). Risk, vulnerability, resistance, and resilience: Towards an integrative model of posttraumatic adaptation. In M.J. Friedman, T.M. Keane, and P.A. Resick (eds.), *Handbook of PTSD: Science and Practice.* (pp. 497–520). New York: Guilford.

Luthar, S.S., Cicchetti, D., and Becker, B. (2000). The construct of resilience: A critical evaluation and guidelines for future work. *Child Development, 71*(3), 543–562.

Masten, A.S., and Powell, J.L. (2003). A resiliency framework for research, policy and practice. In S.S. Luthar (ed.), *Resiliency and vulnerability: Adaptation in the context of childhood adversities* (pp. 1–25). New York: Cambridge University Press.

Pat-Horenczyk, R., and Brom, D. (2007). The multiple faces of post traumatic growth. *Journal of Applied Psychology, 56*(3), 379–385.

Schok, M.L., Kleber, R.J., Elands, M.E., and Weerts, J.M.P. (2008). Meaning as a mission: Review of empirical studies on appraisals of war and peacekeeping experiences. *Clinical Psychology Review, 28*, 357–365.

Schore, A.N. (2002). Dysregulation of the right brain: A fundamental mechanism of traumatic attachment and the psychopathogenesis of posttraumatic stress disorder. *Australian and New Zealand Journal of Psychiatry, 36*(1), 9–30.

Taylor, S.E. (1983). Adjustment to threatening events: A theory of cognitive adaptation. *American Psychologist, 38*, 1161–1173.

Thompson, S.C., Armstrong, W., and Thomas, C. (1998). Illusions of control, underestimations and accuracy: A control heuristic explanation. *Psychological Bulletin, 123*, 143–161.

van der Hart, O., Nijenhuis, E.R.S., and Steele, K. (2006). *The haunted self: Structural dissociation and the treatment of complex traumatization*. New York: Norton.

van der Velden, P.G., Kleber, R.J., Christiaanse, B., Gersons, B.P.R., Marcelissen, F.G.H., Drogendijk, A.N., et al. (2006). The independent predictive value of peritraumatic dissociation for post-disaster intrusions and avoidance reactions and PTSD severity: A four-year prospective study. *Journal of Traumatic Stress, 19*(4), 493–506.

Wong, P.T.P., and Weiner, B. (1981). When people ask "why" questions and the heuristics of attributional search. *Journal of Personality and Social Psychology, 40*, 650–663.

Chapter 9

Resiliency and resource loss in times of terrorism and disaster

Lessons learned for children and families and those left untaught

Stevan E. Hobfoll, Katie J. Horsey, and Brittain E. Lamoureux

Terrorism and disaster create circumstances that challenge individuals, families, organizations, and the very social fabric of society. The West has been complacent about terrorism and mass casualties because they have often happened elsewhere or have had manageable consequences. Even the California earthquake in 1994 and the major hurricanes Hugo (1989) and Andrew (1992) caused relatively little loss of life or major injury due to the sophisticated building structures and warning systems available. The tragedies of the attacks of September 11 in 2001 and Hurricane Katrina in 2005 have ended this complacency and resulted in a new awareness that it can happen here and that we need to better understand the consequences of mass casualty and develop preventive and treatment interventions. Of course this is a lesson that much of the world knew before, but lacked scientific resources to fully address.

This chapter focuses on the impact of mass casualty situations on children and families, with particular emphasis on factors that affect resiliency. We will use Conservation of Resources (COR) theory (Hobfoll 1988, 1998, 2002) as a theoretical backdrop to frame an understanding of the impact of mass casualty and place it in context that can lead to intervention strategies. It is our argument that clinical science to date has contributed greatly to an understanding of individual trauma and its treatment, but that the clinical paradigm is quickly overstretched even on the individual level when traumas affect more than emotions and cognitions and when they impact large numbers of people in a given period (de Jong 2002a, 2002b). On the family and systems level, the clinical paradigm is still an important part of the overall puzzle, but only if integrated into systems-level constructions of events and how they impact people. Further, although psychological research on stress has often focused on resiliency, this notion needs to be better integrated into clinical and public health models.

A great deal of research has indicated that COR theory is useful in understanding the responses not only of individuals, but of families and communities, and their interconnected nature, to situations of disaster and terrorism (Benight and Harper 2002; Benight et al. 1999; Burnett et al. 1997; Hobfoll 2001; Hobfoll et al. 2006; Ironson et al. 1997; Sattler 2006; Sattler et al. 2002; Smith and Freedy 2000). In the specific context of disaster and mass casualty traumas, there is a massive loss of resources on a systemic level within the infrastructures of the community and society at large and how those losses translate to individuals trying to cope with trauma (Collins and Collins 2005; Klingman and Cohen 2004). The loss of resources at the highest level of a community branches down to great losses for families and individuals. When we try to understand resiliency, however, it is the ability to sustain resources and to sustain the social ecology that allows those resources to be invested in service of the self, the family, and the society that is critical. COR theory enables us to understand this interconnected nature of society, families, and the individual.

Principles of COR theory

COR theory rests on the basic tenet that individuals strive to obtain, retain, foster, and protect those things they value. This state of active acquisition and preservation of resources is fundamental to resiliency and adaptation. These centrally valued entities are termed resources and they include object, condition, personal, and energy resources. Object resources include resources that have a physical presence and are either necessary for survival or highly valued within a culture. This includes such objects as shelter, transportation, and the means to process food (stove, refrigerator) and perform hygiene (washing machine, plumbing). Condition resources are valued as they either are important for survival or bring status that is secondarily linked to survival. This includes marriage, a supportive social network, job security, and educational status. Personal resources can be divided into two categories, personal traits and skills. Clearly there may be many traits and skills possessed by individuals, but those resources highlighted by COR theory are linked to either survival or resiliency. This includes such traits as optimism (Carver 2000), self-efficacy (Benight and Bandura 2004) and self-esteem (Rosenberg 1965), and such skills as those necessary for work (e.g. job skills) and social skillfulness. Finally, energy resources are those that have value due to their ability to be used or exchanged for object or condition resources or for their protection and maintenance. This includes such resources as knowledge, credit, money, and insurance.

Underlying this motivational principle, that individuals strive to obtain, retain, foster, and protect those things they value to support the individual, nested in families, nested in the tribe, it can be seen that resilience in the face of loss and the threat of loss will be fundamentally related to the strength of the resource reservoir available to the individual, social group, and society. This strength, in turn, will depend on amount of resources, their fit with the demands of the mass casualty circumstances, and their flexibility. This approach is quite the opposite of a learned helplessness perspective as it suggests that the motivation to secure, protect, and garner resources is an ongoing process that is difficult to extinguish .

COR theory rests on several principles and corollaries that have been delineated in the past (Hobfoll 1988, 1989, 1998). It is important to underscore that although COR theory involves, in part, the element of appraisal, unlike other stress theories (Lazarus and Folkman 1984), these appraisals are first and foremost delineated by the culture, not the individual. That is, what individuals find stressful, what they value, and the behaviors they perform individually, in families, and organizationally are principally determined by their shared culture. Individual, idiographic appraisals are important, but quite secondary to shared ones. Likewise, appraised resources will have limited value if not underpinned by actual resources as the demand on resources will quickly outstrip any perceived resources that are not buttressed by the real thing. These principles are as follows.

Principle 1: The primacy of resource loss

The first principle of COR theory is that resource loss is disproportionately more salient than resource gain

This state of affairs offers several challenges for the promotion of resiliency. On one hand it is true that if the demand on resources is not overwhelming or chronic then most people will do well, especially after they are given some time and support for natural recovery (Bonanno 2004). Yet, because those who lack strong resource reservoirs are the most vulnerable, resiliency will require targeted attention to fill in these critical gaps so as to prevent the quick acceleration of such loss cycles. For fostering resiliency it can be seen that prevention of significant losses is critical. It will always be an uphill battle if key resources are lost. This means that the strategy of proactive coping (Schwarzer and Taubert 2002) should be instituted as early as possible. To the extent that people are involved in limiting resource loss cycles, they will not only be less devastated, but also be beginning the key process of turning loss cycles into gain cycles and fostering their own and their group's resiliency.

Principle 2: Resource investment

The second principle of COR theory is that people must invest resources to protect against resource loss, recover from losses, and gain resources

A related corollary of this (Corollary 1) is that those with greater resources are less vulnerable to resource loss and more capable of orchestrating resource gain. Conversely, those with fewer resources are more vulnerable to resource loss and less capable of resource gain.

Promoting resiliency therefore demands special attention to the resources required to facilitate adaptation, always keeping in mind that people do best when their resiliency is emphasized, rather than their pathology. For example, immigrants' natural resources can aid them if they are provided accelerated access to services through language facilitation and the provision of structural resources that their immigrant status might have limited. This might mean providing legal services or advice on the use of state assistance that might not be in their repertoire or resource armamentarium. The principle underlying this approach is to consider what key or catalysing resources might be added to potentiate the resources they already possess. This further encourages supporting their ability to cope and places them within a resiliency rather than a deviancy paradigm.

In response to the World Trade Center attacks in New York City on September 11, 2001, thousands of children were affected by exposure to the events not only through the media, but also by having family members who were killed or injured in the attacks, witnessing the planes flying into the towers, and watching bodies fall horrifically to the ground (Henry et al. 2004; Hoven et al. 2005; Lengua et al. 2006). In the allocation of much needed resources to help these children in the weeks and months following the attacks, it has been noted that those schools that were able to invest the necessary resources, in extra teachers, health care workers, and the like, produced better outcomes for their children (Klingman and Cohen 2004). However, it has become evident that the invested resources were not nearly sufficient to answer the needs of so many children and families who had experienced such trauma. Similarly, underestimation of the need for resources is also evident in Israeli schools in which counselors provide support to children who have been exposed to ongoing terror. Klingman (2002) stressed the importance of being aware that the counselors' personal resources can become taxed. One must consider that in response to terrorism, mass casualty, and disaster, mental health care responders have often been personally affected by the trauma while also experiencing ongoing secondary stressors due to working with victims for weeks or months following the trauma. Investing in a response plan, not only for the victims, but also for the health care workers, can promote the resilience and recovery of communities following disasters (Bell et al. 2002; Klingman 2002; Klingman and Cohen 2004).

The elements of resiliency against the breakdown process have been shown in various ways in research on families and children. Those with resources such as hardiness, stress-resistance, ego resilience, and ego strength have been found to have greater capacity to withstand stress and trauma than those who do not have such resources (Schoon 2006). This might easily be seen as tautological, calling those who thrive hardy, but research also shows that these traits are underpinned by a certain behavioral style and way of seeing challenges. Specifically, to the extent that people have a history of success with adversity, they will believe that they can solve problems, survive for another day, and begin the cycle of rebuilding, either on their own or with the help of significant others.

For children, it is critical to emphasize that they will require adult role models and ecologies that support their resiliency efforts, as their personal traits and style are still at formative stages. Furthermore, characteristics of parents and families such as higher economic status, knowledge, physical wellness, self-esteem, flexibility, and self-efficacy function as resources that parents can utilize to buffer both their own stress and that of their children (McKenry and Price 2005). Such resources take time and effort to invest in the accumulation and the extension from the community to parents, and then to the child. Within the family, parents must invest time to impart values, flexibility, capability, and knowledge to their children through modeling and other means to help them become resilient to trauma and the loss of resources (McKenry and Price 2005). Additionally, parents can work to promote family cohesion, or unity within the family (McCubbin and McCubbin 1988), as a resource to buffer against the negative impact and potential losses subsequent to a traumatic event. A lack of such cohesion has been associated with increased conflict and a deterioration of the benefits of the social support generally provided by family members (McKenry and Price 2005). Family level resources, which facilitate the adaptation of family members to the consequences of crises, are vital in protecting individuals and children from the aftermath of mass casualties.

Principle 3: Paradoxical

Although resource loss is more potent than resource gain, the salience of gain increases under situations of resource loss

This principle is especially meaningful when considering a resiliency, rather than a pathology-based approach. The paradoxical increase in the saliency of resource gain is accentuated during traumatic situations. This occurs because under conditions of great loss, even small gains may elicit a sense of positive expectancy and hope. Resource gains that might under normal circumstances be appraised as trivial may objectively offer a lifeline to survival (e.g. "I am not alone," "Rescuers are on their way") or may be imbued with meaning (e.g. "People still care").

Although resource gain is less salient than resource loss (Hobfoll et al. 1999), small protective gains from the community or from families and neighbors can have an effect on the resiliency of children in response to terror. For example, one study showed that children who were able to maintain routine by getting parental encouragement were much less likely to demonstrate symptoms of posttraumatic stress (Pat-Horenczyk et al. 2006). This suggests that interventions should aim to promote resource gain, as well as elicit resources that individuals had previous to the trauma (Collins and Collins 2005), to help families and children cope with their situation.

Resource loss and gain spirals

The first two principles of COR theory concerning loss primacy and investment of resources lead in turn to two further corollaries pertaining to resource loss and gain spirals (Hobfoll 1988, 1998).

First, corollary 2 of COR theory states that not only are those who lack resources more vulnerable to resource loss, but also initial loss begets future loss. It follows that promoting resiliency requires moving quickly to prevent the acceleration of loss cycles before they gain such strength and momentum that they devastate individuals and social groups. As intervention systems also have finite resources, this means that intervention must be strategic, choosing its battles wisely. The basic strategy remains the same, however; intervention must move early, powerfully, and in a key strategic direction. Often this means moving from traditional treatment to supporting the individual and family in their natural ecologies – that is, keeping the family, schools, and the workplace operating wherever possible. Even if the workplace must be altered, the benefit of financial remuneration and the psychosocial reward of working and feeling useful remain. For example, using displaced workers to participate in rebuilding, to act as temporary teachers and directors of sports activities for children, to form watch groups, and to make the decisions necessary for recovery are functional work roles that are often available in even severe mass casualty situations. This is quite opposite of the "do for them" approach that government and aid agencies often take.

Second, corollary 3 mirrors corollary 2, stating that those who possess resources are more capable of gain, and that initial resource gain begets further gain. However, because loss is more potent than gain, loss cycles will be more impactful and more accelerated than gain cycles.

Resilience factors are important in understanding resource gain in the face of trauma. Resilience resources, like others, need to be considered on a tiered spectrum, within the individual, the family, and the community. Research has indicated that personal characteristics such as learning and problem-solving skills, having an engaging personality, self-efficacy, mastery motivation, and previous successful coping experiences are all resources that have been shown to moderate childhood stress in general (Rutter 1985). In addition to these internal characteristics, other resiliency resources for children are having a loving parent, having a good social support network, and knowing how to engage with their environment to get necessary resources if a situation demands it (e.g. knowing who to call if something happens to their parents) (Pynoos et al. 2006). Those who have these resources are able to engage their environment, including parents and other caregivers, and tap into resources that those who do not possess such abilities are not able to access. Thus, those who have more resources initially are more likely to experience resource gain. Yet, even though children may have resilience factors and resources, the losses experienced, such as those in the aftermath of the 2004 tsunami, may be so devastating that the gains function mostly as an agent for halting the course of resource loss spirals.

Protection of the protective shield

Situations of mass casualties challenge both the reality and the perception of what has been called the "protective shield" (Bell et al. 2002; Pynoos et al. 1995). This is especially critical for children, whose well-being is largely based on the belief that their parents and the social institutions that they interact with (e.g. schools, the police) will make them safe. In circumstances of ongoing societal threat, this belief may never be established, and this is true for the inner cities of the United States as well as for countries in Africa torn by years of tribal warfare and genocide. In other places, such as Palestine, the belief that parents can provide a protective shield can disintegrate when children see their parents as incapable of protecting them from threats from Israel, or from political factions within Israel.

This protective shield is constituted by a web of resources that the family and culture naturally provide to children in safe circumstances. It is certainly a perceived shield, but such perceptions are very much reality-based. These resources are in part material (e.g. food, clothing) and in part condition (e.g. safe schools, safe streets) resources. They are also a reflection of personal resources. However, psychology more often than not errs here, in thinking that hope, self-efficacy, and optimism (Bandura 1997; Scheier and Carver 1985) are appraised, rather than largely the reflection of actual life circumstances. Such appraisals are secondary to the reality that there is hope of future success, that there is reason to be optimistic, and that self-efficacy can bring about valued ends. In this regard, for example, research on young adult inner-city women showed that, far from being a stable personal characteristic, self-efficacy is fragile in the face of economic resource loss (Hobfoll et al. 2003). Loss of economic and material resources resulted in decrements in both social support and self-efficacy, which, in turn, resulted additively in increased depression. Childhood in particular is the time in life when such personal traits are being shaped, and they are shaped by the reality of how the children themselves are able to achieve their goals and protect themselves and how much their parents and the institutions that surround them (e.g. schools, police, the government) help them meet their goals and keep them safe.

Pynoos and Nader (1988) and Bell and colleagues (Bell and McKay 2004; Bell et al. 2002) have suggested that the adult protective shield for children is critical for sustaining resilience in communities that have been ravaged by disaster and war. The adult protective shield promotes a sense of safety and security vital to the initial response to mass trauma (Klingman and Cohen 2004; Lieberman and Pawl 1990). Bell and McKay (2004) proposed an infrastructure for promoting children's mental health that incorporates field principles for dealing with destruction and mass casualties, including re-establishing the protective shield. The authors noted that other issues also need to be addressed in response to community-wide disaster, such as rebuilding the village, providing access to health care, improving bonding, attachment, and connectedness dynamics within the community and between stakeholders, improving self-esteem, increasing the social skills of target recipients, and minimizing the residual effects of trauma. Such provisions of needed resources are important within an integrated effort to re-establish infrastructures for children and families following a disaster, both personally and interpersonally.

In line with this, a body of research has suggested that trauma and the intersection of children and families should also be viewed in the context of developmental stages (Pynoos et al. 1999). Within this framework, development interacts with children's appraisals of traumatic events, as well as their ongoing appraisals of community and family responses, and ultimately the posttrauma psychological functioning of these children. This highlights the importance of the protective shield developmentally, so that children are able to regain resources such as security and safety, which may be more important at different levels of development.

Resource caravans

The concept of resource caravans is critical and typically ignored. This largely stems from the fact that social scientists typically study their pet construct, be it social support, optimism, self-esteem, self-efficacy, or hope. Like caravans in the desert, resources aggregate in caravans that are interconnected across time. Research suggests that self-esteem, optimism, and self-efficacy are highly correlated (Cozzarelli 1993) and impact individuals along similar recuperative pathways after disaster (Sumer et al. 2005). When you have one personal resource you are likely to have the others. Even social support, which is a reflection of the social environment, is highly correlated with possessing strong personal resources (Hobfoll 2002).

This also explains why those who are more resilient can resist much of the negative impact of even mass trauma if it does not cause massive resource loss to them directly. They have an array of resources that are likely to fit or be adaptive to the situation. There are situations where different resources might best fit the situational demands, and the caravan of resources allows for the use of this tool box of resources. Even if some resources are damaged, others are likely to be available. Children in particular are dependent on the resource caravans that are supplied to them by families and institutions.

Moreover, the developmental process is formative in aiding them to create their own resource caravans (McKenzie and Frydenberg 2004).

Because children are especially susceptible to resource loss through disruption within the family, special attention needs to be paid to their access to resources in response to disasters. Children's psychological and physical well-being is greatly reflective of their parents' well-being following mass trauma (Issroff 2006; Klingman and Cohen 2004; Norris et al. 2002; Scheeringa and Zeanah 2001). Following the initial reaction to the trauma, however, children need special attention from parents to reinstate lost resources, such as a social network if they have become isolated for safety, or a routine, if upset by such an event. These secondary issues, moderated by parental behavior, can be especially important in shaping children's ability to cope and develop in the time of crisis (Issroff 2006; McKenry and Price 2005; Pynoos et al. 2004). In a study of ongoing terror, the loss of routine was found to be an important predictor of posttraumatic stress in junior high and high school students in Jerusalem (Pat-Horenczyk et al. 2006). When parents encouraged children to maintain their routine, and they therefore did so, there was much less post-traumatic stress, suggesting further that parents play a vital role in the process by which children and families themselves can maintain resources as well as foster their own coping.

The family is also tied to the community to obtain necessary resources for children's developmental progress. After a disaster, the loss of books, materials, schools, and the mere time and availability of developmental fostering can cascade into a cycle of loss for children. Not only are children without schools, but also, without school, they are without books and resources necessary to learn and progress through natural development. As an example, after Hurricane Katrina, thousands of children were displaced and without school for weeks and even months at a time. Due to their lack of access to such resources, they subsequently lost potential skill sets necessary to progress through natural schooling. Many children had to repeat the year of school they were in when the hurricane occurred. Developmental theories suggest that children are unable to progress to a new developmental stage without first accomplishing the goals of the present stage (Collins and Collins 2005). In war zones it is even more apparent that children are sometimes held back from progressing for years at a time. With such a massive loss of resources on all levels within the family and community, it may become impossible to halt this process whereby there is a failure to develop resource caravans, thus preventing many children from staying at the developmental and skill level of other children their age, not to mention the potential psychological damage as well.

A developed Western nation like the United States possesses ample institutional safeguards for these caravans, which are linked to broader social structures. These include the police, emergency services, the National Guard, and the formidable resources of the local, state, and US government. What may have been underestimated, however, in the disaster of Katrina was the strength of the linkages between individuals and families and these broader governmental resources, especially for the poor and ethnic minorities. Because individuals and families normally do not rely on these public resources, the linkages are loose and ill-defined. When barriers of distance, roads, personnel, and material logistics are strained, as in the post-September 11 environment of New York, there is rather rapid reassignment of public resources for the public good. Expecting that this model would serve when there was a combined breakdown of individual, family, and government resources was an error that cost thousands of lives, helped destroy a major American city, and will likely lead to long-term mental health and social consequences. At the time of the writing of this chapter, the murder rate in New Orleans was epidemic and youth violence outstripped the already high pre-disaster levels in this troubled city (Times-Picayune 2007).

Conclusions

The halting or slowing of resource loss and reconstituting of valuable pre-trauma resources are essential to re-establishing physical and psychological well-being and promoting resiliency. For those children and families who are having difficulty recovering independently, more intensive interventions offer effective and efficient ways of guiding them through the recovery process. Therapeutic exposure and habituation to traumatic stimuli, restructuring maladaptive trauma-related cognitions, and effective anxiety management lead to important increases in the personal resources of optimism, self-esteem, and self-efficacy. These personal resources are essential to adaptive coping and recovery, as well as treatment progress. However, personal resources are integrally tied to material, condition and energy resources. Their interwoven nature makes it compulsory to work on them collectively and demands the use of non-traditional approaches. Partnerships with other organizations, professionals, non-professionals and the victims themselves are essential for recovery and psychosocial advancement following disaster and mass casualties. Finding common themes and pathways for intervention is of paramount importance both because of the size of the likely demand and need, and also because these will be more effective than idiographic individualistic approaches, which are best used for individuals with severe disorders who have not managed a natural recovery even when properly supported.

Intervention following disaster or mass casualties should focus on supporting or enhancing the natural recovery process. Importantly, interventions should be tailored to the specific circumstances at hand, as the characteristics of the traumatic event and the community involved should guide relief and intervention efforts. These efforts should make use of the existing infrastructure, such as schools or other community institutions, when possible. Though several effective interventions for children alone have been developed, treatment should ideally involve parents or primary caregivers to promote family stability and parental support. Strengthening individuals, families, and communities in these ways facilitates recovery from disaster and mass casualties and increases resilience and preparedness for future traumatic events.

References

Bandura, A. (1997). *Self-efficacy: The exercise of control.* New York: W.H. Freeman/ Times Books/Henry Holt.

Bell, C.C., and McKay, M.M. (2004). Constructing a children's mental health infrastructure using community psychiatry principles. *Journal of Legal Medicine, 25,* 5–22.

Bell, C.C., Flay, B., and Paikoff, R. (2002). Strategies for health behavior change. In J.C. Chunn (ed.), *The health behavioral change imperative: Theory, education, and practice in diverse populations* (pp. 17–39). New York: Plenum-Kluwer.

Benight, C.C., and Bandura, A. (2004). Social cognitive theory of posttraumatic recovery: The role of perceived self-efficacy. *Behaviour Research and Therapy, 42,* 1129–1148.

Benight, C.C., and Harper, M.L. (2002). Coping self-efficacy perceptions as a mediator between acute stress response and long-term distress following natural disasters. *Journal of Traumatic Stress, 15,* 177–186.

Benight, C.C., Ironson, G., Klebe, K., Carver, C.S., Wynings, C., Burnett, C.S., et al. (1999). Conservation of resources and coping self-efficacy predicting distress following a natural disaster: A causal model analysis where the environment meets the mind. *Anxiety, Stress and Coping, 12,* 107–126.

Bonanno, G.A. (2004). Loss, trauma, and human resilience: Have we underestimated the human capacity to thrive under extremely aversive events? *American Psychologist, 59,* 20–28.

Burnett, K., Ironson, G., Benight, C., Wynings, C., Greenwood, D., Carver, C.S., et al. (1997). Measurement of perceived disruption during rebuilding following Hurricane Andrew. *Journal of Traumatic Stress, 10,* 673–681.

Carver, C.S. (2000). Optimism and pessimism. In A.E. Kazdin (ed.), *Encyclopedia of psychology, Volume 6.* (pp. 1–3). Washington, DC: American Psychological Association.

Collins, B.G., and Collins, T.M. (2005). *Crisis and trauma: Developmental-ecological intervention.* Boston, MA: Lahaska Press.

Cozzarelli, C. (1993). Personality and self-efficacy as predictors of coping with abortion. *Journal of Personality and Social Psychology, 66,* 1224–1236.

de Jong, J.T.V.M. (ed.) (2002a). *Trauma, war and violence: Public mental health in sociocultural context.* New York: Plenum-Kluwer.

de Jong, J.T.V.M. (2002b). Public mental health, traumatic stress and human rights violations in low-income countries: A culturally appropriate model in times of conflict, disaster and peace. In J. de Jong (ed.), *Trauma, war and violence: Public mental health in sociocultural context* (pp. 1–91). New York: Plenum-Kluwer.

Henry, D.B., Tolan, P.H., and Gorman-Smith, D. (2004). Have there been lasting effects associated with the September 11, 2001, terrorist attacks among inner-city parents and children? *Professional Psychology: Research and Practice, 35,* 542–547.

Hobfoll, S.E. (1988). *The ecology of stress.* New York: Hemisphere.

Hobfoll, S.E. (1989). Conservation of resources: A new attempt at conceptualizing stress. *American Psychologist, 44*(3), 513–524.

Hobfoll, S.E. (1998). *Stress, culture, and community: The psychology and philosophy of stress.* New York: Plenum.

Hobfoll, S.E. (2001). The influence of culture, community, and the nested-self in the stress process: Advancing Conservation of Resources Theory. *Applied Psychology: An International Review, 50,* 337–370.

Hobfoll, S.E. (2002). Alone together: Comparing communal versus individualistic resiliency. In E. Frydenberg (ed.), *Beyond coping: Meeting goals, visions, and challenges* (pp. 63–81). New York: Oxford University Press.

Hobfoll, S.E., Lavin, J., and Wells, J.D. (1999). When it rains it pours: The greater impact of resource loss compared to gain on psychological distress. *Personality and Social Psychology Bulletin, 25,* 1172–1182.

Hobfoll, S.E., Johnson, R.J., Ennis, N., and Jackson, A.P. (2003). Resource loss, resource gain and emotional outcomes among inner city women. *Journal of Personality and Social Psychology, 84,* 632–643.

Hobfoll, S.E., Canetti-Nisim, D., and Johnson, R.J. (2006). Exposure to terrorism, stress-related mental health symptoms, and defensive coping among Jews and Arabs in Israel. *Journal of Consulting and Clinical Psychology, 74,* 207–218.

Hoven, C.W., Duarte, C.S., Lucas, C.P., Wu, P., Mandell, D.J., Goodwin, R.D., et al. (2005). Psychopathology among New York City public school children 6 months after September 11. *Archives of General Psychiatry, 62,* 545–552.

Ironson, G., Wynings, C., Schneiderman, N., Baum, A., Rodriguez, M., Greenwood, D., et al. (1997). Posttraumatic stress symptoms, intrusive thoughts, loss, and immune function after Hurricane Andrew. *Psychosomatic Medicine, 59,* 128–141.

Issroff, J. (2006). How the effects of traumatic experiences are passed unto the following generations. In T.G. Plante (ed.), *Mental disorders of the new millennium: Volume 2. Public and social problems* (pp. 235–262). Westport, CT: Praeger/Greenwood.

Klingman, A. (2002). Children under stress of war. In A.M. La Greca, W.K. Silverman, E.M. Vernberg, and M.C. Roberts (eds.), *Helping children cope with disasters and terrorism* (pp. 359–380). Washington, DC: American Psychological Association.

Klingman, A., and Cohen, E. (2004). *School-based multisystemic interventions for mass trauma.* New York: Plenum-Kluwer.

Lazarus, R.S., and Folkman, S. (1984). *Stress, appraisal and coping.* New York: Springer.

Lengua, L.J., Long, A.C., and Meltzoff, A.N. (2006). Pre-attack stress-load, appraisals, and coping in children's responses to the 9/11 terrorist attacks. *Journal of Child Psychology and Psychiatry, 47,* 1219–1227.

Lieberman, A.F., and Pawl, J.H. (1990). Disorders of attachment and secure base behavior in the second year of life: Conceptual issues and clinical intervention. In M.T. Greenberg, C. Dante, and E. Mark (eds.), *Attachment in the preschool years: Theory, research, and intervention* (pp. 375–397). Chicago, IL: University of Chicago Press.

McCubbin, H.I., and McCubbin, M.A. (1988). Typology of resilient families: Emerging roles of social class and ethnicity. *Family Relations, 37,* 247–254.

McKenry, P.C., and Price, S.J. (2005). *Families and change: Coping with stressful events and transitions,* 3rd edition. Thousand Oaks, CA: Sage.

McKenzie, V., and Frydenberg, E. (2004). Young people and their resources: How they cope. In E. Frydenberg (ed.), *Thriving, surviving or going under: Coping with everyday lives* (pp. 189–206). Greenwich, CT: Information Age Publishing.

Norris, F.H., Friedman, M.J., Watson, P.J., Byrne, C.M., Diaz, E., and Kaniasty, K. (2002). 60,000 disaster victims speak: Part I. A review of the empirical literature, 1981–2001. *Psychiatry: Interpersonal and Biological Processes, 65*(3), 207–239.

Pat-Horenczyk, R., Schiff, M., and Doppelt, O. (2006). Maintaining routine despite ongoing exposure to terrorism: A healthy strategy for adolescents? *Journal of Adolescent Health, 39*, 199–205.

Pynoos, R.S., and Nader, K. (1988). Psychological first aid treatment approach to children exposed to community violence: Research implications. *Journal of Traumatic Stress, 1*, 445–473.

Pynoos, R.S., Steinberg, A.M., and Wraith, R. (1995). A developmental model of childhood traumatic stress. In D. Cicchetti and D.J. Cohen (eds.), *Developmental Psychopathology: Volume 2. Risk, disorder, and adaptation* (pp. 72–95). Oxford: Wiley.

Pynoos, R.S., Steinberg, A.M., and Piacentini, J.C. (1999). A developmental psychopathology model of childhood traumatic stress and intersection with anxiety disorders. *Biological Psychiatry, 46*, 1542–1554.

Pynoos, R.S., Steinberg, A.M., Grete, D., Goenjian, A.K., Chen, S., and Brymer, M.J. (2004). Reverberations of danger, trauma and PTSD on group dynamics. In B. Sklarew, S.W. Twemlow, and S.M. Wilkinson (eds.), *Analysts in the trenches: Streets, schools, war zones* (pp. 1–22). Hillsdale, NJ: Analytic Press.

Pynoos, R.S., Steinberg, A.M., Schreiber, M.D., and Brymer, M.J. (2006). Children and families: A new framework for preparedness and response to danger, terrorism and trauma. In L.A. Schein, H.I. Spitz, G.M. Burlingame, P.R. Ruskin, and S. Vargo (eds.), *Psychological effects of catastrophic disasters: Group approaches to treatment*. New York: Haworth.

Rosenberg, M. (1965). *Society and the adolescent self-image*. Princeton, NJ: Princeton University Press.

Rutter, M. (1985). Resilience in the face of adversity: Protective factors and resistance to psychiatric-disorder. *British Journal of Psychiatry, 147*, 598–611.

Sattler, D.N. (2006). Family resources, family strains, and stress following the Northridge earthquake. *Stress, Trauma, and Crisis, 9*, 187–202.

Sattler, D.N., Preston, A.J., Kaiser, C.F., Olivera, V.E., Valdez, J., and Schlueter, S. (2002). Hurricane Georges: A cross-national study examining preparedness, resource loss, and psychological distress in the U.S. Virgin Islands, Puerto Rico, Dominican Republic, and the United States. *Journal of Traumatic Stress, 15*, 339–350.

Scheeringa, M., and Zeanah, C.H. (2001). A relationship perspective on PTSD in infancy. *Journal of Traumatic Stress, 14*, 799–815.

Scheier, M.F., and Carver, C.S. (1985). Optimism, coping, and health: Assessment and implications of generalized outcome expectancies. *Health Psychology, 4*, 219–247.

Schoon, I. (2006). *Risk and resilience: Adaptations in changing times*. New York: Cambridge University Press.

Schwarzer, R., and Taubert, S. (2002). Tenacious goal pursuits and striving toward personal growth. In E. Frydenberg (ed.), *Beyond coping: Meeting goals, visions, and challenges* (pp. 19–35). New York: Oxford University Press.

Smith, B.W., and Freedy, J.R. (2000). Psychosocial resource loss as a mediator of the effects of flood exposure on psychological distress and physical symptoms. *Journal of Traumatic Stress, 13*, 349–357.

Sumer, N., Karanci, A.N., Berument, S.K., and Gunes, H. (2005). Personal resources, coping self-efficacy, and quake exposure as predictors of psychological distress following the 1999 earthquake in Turkey. *Journal of Traumatic Stress, 18*, 331–342.

Times-Picayune (2007). Thousands march to protest city's alarming murder rate, January 12 (www.nola.com/news/t-p/frontpage/index.ssf?/base/news-7/1168586093261300.xml&coll=1#continue) (accessed January 18, 2007).

Chapter 10

Ecological resilience
Working with child-related psychosocial resources in war-affected communities

Wietse A. Tol, Marc D. Jordans, Ria Reis, and Joop de Jong

Across a variety of scientific disciplines within medicine and the social sciences, theories have been proposed that attempt to explain people's ability to maintain well-being in the face of stressful situations. Alongside a more dominant paradigm in which the focus lies on studying the disruption of well-being, a multiplicity of "resource" theories have investigated which assets contribute to the retention of psychosocial health amidst adversity.[1] Some examples of such constructs are resilience, personality hardiness, sense of coherence, self-efficacy, recovery, and recently, post-traumatic growth (Almedom 2005). This chapter provides an overview of the construct of resilience from an ecological perspective, applied to psychosocial well-being of children living in areas of armed conflict. First, the concept of resilience and the ecological perspective are described for this field of science and practice, followed by an explanation of how "ecological resilience" is conceptualized in this chapter. Second, an overview is given of research findings on resilience at different social and ecological levels (family, peers, school, community). Each section discusses research findings about children living in areas of armed conflict, findings from a recent qualitative study in Burundi, Indonesia, and Sri Lanka,[2] and examples of how ecological resilience has been translated into psychosocial programming. These sections are followed by a general discussion of how to integrate ecological resilience into psychosocial programming, with an emphasis on pre-programming assessment. The chapter ends with a discussion of some limitations of this approach, including the current lack of evidence to guide the field.

Resources and resilience

Although there is significant controversy regarding the specific construct and definition of resilience (Layne et al., Chapter 2 in this volume), it has been defined as "good outcomes in spite of serious threats to adaptation or development" (Masten 2001, p. 2) and "a dynamic process encompassing positive adaptation within the context of significant adversity" (Luthar et al. 2000, p. 543). In this sense, resilience as a construct can be considered to fit in the category of Integrated Resource Models as categorized by Hobfoll (2002).

Currently, there has been increased attention to the construct of resilience in the field of psychosocial interventions for children affected by armed conflict (Apfel and Simon 1996; Loughry and Eyber 2004). Children living in areas of armed conflict have been shown to be at increased risk for a range of psychiatric problems, such as posttraumatic stress disorder, major depressive disorder, anxiety disorders, aggression, dissociative disorders, somatization problems, substance abuse (adolescents), disturbed academic functioning and interference in developmental tasks (for reviews see Barenbaum et al. 2004; Berman 2001; Joshi and O'Donnell 2003; Shaw 2003; Stichick 2001). Researchers in this new field, however, have been increasingly critical of an overemphasis on Western biomedical disease constructs as classified in the *Diagnostic and Statistical Manual* (DSM-IV; American Psychiatric Association 1994) and the International Classification of Diseases (ICD-10; World Health Organization 1990), especially in low-income countries, where the great majority of armed conflicts take place. A paradigm shift has been called for in studying the psychosocial impact of war on children, from describing the impact in terms of psychiatric classification systems to examining the effects of chronic stress situations, protective and mediating factors, and the roles of cultural context, gender, and type of conflict situation (e.g. Berman 2001; de Jong 2002; Lustig et al. 2004; Stichick 2001).

Although attention has been called to resilience processes in children in situations of armed conflict, only a limited number of studies have investigated this issue. Moreover, research into the resilience construct itself has been criticized for lacking cultural sensitivity (McAdam-Crisp 2006) and for its assumption of the universality of childhood experiences. Boyden (2003), for instance, points to the ethnographic evidence showing that social constructions of childhood are extremely variable and context-specific. She provides the example of Bangladesh, where someone up to puberty may be called a child if they go to school and have no social or economic responsibilities. Similarly, a boy or girl who works will no longer be called a child even at age 6 Boyden (2003).

An ecological perspective

In addition to this renewed attention to the concept of resiliency in this field, there has been an increased focus on the larger social environment in which children live – a direction that has been visible in resilience research as well. This attention to ecological variables is not new, as it stems from sociology (Blakely and Woodward 2000). A renewed interest in ecological variables can be observed in a variety of disciplines, for instance, the stress literature's interest in social support (Coyne and Downey 1991) and the public health literature's interest in ecological variables (Earls and Carlson 2001) such as social capital (De Silva et al. 2005, 2007). In studying children in adversity, ecological approaches have been used to research the possible exposure to and impact of child maltreatment (Cicchetti and Lynch 1993; Freisthler et al. 2006; Lynch and Cicchetti 1998; Zielinski and Bradshaw 2005), child abuse (Wilson-Oyelaran 1989), community and interpersonal violence (Aisenberg and Ell 2005; Almgren 2005; Garbarino 2001; Hughes et al. 2005), as well as the perpetration of violence by youth (Banyard et al. 2006). The increased sophistication of statistical methods in accounting for latent and nested patterns in data (e.g. multilevel approaches, structural equational modeling) has greatly enhanced the possibility of observing ecological effects in quantitative studies (Blakely and Woodward 2000; Kawachi and Subramanian 2006; Susser and Susser 1996).

The literature on children living in areas of armed conflict has increasingly referred to the ecological model as initially outlined by Bronfenbrenner (1979). Bronfenbrenner considered his theory of human development to be a possible theoretical breakthrough in the perceived dilemma between the "hard" scientific psychometric practices in laboratories on the one hand, and the relevance of research results for policy and practice on the other. Bronfenbrenner advocates that children be studied with experimental methods in their natural environment, taking into account the environmental influences on children's development. He defined human development as:

> The process through which the growing person acquires a more extended, differentiated, and valid conception of the ecological environment, and becomes motivated and able to engage in activities that reveal the properties of, sustain, or restructure that environment at levels of similar or greater complexity in form and content.
>
> (Bronfenbrenner 1979, p. 27)

This ecological environment is conceptualized as a nested number of systems around the individual child:

- the *micro-system*, consisting of the direct activities, roles, and interpersonal relations in a certain setting (e.g. the home, the school)
- the *mesosystem*, which is comprised of the interrelations among two or more of these settings (e.g. relations between home, school, and peer group)
- the *exosystem*, in which the child does not actively participate but which influences and is influenced by the developing person (e.g. the parents' workplaces)
- the *macrosystem*, which are consistencies in the form of culture or subculture in the micro-, exo-, and mesosystems (Bronfenbrenner 1979).

The emphasis on the broader social environment, as well as the focus on interrelationships and more complicated structures of cause and effect, can be seen in reconceptualizations of these theoretical standpoints in connection with current research on childhood adversity. Rather than the systems proposed by Bronfenbrenner (1979), current ecological theories more often see the child as nested within a system of social ecological levels, such as the individual child, the family, peer groups, school, and community (e.g. Earls and Carlson 2001; Lynch and Cicchetti 1998; Zielinski and Bradshaw 2005).

Ecological resilience

For the purpose of this chapter we view ecological resilience as those assets and processes on all social ecological levels that have been shown to be associated with good developmental outcomes after exposure to situations of armed conflict.[3] As this working definition shows, we discuss the consequences of ecological resilience for children's *individual* functioning. Although resilience can be argued to be a function of the social ecological levels *themselves* (e.g. the plasticity of a community in reforming communal social connections disrupted by war could be termed "community resilience"), we do not discuss it as such here. Rather, we see ecological resilience as a reservoir of factors at different social and ecological levels that can enhance psychosocial well-being. Children under strain can seek out and utilize resources from this reservoir to enhance their chances of retaining or obtaining psychosocial well-being.

We can see several reasons for the importance of ecological resilience in the field of psychosocial interventions for children in areas of armed conflict. First, such a perspective would make it easier for practitioners to answer the call for more culturally sensitive psychosocial interventions, rather than simply introduce models from high-income settings (Bracken et al. 1995; Summerfield 2000). Interventions that produce a better fit between methodology and context are less likely to undermine the pre-existing coping capabilities of communities by introducing outside resources. Second, it has been observed that war has consequences on social levels that have been termed "collective trauma" (Abramowitz 2005). Working with ecological resilience could provide appropriate ways of dealing with these consequences. Third, it has been argued that psychosocial interventions should follow a public health or primary care approach, encompassing universal, selective, and indicated interventions (Dawes and Cairns 1998; de Jong 1996, 2002). An ecological perspective would enable practitioners to identify aspects of the social environment that could be reinforced as part of broader interventions at a more universal level. In addressing the damaged social fabric of communities, for instance, psychosocial interventions could aid in parenting the reoccurrence of violent conflict. Fourth, integrating ecological resilience in psychosocial programming avoids the risk of overemphasizing universal conceptualizations of childhood and viewing children and communities as passive recipients of aid (Boyden 2003). Through the methodology described below (pp. 173–175), planners involve children from the start in planned interventions, taking into account their agency. From the beginning children are seen as knowledgeable partners for both the possible consequences of armed violence and the strengths and gaps in resources. Taking the existing resources as a starting point is also argued to make interventions more sustainable over a prolonged period of time. Finally, settings of armed conflict often involve many children exposed to a large number of stressors in settings with very few available health professionals (de Jong et al. 2003). Working to enhance available resources at the school and community level can then form an appropriate way of reaching a substantial number of families.

Family-level resilience

Much has been written about resources at the family level, and it is not our intention to summarize that literature here (for reviews see Rutter 1999; Walsh 1996, 2002). Rather, we would like to focus on what is known about possible relevant family resource mechanisms at play in low-income conflict-affected settings, and provide some examples of how interveners could use this knowledge in the design of psychosocial projects.

The importance of family relationships has been part of studying the psychosocial impact of war on children from its inception. Anna Freud and Burlingham (1943) found that children who were physically close to their parents during aerial bombings fared better than children separated from their parents. In line with attachment theory, Garbarino et al. (1991), provided further support for the importance of a stable, open relationship with a caregiver, as did David Kinzie and his team (as cited in Wallen and Rubin 1997) for children who survived the Pol Pot regime. Moreover, research has shown the important effects of the mother's psychosocial problems on children's functioning in war situations (Bryce et al. 1989; Qouta et al. 2005). Laor et al. (2001) have shown that the mother's symptoms continued to be associated with the child's symptoms five years after SCUD missile attacks. Besides the importance of relationships with a caregiver, research findings have shown the relevance of more general characteristics of the family, such as hardiness and cohesion in times of war (Jovanovic et al. 2004; Stichick Betancourt 2004). In one of the few studies on parenting practices, associations between traumatic exposure, perceived parenting (on three dimensions: punishment and rejection, intimacy and love, strictness and control) and psychological adjustment were examined in a Palestinian sample (Punamaki et al. 1997). Although it is hard to interpret the findings because of the small sample size, the study suggests not only the importance of perceived good parenting for children's well-being, but also the risks of poor parenting.

Although in need of cross-cultural validation, a promising overarching conceptualization of resources at this level is Walsh's conceptualization of "family resilience" (Walsh 2002), which is grounded in ecological and developmental theories (Walsh 1996). She distinguishes several key processes in family resilience:

- belief systems, consisting of the ability to make sense of adversity, retaining a positive outlook, and the dimension of spirituality
- organizational patterns, consisting of flexibility, connectedness, and social and economic resources
- communication processes, consisting of clarity, open emotional sharing, and collaborative problem-solving (Walsh 2002).

In our qualitative research with children in armed conflict zones in north-western Burundi, the Poso region of Sulawesi (Indonesia), and northern Sri Lanka, we observed the importance of resilience factors at the family level (Tol et al. 2007). In addition to the above-mentioned resilience factors, children, families, and community members mentioned the importance of assistance from siblings and extended family. For instance, in the case of Burundian child-headed households, when parents were killed during the civil war, sisters were observed to actively encourage education for siblings who were about to drop out from school. In northern Sri Lanka, extended family members, such as aunts and uncles, were often able to provide distraction from grief after the death or "disappearance" of fathers, as well as provide a stable supporting relationship when single mothers were focusing on their families' economic survival.

Examples of working with resilience at the family level include psychoeducation and consciousness, raising for caregivers and other family members, tracing family members in cases of displacement, various forms of family therapy, assisting in parenting practices, and helping families obtain economic resources. Macksoud (1993), for instance, has written a useful manual for UNICEF on how parents and teachers can understand and deal with wartime stresses for children of different ages.

Peer-level resilience

Positive peer relations have been studied as protective factors for children in adversity (Bolger et al. 1998; Criss et al. 2002; Zielinski and Bradshaw 2005), including children exposed to community violence in the United States (Morrison 2000; Schwartz et al. 2003). In her review, Morrison (2000) comments on the scarcity of research on the role of social support, including peer support, in the community violence literature. The sparse findings available suggest that peer support seems to be associated with more favorable outcomes for children exposed to community violence, for instance by moderating effects on anxiety (Hill and Madhere 1996; Hill et al. 1996), and by being associated with more competent classroom behavior (Hill and Madhere

1996), more positive future expectations, more self-reliance, and better inter-personal relations (O'Donnell et al. 2002).

In our research in Burundi, Indonesia, and Sri Lanka we found that peers supported each other in several ways. Besides assistance in basic needs (e.g. where pupils in northwestern Burundi would ask their parents to feed class-mates), peers would support each other through play, support in education, and individual emotional support (e.g. advice-giving and encouragement). In central Sulawesi, however, we found that the communal violence had dam-aged the social fabric especially at the peer level. Because of the religious lines along which violence occurs and around which communities have become segregated, mistrust, awkwardness and sensitivity were felt to have arisen in Muslim–Christian peer interpersonal contacts. It is in such cases that plan-ning attention might be focused on the development of stronger trusting peer relations, aimed at the prevention of violence later on.

Another example of psychosocial planning aimed at working with positive peer relations is children's and youth clubs. This is currently an approach of increasing popularity, partly because it involves a degree of child participa-tion (Ackermann et al. 2003; Ispanovic-Radojkovic 2003; UNICEF 2003). Child participation in planning for children affected by armed conflict has been advocated as a means of avoiding working with children as passive victims and seeing them as lacking capacity as social actors, but so far only anecdotal evidence supports this claim (Morris et al. 2007). Children's agency is a theme currently interesting anthropologists studying childhood and violence (Das and Reynolds 2003). Hart (2002, 2003) has evaluated child participatory activities in humanitarian assistance in three conflict-affected settings, including children's club activities in eastern Sri Lanka and Nepal. Beneficial effects observed through qualitative research were the possibility of engaging in community development and peace building, increased social competence and confidence, increased effectiveness as a group, and positive changes in psychosocial well-being, including rebuilding social ties shattered by conflict (Hart 2002, 2003).

School-level resilience

School can offer a protective environment for children in settings of armed conflict in several ways. First, school provides a structure with routine activ-ities that could add a sense of predictability in a chaotic situation. Second, the school environment is a source of possible relationships, with both teachers and peers. Supportive relationships with teachers have been men-tioned as important predictors of psychological well-being for traumatized children (Barenbaum et al. 2004) and teachers can provide a role model for dealing with stressful situations. Third, school enhances skills, knowledge and values that have a role in individual and community development. Fourth, these skills and knowledge in turn are able to increase children's self-confidence. School attendance has been associated with competence in El Salvador, for instance (Flores 2004). Skills and attitudes aimed at the prevention of further armed conflict have been promoted in peace education and reconciliation skills, such as negotiation, problem-solving, critical thinking and communication skills (Miller and Affolter 2002; Tolfree 1996). Fifth, school can provide opportunities for recreational and sports activities, which are deemed important in relation to psychosocial well-being of children in war situations (Aguilar and Retamal 1998). Finally, schools have been advocated as one of the best public health settings in which to implement psychosocial interventions for children in settings of armed conflict (Saltzman et al. 2003; Shaw 2003). Research on school-based programs for children affected by Hurricane Iniki and violence in the United States (Chemtob et al. 2002a, 2002b; Stein et al. 2003), as well as school-based programs in the occupied Palestinian territory and Bosnia (Khamis et al. 2004; Layne et al. 2000) has shown promising results. Accordingly, a significant number of psychosocial initiatives use the school as their base (for an overview see Jaycox et al. 2006).

Resources identified in our qualitative research in Burundi, Indonesia, and Sri Lanka not only support the literature on the importance of the school environment, but also point to the difficulties inherent in the school situation in these settings. In all three settings teachers were felt to be possible sources of support in providing an individual emotionally supporting relationship, as well as moral and religious instruction in circumstances of perceived damage to children's moral fabric. In general, education was deemed central in helping children achieve their aspirations. Moreover, teachers were often able to work with resources at the family and peer level, by actively trying to increase unity in schools (Sri Lanka), promoting reconciliation (Indonesia), and encouraging family visits aimed at advising parents and caregivers. Besides the lack of proper school facilities and teachers in most settings, there were a number of barriers preventing children from attending school, including poverty, security concerns, and displacement. Even when in school, pupils had difficulties in fully participating due to concentration difficulties, involvement in armed struggles (Sri Lanka), and lack of equipment (school uniforms, stationery). Furthermore, in all three settings there was an ambivalent relationship between parents and teachers, where the teachers would blame parents for not caring enough about the children's education or not paying school fees, and the parents would blame the teachers for not understanding their children's concerns or for severe corporal punishment.

Community-level resilience

According to the ecological theory of Bronfenbrenner (1979), the macrosystem involves consistencies in the form of culture or subculture in the micro-, exo-, and mesosystems. In research on children in adversity, an ecological lens has more often meant that researchers have tried to identify risk and protective factors at the neighborhood or community level. In cases of child maltreatment, such factors have been neighborhood poverty, large numbers of single-parent households, and residential instability (Zielinski and Bradshaw 2005).

A possibly useful theoretical framework at this level is the sociological concept of social capital. Although social capital has been conceptualized as bringing benefits in social control as well as family support, we focus here on its function as a source of benefits through extra-familial networks. The idea that involvement and participation in groups can have positive consequences for the individual and the community is a "staple notion" in the history of sociology (Portes 1998). Although social status is defined differently, there is currently a consensus in the literature it is "the ability of actors to secure benefits by virtue of memberships in social networks or other social structures" (Portes 1998, p. 6). Preliminary evidence suggests associations between social capital and psychosocial outcomes for children in high-income countries in general (Van der Linden et al. 2003) and in adversity (Runyan et al. 1998), as well as for children in communities affected by HIV-AIDS and genocide in Rwanda (Thurman et al. 2006).

Besides social networks at the neighborhood and community level, which were helpful in providing direct assistance (including material assistance and assistance in performing rituals) and linkages to other resources, we found a host of other resources available in our qualitative study in Burundi, Indonesia, and Sri Lanka. Although weakened, the help of wise elder men (*abashingantahe*) in Burundi was sought in cases of family disputes and conflicts over land, which often plagued children orphaned by the civil war. Faith healing (Christian, Hindu, and Muslim) and traditional healing practices (massage herbalists in central Sulawesi and spirit healers) were generally consulted in all three settings to deal with children's problems involving spirits, fears, concentration, behavior, relationships, and bodily complaints. Moreover, churches, mosques and affiliated educational institutions were felt to provide healing opportunities and moral clarity in a climate of perceived moral decline.

Dawes and Cairns (1998) commented on the notion of using cultural practices to aid in restoring the social fabric. Examples of such cultural practices are the empowerment of traditional leadership, and the use of traditional healers and local cleansing rituals for reintegrating former child soldiers in communal life (Honwana 1997). Taking a broader perspective, it has been argued that for the restoration of the social fabric, society as a whole needs to come to terms with wrongs done in the past, for instance through mechanisms like the South African Truth and Rehabilitation Commission.

Integrating ecological resilience in psychosocial planning

We have given some examples of how ecological resilience has been translated into psychosocial planning for children affected by armed conflict. Current reviews, however, agree on an unfortunate lack of research evidence for making detailed intervention recommendations (Layne et al. 2007; Morris et al. 2007). In light of this lack of evidence, we outline below only some general principles on how to integrate ecological resilience into planning, emphasizing the importance of assessment. It is through careful participatory assessment that we believe resources available at different social ecological levels can be identified and the interaction between them observed. Moreover, it has been our observation that damage to the social fabric and the resources is variable, depending in part on pre-conflict family and community characteristics and the type of conflict situation. This means that assessment is crucial for identifying context-specific vulnerabilities and strengths in the social ecological system to guide planning. To organize this section, we have structured psychosocial programming into five phases, outlined in Table 10.1.

Although the assessment of needs prior to planning sounds like common sense, reviewing current practices shows that this is not commonly done (e.g. Marsden and Strang 2006). Several guidelines exist for the assessment of needs, including the section on assessment in the guidelines of the Inter-Agency Standing Committee (IASC) Task Force on Mental Health and Psychosocial Support in Emergency Settings. This document stresses the need to coordinate assessments between agencies, suggests topics for inclusion in the collection of information, and provides guidelines for conducting an assessment in an ethical and appropriately participatory manner (IASC 2006). Regarding methodology, we found that a combination of key informant interviews,

Table 10.1 Overview of phases in psychosocial programming from an ecological resilience perspective

1 Identification
Assessment of needs and resources on all social-ecological levels

2 Negotiation
Discussions to reach a consensus intervention framework based on the identification phase, encompassing elements of local and outside healing strategies.

3 Formulation
Deciding on the plan of action.

4 Implementation
Execution.

5 Evaluation
Looking at project outcomes and documenting lessons learned for future implementation.

illness narratives, and focus group discussions worked well in identifying problems and resources on different social ecological levels and provided sufficient opportunities for triangulation. This can be done relatively quickly if local staff are trained in qualitative data collection. A possible tool for synthesizing information collected is drawing of nested circles on a large sheet of paper, representing the child embedded in the family, peer setting, school, and community. With the use of +, −, and → symbols, the resources, needs, and transactions between the social ecological levels can be summarized for discussion. In addition, the Psychosocial Working Group (2004) advocates integrating power mapping into assessments, to identify vulnerable groups which lack a voice in community discussions. It also encourages linking assessments to the rapid provision of effective support and services.

The second phase involves the beginning of a negotiation process between representatives of the target population, agency staff from the specific setting, and outside interveners on the framework to be used for intervention and its specific strategies. The results from the needs assessment should guide this negotiation process. The negotiation entails discussing which types of interventions might be appropriate for the problems identified in the needs assessment, including local and foreign traditions. Discussion can take place through dialogue, with the possible use of visual aids and examples to explain more abstract concepts such as consciousness raising (e.g. examples of booklets) or working with community relationships (e.g. drawing a social map with religious facilities, power structures, etc). The word negotiation is used here to focus attention on the asymmetrical power relations that often exist between staff living in the armed conflict setting and foreign interveners (Dawes and Cairns 1998). We argue that the aim of this exercise is not necessarily to arrive at the interventions that are the most "local", but rather to a package that is thought to be the most effective.

Implementation requires the formulation of a plan of action involving representatives of the target group. Although we cannot summarize the multitude of existing psychosocial guidelines here, we list four principles of successful ecological resilience interventions, as proposed by Sandler (2001):

- work with multiple resources to reduce the negative effects of exposure to adversity
- deliver the resources that match the needs of the target population, keeping in mind the public health concepts of universal, selective, and indicated interventions
- work at multiple levels to promote the development of resources
- keep in mind that "successful interventions do not simply build skills, they promote a sense of efficacy, support, and self-worth, and they prevent future adversities" (Sandler 2001, p. 48).

For the formulation of a plan of action, the Logical Framework Approach

(LFA) is used most often at present (e.g. Örtengren 2004). Monitoring and evaluation are necessary throughout the project cycle. An ecological perspective on resilience entails that indicators must be chosen to reflect the possible changes at multiple social ecological levels and not only assess individual change (e.g. membership in civil organizations to indicate social capital, ability of families to recognize children's psychosocial concerns, number of parents actively involved in school committees).

At the end of the program an evaluation is needed. A useful guide for evaluation of psychosocial programming is a publication by the Save the Children Federation (Duncan and Arntson 2004), which is based on the LFA. The Psychosocial Working Group stresses the need for strong evaluations for this new field to strengthen knowledge of the best practices, which, it observes, is hampered by isolation and inter-agency competition (Psychosocial Working Group 2004).

Conclusion

In this chapter we have attempted to provide an overview of ecological resilience and the research evidence currently supporting it, as well as suggestions and further reading for integrating ecological resilience into psychosocial programming for children affected by armed conflict.

Since we have presented the resources in separate sections, we would like to argue here against possible misinterpretations that might arise from this separation. First, it is likely that resources at different social ecological levels are connected, and that access to resources at one level is associated with access to resources at other levels (Hobfoll 2002). An important suggestion of Bronfenbrenner's ecological theory, that is somewhat obscured in more recent discussions, is the existence of similarities between systems in a culture or subculture (Bronfenbrenner's (1979) macro-level). This describes well our observations of an all-permeating sense of destruction, loss of hope, and damage to the moral and social fabric in parts of northwestern Burundi. Second, one of the main proposals of the ecological model is that transactions take place between the different ecological levels. For instance, in central Sulawesi, we found that the communal violence, displacement, and associated neglect of plantations had greatly affected families' opportunities to economically provide for their children, including the ability to pay school fees. This inability sometimes led to verbal abuse by teachers, which caused the children to feel stigmatization, shame, and sadness. These children would then drop out of school, form groups, and engage in early sexual behaviors, smoking, and drinking, leading to a feeling of communal moral decline.

Similarly, resilience factors at one social ecological level can interact with factors at other levels. For example, in Burundi high school dropout rates had a variety of causes including lack of financial resources and large gaps in education due to displacement and dissatisfaction with schooling. Church and other initiatives worked with children with a lack of schooling, to teach them skills necessary for earning a living. Such interventions gave the children a sense of accomplishment and kept them from joining groups of dropouts who were living on the streets.

Furthermore, even though we stress the importance of social resources for the psychosocial well-being of children in armed conflict settings, it is important also to not overestimate available local resources. On the one hand, this could risk imposing the idea of cultures as static entities, rather than the possibility of engaging dynamically with cultural practices. On the other hand, it could risk neglecting the problems in social organizations, which has sometimes led to the existence of armed violence in the first place. Issues such as marginalized groups, stigmatization, and the abuse of political power should, we argue, not be reified in an attempt to work in as culturally sensitive a manner as possible. In this sense a middle stance between neglect and overestimation of available social resources is suggested.

An ecological perspective on resilience posits a system of interrelated social ecological levels, at which resources can be found that contribute to good developmental outcomes of children living in areas of armed conflict. In this chapter we have not tried to explain why some children would be able to utilize such resources and others not. Other contributions in this book might clarify this important question, for instance by utilizing the rich resilience literature in the field of child developmental studies.

In conclusion, one of the main problems in this field is a lack of research evidence on basic principles for psychosocial programming and a lack of translation of research findings into intervention methodology (Layne et al. 2007; Morris et al. 2007). In our opinion, future studies should focus on how resilience processes at different social ecological levels can be effectively incorporated into psychosocial programs for children living in areas of armed conflict. Multilevel statistical techniques can be of assistance in this effort. At present there is evidence suggesting the importance of the family, but on the other social-ecological levels there is only scant research evidence to support the association of resilience with psychosocial well-being. For a field in which there are considerable theoretical debates about such issues as the cross-cultural appropriateness of theories underlying assistance, research evidence could enhance the availability of effective practices to counter the suffering of large numbers of children who have been exposed to the horrors of armed conflict.

Notes

1   Following the Psychosocial Working Group's formulation, the word psychosocial is used here to emphasize the close connection between psychological aspects of human functioning and wider social experience (Psychosocial Working Group 2003).

2   In short, this study involved examining not only the psychosocial consequences
    of armed violence from an emic perspective, but also the resources available to
    deal with these consequences. Trained local assessors in each of the three settings
    (northwestern Burundi, the Poso region of central Sulawesi, Indonesia, and the
    Jaffna District of Sri Lanka) conducted focus group discussions (children, parents,
    teachers), key informant interviews with those providing support to children in
    communities (traditional healers, religious clergy and healers, teachers, principals,
    midwives, etc.), and semi-structured interviews with families identified as
    afflicted). Interviews were tape-recorded, transcribed, translated and analysed
    using ATLAS.ti qualitative data analysis software. This study took place as pre-
    paration for an ongoing efficacy study (randomized controlled trial) to select,
    adapt, and construct instrumentation.
3   Both terms "ecological" and "resilience" have been imported into the social and
    medical sciences from the natural sciences. The term *resilience* refers to the ability
    of metals to return to their original shape after applying pressure, imported from
    the field of engineering (Layne et al. 2007). Subsequently, this term was introduced
    into the (biological) ecological literature by C.S. Holling, who defined *ecological
    resilience* as the amount of disturbance a system can absorb without changing
    state. Other definitions from the ecological literature have stressed the ability of a
    system to change into another stable structure after disruption (Gunderson 2000).

References

Abramowitz, S.A. (2005). The poor have become rich, and the rich have become poor:
    Collective trauma in the Guinean Langette. *Social Science and Medicine, 61*(10),
    2106–2118.
Ackermann, L., Feeny, T., Hart, J., and Newman, J. (2003). Understanding and evalu-
    ating children's participation: A review of contemporary literature. PLAN UK/
    PLAN International (www.plan-uk.org/pdfs/literaturereview.pdf).
Aguilar, P., and Retamal, G. (1998). *Rapid educational response in emergencies:
    A discussion document.* Geneva: International Bureau of Education.
Aisenberg, E., and Ell, K. (2005). Contextualizing community violence and its effects:
    An ecological model of parent–child interdependent coping. *Journal of Inter-
    personal Violence, 20*(7), 855–871.
Almedom, A.M. (2005). Resilience, hardiness, sense of coherence, and posttraumatic
    growth: All paths leading to "light at the end of the tunnel"? *Journal of Loss and
    Trauma, 10*, 253–265.
Almgren, G. (2005). The ecological context of interpersonal violence: From culture
    to collective efficacy. *Journal of Interpersonal Violence, 20*(2), 218–224.
American Psychiatric Association (APA) (1994). *Diagnostic and statistical manual
    of mental disorders*, 4th edition. Washington, DC: APA.
Apfel, R.J., and Simon, B. (1996). *Minefields in their hearts: The mental health
    of children in war and communal violence.* New Haven, CT: Yale University Press.
Banyard, V.L., Cross, C., and Modecki, K.L. (2006). Interpersonal violence in
    adolescence: Ecological correlates of self-reported perpetration. *Journal of
    Interpersonal Violence, 21*(10), 1314–1332.
Barenbaum, J., Ruchkin, V., and Schwab-Stone, M. (2004). The psychosocial aspects
    of children exposed to war: Practice and policy initiatives. *Journal of Child
    Psychology and Psychiatry, 45*(1), 41–62.

Berman, H. (2001). Children and war: Current understandings and future directions. *Public Health Nursing, 18*(4), 243–252.

Blakely, T.A., and Woodward, A.J. (2000). Ecological effects in multilevel studies. *Journal of Epidemioligy and Community Health, 54*, 367–374.

Bolger, K.E., Patterson, C.J., and Kupersmidt, J.B. (1998). Peer relations and self-esteem among children who have been maltreated. *Child Development, 69*(4), 1171–1197.

Boyden, J. (2003). Children under fire: Challenging assumptions about children's resilience. *Children, Youth and Environment, 13*(1).

Bracken, P.J., Giller, J.E., and Summerfield, D. (1995). Psychological responses to war and atrocity: The limitations of current concepts. *Social Science and Medicine, 40*(8), 1073–1082.

Bronfenbrenner, U. (1979). *The ecology of human development: Experiments by nature and design.* Cambridge, MA: Harvard University Press.

Bryce, J.W., Walker, N., Ghorayeb, F., and Kanj, M. (1989). Life experiences, response styles and mental health among mothers and children in Beirut, Lebanon. *Social Science and Medicine, 28*(7), 685–695.

Chemtob, C.M., Nakashima, J., and Carlson, J.G. (2002a). Brief treatment for elementary school children with disaster-related posttraumatic stress disorder: A field study. *Journal of Clinical Psychology, 58*(1), 99–112.

Chemtob, C.M., Nakashima, J.P., and Hamada, R.S. (2002b). Psychosocial intervention for postdisaster trauma symptoms in elementary school children: A controlled community field study. *Archives of Pediatric and Adolescent Medicine, 156*, 211–216.

Cicchetti, D., and Lynch, M. (1993). Toward an ecological/transactional model of community violence and child maltreatment: Consequences for children's development. *Psychiatry, 56*, 96–118.

Coyne, J.C., and Downey, G. (1991). Social factors and psychopathology: Stress, social support, and coping processes. *Annual Review of Psychology, 42*, 401–425.

Criss, M.M., Pettit, G.S., Bates, J.E., Dodge, K.A., and Lapp, A.L. (2002). Family adversity, positive peer relationships, and children's externalizing behavior: A longitudinal perspective on risk and resilience. *Child Development, 73*(4), 1220–1237.

Das, V., and Reynolds, P. (2003). *The child on the wing: Children negotiating the everyday in the geography of violence.* Baltimore, MD: Johns Hopkins University.

Dawes, A., and Cairns, E. (1998). The Machel study: Dilemmas of cultural sensitivity and universal rights of children. *Peace and Conflict: Journal of Peace Psychology, 4*(4), 335–348.

de Jong, J.T.V.M. (1996). A comprehensive public mental health programme in Guinea-Bissau: A useful model for African, Asian and Latin-American countries. *Psychological Medicine, 26*(1), 97–108.

de Jong, J.T.V.M. (ed.) (2002). *Trauma, war, and violence: Public mental health in socio-cultural context.* New York: Plenum-Kluwer.

de Jong, J.T.V.M., Komproe, I.H., and Van Ommeren, M. (2003). Common mental disorders in postconflict settings. *Lancet, 361*(9375), 2128–2130.

De Silva, M.J., McKenzie, K., Harpham, T., and Huttly, S.R.A. (2005). Social capital and mental illness: A systematic review. *Journal of Epidemiology and Community Health, 59*, 619–627.

De Silva, M.J., Huttly, S.R., Harpham, T., and Kenward, M.G. (2007). Social capital and mental health: A comparative analysis of four low income countries. *Social Science and Medicine, 64*(1), 5–20.

Duncan, J., and Arntson, L. (2004). *Children in crisis: Good practices in evaluating psychosocial programming.* Westport, CT: Save the Children Federation.

Earls, F., and Carlson, M. (2001). The social ecology of child health and wellbeing. *Annual Review of Public Health, 22*, 143–166.

Flores, J.E. (2004). Schooling, family, and individual factors mitigating psychosocial effects of war on children. *Current Issues in Comparative Education, 2*(1), 23–42.

Freisthler, B., Merritt, D.H., and LaScala, E.A. (2006). Understanding the ecology of child maltreatment: A review of the literature and directions for future research. *Child Maltreatment, 11*(3), 263–280.

Freud, A., and Burlingham, D. (1943). *War and children.* New York: Ernst Willard.

Garbarino, J. (2001). Violent children: Where do we point the finger of blame? *Archives of Pediatrics and Adolescent Medicine, 155*(1), 17–23.

Garbarino, J., Kostelny, K., and Dubrow, N. (1991). *No place to be a child: Growing up in a war zone.* Toronto: Lexington.

Gunderson, L.H. (2000). Ecological resilience: In theory and application. *Annual Review of Ecology and Systematics, 31*, 425–439.

Hart, J. (2002). *Participation of conflict-affected children in humanitarian action: Learning from eastern Sri Lanka.* Oxford: Refugee Studies Centre.

Hart, J. (2003). *Participation of conflict-affected children in humanitarian action: Learning from Nepal.* Oxford: Refugee Studies Centre.

Hill, H.M., and Madhere, S. (1996). Exposure to community violence and African-American children: A multidimensional model of risk and resources. *Journal of Community Psychology, 24*, 26–43.

Hill, H.M., Levermore, M., Twaite, J., and Jones, L.P. (1996). Exposure to community violence and social support as predictors of anxiety and social emotional behavior among African-American children. *Journal of Child and Family Studies, 5*(4), 399–414.

Hobfoll, S.E. (2002). Social and psychological resources and adaptation. *Review of General Psychology, 6*(4), 307–324.

Honwana, A.M. (1997). Healing for peace: Traditional healers and post-war reconstruction in southern Mozambique. *Peace and Conflict: Journal of Peace Psychology, 3*(3), 293–305.

Hughes, H.M., Humphrey, N.N., and Weaver, T.L. (2005). Advances in violence and trauma: Toward comprehensive ecological models. *Journal of Interpersonal Violence, 20*(1), 31–38.

IASC (2006). IASC guidance on mental health and psychosocial support in emergency settings: Fourth working draft (peer review version).

Ispanovic-Radojkovic, V. (2003). Youth clubs: Psychosocial intervention with young refugees. *Intervention, 1*(3), 38–44.

Jaycox, L.H., Morse, L.K., Tanielian, T., and Stein, B.D. (2006) How schools can help students recover from traumatic experiences: A toolkit for supporting long-term recovery [electronic version]. Retrieved from www.rand.org/pubs/technical_reports/2006/RAND_TR413.pdf

Joshi, P.T., and O'Donnell, D.A. (2003). Consequences of child exposure to war and terrorism. *Clinical Child and Family Psychology Review, 6*(4), 275–292.

Jovanovic, N., Aleksandric, B.V., Dunkic, D., and Todorovic, V.S. (2004). Family hardiness and social support as predictors of posttraumatic stress disorder. *Psychiatry, Psychology, and Law, 11*(2), 263–268.

Kawachi, I., and Subramanian, S.V. (2006). Measuring and modeling the social and geographical context of trauma: A multilevel modeling approach. *Journal of Traumatic Stress, 19*(2), 195–203.

Khamis, V., Macy, R., and Coignez, V. (2004). *The impact of the classroom/community/camp-based intervention (CBI) program on Palestinian children.* Save the Children, USA.

Laor, N., Wolmer, L., and Cohen, D.J. (2001). Mother's functioning and children's symptoms 5 years after a SCUD missile attack. *American Journal of Psychiatry, 158*, 1020–1026.

Layne, C.M., Saltzman, W.R., Burlingame, G.M., Houston, R.F., and Pynoos, R.S. (2000). *Evaluation of program efficacy of UNICEF school-based psychosocial program for war-exposed adolescents as implemented during the 1999–2000 school year.* UNICEF.

Layne, C.M., Warren, J.S., Watson, P.J., Shalev, A.I., Friedman, T.M., Keane, T.M., et al. (2007). Risk, vulnerability, resistance, and resilience: Towards an integrative conceptualization of posttraumatic adaptation. In M.J. Friedman, T.M. Keane, and P.A. Resick (eds.) *Handbook of PTSD: Science and Practice.* New York: Guilford.

Loughry, M., and Eyber, C. (2004). *Psychosocial concepts in humanitarian work with children: A review of the concepts and related literature.* Washington, DC: National Academies Press.

Lustig, S.L., Kia-Keating, M., Grant-Knight, W., Geltman, P., Ellis, H., Kinzie, J.D., et al. (2004). Review of child and adolescent refugee mental health. *Journal of the American Academy of Child and Adolescent Psychiatry, 43*(1), 24–36.

Luthar, S.S., Cicchetti, D., and Becker, B. (2000). The construct of resilience: A critical evaluation and guidelines for future work. *Child Development, 71*(3), 543–562.

Lynch, M., and Cicchetti, D. (1998). An ecological-transactional analysis of children and contexts: The longitudinal interplay among child maltreatment, community violence, and children's symptomatology. *Developmental Psychopathology, 10*, 235–257.

McAdam-Crisp, J.L. (2006). Factors that can enhance and limit resilience for children at war. *Childhood, 13*(4), 459–477.

Macksoud, M.S. (1993). *Helping children cope with the stresses of war: A manual for parents and teachers.* UNICEF.

Marsden, R., and Strang, A. (2006). *Assessing psychosocial needs: What are we looking for and why? Assessing psychosocial needs in Sri Lanka post-tsunami.* Edinburgh: Institute of International Health and Development, Queen Margaret University College.

Masten, A.S. (2001). Ordinary magic: Resilience processes in development. *American Psychologist, 56*(3), 227–238.

Miller, V.W., and Affolter, F.W. (2002). *Helping children outgrow war.* USAID.

Morris, J., Van Ommeren, M., Belfer, M., Saxena, S., and Saraceno, B. (2007). Helping children in crisis: A child-focused review of the Sphere standard on mental and social aspects of health. *Disasters, 31*(1), 71–90.

Morrison, J.A. (2000). Protective factors associated with children's emotional responses to chronic community violence exposure. *Trauma, Violence and Abuse,* *1*(4), 299–320.

O'Donnell, D.A., Schwab-Stone, M., and Muyeed, A.Z. (2002). Multidimensional resilience in urban children exposed to community violence. *Child Development,* *73*(4), 1265–1282.

Örtengren, K. (2004). *The logical framework approach: A summary of the theory behind the LFA method.* Stockholm: Sida.

Portes, A. (1998). Social capital: Its origins and applications in modern sociology. *Annual Review of Sociology, 24,* 1–24.

Psychosocial Working Group (2003). *Psychosocial intervention in complex emergencies: A conceptual framework.* Oxford: Refugee Studies Centre.

Psychosocial Working Group (2004). *Considerations in planning psychosocial programs.* Oxford: Refugees Studies Centre.

Punamaki, R.L., Qouta, S., and el Sarraj, E. (1997). Models of traumatic experiences and children's psychological adjustment: The roles of perceived parenting and the children's own resources and activity. *Child Development, 68*(4), 718–728.

Qouta, S., Punamaki, R.L., and el Sarraj, E. (2005). Mother-child expression of psychological distress in war trauma. *Clinical Child Psychology and Psychiatry,* *10*(2), 135–156.

Runyan, D.K., Hunter, W.M., Socolar, R.R.S., Amaya-Jackson, L., English, D., Landsverk, J., et al. (1998). Children who prosper in unfavorable environments: The relationship to social capital. *Pediatrics, 101,* 12–18.

Rutter, M. (1999). Resilience concepts and findings: Implications for family therapy. *Journal of Family Therapy, 21,* 119–144.

Saltzman, W.R., Layne, C.M., Steinberg, A.M., Arslanagic, B., and Pynoos, R.S. (2003). Developing a culturally and ecologically sound intervention for youth exposed to war and terrorism. *Child and Adolescent Psychiatric Clinics of North America, 12,* 319–342.

Sandler, I. (2001). Quality and ecology of adversity as common mechanisms of risk and resilience. *American Journal of Community Psychology, 29*(1), 19–61.

Schwartz, D., Hopmeyer-Gorman, A., Toblin, R.L., and Abou-ezzeddine, T. (2003). Mutual antipathies in the peer group as a moderating factor in the association between community violence exposure and psychosocial maladjustment. *New Directions in Child and Adolescent Development, 102,* 39–54.

Shaw, J.A. (2003). Children exposed to war/terrorism. *Clinical Child and Family Psychology Review, 6*(4), 237–246.

Stein, B.D., Jaycox, L.H., Kataoka, S.H., Wong, M., Tu, W., Elliott, M.N., et al. (2003). A mental health intervention for schoolchildren exposed to violence: A randomized controlled trial. *Journal of the American Medical Association,* *290*(5), 603–611.

Stichick, T. (2001). The psychosocial impact of armed conflict on children: Rethinking traditional paradigms in research and intervention. *Child and Adolescent Psychiatric Clinics of North America, 10*(4), 797–814.

Stichick Betancourt, T. (2004). *Working paper #22: Connectedness, social support and mental health in adolescents displaced by the war in Chechnya.* Cambridge, MA: MIT-Mellon Program on NGOs and Forced Migration.

Summerfield, D. (2000). Childhood, war, refugeedom and "trauma": Three core questions for mental health professionals. *Transcultural Psychiatry, 37*(3), 417–433.

Susser, M., and Susser, E. (1996). Choosing a future for epidemiology: II. From black box to Chinese boxes and eco-epidemiology. *American Journal of Public Health, 86*(5), 674–677.

Thurman, T.R., Snider, L., Boris, N., Kalisa, E., Nkunda Mugarira, E., Ntaganira, J., et al. (2006). Psychosocial support and marginalization of youth-headed households in Rwanda. *AIDS Care, 18*(3), 220–229.

Tol, W.A., Reis, R., Susanty, D., Sivayokan, S., Sururu, A., and de Jong, J.T.V.M. (2007). Children and armed conflict in Burundi, Indonesia, and Sri Lanka: A qualitative ecological analysis of psychosocial impact and resources. Manuscript submitted for publication.

Tolfree, D. (1996). *Restoring playfulness: Different appoaches to assisting children who are psychologically affected by war or displacement*. Stockholm: Rädda Barnen.

UNICEF (2003). *The state of the world's children 2003*. New York: UNICEF.

Van der Linden, J., Drukker, M., Gunther, N., Feron, F., and Van Os, J. (2003). Children's mental health service use, neighborhood socioeconomic deprivation, and social capital. *Social Psychiatry and Psychiatric Epidemiology, 38*, 507–514.

Wallen, J., and Rubin, R.H. (1997). The role of the family in mediating the effects of community violence on children. *Aggression and Violent Behavior, 2*(1), 33–41.

Walsh, F. (1996). The concept of family resilience: Crisis and challenge. *Family Relations, 35*, 261–281.

Walsh, F. (2002). A family resilience framework: Innovative practice applications. *Family Relations, 51*, 130–137.

Wilson-Oyelaran, E.B. (1989). The ecological model and the study of child abuse in Nigeria. *Child Abuse and Negect, 13*, 379–387.

World Health Organization (WHO) (1990). *International classification of diseases: 10th revision*. Geneva: WHO.

Zielinski, D.S., and Bradshaw, C.P. (2005). Ecological influences on the sequelae of child maltreatment: A review of the literature. *Child Maltreatment, 11*(1), 49–62.

Chapter 11

Bolstering resilience

Benefiting from lessons learned

Donald Meichenbaum

Prologue

The central issue of this book is how to provide both prevention and treatment interventions designed to bolster resilience and build on existing and potential strengths in diverse, victimized, and high-risk groups of children, youth, families, and communities. What can be done at the primary prevention level, which focuses on the universal implementation of intervention for all children (for example, youth violence prevention, gun safety, and family strengthening interventions may reduce the risk of all children's exposure to psychological trauma and victimization)? What can be done at the secondary prevention level, which targets children and youth already at risk (for example, children who are living in high-risk poverty environments or high-risk situations with exposure to repeated natural disasters or ongoing violence)? What can be done at the tertiary level, which provides interventions for selected populations of children and youth who present with persistent needs and challenging behaviors, and who require comprehensive wrap-around services (for example, incarcerated youth who have a history of neglect and victimization, or children and youth who present with the psychiatric sequelae of sexual and physical abuse)?

The answers to these challenging questions should be informed by research on the developmental nature of risk and resilience, and studies that translate this research literature's findings into demonstrably effective methods of prevention and treatment. What are the lessons learned that should guide the development and evaluation of interventions addressing childhood victimization?

Lessons to be learned about resilience

First, there is a need to reduce or remove exposure to multiple risk factors, and a need to address the cumulative complex impact of multiple victimization experiences.

It is estimated that 25 percent of American youth experience serious traumatic events by their sixteenth birthday (Costello et al. 2002). Children and youth frequently experience different types of victimization on multiple occasions, rather than being exposed to singular experiences. There is an overlap of different types of victimization experiences, such as living in high-risk crime-saturated poverty areas, witnessing violence at home, or experiencing neglect and abuse. Most instances of exposure to violence occur within a youth's immediate environment (home, school, neighborhood) and are most often perpetrated by a family member or acquaintance (Finkelhor et al. 2005; Garbarino et al. 1992).

Second, there is a need to systematically assess for the cumulative exposure to adverse childhood experiences (Edwards et al. 2005; Finkelhor et al. 2005). Moreover, interventions to nurture resilience need to target multiple systems, including child welfare, children's mental health, public health, schools, social services, and juvenile justice.

Research indicates that it is the total number of risk factors present that is more important than the specificity of risk factors that impact developmental outcomes. Risk factors often co-occur and pile up over time. For example, Sameroff et al. (1992) studied the influence of social and family risk factors on the stability of intelligence from preschool to adolescence. They found that the pattern of risk was less important than the total amount of risk present in the child's life.

Third, there is a need to address explicitly the academic needs of victimized children, and work on enhancing their "school connectedness" or feeling of membership in the school they attend, by the use of mentoring programs (Dubois and Karcher 2005). Exposure to chronic traumatic stressors in the developing years can cause changes that impact memory and cognition. More specifically, exposure to violence can reduce the youth's ability to focus attention, organize and process information, as well as contribute to decreased IQ and reading ability, lower academic performance, increased days of school absence and decreased rates of high school graduation. The rates of suspensions and expulsions from school are also associated with the students' exposure to community violence (Wong et al. 2007). Moreover, low-income and ethnic minority youth disproportionately experience higher rates of violence with the consequent academic sequelae for which they usually do not receive intervention (Delaney-Black et al. 2002; Grogger 1997; Hurt et al. 2001). Violence exposure is associated with higher rates of school suspensions and expulsions and lower rates of attendance.

Fourth, there is a need to provide traumatized children with skills training to compensate for self-regulatory deficits, and with "metacognitive prosthetic devices" to compensate for the neurobiological deficits that follow chronic traumatic experiences (Ford 2005). Exposure to recurrent or prolonged trauma, especially if the onset occurs during early childhood, can cause neurobiological changes such as alterations in the volume and activity levels of major brain structures, such as the corpus callosum, and the limbic system;

impairment of the left hemisphere cortical functioning; altered hypothalamic–pituitary axis functioning and increased hypersensitivity to cortisol levels; and increased sympathetic nervous system activity (De Bellis 2002).

Such bodily changes can result in exaggerated startle responses, PTSD, a compromised immune system, increased vulnerability to depression and a failure to develop self-regulatory functions, especially in the development of language, attentional and memory capabilities (Curtis and Cicchetti 2003; De Bellis 2002; De Bellis et al. 1999; Fletcher 1996; Streech-Fisher and Van der Kolk 2000).

Metacognitive supports may include the use of advanced organizers, memory prompts, self-instructional training, and other forms of cognitive-behavioral interventions (described on www.teachsafeschools.org). In addition, there is a need to reduce high-risk behaviors that can lead to revictimization, such as substance abuse, aggressive behaviors, sensation-seeking behaviors, and sexual acting-out behaviors (Alvord and Grados 2005; Grotberg 2003).

Fifth, helpers need to make special efforts to develop and monitor a collaborative therapeutic alliance with traumatized youth and address behaviors that interfere with therapy (Bertolino 2003; Miller et al. 2007). Trauma exposure can have a negative impact on the development of attachment behaviors. For example, abused teenage girls are more likely to hold in their feelings and have extreme emotional reactions. They have fewer adaptive coping strategies and have problems handling strong emotions, particularly anger. They have limited expectations that others can be of help. They show deficits in the ability to self-soothe and modulate negative emotions (Berman et al. 1996; Haggerty et al. 1996; Kendler et al. 2000). As Masten and Reed (2002, p. 95) observe:

> The best documented asset of resilience is a strong bond to a competent caring adult, which need not be a parent. For children who do not have such an adult involved in their lives, it is the first order of business. Children also need opportunities to experience success at all ages.

Sixth, there is a need to incorporate into resilience-bolstering interventions the attributes and circumstances that can contribute to people's abilities to cope effectively in the face of adversities and difficulties. Not all children and youth who are exposed to traumatic events develop behavioral and mental health problems. In fact, resilience appears to be the general rule of adaptation. This conclusion holds whether the children who are studied have experienced premature birth, physical illness or surgery, maltreatment (abuse or neglect), are the offspring of mentally ill, alcoholic, or criminally involved parents, are exposed to marital discord, domestic violence, poverty, or the trauma of war or natural disasters (DeAngelis 2007; Masten 2001, 2004; Masten and Gewirtz 2006). As Bernard (1995) observes, between half and two-thirds of children living in such extreme circumstances grow up and "overcome the odds", going on to achieve successful and well-adjusted lives.

The Search Institute (www.Search-Institute.org) has enumerated some forty developmental assets that are the building blocks of positive youth development. Interventions should nurture these assets, some of which are listed here:

- A commitment to learning, a motivation to do well in school, feeling connected to school, participating in school activities, completing homework, reading for pleasure.
- Positive values and a prosocial attitude of being empathic, understanding, honest, and responsible, and practicing self-restraint with regard to addictive substances and sexual activity.
- Social competence, as reflected in the ability to resolve conflicts peacefully, resist negative peer pressure and make friends.
- Positive identity, which includes assets such as having high self-esteem, a sense of purpose in life, and plans for the future.

Resilience is not a trait that a child is born with or automatically keeps once it is achieved. Resilience is a complex interactive process that entails characteristics of the child, the family, extra-familial relationships, and school and community factors.

Seventh, when considering the features of so-called resilient children, it is important to keep in mind that children may be resilient in one domain of their lives, but not in other areas (e.g. academic, social, self-regulating behaviors). As Zimmerman and Arunkumar (1994) observe:

> Resilience is not a universal construct that applies to all life domains . . . [children] may be resilient to specific risk conditions, but quite vulnerable to others . . . [Resilience] is a multidimensional phenomenon that is context specific and involves developmental changes.
>
> (p. 4)

Resilience should be viewed as being 'fluid over time'. The relative importance of risk and protective factors changes at various stages of life. A child who may be resilient at one developmental stage may not necessarily be resilient at the next one. Developmental transition points at school, and during puberty are particularly sensitive times for the impact of traumas. Protective efforts at bolstering resilience should be sensitive to these developmentally vulnerable periods.

Eighth, the factors that influence resilience differ for males and females, and interventions need to be gender-sensitive. Protective factors differ across gender, race, and culture. For instance, girls tend to bolster their resilience by building strong, caring relationships, while boys are more likely to build resilience by learning active problem-solving (Bernard 1995). Further evidence that resilience may have gender differences comes from the longitudinal research by Werner and Smith (1992), who found that scholastic competence at age 10 was more strongly associated with successful transition to adult responsibilities for men than for women. In contrast, factors such as high self-esteem, self-efficacy, and a sense of personal control were more predictive of successful adaptation among the women than the men. In the stress domain, males were more vulnerable to separation and loss of caregivers in the first decade of life, while girls were more vulnerable to family discord and loss in the second decade of life.

Another source of variability to be considered in resilience-based interventions is the cultural background. For instance, Kataoka et al. (2006) provide a description of how a culturally sensitive faith-based community intervention can be used to bolster the resilience of children who have been exposed to neighborhood violence. They combined an evidence-based intervention (Cognitive-Behavioral Intervention for Trauma in Schools – CBITS) with spirituality, as reflected in the use of the religious coping strategies of prayer, religious relaxation imagery and local faith-based healers. As one mother commented, "My boy was very afraid and from that day he was terrorized. He wouldn't go outside. I remember at night he would pray and ask Jesus to give him comfort" (Kataoka et al. 2006, p. 90). Nonetheless, faith and spirituality operate as a stronger protective factor in some cultures than in others.

Ninth, it is important for mental health care providers to build upon the specific positive behaviors and coping techniques that individuals already use to deal with suffering and disability, and capitalize on, and nurture their innate self-healing capacities. Health care providers can aid survivors in enhancing their coping skills by pointing out techniques, already in place that they have utilized in the recovery process.

There are multiple pathways to resilience. Resilient children and youth possess multiple skills in varying degrees that help them cope with adversities. These response skills can be strengthened, as well as learned. Among other skills resilient individuals make wise choices and they take advantage of opportunities (e.g. continuing their education, learning new skills, joining the military, choosing healthy life partners, and breaking away from deviant peers) (Werner and Smith 2001).

To help survivors, health care providers can encourage and recommend altruistic behaviors, independent activities, and the use of spirituality. By helping others, survivors are in effect helping themselves. Encouraging independent activities, such as schoolwork, or work in general, enhances the recovery process. Using spirituality, survivors can reclaim values, and foster meaning and hope (Kataoka et al. 2006; Mollica 2006).

For example, at a recent clinical consultation, a youth who had a remarkable history of victimization was encouraged and challenged to use his talent and interest in poetry as a form of healing and a way to transform his life. There is a need to help victimized youth use their "islands of competence" to foster a sense of accomplishment.

Finally, most victimized children and youth do not receive services, and very few are treated with evidence-based interventions. For example, only 25 per cent of children with emotional and behavioral problems in the United States receive specific mental health services.

The hopeful news is that there are now several evidence-based interventions that have been employed successfully with traumatized children. Schools are the best settings to identify at-risk children, and provide mental health interventions (Alvord and Grados 2005; Battistich et al. 1996; Cohen et al. 2006; Cowen 2000; Doll and Lyon 1998; Eber et al. 1996; Ennett et al. 2003; Huang et al. 2005; Jennings et al. 2000; Rutter et al. 1979; Stein et al. 2003; Tobler and Stratton 1997; Weisz et al. 2005; Wong et al. 2007).

Conclusion

The research literature on resilience in children has yielded important lessons and guidelines to follow when implementing prevention and treatment interventions. But it will take more than research to bolster the resilience of victimized children. It will take political leadership and public commitment.

References

Alvord, M.K., and Grados, J.J. (2005). Enhancing resilience in children: A proactive approach. *Professional Psychology: Research and Practice, 36*, 238–245.

Battistich, V., Scheps, E., Watson, W., and Solomon, D. (1996). Preventative effects for the Child Development Project. *Journal of Applied Developmental Psychology, 11*, 12–35.

Berman, S.L., Kurtines, W.M., Silverman, W.K., and Serafini, L.T. (1996). The impact of exposure to crime and violence on urban youth. *American Journal of Orthopsychiatry, 66*, 329–336.

Bernard, B. (1995). *Fostering resiliency in kids: Protective factors in the family, school and community.* San Francisco, CA: Far West Laboratory for Educational Research and Development.

Bertolino, B. (2003). *Change-oriented therapy with adolescents and young adults.* New York: Norton.

Cohen, J.A., Mannarino, A.P., and Deblinger, E. (2006). *Treating trauma and traumatic grief in children and adolescents.* New York: Guilford.

Costello, E.J., Erkanli, A., Fairbank, J.A., and Angold, A. (2002). The prevalence of potentially traumatic events in childhood and adolescence. *Journal of Traumatic Stress, 15*(2), 99–112.

Cowen, E. (2000). Psychological wellness: Some hopes for the future. In D. Cicchetti, J. Rappaport, I. Sandler, and R.P. Weissberg (eds.), *The promotion of wellness in adolescents* (pp. 477–503). Washington, DC: Child Welfare League of America Press.

Curtis, W.J., and Cicchetti, D. (2003). Moving research on resilience into the 21st century: Theoretical and methodological considerations in examining biological contributions to resilience. *Development and Psychopathology, 15*, 773–810.

DeAngelis, T. (2007). A new diagnosis for childhood trauma? *Monitor on Psychology, 38*(3), 32–34.

De Bellis, M.D. (2002). Developmental traumatology. *Psychoneuroendocrinology, 27*, 155–170.

De Bellis, M.D., Baum, A.S., Birmaher, B., Keshavan, M.S., Eccard, C.H., Boring, A.M., et al. (1999). Developmental traumatology. Part 1: Biological stress systems. *Biological Psychiatry, 45*(10), 1259–1270.

Delaney-Black,V., Covington, C., Ondersma, S.J., Nordstrom-Klee, B., Templin, T., Ager, J., et al. (2002) Violence exposure, trauma, and IQ and/or reading deficits among urban children. *Archives of Pediatrics and Adolescent Medicine, 156*(3), 280–285.

Doll, B., and Lyon, M.A. (1998). Risk and resilience: Implications for delivery of educational and mental health services in schools. *School Psychology Review, 27*, 348–363.

Dubois, D.L., and Karcher, M.J. (eds.) (2005). *Handbook of youth mentoring.* Thousand Oaks, CA: Sage.

Eber, L., Osuch, R., and Reddott, C. (1996). School-based application of the wrap-around process: Early results in service provision and student outcomes. *Journal of Child and Family Studies, 5*, 83–99.

Edwards, V.J., Anda, R.F., Dube, S.R., Dong, M., Chapman, D.P., and Felitti, V.J. (2005). The wide-ranging health outcomes of adverse childhood experiences. In K.A. Kendall-Tackett and S.M. Giaromoni (eds.), *Child victimization* (pp. 8–12). Kingston, NJ: Civic Research Institute.

Ennett, S.T., Ringwalt, C.L., Thorne, J., Rohrbach, L.A., Vincus A., Simons-Rudolph A., et al. (2003). A comparison of current practice in school-based substance use prevention programs with meta-analysis findings. *Prevention Science, 4*(1), 1–14.

Finkelhor, D., Ormrod, R., Turner, H., and Hamby, S.L. (2005). The victimization of children and youth: A comprehensive national survey. *Child Maltreatment, 10*(1), 5–25.

Fletcher, K.E. (1996). Childhood posttraumatic stress disorder. In E. Mash and R. Barkley (eds.), *Child psychopathology* (pp. 242–276). New York: Guilford.

Ford, J.D. (2005). Treatment implications of altered neurobiology, affect regulation and information processing following child maltreatment. *Psychiatric Annals, 35*, 410–419.

Garbarino, J., Dubrow, N., Kostelny, K., and Pardo, C. (1992). *Children in danger: Coping with the consequences of community violence.* San Francisco, CA: Jossey-Bass.

Grogger, J. (1997). Local violence and educational attainment. *Journal of Human Resources, 32*, 659–682.

Grotberg, E.H. (ed.) (2003). *Resilience for today: Gaining strength from adversity.* Westport, CT: Praeger.

Haggerty, J., Sherrod, L., Garmezy, N., and Rutter, M. (1996). *Stress, risk and resilience in children and adolescents.* New York: Cambridge University Press.

Huang, L., Stoul, B., Friedman, R., Mrazek, P., Friesen, B., Pires, S., et al. (2005).

Transforming mental health care for children and their families. *American Psychologist, 60*(6), 615–627.

Hurt, H., Malmud, E., Brodsky, N.L., and Giannetta, J. (2001). Exposure to violence: Psychological and academic correlates in child witnesses. *Archives of Pediatrics and Adolescent Medicine, 155,* 351–356.

Jennings, J., Pearson, G., and Harris, M. (2000). Implementing and maintaining school-based mental health services in a large urban school district. *Journal of School Health, 70,* 201–205.

Kataoka, S.H., Fuentes, S., O'Donoghue, V.P., Castillo-Campos, P., Bonilla, A., Halsey, K., et al. (2006). A community participatory research partnership: The development of a faith-based intervention for children exposed to violence. *Ethnicity and Disease, 16*(1), 89–97.

Kendler, K.S., Bulik, C.M., Silberg, J., Hettema, J.M., Myers, J., and Prescott, C.A. (2000). Childhood sexual abuse and adult psychiatric and substance abuse disorders in women: An epidemiological and co-twin control analysis. *Archives of General Psychiatry, 57*(10), 953–959.

Masten, A.S. (2001). Ordinary magic: Resilience processes in development. *American Psychologist, 56,* 227–238.

Masten, A.S. (2004). Regulatory processes, risk and resilience in adolescent development. *Annals of the New York Academy of Sciences, 1021,* 310–319.

Masten, A.S., and Gewirtz, A.H. (2006). Resilience in development: The importance of early childhood. In R.E. Tremblay, R.E. Barr, and D.V. Peters (eds.), *Encyclopedia on early childhood development* (pp. 1–6). Retrived from Centre of Excellence for Early Childhood Development website (www.excellence-earlychildhood.ca/documents/masten-gewirtzangxp.pdf).

Masten, A.S., and Reed, M.G. (2002). Resilience in development. In S.R. Snyder and S.J. Lopez (eds.), *The handbook of positive psychology.* Oxford: Oxford University Press.

Miller, A.L., Rathus, J.H., and Linehan, M.M. (2007). *Dialetical behavior therapy with suicidal adolescents.* New York: Guilford.

Mollica, R.F. (2006). *Healing invisible wounds: Paths to hope and recovery in a violent world.* New York: Harcourt.

Rutter, M.B., Maughan, P., Mortimore, J., Ouston, J., and Smith, A. (1979). *Fifteen thousand hours.* Cambridge, MA: Harvard University Press.

Sameroff, A.J., Seifer, R., Baldwin, A., and Baldwin, C. (1992). Stability of intelligence from preschool to adolescence: The influence of social and family risk factors. *Child Development, 64,* 80–97.

Stein, B.D., Jaycox, L.H., Kataoka, S.H., Wong, M., Tu, W., Elliott, M.N., et al. (2003). A mental health intervention for schoolchildren exposed to violence: A randomized controlled trial. *Journal of the American Medical Association, 290*(5), 603–611.

Streech-Fisher, A., and Van der Kolk, B.A. (2000). Down will come baby, cradle and all: Diagnostic and therapeutic implications of chronic trauma on child development. *Australian and New Zealand Journal of Psychiatry, 34,* 903–918.

Tobler, N.S., and Stratton, H.H. (1997). Effectiveness of school-based drug prevention programs: A meta-analysis of the research. *Journal of Primary Prevention, 18,* 71–128.

Weisz, J.R., Sandler, I.N., Durlak, J.A., and Anton, B.S. (2005). Promoting and protecting youth mental health through evidence-based prevention and treatment. *American Psychologist, 60*(6), 628–648.

Werner, E.E., and Smith, R. (1992). *Vulnerable but invincible: A longitudinal study of resilient children and youth.* New York: Adams, Bannistar and Cox.

Werner, E.E., and Smith, R. (2001). *Journeys from childhood to midlife: Risk, resilience, and recovery.* Ithaca, NY: Cornell University Press.

Wong, M., Rosemond, M.E., Stein, B.D., Langley, A.K., Kataoka, S.H., and Nadeem, E. (2007). School-based mental health intervention for adolescents exposed to violence. *The Prevention Researcher, 14*(1), 17–20.

Zimmerman, M.A., and Arunkumar, R. (1994). Resiliency research: Implications for schools and policy. *Social Policy Report of the SRCD, 8,* 1–17.

Part III

Recovery

Empirically based systemic
interventions for traumatized
children

Chapter 12

Prevention and treatment interventions for traumatized children

Restoring children's capacities for self-regulation

Julian D. Ford, David B. Albert, and Josephine Hawke

As a result of their sensitized biological alarm systems, traumatized children (as well as their directly or indirectly traumatized caregivers; see Chapter 4 by Cohen in this volume) often have difficulty identifying and reacting to stressors. They may overreact to perceived threats when, objectively speaking, a threat is minor or even nonexistent. Conversely, they may "shut down" in the face of an actual threat. They may feel chronically aroused, or they may have difficulty identifying how they are feeling. When faced with uncomfortable affect states, they may lack the internal resources to change how they are feeling. As a result, older children and adolescents may begin relying on the assistance of alcohol, drugs, or other potentially harmful means to modulate their feelings. Therefore, prevention and treatment interventions for post-traumatic dysregulation should, in a developmentally appropriate manner, guide both the child and caregiver(s) in learning and becoming familiar and skillful in using self-regulation skills. They should also provide the child and the caregivers with a framework within which to understand symptoms and problems as having developed as a trajectory in which self-protection has overshadowed healthy development – and therefore as a path that, if changed gradually by learning and using self-regulation skills, can be shifted back toward the original developmental trajectory of personal growth. Thus, skills and perspectives acquired in psychoeducation or psychotherapy for trauma-tized children and caregivers are a way of reclaiming the child's strengths and capacities rather than repairing deficits.

While drawing on the risk, protective, and resistance/resilience factors for children exposed to psychological trauma described in previous sections of this book, we will focus on a theoretical model of posttraumatic self-regulation that emphasizes *trajectories* of change. We use the term "trajector-ies" in several ways in this chapter, depending on whether we are discussing normal development or posttraumatic or psychological problems or recovery. The common denominator is that "trajectory" refers to a pathway of change over time that, if identified, can be intentionally modified with intervention. We will describe how the model has been operationalized clinically in proven or promising empirically based prevention and treatment interventions, including our intervention research with children, adolescents, and families in the child welfare, mental health, and juvenile justice systems.

Self-(dys)regulation as a common feature underlying posttraumatic trajectories

In order to understand the role of psychological trauma and posttraumatic stress, resistance, and resilience in forming or deforming childhood developmental and pathological trajectories, self-regulation offers an organizing framework. Despite controversy about the role that traumatic stress plays in the etiology of psychiatric disorders (Edwards et al. 2003; Seedat et al. 2003), posttraumatic deficits in self-regulation capacities have been implicated in numerous childhood psychiatric disorders, including anxiety disorders (Cortes et al. 2005), mood disorders (Stuewig and McCloskey 2005), and disruptive behavior disorders (Ford et al. 2000). Impulse and emotion (dys)regulation profoundly influences healthy, pathological, and posttraumatic childhood trajectories (Campos et al. 1989; McFarlane 2000; Riggs et al. 2003; Widiger and Samuel 2005). Relational self-regulation ("attachment") underlies the acquisition of impulse/affect regulation, as well as laying the foundation for social competence (Bowlby 1969). Childhood exposure to developmentally adverse interpersonal psychological trauma fundamentally compromises self-regulation (Cicchetti and Toth 1995; Ford 2005; Van der Kolk et al. 2005).

Young infants enter the world with relatively few strategies for modulating arousal, primarily non-nutritive sucking and gaze aversion (Mangelsdorf et al. 1995). As infants mature, they develop an expanded repertoire of self-regulation strategies (Kopp 1989). While there are temperamental individual differences in infants' emotion-regulation capacities, self-regulation is malleable in childhood (Kopp 1989) on the basis of experience-dependent change in cognitive, motoric, and social capacities (Campos et al. 1989).

A child's developmental trajectory can be viewed as the progressive achievement or impairment (when inborn or environmental adversities interfere) of self-regulation competencies that become more fully elaborated and mastered over the course of childhood and adolescence. Psychological trauma is one of many environmental adversities that may alter a healthy developmental trajectory and lead to a pathological one. However, psychological trauma is relatively unique among all the environmental adversities in that it tends to rapidly and automatically elicit changes in self-regulation that are helpful for surviving life-threatening harm but detrimental to ordinary psychosocial functioning (e.g. extremes of arousal, detachment from social relationships).

Traumatic stress may interfere with growth and development in any or all of these domains. Young children (birth to preschool age) are especially vulnerable to the effects of chronic exposure to traumatic stress. Very young children must rely upon caregiver(s) for assistance in self-soothing when uncomfortably aroused. Such "co-regulation" is the first phase in achieving self-regulation (Mikulincer et al. 2003). Co-regulation depends upon and enhances attachment, and has been referred to as the dyadic regulation of emotion (Sroufe 1996). Schore (2001) describes caregivers as the "external psychobiological regulator of the 'experience-dependent' growth of the infant's nervous system." If a caregiver is too stressed (e.g. due to socio-economic adversity, family conflict, or trauma) or temperamentally unable to engage in co-regulation, the child must cope with her or his own shifting arousal states and with the effect of the caregiver's unmodulated arousal states. Schore (2001) argues that early life deficits in co-regulation may lead to a "chaotic alteration" of the neurobiological network responsible for emotion processing, such that affect regulation is lastingly compromised.

The neurobiological mechanisms underlying impaired self-regulation include the body's systems for arousal and healing (e.g. the hypothalamic-pituitary-adrenal axis and immune system; Heim and Nemeroff 2001; Kaufman et al. 2001), threat detection (e.g. the amygdala; Schmahl et al. 2003), and memory organization and retrieval (e.g. hippocampus, prefrontal cortex; Pederson et al. 2004; Schmahl et al. 2003; Tupler and De Bellis 2006). These are the same neurobiological systems that serve as a foundation for healthy self-regulation; thus, the psychobiological competencies that underlie self-regulation (i.e. emotion/arousal and relational regulation; information processing) are likely to be undermined by developmentally adverse trauma (Ford 2005). Children have a remarkable ability to adapt when challenged by traumatic stressors. However, adaptation to developmentally adverse trauma comes at a cost: heightened risk of biological/affective/behavioral dysregulation that occurs because bodily responses to traumatic stressors essentially involve the activation of an internal alarm system that, if triggered by repetitive survival threats, continues to be activated (or has a greatly reduced threshold for reactivation) long after the stressor is no longer present. It is as if the body cannot stop attempting to detect and mobilize to respond to threats – as if the "alarm" will not turn off or gets turned on by even minor stressors, events, or bodily states.

In this posttraumatic "alarm" state, ordinary self-regulatory processes are disrupted because perception, emotion, memory, and decision-making have become narrowly focused on detecting and reacting to ill-defined external threats (Mason et al. 2002) instead of the normal developmental tasks of creative exploration and play, learning and remembering, and consciously planning and pursuing goals. The problem is not only persistent anxiety, but a disorganization of or "oscillation" between extreme states of confusion and distress – like living with an inner alarm that the child and caregivers neither understand nor know how to self/co-regulate (Antelman et al. 1997). This dysregulated "alarm" state may involve addictive cravings (Jacobsen et al. 2001), pain (Price 2000), aggression (Davidson et al. 2000), despair (Hindmarch 2001), or dissociation (Sar et al. 2001).

With self-regulation as an organizing framework, interventions for trauma-tized children can be understood as ways of assisting the social support system (e.g. parents, teachers, therapists, peers) to provide the child with co-regulation through experiences that jointly involve:

- balancing arousal with focused attention
- recognizing specific traumatic stress reactions and trigger stimuli
- identifying and experimenting with self-relevant emotions, thoughts, goals, and actions
- achieving a sense of accomplishment and personal worth.

In essence, treatment and prevention might be conceptualized as enabling children to gain conscious control over their neurobiological "alarm" systems, which were sensitized by developmentally adverse traumas but now (with the important exception of children still in danger, e.g. ongoing domestic or community violence) are highly reactive to sub-traumatic stressors (Ford 2005). Risk factors may increase, and protective factors may mitigate further exposure to trauma and the severity of trauma-related reactivity – thereby disrupting self-regulation and reducing posttraumatic resistance, resilience, and recovery. Thus, trajectories of posttraumatic adaptation may be thought of as patterns of either increased (i.e. resistance, resilience, recovery) or decreased (i.e. deterioration, morbidity) self-regulation, with risk and protective factors driving the direction and slope of change.

Impact of traumatic stress on children's development of self-regulatory capacities

Trauma occurs in the lives of 25 percent (Costello et al. 2002) to 43 percent (Silverman et al. 1996) of children in the United States, and is even more prevalent in many developing countries (e.g. 80 percent among South African and Kenyan tenth graders (15–16 year olds); Seedat et al. 2004). In a nation-ally representative sample of 2–17 year olds, almost three-quaters reported at least one form of victimization in the past year and almost one-quater reported four or more types (i.e. poly-victimization; Finkelhor et al. 2007). Poly-victimization was associated with particularly severe traumatic stress symptoms and functional (i.e. self-regulatory) impairment.

In the United States, PTSD is rare among young children (ages 0–4; about 1 child in every 167) and school-age and adolescent children (about 1 child in every 100; Egger and Angold 2006), compared to adults (about 4 adults in every 100; Kessler et al. 2005). Comparable estimates are just under 1 percent of Puerto Rican children (Canino et al. 2004) and just over 1 percent of Bangaladeshi children (although those living in slums were more likely to have PTSD, 3.2 percent; Mullick and Goodman 2005). Prevalence estimates were higher (7.6 percent) in a more recent survey of adolescents, more than half of whom were directly or indirectly exposed to terrorist incidents (Pat-Horenczyk et al. 2007a). Other studies found PTSD to be less common, affecting only 1 percent of British (Meltzer et al. 2003) and Brazilian (Goodman et al. 2005) children. In addition to PTSD, children exposed to psychological trauma are at risk for varied functional impairments due to both internalizing (e.g. depression; Finkelhor et al. 2007) and externalizing (e.g. risk taking; Pat-Horenczyk et al. 2007) behavior problems.

Evidence from retrospective studies such as the Adverse Childhood Experiences Study (Edwards et al. 2003), and prospective studies of posttraumatic change in childhood (Cortes et al. 2005), suggest that each trauma survivor varies substantially over her or his lifespan in psychosocial resistance to trauma, and recovery from posttraumatic stress (Layne et al., Chapter 2 in this volume). We hypothesize that children who are able to modulate acute stress reactions and continue (or resume) self-regulating psychobiologically are resistant/resilient – and therefore that enhancing self-regulation is a primary goal for effective interventions.

In considering how trauma-resistant/resilient children may differ from children whose functional capacities are overwhelmed by trauma, we will focus on trajectories of adaptation over time rather than on static outcomes at any time-point. Following the model of Layne and colleagues (Chapter 2 in this volume), we will consider:

- *resistance:* maintaining functionality and self-regulation
- *resilience:* transient loss followed by regaining of functionality and self-regulation
- *remission:* chronic posttraumatic dysregulation followed by recovery of adequate, although not necessarily equivalent to premorbid, functionality.

Adult trauma survivors have been shown to follow several distinct trajectories in the course of their lives depending, on fluctuations in the nature and severity of their symptoms and functioning (e.g. minimal, moderate, or severe impairment; Breslau et al. 2004). It is likely that child trauma survivors also experience differing trajectories that are complicated by age-dependent developmental processes. Empirical verification of this hypothesis with longitudinal prospective studies of children is needed. If correct, the trajectory hypothesis implies that assessing symptoms and functioning only at arbitrary time (e.g. at the beginning of an episode of treatment and again following the conclusion of treatment) will understate or entirely miss key changes in children's posttraumatic trajectories. In designing and evaluating prevention and treatment interventions for traumatized children, trajectories of pre- and posttraumatic symptoms, functioning, and development must therefore be assessed as an alternative to static "snapshots" of a child's current symptoms or functioning.

Trajectories of development, psychopathology, and posttraumatic self-regulation

One in two Americans will meet the criteria for a psychiatric disorder at some point in their lives; more than half of them will have an anxiety disorder, including PTSD (7 percent overall prevalence; Kessler et al. 2005). First onset of single psychiatric disorders usually occurs in childhood, while adult onset psychiatric disorders tend to be comorbidities of existing disorders (Kessler et al. 2005). In infancy, temperamental reactivity, withdrawal, and poor attention control place children at risk for problematic anxiety as toddlers, but only if their primary caregiver is disengaged or insensitive (Crockenberg and Leerkes 2006). Another study found that some risk or protective factors for externalizing and internalizing problems are associated with or buffer against a trajectory of increasing problems from kindergarten to early adolescence (Lansford et al. 2006) for externalizing problems (male gender, African American ethnicity; poverty; poor early childhood social competence, and harsh, absent, or poorly informed parenting in early adolescence) and internalizing problems (poverty, poor early childhood social competence, non-proactive parenting). Thus, regardless of trauma, some risk and protective factors are associated with problematic childhood trajectories.

In addition, psychological trauma may make other risk and protective factors particularly salient. Lansford et al. (2006) identified risk and protective factors for problem trajectories that applied only to maltreated children. Unilateral parental decision-making was associated with a trajectory of increasing externalizing problems only if a child had been maltreated. Similarly, family stress and dispositional hostility were related to a trajectory of increasing internalizing problems only for maltreated children. While requiring replication (e.g. with other forms of trauma and positive as well as problematic forms of adaptation; across geographic areas and socioeconomic strata), these findings suggest that the effects of risk and protective factors on children's developmental trajectories may be moderated by trauma.

Similarly, research indicates that combinations of psychiatric disorders (comorbidity) are not static, but fluctuate during childhood and adulthood. Epidemiological studies show that changes in one disorder can be accompanied by homotypic or heterotypic shifts across disorders, as well as for sub-threshold conditions or symptoms (Costello et al. 2003; Lewinsohn et al. 2004; Wittchen et al. 2000). Psychosocial impairment related to comorbidity may change as well, not only due to the identified primary disorders but also due to a waxing or waning of sub-threshold conditions (Lewinsohn et al. 2004) or longstanding personality disorders (Shea et al. 2004). These findings raise the fundamental question of how emotional and behavioral problems wax and wane from less severe, isolated problems to complex pervasive disorders, and how psychological trauma may affect trajectories of psychopathology. Interventions to prevent or treat posttraumatic impairment in childhood may be less than optimally effective if they do not address trajectories of risk, impairment, protective factors and resilience.

Research and clinical observations concerning possible trajectories of symptoms and impairment following exposure to trauma in childhood are sparse, but suggest that there are several potential trajectories that may be associated with risk and protective factors and functional outcomes before, during, and after trauma (McFarlane 2000). Perkonigg et al. (2005) conducted the Early Developmental Stages of Psychopathology study with a community sample of 14–24 year olds, and found that only half of the 125 cases of PTSD remitted during a 3–4-year follow-up. Exposure to new traumas in the follow-up period and avoidant symptoms or comorbid somatoform or anxiety disorders at baseline distinguished those with chronic PTSD; those who remitted reported less severe PTSD symptoms and a greater sense of self-competence at baseline. Schell et al. (2004) reported a similar decline in PTSD symptoms among young adults exposed to community violence, but found hyperarousal rather than avoidance to be the symptoms most predictive of chronicity. Thus, the role of trauma exposure and PTSD symptoms in trajectories of change remains of great interest but largely unknown. Further, the absence of additional repeated assessments over a longer time period rule out definitive conclusions as to whether the observed effects reflect fluctuating symptoms that could be characterized as distinct trajectories of change.

Recently, the US Homeless Families study explicitly identified trajectories of change in PTSD symptoms among homeless women caring for children across several repeated assessments over fifteen months. Independent of interventions received in the study, five statistically distinguishable patterns of change over time were documented, including four with relatively unchanging symptoms at low, mild, moderate and high severity levels, and one with initial moderately severe symptoms which improved over time (Sacks et al., in review; see also Orcutt et al. 2004). The distinguishing characteristics of women in the improved trajectory subgroup were achieving employment and stable residence with children living at home, and low levels of perceived relationship conflict. Paradoxically, the women whose PTSD symptoms improved over time tended *not* to be receiving services for mental health or trauma problems. Sacks et al. (in review) interpret this finding as meaning that trauma or mental health services for homeless mothers need to focus explicitly on increasing resilience (i.e. improved income, stable safe residence, unification with children) and reducing risk (e.g. ameliorating support system conflict), particularly when the mother suffers from chronic and severe PTSD.

Trajectories of change in traumatic stress symptoms among children are less well documented. Patterson's (1993) research suggests a trajectory of deterioration beginning with early childhood internalizing problems (depression, anxiety) and followed sequentially by escalating externalizing problems (e.g. inattention, oppositionality, impulsiveness), social isolation and deviant peer group affiliations, and ultimately conduct disorder. Ford (2002) described how traumatic victimization could be either a contributor to or result of further escalation at any point in the development of this trajectory (Ford et al. 2000), though prospective studies testing this hypothesis are needed. Other studies document a trajectory of chronic traumatic stress and deteriorating functioning. For example, permissive or hostile parenting styles have been found to be associated with deterioration in traumatic stress and socioeducational adaptation, while authoritative parenting, by contrast, was related to stable adjustment, among children living in violent families (Rea and Rossman 2005).

Helping children and caregivers move from reactivity to regulation

How, then, can prevention and treatment interventions guide traumatized children and caregiver(s) in learning and becoming familiar and skillful in using self-regulation skills? We will describe a framework for psychoeducation and psychotherapy designed to help children and caregivers to understand symptoms and problems as having developed as a trajectory in which self-protection has overshadowed healthy development – and therefore as a path that can be changed gradually by learning and using self-regulation skills. This approach shifts the focus of intervention from repairing damage or deficits (of the child or caregiver) to assisting each of them in reclaiming and building their psychosocial capacities.

Phase-oriented prevention and treatment interventions for traumatized children

In order to enable children and caregivers to initiate (or resume) a life trajectory leading to increased self-regulation, there is wide acceptance of and a growing evidence base to support a phase-oriented approach to prevention or treatment interventions (Ford et al. 2005). Phase one focuses on enhancing safety and stabilization by enhancing affect dysregulation, impulse control, safety (in relation to self and others), reflective thinking (versus pathological dissociation), and healthy relationships. Phase two involves processing trauma-related emotions, cognitive schemas, and memories, and developing a more coherent, integrated life narrative that charts a course for a trajectory of posttraumatic growth. Phase three addresses the challenges posed by adopting a different life trajectory in social, vocational, recreational, and spiritual pursuits. We next apply the three-phase model to traumatized children.

Especially for children who may have yet to develop the cognitive or developmental capacities to make sense of their traumatic experiences and to integrate them into their life stories, posttraumatic decline is persistent, recurrent, and difficult to transform into growth. Consequently, phase-oriented treatment often takes the form of a recursive spiral (Kepner 1995; Vila et al. 1999) in which the therapist guides the child and caregivers in sustaining (or regaining) self-regulation during periods of fluctuating rather than static risk and protective factors, and ebbing and flowing resistance, resilience, and recovery. The therapist must be aware of trajectories that are influenced by the dynamic nature and interaction of many ongoing influences, including biological and environmental vulnerability (risk) and adaptation (protective), environmental adversity (stressors and trauma), psychiatric morbidity, posttraumatic comorbidity, and healthy psychobiological development.

Family systems: from dysregulation to co-regulation

As mentioned above, a key component of self-regulation for traumatized children (and their caregivers) is the ability to modulate arousal, emotion, and information processing so as to be able to think clearly and act effectively when experiencing the psychobiological reactivity that underlies emotional, cognitive, and behavioral dysregulation. The central organizing structure for a child's perception and response to danger is the attachment system (Bowlby 1969). Thus, interventions – especially with young children – should educate and directly involve caregiver(s) (DeRosa and Pelcovitz, Chapter 14 in this volume; Saltzman et al., Chapter 15 in this volume). Moreover, interventions must address difficulties that caregivers have in their own self-regulation as well as the child's regulatory capacities (Cohen, Chapter 4 in this volume; Van Horn and Lieberman, Chapter 13 in this volume). Young children, and dyrsregulated children of any age, cannot be expected to manage negative affective states entirely on their own, but they can acquire autonomous self-regulation if they experience a period of consistent ongoing co-regulation. Entire family systems can become dysregulated in the wake of trauma (Saltzman et al., Chapter 15), especially developmentally adverse interpersonal trauma such as abuse, domestic violence, or war violence.

    Therefore, posttraumatic family therapy can be construed as an opportunity to assist the entire family system to regain (or develop for the first time) the capacity to self-regulate through the use of cognitive, behavioral, affective, and relational interventions that involve the therapist first modeling co-regulation in their interactions with the caregiver as well as the child, and then assisting caregivers in providing reliable, sensitive, empathic co-regulation for the child (Van Horn and Lieberman, Chapter 13). This is not an encouragement of dependency on the part of the caregiver or the child, but rather a systematic rebuilding of a trajectory that leads from stress and distress to co-regulation (i.e. feeling secure enough to inhibit and transform impulsive/reactive feelings, thoughts, and actions into reflective, goal-oriented choices) to self-regulation (i.e. being able to autonomously sustain self-regulation, while continuing to "ground" oneself in healthy reciprocal relationships).

It may also be advisable to work individually with a caregiver, especially when that caregiver has her or his own difficulties with self-regulation. Research suggests that mothers with their own histories of childhood trauma may have particular difficulty engaging in healthy co-regulation with their children, and that this difficulty may stem from what has been termed maternal "hostile helplessness" (Lyons-Ruth et al. 2005). Providing caregivers with opportunities to experience therapeutic co-regulation, learn self-regulation skills, and develop self-efficacy may increase their ability to help their children do the same.

Peer group and school systems: from alienation to achievement

Dysregulation frequently lies at the root of interpersonal problems in childhood. The relationship between self-regulation and social functioning is a complex one, with the potential for synergy or entropy. Just as interventions for posttraumatic dysregulation in young children should focus on enhancing primary social relationships (attachment relationships and working models; Bowlby 1969), interventions with older children should focus on relationships with peers and adults in school, recreational, and work contexts (DeRosa and Pelcovitz, Chapter 14). Exposure to traumatic stress may hinder a child's ability to successfully navigate in these social settings. This is especially true if the child's difficulties with self-regulation contribute to the development of a disruptive behavior disorder, such as attention deficit hyperactivity disorder (ADHD) or oppositional-defiant disorder (ODD) (Ford et al. 2000). While only one of many possible contributing factors, "traumatic life events" have been implicated in the etiology of disruptive behavior disorders (Slutske et al. 1998). Once a child manifests a disruptive behavior disorder, the risk exists that the disorder will become a chronic one. Patterson (1993) describes a "cascade" of events set in motion by a child's disruptive behaviors, whereby the child's impulsivity alienates others, resulting in feelings of rejection and demoralization, which in turn prompt the child to escalate his or her disruptive behaviors. Ford (2002) applied this cascade model to describing a potential sequence of posttraumatic decline in childhood that begins with anxiety and depression, progresses to more debilitating problems with the modulation of attention and arousal (which may be comorbid with, or mistaken for, ADHD), and devolves into isolation or deviant peer associations and increased risk of social and academic failure.

It is important to keep in mind that social and academic failure may play a significant role in a child's level of frustration, self-esteem, and dysregulated (anxious, depressed, or disruptive) behaviors. Children who have been exposed to traumatic stress may be at risk for academic problems (Lipschitz et al. 2000). The developmental alterations that occur in the wake of traumatic stress exposure may affect capacities that are essential for academic success, such as focused attention and the capacity for reflection (Cook-Cottone 2004). Interventions, should therefore, include self-regulation skill-building explicitly designed for use in the classroom (DeRosa and Pelcovitz, Chapter 14). When feasible, and especially when treating young school-age children, it is useful to include key adults (such as teachers, mentors, coaches) who may serve as role models for regulation and secure attachment as well as facilitators of peer relationships. Community-based interventions that provide opportunities to learn and practice self-regulation skills in structured activities (e.g. athletics, theater, hobby and social clubs) provide further opportunities to help children and adolescents develop by scaffolding from co-regulation to interactive self-regulation.

Conclusion

In sum, while extremely complex and still relatively nascent, the science of posttraumatic risk and resilience suggests that recovery from early life trauma depends upon strengthening the child's capacities to detect threats and achieve a regulated response of activating bodily and behavioral defenses while conserving the bodily resources that are necessary for development and growth. With further research and continued clinical innovation, it may be possible to develop psychosocial and biological interventions that reliably restore children's robust capacities for self-regulation. Understanding how the biopsychosocial functions involved in stress adaptation and self-regulation develop early in life, and how this trajectory of health self-development is altered by traumatic stressors, thus represents an important agenda for researchers and clinicians alike.

References

Antelman, S., Caggiula, A., and Gershon, S. (1997). Stressor-induced oscillation: A possible model of the bidirectional symptoms in PTSD. In R. Yehuda and A. McFarlane (eds.), *Psychobiology of posttraumatic stress disorder* (pp. 296–304). New York: New York Academy of Sciences.

Bowlby, J. (1969). *Attachment and loss: Volume 1. Attachment.* New York: Basic Books.

Breslau, N., Peterson, E., Poisson, L., Schultz, L., and Lucia, V. (2004). Estimating posttraumatic stress disorder in the community: Lifetime perspective and the impact of typical traumatic events. *Psychological Medicine, 34,* 889–898.

Campos, J.J., Campos, R.J., and Barrett, K.C. (1989). Emergent themes in the study of emotional development and emotion regulation. *Child Development, 25*(3), 394–402.

Canino, G.J., Shrout, P., Rubio-Stipec, M., Bird, H., Bravo, M., Ramirez, R., et al. (2004). The DSM-IV rates of child and adolescent disorders in Puerto Rico. *Archives of General Psychiatry, 61,* 85–93.

Cicchetti, D., and Toth, S. (1995). A developmental psychopathology perspective on child abuse and neglect. *Journal of the American Academy of Child and Adolescent Psychiatry, 34*, 541–565.

Cook-Cottone, C. (2004). Childhood posttraumatic stress disorder: Diagnosis, treatment, and school reintegration. *School Psychology Review, 33*, 127–140.

Cortes, A., Saltzman, K., Weems, D., Regnault, H., Reiss, A., and Carrion, V. (2005). Development of anxiety disorders in a traumatized pediatric population: A preliminary longitudinal evaluation. *Child Abuse and Neglect, 29*, 905–914.

Costello, E.J., Erklani, A., Fairbank, J., and Angold, A. (2002). The prevalence of potentially traumatic events in childhood and adolescence. *Journal of Traumatic Stress, 15*, 99–112.

Costello, E.J., Mustillo, S., Erkanli, A., Keeler, G., and Angold, A. (2003). Prevalence and development of psychiatric disorders in childhood and adolescence. *Archives of General Psychiatry, 60*(8), 837–844.

Crockenberg, S., and Leerkes, E. (2006). Infant and maternal behavior moderate reactivity to novelty to predict anxious behavior at 2.5 years. *Development and Psychopathology, 18*, 17–34.

Davidson, R., Putnam, K.M., and Larson, C.L. (2000). Dysfunction in the neural circuitry of emotion regulation – a possible prelude to violence. *Science, 289*, 591–594.

Edwards, V.J., Holden, G., Felitti, V., and Anda, R.F. (2003). Relationship between multiple forms of childhood maltreatment and adult mental health in community respondents: Results from the Adverse Childhood Experiences Study. *American Journal of Psychiatry, 160*, 1453–1460.

Egger, H., and Angold, A. (2006). Common emotional and behavioral disorders in preschool children. *Journal of Child Psychology and Psychiatry and Allied Disciplines, 47*, 313–337.

Finkelhor, D., Ormrod, R., and Turner, H. (2007). Poly-victimization: A neglected component in child victimization. *Child Abuse and Neglect, 31*, 7–26.

Ford, J.D. (2002). Traumatic victimization in childhood and persistent problems with oppositional-defiance. *Journal of Trauma, Maltreatment, and Aggression, 11*, 25–58.

Ford, J.D. (2005). Treatment implications of altered affect regulation and information processing following child maltreatment. *Psychiatric Annals, 35*(5), 410–419.

Ford, J.D., Racusin, R., Ellis, C., Daviss, W.B., Reiser, J., Fleischer, A., et al. (2000). Child maltreatment, other trauma exposure, and posttraumatic symptomatology among children with oppositional defiant and attention deficit hyperactivity disorders. *Child Maltreatment, 5*, 205–217.

Ford, J.D., Courtois, C., van der Hart, O., Nijenhuis, E., and Steele, K. (2005). Treatment of complex posttraumatic self-dysregulation. *Journal of Traumatic Stress, 18*, 467–477.

Goodman, R., dos Santos, D., Nunes, A., Miranda, D., Fleitlich-Bilyk, B., and Filho, N. (2005). The Ilha de Maré study: A survey of child mental health problems in a predominantly African-Brazilian rural community. *Social Psychiatry and Psychiatric Epidemiology, 40*, 11–17.

Heim, C., and Nemeroff, C. (2001). The role of childhood trauma in the neurobiology of mood and anxiety disorders. *Biological Psychiatry, 49*(12), 1023–1039.

Hindmarch, I. (2001). Expanding the horizons of depression. *Human Psychopharmacology: Clinical and Experimental, 16*, 203–218.

Jacobsen, L., Southwick, S., and Kosten, T. (2001). Substance use disorders in patients with posttraumatic stress disorder. *American Journal of Psychiatry, 158*, 1184–1190.

Kaufman, J., Martin, A., King, R., and Charney, D. (2001). Are child-, adolescent-, and adult-onset depression one and the same disorder? *Biological Psychiatry, 49*, 980–1001.

Kepner, J. (1995). *Healing tasks: The psychotherapy of adult survivors of childhood abuse.* San Francisco, CA: Jossey-Bass.

Kessler, R.C., Berglund, P., Demler, O., Jin, R., Merikangas, K., and Walters, E. (2005). Lifetime prevalence and age-of-onset distributions of DSM-IV disorders in the National Comorbidity Survey Replication. *Archives of General Psychiatry, 62*, 593–602.

Kopp, C. (1989). Regulation of distress and negative emotions: A developmental view. *Developmental Psychology, 25*, 343–354.

Lansford, J.E., Malone, P.S., Castellino, D.R., Dodge, K.A., Pettit, G.S., and Bates, J.E. (2006). Trajectories of internalizing, externalizing, and grades for children who have and have not experienced their parents' divorce or separation. *Journal of Family Psychology, 20*, 292–301.

Lewinsohn, P., Shankman, S., Gau, G., and Klein, D. (2004). The prevalence and co-morbidity of subthreshold psychiatric conditions. *Psychological Medicine, 24*, 613–622.

Lipschitz, D.S., Rasmusson, A., Anyan, W., Cromwell, P., and Southwick, S. (2000). Clinical and functional correlates of posttraumatic stress disorder in urban adolescent girls at a primary care clinic. *Journal of the American Academy of Child and Adolescent Psychiatry, 39*, 1104–1111.

Lyons-Ruth, K., Yellin, C., and Melnick, S. (2005). Expanding the concept of unresolved mental states. *Development and Psychopathology, 17*, 1–23.

McFarlane, A.C. (2000). Posttraumatic stress disorder. *Journal of Clinical Psychiatry, 61*, 15–23.

Mangelsdorf, S.C., Shapiro, J.R., and Marzolf, D. (1995). Developmental and temperamental differences in emotion regulation in infancy. *Child Development, 66*, 1817–1828.

Mason, J.W., Wang, S., Yehuda, R., Lubin, H., Johnson, D.R., Bremner, J.D., et al. (2002). Marked lability in urinary cortisol levels in subgroups of combat veterans with posttraumatic stress disorder during an intensive exposure treatment program. *Psychosomatic Medicine, 64*, 238–246.

Meltzer, H., Gatward, R., Goodman, R., and Ford, T. (2003). Mental health of children and adolescents in Great Britain. *International Review of Psychiatry, 15*, 185–187.

Mikulincer, M., Shaver, P.R., and Pereg, D. (2003). Attachment theory and affect regulation: The dynamics, development, and cognitive consequences of attachment-related strategies. *Motivation and Emotion, 27*(2), 77–102.

Mullick, S., and Goodman, R. (2005). The prevalence of psychiatric disorders among 5–10 year olds in rural, urban, and slum areas in Bangladesh. *Social Psychiatry and Psychiatric Epidemiology, 40*, 663–671.

Orcutt, H., Erickson, D., and Wolf, J. (2004).The course of PTSD symptoms among Gulf War veterans: A growth mixture modeling approach. *Journal of Traumatic Stress, 17*, 195–202.

Pat-Horenczyk, R., Abramovitz, R., Doppelt, O., Brom, D., Daie, A., and Chemtob, C. (2007a). Adolescent exposure to recurrent terrorism in Israel: Posttraumatic distress and functional impairment. *American Journal of Orthopsychiatry, 77*(1), 76–85.

Pat-Horenczyk, R., Peled, O., Miron, T., Brom, D., Villa, Y., and Chemtob, C. (2007b). Risk taking behaviors among Israeli adolescents exposed to recurrent terrorism. *American Journal of Psychiatry, 164*, 66–72.

Patterson, G.R. (1993). Orderly change in a stable world: The antisocial trait as chimera. *Journal of Consulting and Clinical Psychology, 155*, 862–870.

Pederson, C.L., Maurer, S.H., Kaminski, P.L., Zander, K.A., Peters, C.M., Stokes-Crowe, L.A., et al. (2004). Hippocampal volume and memory performance in a community-based sample of women with posttraumatic stress disorder secondary to child abuse. *Journal of Traumatic Stress, 17*, 37–40.

Perkonigg, A., Pfister, H., Stein, M.B., Höfler, M., Lieb, R., Maercker, A., et al. (2005). Longitudinal course of posttraumatic stress disorder and posttraumatic stress disorder symptoms in a community sample of adolescents and young adults. *American Journal of Psychiatry, 162*, 1320–1327.

Price, D. (2000). Psychological and neural mechanisms of the affective dimension of pain. *Science, 288*, 1769–1772.

Rea, J., and Rossman, B. (2005). Children exposed to interparental violence: does parenting contribute to functioning over time? *Journal of Emotional Abuse, 5*, 1–28.

Riggs, D., Rukstalis, M., and Volpicelli, J. (2003). Demographic and social adjustment characteristics of patients with comorbid posttraumatic stress disorder and alcohol dependence. *Addictive Behaviors, 28*, 1717–1730.

Sacks, J., Weinreb, L., Ford, J.D., Rog, D., McMullen, L., Holpuka, S., and Fischer, P. (in review). Trauma in the lives of homeless mothers: Findings of the CMSH/CSAT Homeless Families Program.

Sar, V., Unal, S., Kiziltan, E., Kundakei, T., and Ozturk, E. (2001). SPECT study of regional cerebral blood flow in dissociative identity disorder. *Journal of Trauma and Dissociation, 2*(2), 5–20.

Schell, T., Marshall, G., and Jaycox, L. (2004). All symptoms are not created equal. *Journal of Abnormal Psychology, 113*, 189–197.

Schore, A. (2001). The effects of early relational trauma on right brain development, affect regulation, and infant mental health. *Infant Mental Health Journal, 22*, 201–269.

Schmahl, C.G., Vermetten, E., Elzinga, B.M., and Bremner, J. (2003). Magnetic resonance imaging of hippocampal and amygdala volume in women with childhood abuse and borderline personality disorder. *Psychiatry Research, 122*(3), 193–198.

Seedat, S., Stein, M.B., Oosthuizen, P., Emsley, R., and Stein, D. (2003). Linking posttraumatic stress disorder and psychosis: A look at epidemiology, phenomenology, and treatment. *Journal of Nervous and Mental Disease, 191*, 675–681.

Seedat, S., Nyamai, C., Njenga, F., Vythilingum, B., and Stein, D.J. (2004). Trauma exposure and posttraumatic stress symptoms in urban African schools: Survey in CapeTown and Nairobi. *British Journal of Psychiatry, 184*, 169–175.

Shea, M.T., Stout, R., Yen, S., Pagano, M., Skodol, A., Morey, L. et al. (2004). Associations in the course of personality disorders and Axis I disorders over time. *Journal of Abnormal Psychology, 113*, 499–508.

Silverman, A.B., Reinherz, H.Z., and Giaconia, R.M. (1996). The long-term sequelae of child and adolescent abuse: A longitudinal community study. *Child Abuse and Neglect, 20*(8), 709–723.

Slutske, W., Heath, A., Dinwiddle, S., Madden, P., Bucholz, K., Dunne, M. et al. (1998). Common genetic risk factors for conduct disorder and alcohol dependence. *Journal of Abnormal Psychology, 107*, 363–374.

Sroufe, L.A. (1996). *Emotion development: The organization of emotional life in the early years.* New York: Cambridge University Press.

Stuewig, J., and McCloskey, L. (2005). The relation of child maltreatment to shame and guilt among adolescents. *Child Maltreatment, 10*, 324–336.

Tupler, L., and De Bellis, M. (2006). Segmented hippocampal volume in children and adolescents with posttraumatic stress disorder. *Biological Psychiatry, 59*, 523–529.

Van der Kolk, B.A., Roth, S., Pelcovitz, D., Sunday, S., and Spinazzola, J. (2005). The disorders of extreme stress. *Journal of Traumatic Stress, 18*, 389–399.

Vila, G., Porche, L., and Mouren-Siméoni, M. (1999). An 18-month longitudinal study of posttraumatic disorders in children who were taken hostage in their school. *Psychosomatic Medicine, 61*, 746–754.

Widiger, T., and Samuel, D. (2005). Diagnostic categories or dimensions? *Journal of Abnormal Psychology, 114*, 494–504.

Wittchen, H.U., Lieb, R., Pfister, H., and Schuster, S. (2000). The waxing and waning of mental disorders. *Comprehensive Psychiatry, 41*, 122–132.

Chapter 13

Using dyadic therapies to treat traumatized young children

Patricia Van Horn and Alicia F. Lieberman

Relationships are central to the healthy development of infants, toddlers, and preschoolers. Babies internalize the patterns of their earliest caregiving as they learn to calm and soothe themselves. From the security of their earliest relationships, babies begin to explore the world and take on the mental and emotional challenges it presents. Without caring relationships, babies and young children cannot learn to calm and regulate their emotions, trust in the responsiveness of other human beings, or learn and grow.

Trauma can be profoundly disruptive of these essential relationships and, therefore, children's development. Young children have the developmentally appropriate expectation that those who care for them will assess oncoming danger and protect them from overwhelming fear and terror, providing a protective shield to fend off unbearable levels of stimulation (Freud 1920/ 1955; Marans and Adelman 1997; Pynoos et al. 1999). Bowlby (1969/1982), the developer of attachment theory, demonstrated that both this expectation and the mother's role of providing the baby a sense of security in circumstances of threat and danger are biologically determined. When young children experience the overwhelming sights, sounds, and internal sensations that make up a traumatic experience, their expectation of protection is betrayed. Their trust in their caregivers, the *sine qua non* of children's healthy development, is at least momentarily shattered.

Janoff-Bulman (1992) described the existential crisis that traumatic life experiences create in adults as their assumptions of benevolence, meaning, and self-worth are shattered. For young children, the shattering of trust in caregivers presents a similar existential crisis. The relationship with the caregiver is the source of the child's developing assumptions that the world is a benevolent place, that life has meaning, and that the self is worthy. If young children are to be restored to positive and hopeful developmental trajectories after trauma, the ruptures in their relationships with those who care for them must be mended. Psychological interventions that focus on the quality of children's relationships with their caregivers hold particular promise.

In this chapter we review a range of interventions that make use of the parent–child relationship to repair the developmental disruptions that follow trauma. Two interventions, Child–Parent Psychotherapy (CPP) and Parent–Child Interaction Therapy (PCIT) have been demonstrated efficacious with preschoolers exposed to family violence and with physically abused preschoolers. We will explore these in detail, discussing their theoretical foundations, modes of intervention, and evidence base. We will also briefly discuss other relationship-based interventions that stand apart, either because they are not dyadic interventions or because they have been tested with high-risk rather than traumatized populations.

Several trauma treatments that have been used with preschool children are beyond the scope of this chapter because they do not focus on the caregiver–child relationship as an agent of change. These include such well-researched and well-supported treatments as Trauma-Focused Cognitive Behavioral Therapy (TF-CBT) for sexually abused children (Cohen et al. 2004) and Abuse-Focused Cognitive Behavioral Therapy for physically abused children (Kolko 1996). Similarly, we will not discuss a new cognitive behavioral therapy for traumatized preschool children (Scheeringa et al. 2002). This intervention, modeled after TF-CBT, is currently undergoing a randomized trial. All of these treatment models, although they contain parent components, focus clinical attention on the child's symptoms rather than the caregiver–child relationship.

Treatment targets, intervention strategies, and agents of change

The treatment modalities that we discuss in this chapter vary widely, from the psychodynamic to the behavioral. All of them have as their ultimate aim the mental health of the child. To distinguish among the modalities, we focus on three dimensions: what the modality targets for change both as its outcome and in its moment-to-moment interventions, whether the interventions are determined a priori by theory or emerge spontaneously in response to clinical material, and whom the modality identifies as the agent of change. Our goal in defining the modalities on these dimensions is not to demonstrate the superiority of one over the other, but to offer guidance for clinicians seeking to understand which treatment method may be most useful for a particular child, or most consistent with the clinician's own beliefs about psychotherapy.

Targets of intervention

Although all psychotherapeutic modalities seek to alter feelings, cognitions, attitudes, and behavior (Strupp 1978), each may privilege one over the others for intervention in the clinical moment. Some modalities consistently target behavior. Others, such as those that target the parent's internal working model of the child, may have multiple targets. Bowlby (1969/1982) defined internal working models as cognitive-affective structures by which an individual determines how the self, the environment, and others are expected to act or react in a given situation. If the target of intervention were to be a mother's working model of her child, therefore, the clinician would target both the mother's thoughts and her feelings.

Moment-to-moment interventions are made in the service of an ultimate outcome that the clinician and client hope to achieve, and the various treatment modalities conceptualize outcomes differently as well. Some target the relief of specific symptoms. Other modalities strive for a broader goal of promoting personality coherence and healthy development.

Treatment strategies: how interventions are determined

The modalities also differ in how specifically they guide the clinician's behavior. Although all acknowledge that the clinician's expertise and interpersonal experience of the client must ultimately guide interventions, there remains a significant difference among the manuals that describe the modalities that we are discussing. Some offer broad principles for the clinician to internalize and follow; others establish a hierarchy of goals and guide the clinician to work on one goal before later goals are attempted, sometimes outlining specific interventions on a session-by-session basis.

All of the modalities we discuss incorporate play in some way, as it is an essential given that play is a crucial tool by which young children experiment with different situations and roles, test various solutions to problems, and master anxiety (Erickson 1950). In some modalities, children play freely, deciding for themselves whether to play out or avoid anxiety-provoking memories. Others structure the child's play within the session. Children may be offered particular materials or urged to play, draw, or speak about particular things. Slade (1994) pointed out that for children whose lives are filled with trauma and chaos, playing freely may be necessary if they are to build coherent internal structures, ideas, and narratives about their lives. For these children, the premature use of language by adults may be disruptive to their play and ultimately disorganizing. We believe that in work with traumatized young children, therapists should hold to Slade's important idea and give children the freedom to choose how and when to play.

Who is the agent of change?

This final dimension describes the function of the therapist. In some modalities, the therapist brings the expertise to the parent or child and guides them to do things that the therapist believes will help the child reach the desired outcome. The therapist is seen as the agent of change for the child, even when the parent and child are together in session. In other modalities, change in the parent–child relationship is seen as the agent of change. The therapist serves as a facilitator, supporting the parent and child in viewing each other differently and behaving differently toward each other, but not teaching either the parent or the child specific skills or ways of being that will bring about change.

Dyadic modalities: Child–Parent Psychotherapy and Parent–Child Interaction Therapy

We consider these modalities together because, although they are dramatically different on all three dimensions described above, they are both structured so that the parent and child are together during the sessions. Both have been used with populations of traumatized young children; both have a sound evidence base.

Child–Parent Psychotherapy

Theory and practice

CPP emerged from a tradition of relationship-based therapies developed to address situations in which infants or young children suffered traumatic experiences at the hands of their parents, or where the parents were themselves so traumatized or otherwise compromised that their responses to the child were disruptive to the child's development or became a source of secondary traumatization for the child. These relationship-based treatments have been referred to as Infant–Parent Psychotherapy (Fraiberg 1980), Toddler–Parent Psychotherapy (Lieberman 1992), and Preschooler–Parent Psychotherapy (Toth et al. 2002). Lieberman (2004) advocated that the name Child–Parent Psychotherapy be used to describe them all. They share an emphasis on the intergenerational transmission of trauma and psychopathology and a focus on translating the parent's and child's feelings and experiences to one another as a means of achieving enhanced emotional reciprocity in the dyad. Interventions are directed at the parent–child relationship itself, particularly addressing the parent's distorted negative attributions to the child, and the mutual adverse expectations that the parent and child have of one another.

CPP is based on psychodynamic theory, including attachment theory (Lieberman and Van Horn 2005). As it has developed for use with trauma-specific populations, it has incorporated components of trauma theory (specifically, methods for helping children and parents cope with expectations and reminders of traumas, and methods for helping them co-create a coherent narrative of their experience), and social learning theory.

The manual for CPP does not prescribe an order in which interventions must occur or in which treatment goals must be addressed. Ports of entry are not determined a priori, but are selected according to what the clinician believes will best advance the goal of helping the parent and child hold realistic, flexible, and reciprocal views of one another and support the child's development. The manual advises beginning with simple interventions, often based on developmental guidance, but beyond that does not dictate an order of intervention. Although the therapist may sometimes use the child's or parent's behavior as a port of entry, most often the cognitive or affective meaning behind the behavior is what is explored as the therapist helps the parent and child understand one another's motivations and helps the parent understand the child's internal world.

CPP uses a variety of treatment modalities. These include:

- promoting developmental progress through play, physical contact, and language
- offering unstructured, reflective, developmental guidance
- modeling appropriate protective behavior
- interpreting feelings and actions
- providing emotional support
- offering crisis intervention and concrete assistance with problems of daily living.

As therapists weave these modalities into a unified treatment, they pay special attention to trauma themes, both in the present and in the parent's past. Therapists help the parent and the child understand the impact of the trauma on their experience of one another, explore ways to modulate their affective responses to traumatic reminders, and place the trauma in perspective in the larger fabric of their lives. Of particular help in this latter activity is the active quest for beneficent memories from the parents' care-receiving pasts that may guide and sustain the parents as they care for their children (Lieberman et al. 2004).

Play holds a special place in CPP. The therapist's role is one of facilitator: to help the parent and child play together and to support the parent as she witnesses the child's play. If the parent is unable to accept the meaning of the child's play, or cannot tolerate the play because it is too evocative of her own trauma, the therapist both creates a space in which the child can tell the story and supports the parent in witnessing the story. The principle behind this use of play with traumatized children is that trauma has disrupted their ability to maintain a working model of parents as reliable protectors. If children are to continue to develop well, the security of their caregiving relationships must be restored. CPP seeks to accomplish this by supporting the parent in witnessing and understanding the child's fears and anxieties as expressed through play, so the parent can help the child grapple with those fears. As children and parents grow more able to play together, children share their concerns and play provides parents with a vehicle to help children examine the distorted expectations created by the trauma, experiment with different outcomes, and place the trauma in perspective. As the parent becomes more fully able to engage in the play, the therapist steps aside, allowing the parent and child to create conditions for change. Although the therapist facilitates the process, the relationship itself is seen as the agent of change.

In CPP the child is provided with a variety of toys, including toys that are evocative of the trauma and will allow the child to play it out. In the first parent–child session, and thereafter if necessary, the parent and therapist work together to use words to tell the child that the trauma is the reason the child is coming to therapy. For example, a child may be told:

> "You saw your daddy hit your mom and make her face bleed. You cried and told him to stop. Your mom is worried that you are still scared about what you saw. You're here to play and talk so you can feel better."

In short, the therapist brings the trauma into the room in the first session, and actively looks for clues in the child's play that reveal themes of the trauma. But the therapist generally does not guide the play toward the trauma. CPP's format allows children to bring up trauma material in their own time. For some children, this is the first session. For others, a period of organizing play may come before active play about the trauma. For others, trauma material may come and go as children work through both the trauma and through developmental concerns that may not be trauma-related (e.g. exploring the wish for and the fear of increased autonomy).

Evidence base

CPP was not initially developed to treat traumatized children. Before it was adapted to include specific trauma-treatment goals, CPP was demonstrated to be efficacious with high-risk groups, including anxiously attached toddlers of immigrant mothers (Lieberman et al. 1991) and toddlers of depressed mothers (Cicchetti et al. 1999). Recently, randomized trials provided evidence for the efficacy of CPP with traumatized children aged 1–5. CPP significantly reduced PTSD symptoms and behavior problems in preschool children exposed to physical violence between their parents (Lieberman et al. 2005); these improvements persisted for six months after treatment ended, with both children and parents who received CPP showing further gains in functioning during the months after treatment compared to a control group that received case management plus treatment as usual in the community (Lieberman et al. 2006). In samples of maltreated toddlers (Cicchetti et al. 2006; Toth et al., in press), and maltreated preschoolers (Toth et al. 2002), CPP was efficacious in improving, respectively, rates of secure attachment and quality of children's representations of their parents compared to control groups of children who received treatment as usual. The strength of CPP's evidence base is that it has emerged from two labs working independently of one another and that it has demonstrated efficacy using a variety of different outcome measures including problem behaviors, PTSD symptoms in both mothers and children, attachment security, and children's representations of their parents.

Parent–Child Interaction Therapy

Theory and practice

PCIT is a short-term, behaviorally based intervention originally designed for families with children aged 2–7 experiencing externalizing behavior problems. Parents are taught specific skills designed to change dysfunctional parent–child relationship patterns (Eyberg 1988; Eyberg and Boggs 1989). The theoretical basis for PCIT has been described in the manual that guides its interventions and elsewhere (Eyberg and Calzada 1998; Hembree-Kigin and McNeil 1995; Herschell and McNeil 2005).

In the first phase of PCIT, therapists teach parents specific skills collectively called PRIDE skills (Praise, Reflection, Imitation, Description, and Enthusiasm) and coach parents to use these skills during play with their children. At the same time, parents are instructed in the behavioral principle of differential attention and taught to decrease commands, questions, and criticisms during play. Commands, questions, and criticisms are seen as ways that parents exercise control, and during the first phase of PCIT parents are expected to follow the child's lead during play episodes. During parent–child sessions that follow the initial teaching session, parent and child play together while a therapist observes from behind a one-way mirror and coaches the parent to apply the skills to increase the child's appropriate behaviors (e.g. sharing and turn-taking) by attending to and praising them, and decreased inappropriate behaviors (e.g. aggressive use of toys, whining) by ignoring them. The treatment goals in this phase are to enhance the parent's skills, build the child's self-esteem, increase the child's prosocial behavior, and improve the parent–child relationship.

Once parents have demonstrated the PRIDE skills at the required level, PCIT proceeds to a second phase in which the therapist trains the parent in behavior-modification practices including giving effective commands, distinguishing compliance from non-compliance, and using time-out effectively as a discipline technique. Parents must demonstrate these skills at a predetermined level before treatment ends. Treatment generally lasts 10–14 weeks, though its actual length depends on the severity of the child's behavior problems and the pace at which the parent acquires and demonstrates the skills required by each phase.

PCIT is a highly structured modality, with the therapist's moment-to-moment interventions determined a priori by theory. PCIT changes children's behavior by teaching parents specific strategies that are designed to diminish children's externalizing behaviors. Children are encouraged to play freely during the parent–child sessions; the therapist coaches the parent to use the powerful motivator of parental approval to change the child's behavior. Parents notice, reflect and enthusiastically praise children's prosocial behaviors many times during each play session. They ignore, thereby extinguishing, mildly troublesome behaviors. Assuming that the parent's skills generalize to interactions outside the therapeutic play sessions, it is expected that the externalizing behaviors that PCIT was designed to target will be extinguished.

In a sense, the therapist is the direct agent of change in PCIT because the therapist coaches the parent's behavior and requires certain levels of behavior change from parents. The therapist does not, however, interact directly with the child. The direct agent of change for the child is the parent, with the therapist-coach acting as an indirect change agent. As the parent's behavior changes, and the parent interacts with the child in ways that will reinforce prosocial behavior and extinguish antisocial behavior, the child's behavior changes. Like CPP, PCIT uses the parent–child relationship to effect change in the child. The techniques that the two modalities use are vastly different, but both of them rely on the parent–child relationship as the mutative factor for the child.

PCIT has been applied without modification to treat physically abused children (Herschell and McNeil 2005; Timmer et al. 2005a, 2005b; Urquiza and McNeil 1996), and has been modified slightly for use with maltreated toddlers aged 12–30 months (Dombrowski et al. 2005). Urquiza and McNeil (1996) point out that physically abusive parents use less effective discipline strategies, including physical discipline, and that they have greater negative expectations of their children than do non-abusive parents. Physically abused children have a wide range of externalizing behaviors, including aggression and non-compliance, and also exhibit poorer self-control and greater distractibility, negative affect, and resistance to directions. Urquiza and McNeil do not posit a causative direction between these factors and child physical abuse. What is important, from the point of view of theorizing whether PCIT should be useful in physically abusive families, is that the interactions between physically abusing parents and their children are dysfunctional, with parents using ineffective strategies to discipline children who have poor self-control and a strong tendency to resist direction. Because PCIT was designed to intervene in precisely these coercive parent–child interactions in non-abusive families, researchers theorized that it might also be effective in families marked by physical abuse of children.

PCIT is different from other trauma treatments in that it does not conceptualize the physical abuse as a trauma or physically abused children as traumatized. The hallmarks of most trauma treatments (Marmar et al. 1993) include helping the traumatized individual achieve and maintain regular levels of affective arousal, re-establishing trust in bodily sensations and emotional cues, and restoring the capacity to respond realistically to threat. Trauma treatments generally also include some opportunity for the traumatized individual to make sense of what has happened to them and place it in perspective by creating a trauma narrative (Cohen et al. 2006). PCIT does not have any of these features, and it does not target PTSD symptoms or other psychiatric symptoms. Its target is externalizing behaviors; its interventions focus on changing parent behavior so that parents become more effective reinforcers of their children's prosocial behavior, leading to more adaptive interactions between parents and children.

Evidence base

PCIT has been well studied and demonstrated efficacious in reducing child behavior problems in non-maltreating families, and in maintaining the positive effects for up to six years post-treatment (Timmer et al. 2005b). More recently, studies in two different labs have shown that PCIT has promise for maltreating families as well. Chaffin et al. (2004) completed a four-year, randomized trial with 110 physically abusive parent–child dyads recruited as they entered the child-welfare system. A modified version of PCIT was effective in reducing negative parenting behaviors as well as rates of reported reabuse, but not neglect, within 850 days after the completion of treatment. Timmer et al. (2005b) conducted a quasi-experimental study of PCIT with 136 child–parent dyads in which 66.9 percent of the children had been maltreated. Although they found PCIT to be associated with reduced child behavior problems, parenting stress, and abuse potential in dyads with and without histories of maltreatment, maltreated children showed less improvement. Of greater concern is the finding that the dyads at highest risk were most likely to end treatment prematurely. Indeed, 63.5 percent of the maltreated children whose parents had reported clinically significant levels of behavior problems left treatment early.

PCIT effectively reduces negative parenting behaviors in maltreating parents. There is little evidence, however, that it reduces the behavior problems of maltreated children, and no study published to date has assessed whether PCIT relieves symptoms of posttraumatic stress. If PCIT continues to be used with children who have suffered traumas, future research should focus on that question, and on developing modifications that would encourage families of maltreated children with severe behavior problems to stay in treatment long enough to reap benefits. Since affective dysregulation frequently follows trauma, modifications that encourage clinicians to focus on the emotional as well as the behavioral experiences of their clients might be explored.

Intervention models demonstrated effective in high-risk populations

The intervention models described below focus on the parent–child relationship, and have demonstrated effectiveness in high risk samples, and may prove effective in addressing relationship disturbances between traumatized young children and their caregivers. Two of the models, Watch, Wait, and Wonder (WWW; Muir 1992) and Interactional Guidance (IG; McDonough 1992), are dyadic in that the therapist focuses on the interactions between the parent and child. Others, including Circle of Security (Cooper et al. 2005) and foster parent intervention (Dozier et al. 2002a, 2002b) focus on intervention with the parent in the interest of the child

Dyadic models: Watch, Wait, and Wonder and Interaction Guidance

Watch, Wait, and Wonder

WWW is a psychodynamically informed treatment led by the child. For the first half of each session the child initiates play. The therapist and parent observe the play and the parent becomes involved only when the child initiates contact. In the remainder of the session, the therapist discusses the play with the parent, not interpreting, but providing a supportive environment in which the parent can reflect on the play and express her own thoughts and feelings about the child's activity and her relationship with the child. Together the parent and therapist try to understand the themes and relationship issues that the child is trying to master. WWW was tested against CPP in a randomized trial of 67 dyads with infants 10–30 months of age referred to a children's mental health clinic either because of chronic self-regulation problems in the infant, failures of attachment, or maternal depression. Both modalities were associated with a reduction in child symptoms, improvement in the quality of the mother–child relationship and reduced parenting stress, while WWW was associated with a greater shift toward attachment security, greater capacities for emotional self-regulation, and increase in cognitive ability in the infants (Cohen et al. 1999).

Although WWW does not have a specific trauma focus, it allows a parent to observe trauma-based themes and relationship dynamics in the child's play and supports the parent's emotional response to the child's trauma play. It allows children to structure a trauma narrative, experiment with rescue fantasies, and play with alternative endings to the narrative in the supportive company of their parents. One risk that might arise in using WWW with a traumatized child is that the model does not permit either the parent or the therapist to intervene if the child becomes "stuck" in posttraumatic play and becomes increasingly anxious. As with any sound treatment model not designed for delivery to a trauma population, WWW might need thoughtful modification for this group.

Interaction Guidance

Interaction Guidance is a brief, behaviorally based, relatively unstructured intervention for hard-to-engage families and their infants (McDonough 2000). The therapist, relying on the family's desire to help and to play a central role in the baby's life, addresses only those negative relationship dynamics that she believes to be of critical importance, focusing instead on what is going well in the parent–infant relationship.

In the first part of each session, the therapist videotapes the parent and child as they play together for about six minutes. Thereafter, the therapist reviews and discusses the videotape with the parent, and highlights specific examples of positive parenting behavior and parent sensitivity in reading infant cues (McDonough 1992, 2000).

IG encourages parents to attend to their children's needs and emotional states and to follow their children's cues. Like PCIT, it focuses on improving parent–child interactions by selective attention to interactions that work well. There may be less room in IG for a specific focus on trauma material because IG therapists focus on successes in the relationship rather than on problems. Whether this approach would work well with trauma populations is an empirical question.

Tending to the relationship outside the dyad

Although neither of the final interventions that we discuss is strictly dyadic, both focus on the relationships between young children and their caregivers. Intervention for foster parents (Dozier et al. 2002a, 2002b) was developed to benefit infants whose short lives have been marked by loss and trauma. Circle of Security (Cooper et al. 2005) was designed to treat at-risk parents and their young children.

Intervention for foster parents (Dozier et al. 2002a, 2002b) works from the premise that infants and young children in foster care give behavioral signals that discourage nurturing care by their foster parents, including turning away or behaving in fussy, resistant ways when distressed. The intervention provides ten didactic sessions, based on a manual, to help foster parents understand and reinterpret the baby's cues, and assist them in overcoming difficulties in providing nurturance. The intervention stresses the importance of providing infants and young children with predictable interpersonal environments that will help the children develop better self-regulatory capacities.

Circle of Security (Cooper et al. 2005) is a group intervention based on attachment theory. Before the intervention begins, the parent participants are assessed with their young children, including a series of interactions that are videotaped. After two initial sessions during which the group leaders present basic information about attachment, group sessions are devoted to watching edited clips from the videotapes. Clips are selected to highlight parents' strengths and limitations so that parents can begin to shift problematic patterns in their relationships with their children. As the therapist and group members view and discuss the tape segments with the participant who is in the "hot seat", the participants' understanding of the emotional meaning that underlies their children's cues increases, as does their ability to respond empathically and contingently to their children's needs.

Summary

Because of the overwhelming nature of their experiences, traumatized infants, toddlers, and preschoolers suffer disruptions in the caregiving relationships that guide their development. Many young children and their caregivers will be able to repair the breaches in their relationships without intervention. Caring, empathic parents are a young child's most powerful source of resilience (Rutter 1999), and parents who can provide sensitive, consistent care to a child following a trauma can often restore the child to a positive developmental trajectory. When intervention is needed, however, it should attend to children's relationships and build in their caregivers the capacity to provide the sensitive care that will enhance the children's development. The interventions that we have discussed in this chapter all have this as their goal, although they move toward that goal using a wide variety of techniques. It is to be expected that some interventions will work better than others with particular families. As with any clinical decision, therapists should decide what intervention might be most suitable using their best clinical judgment and an awareness of the range of interventions available. The right interventions, faithfully applied, will serve traumatized children and help parents take their rightful places as their children's developmental guides.

References

Bowlby, J. (1969/1982). *Attachment and loss: Volume 1. Attachment.* New York: Basic Books.

Chaffin, M., Silovsky, J.F., Funderburk, B., Valle, L.A., Brestan, E.V., Balachova, T., et al. (2004). Parent–child interaction therapy with physically abusive parents: Efficacy for reducing future abuse reports. *Journal of Consulting and Clinical Psychology, 72,* 500–510.

Cicchetti, D., Toth, S.L., and Rogosch, F.A. (1999). The efficacy of toddler–parent psychotherapy to increase attachment security in offspring of depressed mothers. *Attachment and Human Development, 1,* 34–36.

Cicchetti, D., Rogosch, F.A., and Toth, S.L. (2006). Fostering secure attachment in infants in maltreating families through preventive interventions. *Development and Psychopathology, 18,* 623–650.

Cohen, J.A., Deblinger, E., Mannarino, A.P., and Steer, R.A. (2004). A multisite-randomized controlled trial for children with sexual abuse-related PTSD symptoms. *Journal of the American Academy of Child and Adolescent Psychiatry, 43,* 393–402.

Cohen, J.A., Mannarino, A.P., Murray, L.K., and Ingleman, R. (2006). Psychosocial interventions for maltreated and violence-exposed children. *Journal of Social Issues, 62*, 737–766.

Cohen, N.J., Muir, E., Lojkasek, M., Muir, R., Parker, C.J., Barwick, M., et al. (1999). Watch, Wait, and Wonder: Testing the effectiveness of a new approach to mother–infant psychotherapy. *Infant Mental Health Journal, 20*, 429–451.

Cooper, G., Hoffman, K., Powell, B., and Marvin, R. (2005). The Circle of Security Intervention: Differential diagnosis and differential treatment. In L.J. Berlin, Y. Ziv, L. Amaya-Jackson, and M.T. Greenberg (eds.), *Enhancing early attachments: Theory, research, intervention, and policy* (pp. 127–151). New York: Guilford.

Dombrowski, S.C., Timmer, S.G., Blacker, D.M., and Urquiza, A.J. (2005). A positive behavioral intervention for toddlers: Parent–Child Attunement Therapy. *Child Abuse Review, 14*, 132–151.

Dozier, M., Albus, K., Fisher, P., and Sepulveda, S. (2002a). Interventions for foster parents: Implications for developmental theory. *Development and Psychopathology, 14*, 843–860.

Dozier, M., Higley, E., Albus, K., and Nutter, A. (2002b). Intervening with foster infants' caregivers: targeting three critical needs. *Infant Mental Health Journal, 23*, 541–554.

Erickson, E.H. (1950). *Childhood and society*. New York: Norton.

Eyberg, S. (1988). PCIT: Integration of traditional and behavioral concerns. *Child and Family Behavior Therapy, 10*, 33–46.

Eyberg, S., and Boggs, S.R. (1989). Parent training for oppositional preschoolers. In C.E. Shafer and J.M. Briesmeister (eds.), *Handbook of parent training: Parents as co-therapists for children's behavior problems* (pp. 105–132). New York: Wiley.

Eyberg, S.M., and Calzada, E.J. (1998) Parent–Child Interaction Therapy: Procedures manual. Unpublished manuscript, University of Florida.

Fraiberg, S. (1980). *Clinical studies in infant mental health*. New York: Basic Books.

Freud, S. (1955). Beyond the pleasure principle. In J. Strachey (ed. and trans.), *The standard edition of the complete psychological works of Sigmund Freud*, Volume 18. London: Hogarth Press. (Original work published 1920.)

Hembree-Kigin, T.L., and McNeil, C.B. (1995). *Parent–child interaction therapy*. New York: Plenum.

Herschell, A.D., and McNeil, C.B. (2005). Theoretical and empirical underpinnings of parent–child interaction therapy with child physical abuse populations. *Education and Treatment of Children, 28*, 142–162.

Janoff-Bulman, R. (1992). *Shattered assumptions: Toward a new psychology of trauma*. New York: Free Press.

Kolko, D.J. (1996). Individual cognitive-behavioral treatment and family therapy for physically abused children and their offending parents: A comparison of clinical outcomes. *Child Maltreatment, 1*, 322–342.

Lieberman, A.F. (1992). Infant–parent psychotherapy with toddlers. *Development and Psychopathology, 4*, 559–574.

Lieberman, A.F. (2004). Child–parent psychotherapy: A relationship-based approach to the treatment of mental health disorders in infancy and early childhood. In A.J. Sameroff, S.C. McDonough, and K.L. Rosenblum (eds.), *Treating parent-infant relationship problems* (pp. 97–122). New York: Guilford.

Lieberman, A.F., and Van Horn, P. (2005). *"Don't hit my mommy!": A manual for child-parent psychotherapy with young witnesses of family violence.* Washington, DC: ZERO TO THREE Press.

Lieberman, A.F., Weston, D., and Pawl, J.H. (1991). Preventive intervention and outcome with anxiously attached dyads. *Child Development, 62,* 199–209.

Lieberman, A.F., Padrón, E., Van Horn, P., and Harris, W. (2004). Angels in the nursery: The intergenerational transmission of benevolent parental influences. *Infant Mental Health Journal, 26,* 504–520.

Lieberman, A.F., Van Horn, P., and Ghosh Ippen, C. (2005). Toward evidence-based treatment: Child–parent psychotherapy with preschoolers exposed to marital violence. *Journal of the American Academy of Child and Adolescent Psychiatry, 44,* 1241–1248.

Lieberman, A.F., Ghosh Ippen, C., and Van Horn, P. (2006). Child–parent psychotherapy: 6-month follow-up of a randomized controlled trial. *Journal of the American Academy of Child and Adolescent Psychiatry, 45,* 913–918.

McDonough, S. (1992). Interactional guidance manual. Unpublished manuscript. Brown University, East Providence, RI.

McDonough, S. (2000). Interaction guidance: An approach for difficult-to-engage families. In C.H. Zeanah, Jr. (ed.), *Handbook of infant mental health,* 2nd edition (pp. 485–493. New York: Guilford.

Marans, S., and Adelman, A. (1997). Experiencing violence in a developmental context. In J.D. Osofsky (ed.), *Children in a violent society* (pp. 202–222). New York: Guilford.

Marmar, C., Foy, D., Kagan, B., and Pynoos, R. (1993). An integrated approach for treating posttraumatic stress. In J.M. Oldham, M.B. Riba, and A. Tasman (eds.), *American psychiatry press review of psychiatry, Volume 12.* Washington, DC: American Psychiatric Press.

Muir, E. (1992). Watching, waiting, and wondering: Applying psychoanalytic principles to mother–infant intervention. *Infant Mental Health Journal, 13,* 319–328.

Pynoos, R.S., Steinberg, A.M., and Piacentini, J.C. (1999). A developmental model of childhood traumatic stress and intersection with anxiety disorders. *Biological Psychiatry, 46,* 1542–1554.

Rutter, M. (1999). Resilience concepts and findings: Implications for family therapy. *Journal of Family Therapy, 21,* 119–144.

Scheeringa, M.S., Amaya-Jackson, L., and Cohen, J. (2002). Preschool PTSD treatment. Unpublished manuscript. Tulane University, New Orleans, LA.

Slade, A. (1994). Making meaning and making believe: Their role in the clinical process. In A. Slade and D.P. Wolf (eds.), *Children at play: Clinical and developmental approaches to meaning and representation* (pp. 81–107). New York: Oxford University Press.

Strupp, H.H. (1978). Psychotherapy research and practice: An overview. In A.E. Bergin and Y.S.L. Garfield (eds.), *Handbook of psychotherapy and behavior change,* 2nd edition (pp. 3–22). New York: Wiley.

Timmer, S.G., Urquiza, A.J., and Zebell, N. (2005a). Challenging foster caregiver-maltreated child relationships: The effectiveness of parent–child interaction therapy. *Children and Youth Services Review, 28,* 1–19.

Timmer, S.G., Urquiza, A.J., Zebell, N.M., and McGrath, J.M. (2005b). Parent–child interaction therapy: Application to maltreating parent–child dyads. *Child Abuse and Neglect, 29,* 825–842.

Toth, S.L., Maughan, A., Manly, J.T., Spagnola, M., and Cicchetti, D. (2002). The relative efficacy of two interventions in altering maltreated preschool children's representation models: Implications for attachment theory. *Development and Psychopathology, 14*, 877–908.

Toth, S.L., Rogosch, F.A., and Cicchetti, D. (in press). Toddler–parent psychotherapy reorganizes attachment in young offspring of mothers with major depressive disorder. *Journal of Consulting and Clinical Psychology*.

Urquiza, A.J., and McNeil, C.B. (1996). Parent–child interaction therapy: An intensive dyadic intervention for physically abusive families. *Child Maltreatment, 1*, 134–144.

Chapter 14

Group treatment for chronically traumatized adolescents

Igniting SPARCS of change

Ruth DeRosa and David Pelcovitz

Adolescent development sparks remarkable growth and transformation. Neuroscientists have described the significant reorganization of the adolescent brain as "second only to the neonatal period in terms of both rapid biopsychosocial growth as well as changing environmental characteristics and demands" (Schore 2001). Interestingly, while adolescents' physical and mental capacities expand greatly compared to younger children's, they also undergo heightened reactivity to stress (Spear 2000). In fact, research indicates that physiologically, adolescents are especially ill-suited to cope with stress compared to other age groups (Spear 2000). In particular, adolescents face numerous difficulties with self-regulation as a result of a combination of rapid brain development and a variety of developmental stressors associated with increasingly complex family, peer group, and school relationships and responsibilities (Spessot et al. 2004).

As adolescents grow increasingly vulnerable to problems with self-regulation, their rates of risk-taking, accidents, and exposure to violence also increase drastically (Dahl 2004; Kilpatrick et al. 2003). In addition, there is evidence to suggest that adolescents' ability to successfully negotiate and regulate their emotions and behaviors while planning and making decisions (especially in relation to future consequences) does not fully mature until young adulthood (Dahl 2004; Steinberg 2004).

The vulnerabilities inherent in this period of development increase significantly in the face of trauma. There are epidemiological data to suggest that by age 16 as many as one in four adolescents have experienced at least one type of trauma (accidents, loss, disaster, violence, maltreatment, etc.; Costello et al. 2002). According to the World Health Organization (Krug et al. 2002), violence is the leading cause of death worldwide among adolescents and young adults. Much of the interpersonal violence adolescents experience is perpetrated by someone they know and is usually not reported to authorities (65–86 percent; Kilpatrick et al. 2003).

Among survivors of multiple, repeated experiences of child maltreatment (often referred to as complex trauma; Cook et al. 2005), typical clinical presentations include problems with the adolescent's self-concept, emotional and behavioral self-regulation, and academic and interpersonal functioning. These adaptations to complex trauma are not fully captured by the diagnosis of posttraumatic stress disorder and include difficulty with regulation of the following:

- affect and impulses (upset or angered easily, trouble calming down, impulsivity, self-destructive behaviors)
- somatization and physical health (e.g. multiple, chronic physical complaints, autoimmune disorders)
- attention and information processing (dissociation)
- self-perception (e.g. seeing self as damaged, shameful, guilty)
- sense of meaning and purpose in life (hopeless and pessimistic about the future)
- interpersonal relationships (e.g. problems with trust, assertiveness, and unstable relationships).

These areas of functioning are included in the PTSD-associated features section of the DSM-IV (American Psychiatric Association 1994), and have been described in many ways since the early 1990s (e.g. Sequelae of Type II Traumas, Disorder of Extreme Stress Not Otherwise Specified (DESNOS), Complex PTSD, Developmental Trauma Disorder, and Complex Post-traumatic Self-Dysregulation). The prevalence and consistent co-occurrence of these alterations in functioning among survivors of complex trauma have been described in the literature in adults and more recently in children (e.g. Cook et al. 2005; Ford and Kidd 1998; Ford et al. 2005; Hall 1999; van der Kolk et al. 2005; Zlotnick et al. 1996). Investigation of the impact of trauma on these domains of self-dysregulation from a developmental perspective is less robust; researchers in neurobiology and developmental psychopathology have referred to this area of study as "developmental traumatology" (De Bellis 2005).

Given the developmental tasks of adolescence, Glodich and Allen (1998) outlined reasons that group treatment is well suited to this age group. Group members have the benefit of support and problem-solving with their peers in a manner that can be more powerful and received more readily than an intervention delivered by a clinician alone. Group members can also benefit vicariously from their peers and join at their own pace. While results to date are promising, the literature focused on group treatment specifically for adolescents, especially traumatized youth, is sparse. The effectiveness of group therapy with adolescents has been demonstrated in the treatment of depression, anxiety, posttraumatic stress, and traumatic grief (e.g. Garcia-Lopez et al. 2006; Layne et al. 2001; Weisz et al. 2006). While the group modality has been cited as frequently the treatment of choice for youth survivors of child maltreatment (Forseth and Browne 1981), there has been only one published randomized controlled trial (RCT) of psychotherapy specifically for adolescents exposed to chronic interpersonal trauma (Najavits et al. 2006). Some successful open trials have been published with adolescents in the juvenile justice system and survivors of community violence and war (e.g. Chapman et al. 2006; Layne et al. 2001; Ovaert et al. 2003; Salloum et al. 2001; Saltzman et al. 2001). One RCT exists for adolescent cancer survivors (Kazak et al. 2004).

Interventions specifically targeting posttraumatic self-regulatory problems in adolescence may prevent the long-term emotional, social, and financial cost of childhood trauma (e.g. Ballenger et al. 2000; Ford 2005). There is the potential for intervention during the teen years to minimize the risk of harmful alterations in biological stress response systems and brain development often found in adult survivors of chronic maltreatment (Schore 2001; van der Kolk 2003).

This chapter describes a promising practice, a sixteen-week group intervention for chronically traumatized adolescents, which addresses the alterations in functioning described above (Complex PTSD). Structured Psychotherapy for Adolescents Responding to Chronic Stress (SPARCS) was specifically designed for traumatized teens currently living with, or returning to, chaotic, stressful environments, who would benefit from stabilization and increased coping strategies (DeRosa et al. 2006).

Structured Psychotherapy for Adolescents Responding to Chronic Stress (SPARCS): a trauma-focused guide

SPARCS (DeRosa et al. 2006) is a guide for group treatment with traumatized adolescents designed to "spark" active coping by helping participants to identify their strengths and hopes for the future. SPARCS fosters a collaborative approach to explore current problems and the ways that trauma reminders may trigger maladaptive coping strategies. This approach addresses a range of Complex PTSD symptoms by examining how group members' current lives are impacted by difficulties with modulating affect, impulsivity, attention, concentration, dissociation, problematic relationships, and somatic complaints, as well as problems of shame, self-hatred and hopelessness. The broad goals of treatment are to help youths practice the four C's:

- *cultivate* awareness
- *cope* more effectively
- *connect* with others
- *create* meaning.

The development of SPARCS has differed from traditional practice in treatment design. In an effort to enhance its fit with daily practices, SPARCS was created, refined and evaluated in collaboration with multiple clinicians and community agencies over a period of time. Weisz et al. (2005) describe the benefits of this type of approach, called the Deployment-Focused Model of Intervention Development, which involves clinical application and evaluation of treatment methods in the practice setting as an early phase of intervention development, as well as a phase that follows rigorous research testing. Evaluation and testing to assess core components of treatment and mechanisms of change will continue to take place in community-based settings in an effort to facilitate translating treatment theory and techniques into meaningful interventions.

This sixteen-week treatment guide adapted and integrated three empirically informed interventions in an effort to address the topics specifically relevant to exposure to chronic trauma among adolescents. The three interventions are: Dialectical Behavior Therapy for Adolescents (DBT; Miller et al. 2006), TARGET (Ford and Russo 2006), and the UCLA School-Based Trauma/Grief Group Psychotherapy Program (Layne et al. 2001). Weekly one-hour sessions focus on enhancing coping strategies and teaching adolescents how to make choices mindfully even in the face of potential danger. Group members are routinely encouraged to improve access to their innate strengths or "wise mind" through routine mindfulness exercises, roleplays, and activities with movie clips and discussion. Many sessions include colorful handouts that cover practice exercises to try between sessions.

One of the primary tenets of both TARGET and DBT, which is a core component of the SPARCS approach as well, is the premise that therapists must help group members identify their strengths and find the "kernel of wisdom" in their current approach to life, even when at first it appears quite maladaptive. This kind of validation fosters empowerment and can free adolescents to address problems in a different way.

Cultivating awareness

One powerful antidote to the fragmentation and disorientation that trauma can bring is to enhance focus, attention, and grounding in the present moment. Enhancing awareness can be achieved in many different ways. As in DBT treatment, each SPARCS session includes mindfulness exercises designed to help participants practice paying attention in a particular way: Mindfulness is a process of being aware in the moment, and without judgment, of perceptions, feelings, and thoughts (J. Kabat-Zinn and M. Kabat-Zinn 1997). By being more aware of both internal states (thoughts, feelings, physical sensations, and urges) and external experiences (what is going on around them and in their relationships), group members may have more choices about how to respond to both stressful and enjoyable situations. Group members practice not only mentally focusing and concentrating, but also observing, that is, describing and fully participating in the moment without judging themselves, others or the situation. Adolescents practice mindfulness in a number of engaging ways including, for example, blowing bubbles, mindful eating, and listening to music. Clinical research with adults has demonstrated that mindfulness is a powerful intervention in a number of treatment outcome studies (see Baer 2003).

Group members also practice Ford's "SOS" technique to help them decrease arousal and increase focus and sense of control (Ford and Russo 2006). The SOS acronym stands for Slow Down, Orient Yourself, and do a Self-Check. As part of the self-check, participants and group leaders all rate both how stressed-out they are feeling and separately, how in control they are feeling in the moment. It is anticipated that teaching adolescents both mindfulness and SOS skills will assist them in reducing several complex PTSD symptoms, including alterations in regulation of affect and impulses, somatization, attention, and self-perception.

Mindfulness and SOS can have a powerful influence on affect regulation and impulsivity because they enable the person to interrupt reactive and impulsive patterns of thought and action by adopting a non-judgmental reflective position. These exercises also can help adolescents see the link between emotions and the body, which often has become disconnected. As a result of this disconnection, many adolescent survivors report frequent somatic complaints such as headaches and stomach aches, and do not understand how these symptoms reflect their state of mind and how they can be reduced with mindfulness.

Mindfulness practice includes active games like line dancing and playing catch with a softball, as well as quieter activity like observing and describing thoughts and feelings – each requiring focusing and refocusing of one's attention. Mindfulness practice is the key to accessing one's "wise mind" (Miller et al. 2006) otherwise known as intuition. SPARCS leaders repeatedly emphasize that group members *are* wise; they have a wise mind. Sometimes they just need practice getting there. This concept can be empowering and runs counter to trauma survivors' negative self-perceptions of themselves as permanently damaged and ineffective. Interestingly, adolescents in DBT have rated mindfulness skills as the most helpful skills they learned (Miller et al. 2000).

Adolescents are encouraged to identify both adaptive and maladaptive coping strategies they are currently using on a regular basis. Maladaptive coping strategies include problematic behaviors such as drinking, drugs, excessive risk-taking, and self-harm. We call these "MUPS" or things that mess you up. Ford and Russo (2006) describe the vicious cycle that frequently happens among teens struggling with the aftermath of trauma: something stressful happens, like a fight with a boyfriend or girlfriend, that triggers "unfinished emotional business" from the past, which can lead to additional stress and using MUPS (e.g. cutting or aggressive behavior). MUPS may then in turn cause more problems, and make one more vulnerable to additional stress and trauma. Group members often report that they were unaware how much they respond automatically, and not mindfully, to stress when the MUPS take over.

Coping more effectively

SPARCS group leaders introduce many types of skills and coping strategies to help youth manage ongoing extreme stress, including psychoeducation, identifying emotions, thoughts and their connection to somatic complaints, managing intense emotions and triggers, anger management, and problem-solving strategies. Group members are introduced to coping strategies for both immediate crises, managing the moment, and also for longer-term approaches to problem-solving. To help them "manage the moment" when overwhelmed, group members learn different skills to mindfully soothe and distract themselves and then practice them during the session after watching a somewhat distressing film clip.

Connecting with others

Enhancing communication skills and increasing perceived social support are critical components of treatment among chronically traumatized adolescents who often feel alienated, unable to trust anyone and sometimes too ashamed to let others really get to know them. SPARCS includes role plays for group members to practice asking for what they want and listening skills for relationships (Miller et al. 2006), and specific, concrete ways for teens to reach out to others for different kinds of support (Layne et al. 2001). In order to "keep a relationship or get what you want," the adolescent is taught the acronym "MAKE A LINK" (see below).

(be) **M**indful
Act confident
Keep a calm and gentle manner
Express interest

Ask for what you want

Let them know you get their point of view
Include your feelings
Negotiate – give to get
Keep your self respect

Over time, group members practice these skills using scenarios from their lives. The "L", "Let them know you get their point of view", is often the most challenging. While validation does not require that they agree with the other person, group members frequently fear that clarifying and letting other people know they understand their point of view means that they do agree with the other person or are giving in. Often coming from invalidating environments, many group members have little experience or practice with this type of communication. Repeated discussion and debriefing after the role plays is important and can provide an engaging and supportive way to help group members find their thoughtful, assertive voices.

Creating meaning

> Meaning is the sense that, no matter what is going on in your life, you can hang onto things that really matter to you. It is the belief that there are elements and people and views that cannot – no matter what – be taken from you.
>
> (Frankl 1963, p. 154)

With the advent of formal operations, adolescence is a time of idealism and existential questions when youth begin to explore independence, identity, meaning, and purpose in life. Survivors of chronic trauma often struggle to understand why bad things happen, if there is justice in the world, and whether there is a future, be it in school, one's career or one's ability to find happiness in love relationships. A growing body of research suggests that establishing a sense of meaning can play an important role in coping and health outcomes and is a key ingredient in the process of recovery from trauma (e.g. Gall et al. 2005; Goldblatt 2003; Park and Blumberg 2002). Throughout the course of treatment, SPARCS facilitators directly and indirectly ask group members to consider what is most important to them, what they value and hold dear, and how they would like to craft their future. This is explored in depth during the LET'M GO activity. This approach is adapted from the TARGET treatment for trauma survivors (Ford and Russo 2006). LET'M GO is a mnemonic adapted from Ford's Freedom steps, which teach skills to help group members address the traumatic material in the here-and-now. When repeatedly faced with MUPS, ways of coping that mess them up, group members are encouraged to figure out what is working for them and what is not. The LET'M GO steps are intended to help group members identify what they want to hold on to, what is important to them, and, alternatively, what they want to let go of that has been contributing to maladaptive coping. LET'M GO conveys the message that group members have the freedom to make a choice about what they want, and what they want to change, in their lives and relationships – rather than letting other people or the pain from the past choose it for them.

After mindfully completing an SOS, group members work with their peers and group leaders to discuss a recent conflict or problem using the following acronym and corresponding questions.

Losing it	Why am I losing it? What are my triggers?
Emotions	What am I feeling?
Thoughts	What am I thinking?
Meaning	What is really important to me?
Goals	What do I want?
Option	What are my choices?

They explore possible triggers, why someone might lose it ("L") in the situation described, and what someone's emotions ("E") and thoughts ("T") might be at that time. There are different ways for leaders to address and explore meaning-making ("M"). For example, helping group members to:

- figure out what is important to them in the situation based upon their values and beliefs
- think about the connection between things that they've survived in the past and the choices that they make now – making sense of what they have been through and labeling or reframing the experience
- think ahead about what they might want six months from now in a particular situation
- identify the contribution that the group member made to his/her own life, or the lives and welfare of others.

Some common themes for leaders to label in discussions include: justice, fairness, equality, trust, loyalty, honesty, power, freedom, helping others, respect, spirituality, and hope. After identifying possible goals ("G"), group members also identify what options might be available ("O"). Together the group identifies not only possible options for the future, but also, and more importantly, ways that the group member already "made a difference" in the world through choices made or intentions expressed.

Implementation

There are multiple challenges inherent in adopting and implementing a new clinical practice. These challenges may include poor staff engagement and orientation to the treatment before training even begins, inadequate administrative support, and little ongoing case consultation to facilitate problem-solving and support sustainability. In order to successfully implement and sustain the benefits from a group therapy for traumatized youths such as SPARCS, several organizational issues must be addressed.

Orientation and engagement for staff

A first key question is how implementing the group intervention can benefit the staff and clinicians as well as youth clients. Different organizations will have varying concerns and reservations and varying resources to assist them. One clinician, for example, may welcome additional team supervision and/or peer consultation in their work, while another clinician might welcome a structured yet flexible curriculum that will fit the students' class schedules. Organizations should facilitate an open and responsive forum to discuss reservations about starting a new practice, even when implementing the new intervention is required. This approach can help identify challenges and barriers in a proactive rather than reactive fashion. For example, learning a "manualized treatment" may be one concern. Manuals are often considered to be synonymous with a therapist straitjacket, rigid, inflexible and insensitive to client's needs. Validating concerns and discussing ways the intervention and/or the organization will address those problems, both before the new practice begins and over the course of treatment, is critical. Agencies could benefit from identifying who are potential "cheerleaders" or advocates for the new approach. "Cheerleaders" can collaborate with staff to identify their needs and concerns, and purposefully and systematically outline ways in which the new program can begin to address those problems.

Administrative support

Staff need adminstrative support in order to take the time and make the effort required to learn a new intervention and to integrate it into the existing treatment program. Paid expenses and time to attend a workshop have traditionally been the standard. However, this is not a sufficient strategy for ensuring that the new learning becomes part of the fabric of the organization, and that it is adopted in a way that best suits the adolescents' and the staff's needs at a particular agency. It also does not ensure that the investment of resources will result in a program that will continue over time. In order to promote sustainability, systems can actively anticipate barriers to implementation (e.g. scheduling conflicts, little to no time available to learn the new intervention onsite), problem-solve, and design strategies to maximize and spread organizations' strengths (staff commitment and interest in a new intervention, previous experience and expertise, communication). Some examples of solutions to common challenges with implementing a new practice include:

- guaranteeing protected time during the work week separate from routine duties to attend a new team meeting in order to prepare, practice and participate in collaborative learning with others implementing the new practice
- supporting supervisors' efforts to create a learning environment that incorporates roleplays and practice into team meetings
- creating flexible strategies for gathering assessment information for program evaluation (e.g. a pizza party for the adolescents during group

time, an orientation dinner for families, incorporating trauma questionnaires into intake interviews)
- routinely planning joint meetings with administrators, clinicians, and
  support staff with the specific agenda identifying and recording successes
  and to anticipate future challenges. These are but a few examples of
  administrative support that can increase the likelihood that clinicians will
  be productive and successful over time.

Training and consultation needs

As stated previously, in order to effect change, the traditional one-shot workshop training model is insufficient. The Institute for Healthcare Improvement
(IHI: www.ihi.org) has designed a "learning collaborative" model that brings
multiple sites together for multiple trainings over a period of 8–12 months,
with ongoing cross-site consultation. While IHI has demonstrated significant improvements in patient care in primary and emergency care (see
www.ihi.org/results), application of this model to mental health care has
just begun. Initial reports are promising; for example, Gopalan and McKay
(2006) designed a multi-site learning collaborative in an effort to enhance
engagement in child mental-health services. They reported that their collaborative efforts (among agencies and across all levels of agency management) resulted in an increase in intake attendance rates from 65 to 80 percent.
We are currently applying this learning collaborative model in the development of SPARCS. In addition to offering multiple trainings and ongoing
consultation, SPARCS trainers also encourage including staff who will have
ongoing contact with the group members, such as teachers, administrators,
clinicians, intake coordinators, aides, and supervisors. The learning collaborative approach has enabled a number of sites in the National Child
Traumatic Stress Network to adopt SPARCS within their integrated systems
of care.

Individualizing SPARCS

The ways in which group members cope with stress, connect with others,
learn new ways of dealing with life, and make sense of their experiences will
vary depending upon their age (chronological and developmental), culture,
region and gender. Leaders are encouraged to use the SPARCS guide to help
them identify metaphors, examples and activities that will be culturally meaningful to their group. A learning collaborative model provides a rich resource
for generating creative ways to adapt the treatment guide to best fit the needs
of a particular group.

Summary and conclusions

The deployment-focused model (Weisz et al. 2005) provided the framework for developing and enhancing the ecological validity of SPARCS. In keeping with this model, the treatment protocol was grounded in the empirical and theoretical literature on the impact of complex trauma on adolescents, and we proceeded to fine-tune the content based on systematic feedback from community sites working with different populations across the country. As a result, SPARCS has undergone extensive revision as informed by the cultures, successes and challenges faced by a variety of community settings.

The treatment has been implemented in a number of sites, including residential treatment centers, foster care agencies, outpatient clinics, and neighborhood schools. SPARCS has evolved into a more ecologically sensitive treatment and training based on modifications informed by the reality of the treatment being forged and modified in the real world. Consultation with an adult education consultant with extensive experience in the development of manuals also provided guidance regarding format and presentation to maximize user friendliness. Based on feedback we received from some of the first training sites, a model for training has evolved that includes a two-day learning session before the start of group, a one-day training approximately 4–6 weeks after the group begins, bimonthly consultation with therapists and monthly consultation with supervisors. The training itself includes a balance of didactic presentations on adolescent adaptation to chronic trauma, demonstrations and roleplays to practice the core components of the treatment, and active discussion and planning to address barriers to implementation based on their unique setting, culture, and client population. SPARCS trainers collaborate with agency and school staff to help them complete a SPARCS planning worksheet and facilitate a dialogue, and process for anticipating and addressing clinical and administrative challenges.

Some key variables that contribute to high clinician and client satisfaction appear to be a combination of three factors: high level of administrative support, clinical experience and expertise in either trauma-focused treatment or group therapy with adolescents and, perhaps most importantly, enthusiastic clinicians who also receive the clinical and administrative resources needed to embrace a new practice. Clinicians with expertise in either trauma work or adolescent group therapy bring a knowledge base that can greatly improve the SPARCS learning curve and enhance the quality of care. While systematic research is necessary to determine which ingredients of the treatment program are most efficacious, initial impressions suggest that clinicians are enthusiastic about a treatment guided by a manual that includes built-in flexibility and a resilience focus. Resilience is emphasized in SPARCS by focusing the intervention on assisting youths to identify coping strategies and supports that are already working well, as well as new skills. Emphasizing the wisdom and resilience of the youths seems to energize clinicians with a sense of enthusiasm and hope that contrasts with the pessimism and sadness that can accompany therapeutic work with traumatized youngsters.

Adolescent participants in SPARCS groups also seem to embrace a resilience-focused intervention that gives them practical tools for coping with the difficulties in their lives. Other recurring themes expressed by the adolescents include the connection they have felt with their therapists, who actively joined the adolescents in participating in group activities. In keeping with the literature on the efficacy of judicious therapist self-disclosure, the adolescents found that the non-judgmental stance of the therapist, combined with their use of carefully selected personal examples from their own lives, was particularly helpful.

We are currently exploring the efficacy of the treatment using the deployment-focused model in a variety of sites, and are systematically tracking group satisfaction, treatment compliance, and behavioral improvements. Based on our initial pilot work, we are hopeful that the treatment will stand up to the more rigorous standards of randomized clinical trials. As noted earlier, adolescence is a developmental period that includes a unique combination of heightened risk for traumatic exposure at a time when they are exceedingly vulnerable to the negative impact of trauma. An ancient Hebrew proverb states that "a little bit of light can push away much darkness" (Bachya Ibn Paquda 1997). The SPARCS program aims to help traumatized adolescents find that bit of light within themselves and ignite "sparks" of hope.

References

American Psychiatric Association (APA) (1994). *Diagnostic and statistical manual of mental disorders*, 4th edition. DSM-IV. Washington, DC: APA.

Bachya Ibn Paquda, R. (1997). *Duties of the heart/Chovoth Halevavoth*. Jerusalem: Feldheim.

Baer, R.A. (2003). Mindfulness training as a clinical intervention: A conceptual and empirical review. *Clinical Psychology: Science and Practice, 10*(2), 125–143.

Ballenger, J.C., Davidson, J.R.T., Lecrubier, Y., Nutt, D.J., Foa, E.B., Kessler, R.C., et al. (2000). Consensus statement on posttraumatic stress disorder from the international consensus group on depression and anxiety. *Journal of Clinical Psychiatry, 61*(suppl. 5), 60–66.

Chapman, J.F., Ford, J., Albert, D., Hawke, J., and Cruz St. Juste, M. (2006). Taking the fear out of trauma services in correctional settings: The TARGET approach. *CorrectCare: Newsletter of the National Commission on Correctional Healthcare, 1*(14).

Cook, A., Spinazzola, J., Ford, J., Lanktree, C., Blaustein, M., Cloitre, M., et al. (2005). Complex trauma in children and adolescents. *Psychiatric Annals, 35*(5), 390–398.

Costello, E.J., Erkanli, A., Fairbank, J.A., and Angold, A. (2002). The prevalence of potentially traumatic events in childhood and adolescence. *Journal of Traumatic Stress, 15*(2), 99–112.

Dahl, R.E. (2004). Adolescent brain development: A period of vulnerabilities and opportunities. *Annals of the New York Academy of Sciences, 1021*, 1–22.

De Bellis, M.D. (2005). The psychobiology of neglect. *Child Maltreatment, 10*(2), 150–172.

DeRosa, R., Habib, M., Pelcovitz, D., Rathus, J., Sonnenklar, J., Ford, J., et al. (2006). *Structured Psychotherapy for Adolescents Responding to Chronic Stress (SPARCS): A trauma-focused guide.* Manhasset, NY: North Shore University Hospital

Ford, J. (2005). Treatment implications of altered affect regulation and information processing following child maltreatment. *Psychiatric Annals, 35*(5), 410–419.

Ford, J.D., and Kidd, P. (1998). Early childhood trauma and disorders of extreme stress as predictors of treatment outcome with chronic PTSD. *Journal of Traumatic Stress, 11*, 743–761.

Ford, J.D., and Russo, E. (2006). A trauma-focused, present-centered, emotional self-regulation approach to integrated treatment for posttraumatic stress and addiction: Trauma Affect Regulation: Guidelines for Education and Therapy (TARGET). *American Journal of Psychotherapy, 60*, 335–355.

Ford, J.D., Courtois, C.A., Steele, K., Hart, O., and Nijenhuis, E.R.S. (2005). Treatment of complex posttraumatic self-dysregulation. *Journal of Traumatic Stress, 18*(5), 437–447.

Forseth, L.B., and Brown, A. (1981). A survey of intrafamilial sexual abuse treatment centers: Implications for intervention. *Child Abuse and Neglect, 5*, 177–186.

Frankl, V.F. (1963). *Man's search for meaning.* New York: Pocket Books.

Gall, T.L., Charbonneau, C., Clarke, N.H., Grant, K., Joseph, A., and Shouldice, L. (2005). Understanding the nature and role of spirituality in relation to coping and health: A conceptual framework. *Canadian Psychology, 46*(2), 88–104.

Garcia-Lopez, L.J., Olivares, J., Beidel, D., Albano, A.M., Turner, S., and Rosa, A.I. (2006). Efficacy of three treatment protocols for adolescents with social anxiety disorder: A 5-year follow-up assessment. *Journal of Anxiety Disorders, 20*(2), 175–191.

Glodich, A., and Allen, J.G. (1998). Adolescents exposed to violence and abuse: A review of the group therapy literature with an emphasis on preventing trauma reenactment. *Journal of Child and Adolescent Group Therapy, 8*(3), 135–154.

Goldblatt, H. (2003). Strategies of coping among adolescents experiencing interparental violence. *Journal of Interpersonal Violence, 18*(5), 532–552.

Gopalan, G., and McKay, M.M. (2006). The effects of a learning collaborative on engagement in child mental health services. Poster presented at the Society for Social Work and Research, San Antonio, TX, January.

Hall, D.K. (1999). "Complex" posttraumatic stress disorder/disorders of extreme stress in sexually abused children. *Journal of Child Sexual Abuse, 8*(4), 51–71.

Kabat-Zinn, J., and Kabat-Zinn, M. (1997). *Everyday blessings: The inner work of mindful parenting.* New York: Hyperion.

Kazak, A.E., Alderfer, M.A., Streisand, R., Simms, S., Rourke, M.T., Barakat, L.P., et al. (2004). Treatment of PTSD in adolescent survivors of childhood cancer and their families: A randomized clinical trial. *Journal of Family Psychology, 18*(3), 493–504.

Kilpatrick, D.G., Saunders, B.E., and Smith, D.W. (2003). *Youth victimization. Research in brief.* Washington, DC: US Department of Justice, National Institute of Justice.

Krug, E.G., Dahlberg, L.L., Mercy, J.A., Zwi, A., and Lozano, R. (eds.) (2002). *World report on violence and health.* Geneva: World Health Organization.

Layne, C.M., Pynoos, R.S., Saltzman, W.R., Arslanagic, B., Black, M., Savjak, N., et al. (2001). Trauma/grief-focused group psychotherapy: School-based postwar intervention with traumatized Bosnian adolescents. *Group Dynamics: Theory, Reseach and Practice, 5*(4), 277–290.

Miller, A.L., Wyman, S.E., Huppert, J.D., Glassman, S.L., and Rathus, J.H. (2000). Analysis of behavioral skills utilized by suicidal adolescents receiving dialectical behavior therapy. *Cognitive and Behavioral Practice, 7*, 183–187.

Miller, A.L., Rathus, J.H., and Linehan, M. (2006). *DBT for adolescents.* New York: Guilford.

Najavits, L.M., Gallop, R.J., and Weiss, R.D. (2006). Seeking safety therapy for adolescent girls with PTSD and substance use disorder: A randomized controlled trial. *Journal of Behavioral Health Services and Research, 33*(4), 453–463.

Ovaert, L.B., Cashel, M.L., and Sewell, K.W. (2003). Structured group therapy for posttraumatic stress disorder in incarcerated male juveniles. *American Journal of Orthopsychiatry, 73*(3), 294–301.

Park, C.L., and Blumberg, C.J. (2002). Disclosing trauma through writing: Testing the meaning making hypothesis. *Cognitive Therapy and Research, 26*(5), 597–616.

Salloum, A., Avery, L., and McClain, R.P. (2001). Group psychotherapy for adolescent survivors of homicide victims. *Journal of the American Academy of Child and Adolescent Psychiatry, 40*(11), 1261–1267.

Saltzman, W., Layne, C., Pynoos, R., Steinberg, A., and Aisenberg, E. (2001). Trauma and grief-focused intervention for adolescents exposed to community violence: Results of a school-based screening and group treatment protocol. *Group Dynamics: Theory, Research and Practice, 5*(4), 291–303.

Schore, A.N. (2001). Effects of a secure attachment relationship on right brain development, affect regulation, and infant mental health *Infant Mental Health Journal, 22*(1–2), 7–66.

Spear, L.P. (2000). Neurobehavioral changes in adolescence. *Current Directions in Psychological Science, 9*(4), 111–114.

Spessot, A.L., Plessen, K.J., and Peterson, B.S. (2004). Neuroimaging of developmental psychopathologies: The importance of self-regulatory and neuroplastic processes in adolescence. *Annals of the New York Academy of Sciences, 1021,* 86–104.

Steinberg, L. (2004). Risk taking in adolescence: What changes, and why? *Annals of the New York Academy of Sciences, 1021,* 51–58.

van der Kolk, B.A. (2003). The neurobiology of childhood trauma and abuse. *Child and Adolescent Psychiatric Clinics of North America, 12*(2), 293–317.

van der Kolk, B.A., Roth, S., Pelcovitz, D., Sunday, S., and Spinazzola, J. (2005). Disorders of extreme stress: The empirical foundation of complex adaptation to trauma. *Journal of Traumatic Stress, 18*(5), 389–400.

Weisz, J., Jensen, A., and McLeod, B.D. (2005). Deployment and dissemination of child and adolescent psychotherapies: Milestones, methods and a new deployment-focused model. In E.D. Hibbs and P.S. Jensen (eds.), *Psychosocial treatments for child and adolescent disorders: Empirically based strategies for clinical practice,* 2nd edition (pp. 9–39). Washington, DC: APA.

Weisz, J.R., McCarty, C.A., and Valeri, S.M. (2006). Effects of psychotherapy for depression in children and adolescents: A meta-analysis. *Psychological Bulletin, 132*(1), 132–49.

Zlotnick, C., Zakriski, A., Shea, M.T., Costello, E., Begin, A., Pearlstein, T., et al. (1996). The long-term sequelae of sexual abuse: Support for a complex post-traumatic stress disorder. *Journal of Traumatic Stress, 9*(2), 195–205.

Chapter 15

Family-based treatment for child traumatic stress

A review and report on current innovations

William R. Saltzman, Thomas Babayan, Patricia Lester, William R. Beardslee, and Robert S. Pynoos

The experience of trauma has been likened to the surface of a lake after being struck by a stone: the impact of single trauma can ripple throughout many individuals' lives. Indeed, theoreticians and researchers have increasingly noted that childhood trauma is fundamentally a family-level event, both in terms of impact and the prospects for recovery (Catherall 2004; Figley 1989). While a growing body of empirical literature has demonstrated the efficacy of family-based interventions for a range of child mental health problems in multiple contexts (Diamond and Josephson 2005), efficacious models for family-based interventions for children or families affected by psychological trauma have yet to be established (Lester et al. 2003). This represents a significant gap in theory and practice in the field of child traumatic stress.

To help address this gap, this chapter will summarize the evidence concerning the effects of traumatic stress on family systems, including the effects on multiple generations; examine the evidence regarding the efficacy of family-based treatments for treating posttraumatic stress; and describe an innovative family-based approach for treating child and family trauma that is currently being evaluated.

Traumatic stress and the family

Posttraumatic stress impacts on the family

Figley (1989) was the first to set up a conceptual framework for understanding the impact of traumatic stress on families by recognizing four distinct types of effects:

- *simultaneous effects* occur from a trauma that involves the entire family at once, such as a car accident or natural disaster
- *vicarious effects* may arise when trauma is experienced by an individual while separated from the family, as in soldiers at war
- *intrafamilial trauma* involves those instances in which a family member causes the trauma of another, such as child abuse or domestic violence

- chiasmal effects, or what are now known as *secondary stress effects* (Lebow and Rekart 2004), refer to effects experienced by the entire family system as a result of an individual family member's ongoing post-traumatic stress symptoms.

A key point of Figley's typology is that trauma may enter the family system via any of its members, through direct and indirect pathways.

Equally important is the notion that even when there is a shared trauma across the family (as is frequently the case in natural disasters) individual family members usually have distinct levels of actual and perceived exposure to the stressful events, with different degrees of posttraumatic response (Pynoos et al. 1999). Individual reactions to traumatic events are linked to a host of factors, including personal histories of trauma and loss, comorbid psychological difficulties, and differences in temperament and personality (Brewin et al. 2000; Ozer et al. 2003). As a result of discordant levels of exposure and posttraumatic symptoms among family members, individuals may have very different needs and courses of recovery. The "dis-synchrony" of family members' recovery from trauma or loss may then result in heightened levels of stress and conflict within the family (Pynoos et al. 1999). The result is compromised family support and cohesion just when these qualities are most needed to facilitate recovery.

Family impacts on vulnerability and resilience to posttraumatic stress

Lack of social support appears to be one of the most important factors in the development of posttraumatic stress (Brewin et al. 2000; Ozer et al. 2003). For children and adolescents, social support relates directly to the role of the family in the wake of trauma. Indeed, children and adolescents often look to their parents and siblings as sources of support during a variety of stressful situations, including illness and the loss of a loved one (Hawkins and Manne 2004). Chaotic, distant and anxious families tend to increase the risk of PTSD in children (Perry and Azad 1999). These findings are consistent with those of Green et al. (1991), who found children from depressed and chaotic families to be more prone to developing PTSD symptoms after a natural disaster. Greenberg and Keane (2001) found that children who were dissatisfied with familial support after a house fire showed higher rates of PTSD symptoms than those who perceived their familial support as satisfactory. Using data provided by the National Youth Victimization Prevention Study, Boney-McCoy and Finkelhor (1996) identified disturbed parent–child relationships as a powerful predictor of a child developing PTSD symptoms following a trauma. Children from families in which parents reported greater difficulties with communication and supervision, and lower levels of positive interaction in the parent–child subsystem, were more likely to present with posttraumatic stress subsequent to traumatic exposure. Similarly, Brent et al. (1995) showed that of adolescents who had been exposed to a friend's suicide, those who came from families with discordant parent–child relationships tended to be at greater risk of developing symptoms of PTSD.

These findings reveal the importance of healthy family functioning as a source of support for victims of trauma. The presence of trauma-related symptoms in a parent, such as anxiety, avoidance, intrusion, and emotional numbing, have been found to interfere with their ability to maintain family routines and roles (Jordan et al. 1992; Ruscio et al. 2002). Because children depend on their parents for emotional support, role modeling, and physical safety/security, when parents suffer posttraumatic stress symptoms, their children may have difficulty managing their own reactions to the trauma. This appears to be true for those children directly victimized by a traumatic event (Nader et al. 1990), as well as those who simply have been told about a family member's violent or traumatic experience (Steinberg et al. 2004). Parental withdrawal, over-protectiveness, and excessive preoccupation related to the trauma have been identified as relational factors that may indirectly exacerbate a child's traumatic stress symptoms (Scheeringa and Zeanah 2001). In addition, Meiser-Stedman et al. (2006) found parental depression to be positively correlated with posttraumatic stress symptoms in their children.

Just as it is important to understand what makes individuals vulnerable to posttraumatic stress, it also makes sense to study those who are able to thrive in the wake of traumatic experiences. Waller (2001) defines resilience as "a positive adaptation to adversity," such as trauma and other threatening life circumstances.

Research has borne out the value of family support (Jovanovic et al. 2004; Schumm et al. 2004) and healthy family function (Perry and Azad 1999) as sources of resilience in the wake of trauma. Within the family, the parent–child subsystem appears to have the greatest impact on the development of PTSD symptoms in children and adolescents. In a meta-analysis of seventeen studies, Scheeringa and Zeanah (2001) identified a strong association between parent and child functioning posttrauma. A number of these studies note that parents who are able to effectively cope with trauma (their own or their child's) are better able to provide emotional support to their children (Goff and Schwerdtfeger 2004). Because children are sensitive to their parents' reactions to trauma (Steinberg et al. 2004), parents who successfully manage their posttraumatic stress symptoms provide a positive role model for their children (Rossman et al. 1997).

However, the bulk of the studies linking parental and child response to trauma are correlational in nature and cannot substantiate a causal relationship. Nevertheless, these findings suggest practical guidelines for engaging families in enhancing their members' resilience to trauma. For example, it appears that parents do not have to be unaffected by traumatic stress in order to effectively assist their children in coping resiliently with or recovering from trauma. To the extent that they can be assisted to cope with their own traumatic stress reactions, parents are more likely to be able to be emotionally available to and able to provide the modeling and appropriate support that would best benefit their children and family.

A child's traumatic stress experiences or reactions also may be traumatic for the parents. Parents may develop posttraumatic stress symptoms based on their child's experiencing potentially traumatic stressors regardless of whether the parent has been directly exposed to the traumatic event itself (Barnes 1998). For instance, parents whose child experiences a traumatic disaster or illness may also develop posttraumatic stress symptoms (Kazak et al. 2004; Pfefferbaum 1997). In fact, a review of twenty-four studies of posttraumatic stress reactions in parents of childhood cancer survivors shows lifetime prevalence of cancer-related PTSD in the parents ranging from 27 percent to 54 percent (Bruce 2006). This is quite high compared to community prevalence estimates of PTSD among people exposed to at least one traumatic event: 8 percent of men and 20 percent of women (Kessler et al. 1999).

Transgenerational transmission of psychological trauma and traumatic stress

Not only can the effects of trauma travel through an extant family system, but also they can be transmitted to future generations. Children of traumatized parent(s) may be at greater risk of developing PTSD-related symptoms and psychological difficulties if exposed to a trauma themselves (Danieli 1998). This is not surprising given the relationship between parental and child posttraumatic symptomatology. In a longitudinal study of children of Holocaust survivors, Kellerman (2001a) found that the offspring of these traumatized parents shared multiple psychological and interpersonal characteristics that did not meet criteria for diagnosis but were, nevertheless, problematic and impairing. Steinberg et al. (2004) identified similar characteristics belonging to children of survivors of major traumas including depression, anxiety, excessive guilt, phobias, and separation problems. Kellerman (2001b) divided such characteristics into four categories:

- *self*, consisting of low self-esteem, identity issues, over-identification with victim/survivor status, pressure to overachieve in order to make up for parents' losses and carrying the burden of replacing lost relatives
- *cognition*, consisting of expectation of another catastrophe, preoccupation with death and stress when exposed to Holocaust reminders
- *affectivity*, consisting of annihilation anxiety, nightmares of persecution, dysphoric mood related to loss, unresolved conflicts related to guilt and increased vulnerability to stress
- *interpersonal functioning*, consisting of enmeshed or disengaged family

attachments, difficulty creating intimate relationships and dealing with interpersonal conflicts.

A number of theoretical models have been developed to account for the transgenerational transmission of PTSD. Sociocultural models place an emphasis on the process of socialization through parental practices while a family system orientation identifies communication and enmeshment/disengagement factors as primary (Kellerman 2001b). A family systems approach described by Catherall (1998) spotlights the importance of distorted family cognitions, debilitating family myths and dysfunctional family rules. These family generated mechanisms may perpetuate trauma themes for children growing up in such families.

Family-based treatment for posttraumatic stress

Through family therapy, individuals are not only offered the opportunity to improve their own reactions to trauma, but also learn how to effectively support the members of their family suffering from posttraumatic stress. For example, family interventions may serve to raise members' awareness of potentially unsupportive family behaviors such as excessive criticism, giving unsolicited advice and conveying discomfort during attempts to communicate about the trauma (Lebow and Rekart 2004).

Family therapy can be defined as any "psychotherapeutic intervention that directly involves family members beyond the index person" (Pinsof and Wynne 2000). Meta-analytic studies have found family-based treatments to be more effective than no treatment and at least as successful as individual treatments for a variety of psychological disorders (Diamond and Josephson 2005). Some therapeutic approaches engage the family directly, while others intervene with parents to help them promote their children's therapeutic success (Diamond and Josephson 2005). The tightly knit relationship between parental involvement and child/adolescent therapy led Kazdin and Weisz (1998) to declare that most child therapy is "de facto family context therapy".

Since the mid-1990s there have been several empirically based research studies showing the effectiveness of family components used in conjunction with cognitive behavioral approaches for treating child and adolescent posttraumatic stress (Stallard 2006). For example, Kolko (1996) compared cognitive behavioral treatments (CBT), family-based treatments, and community-based services working with children between the ages of 6 and 13 who had recently experienced physical abuse. Individual CBT consisted of separate sessions for parent and child, while family therapy sessions included the entire family. Community-based services included parenting and homemaking skills given in the home. The study showed CBT and family-based treatments consistently outperforming community services. The family-based treatment group showed that treatment gains were retained at greater rates than other interventions after a one-year follow-up survey and were associated with a greater reduction in parent-to-child violence (Kolko 1996). Deblinger et al. (1996) found that parental involvement in cognitive behavioral therapies significantly improved the reduction of PTSD symptoms in those children who had suffered from sexual abuse. It should be noted that the mothers in this case were "non-offending", indicating that they were not the perpetrators of the abuse. Finally, several more recent studies (Kazak et. al. 2004; Lieberman et al. 2005) have pointed to the greater efficacy of cognitive behavioral treatments with family-based components over community-based treatment and no treatment at all.

It is now generally agreed that parental involvement in child and adolescent interventions for posttraumatic stress is beneficial (National Institute for Clinical Excellence 2005; Stallard 2006). Still, many questions remain. Does family therapy for PTSD have unique outcomes compared to other therapeutic approaches? What are the most effective components of family therapy for PTSD? Does the nature of the trauma make a difference in therapeutic outcomes? Despite these questions, it is clear that family therapy holds untapped potential for treating the multiple impacts of posttraumatic stress on the family, especially when the victim of trauma is a child.

The FOCUS Program: a family-based treatment for traumatic stress

Since 2003, staff members at the UCLA Trauma Psychiatry Program (William Saltzman, PhD, Patricia Lester, MD, Robert Pynoos, MPH, MD) in collaboration with William Beardslee, MD from the Harvard Judge Baker Children's Center and Children's Hospital Boston, have developed and piloted the FOCUS Program (Families Overcoming and Coping Under Stress) in multiple settings. Initially, the program was implemented with military families at Camp Pendleton, a Marine Base in California whose forces have sustained more casualties and deaths during the war in Iraq (Operation Iraqi Freedom and Operation Enduring Freedom) than any other US base, and more recently with families impacted by child medical trauma at Miller Children's Hospital in Long Beach, California. An abbreviated version of the program was implemented as an "Enhanced Service" by FEMA for communities across Florida that sustained significant damage from hurricanes in 2004 and 2005. A Robert Woods Johnson grant has recently been awarded to adapt and implement the program for use with police, fire department, and emergency medical personnel who were in New Orleans during Hurricane Katrina in 2005.

The FOCUS Program is unique in providing a structured approach for delivering trauma-focused family therapy that is at once rich with detail and therapeutic activities, and sufficiently flexible to accommodate families of different ethnicity and culture who present with various levels of need and trauma severity. A number of individual and family assessment measures are administered initially and throughout the treatment to index exposure to trauma and loss, symptoms of posttraumatic distress, depression and anxiety, functional impairment, and family cohesion, support and communication. These assessments are used to help specify the sequence and number of sessions to be held to accomplish the program goals.

The intervention is generally delivered over eight sessions: the first three sessions with the parent(s), the fourth and fifth with the children, and the last three sessions with the entire family. The FOCUS Program is not intended for crisis intervention and should be applied after acute stabilization has taken place. For example, in the case of medical trauma, initial outreach is provided to the family in the hospital and arrangements are made to meet after the immediate medical crisis has been resolved and ongoing or rehabilitative treatment is in place. The same is true for the treatment of families that have experienced a natural disaster, been victimized by community violence, or have had a family death.

The FOCUS Program aims to improve child outcomes (reducing post-trauamtic stress, anxiety and depression while improving functioning in key domains) through targeting key intermediate outcomes, both familial (improve family communication and cohesion) and parental (improve communication and support between parents, facilitate consistent care routines and parenting practices, and maintain developmentally appropriate expectations for child reactivity and recovery). The model underlying this intervention is an integration of psychoeducational, narrative, and cognitive-behavioral theory, and builds on previous research that demonstrates the potential of improving child adjustment by improving family coping skills, promoting positive parenting skills, enhancing parent–child communication, and reducing parental emotional distress (Beardslee et al. 2003; Patterson 1992; Rotheram-Borus et al. 2001; Taylor and Biglan 1998).

The intervention is based on the earlier UCLA Trauma/Grief Program, which has been shown to reduce primary trauma-related symptoms, and improve school and interpersonal functioning among participants (Layne et al. 2001, 2002). The FOCUS model also incorporates elements of an intervention for families with parental depression which has been shown to be effective both short-term and long-term in changing attitudes, behaviors, and interactions, and in reducing the long-term risk of mental health problems among children (Beardslee et al. 2003). The FOCUS model also incorporates portions of an intervention for HIV-affected mothers and their children which has demonstrated improvements in emotional and behavioral adjustment and sustained long-term improvements in key functional domains (Lester et al. 2003; Rotheram-Borus et al. 2004).

The content and design of the FOCUS Program was adapted and refined through pilot implementations with military families at Camp Pendleton Marine Base and with children and families impacted by medical trauma, community violence, and traumatic loss who were being seen at Miller Children's Hospital and the UCLA Medical Center. As the program evolved, core therapeutic elements emerged. These included

- psychoeducation regarding trauma and developmentally appropriate expectations for children and adolescents
- enhancement of individual and family coping skills
- development and sharing of individual and family trauma narrative timelines.

Psychoeducation regarding trauma and developmentally appropriate expectations

Prior studies have shown that trauma-focused psychoeducation that includes information about expected reactions to trauma and course of recovery, when linked to coping skill enhancement, can help ameliorate posttraumatic symptomatology in adolescents (Layne et al. 2002). In the current program, psychoeducation is provided separately and collectively to the parents, children and family as a whole. Psychoeducation regarding trauma and loss is woven throughout all of the sessions in the guise of factual information, feedback from assessments, and activities designed to heighten personal and interpersonal awareness.

Feedback is provided from initial and ongoing assessments of trauma exposure, posttraumatic stress, depression, anxiety, traumatic grief and a range of functional indices for individual family members, along with measures of overall family functioning. General information on expected reactions to trauma based on age and developmental level is then customized to the family's specific symptom and functional profile and prioritization of current concerns. The family members and the counselor then use this information to collaboratively craft family goals. The counselor helps parents understand how family trauma or loss and parental distress may be linked to breakdowns in family cohesion, communication, care routines, and other key parenting activities. On the positive side, the counselor also assesses and highlights family strengths, adaptive coping responses, and available resources.

Enhancement of individual and family coping skills

The FOCUS Program is designed to identify and build on the strengths and adaptive coping strategies already present in the family. It starts by helping the parents and family identify and prioritize their current concerns, difficulties, and situations that evoke trauma-related reactions in one or more family members. Families then explore what they individually and collectively do to help themselves feel better and function better. This discussion begins an ongoing dialogue in which the family members report on difficulties and trauma or loss reminders encountered during the week and how they coped with them. The clinician offers new coping strategies to add to their existing "tool kit", such as relaxation and breathing techniques, communication, interpersonal awareness skills, cognitive techniques designed to interrupt distorted and harmful ways of thinking, and problem-solving strategies. Skills are learned in sessions and practiced in homework. Individual skills are built incrementally, focusing first on monitoring and articulation of feeling states, then on identifying the internal and external "triggers" or reminders that contribute to these changes, and then on selecting one or more behavioral responses or strategies to productively deal with the distress.

Development and sharing of individual and family trauma narrative timelines

This is perhaps the most novel element of the FOCUS Program: having individual family members develop their own narratives of the trauma or loss event and share them with the rest of the family through a graphic timeline. This exercise is important for a number of reasons, especially since family members usually have very different levels of exposure, and different experiences of a traumatic situation. This is true even if the family members were all present during the same distressing events. Individual discrepancies are based on differences in proximity and perceived threat, prior trauma and loss history, comorbid psychopathology, gender and personality characteristics. These differences can be extreme when one family member has had severe trauma exposure, as in military families in which one of the parents has experienced combat, injury and death during a wartime deployment.

As a result of their different experiences and reactions, family members typically have very different psychological needs and different courses of recovery. These differences may lead to increased family conflict, decreased empathy and understanding between family members, and decreased family support and tolerance. This becomes especially problematic because most families do not have mechanisms of discourse in place that permit open discussion and acknowledgement of these differences. In many cases, family members frame their silence as a way of protecting each other from worry or from what they perceive as an additional burden on family members already under duress. This was the case for a mother of a 16-year-old boy whose friend was shot while standing next to him at a bus stop after school. The boy and his family did not understand why their mother became increasingly anxious and depressed over the months following the incident nor why she could not get out of bed and demanded to know her son's whereabouts at all times. During a family session six months after the shooting, it was revealed that before the mother was married, she was present during an armed robbery in a small downtown store, and was standing next to her uncle when he was shot and killed. She had never told her husband or family about this experience and insisted that she should not do so even now when the memory and related fears were activated by her son's similar experience. Clearly, it was very important that the mother understand how her previous trauma heightened her reactions in the current case, and equally important for her family to make sense of the mother's seemingly extreme reactions, and to be supportive of her very different course and timetable for recovery.

Mutual understanding and appreciation of differences can help reduce family stress, increase support, and foster individual and family recovery. As illustrated in the case example, only by bringing these discrepant experiences and reactions to the family in an appropriate manner can the resources of the family be fully enlisted in the tasks of support and recovery.

To provide a safe and structured means for family members to develop and share their personal narratives within the family and, ultimately, to develop a consensual "family narrative" of the traumatic event(s), guidelines were developed for eliciting these narratives from children and adults. To facilitate the sharing and contrasting of experiences, a graphic approach using a "narrative timeline" was developed. Parents and children, generally aged 10 and older, are shown how to graph out their single or multiple trauma and loss experiences via a chart that shows time on the horizontal axis and intensity of distress on the vertical axis. Once instructed, clients are usually able to map their experiences on the timeline themselves. Younger children are directed to use art and drawing to convey their experiences and to assemble their narrative on a game board that tracks chronology via a colorful and winding path.

Parental narratives are elicited during the first "parents only" sessions. In most cases, parents learn new aspects of their partner's objective and subjective experience from the narratives. It can also be helpful to use the narrative timeline to track prior trauma and loss experiences that the parent or family has had. Helping the parents appreciate the cumulative load of multiple or repeated stressful experiences can provide an important backdrop for understanding individual and family reactions to the current trauma. For example, in working with a family who had lost a daughter in a car accident, it was pivotal to track the prior experiences of both parents who had endured serial hardships and traumatic events in El Salvador, their country of origin, during the civil war in that country, and during the course of their immigration to the United States.

During the latter parts of the parental sessions, the clinician focuses on the ways in which differences in the parental experiences and reactions, and subsequent misunderstandings may contribute to current difficulties and breakdowns in marital communication and parenting tasks. In fact, by maintaining the primary focus on the family and children's welfare rather than on marital issues, parents are much more open and willing to engage in the therapeutic work. It is also important to spend time preparing the parents for the family sessions. This involves clarifying which portions of the parental narratives should be shared with the children, how to appropriately respond to children's questions and concerns, and how to take a leadership role in the family sessions via good listening and supportive engagement.

Child narratives are elicited during the following two sessions. As mentioned above, art and play activities are incorporated to provide developmentally appropriate means of representing the child's experience. In preparation for the family sessions, children are helped to identify specific concerns and questions that they might want to discuss at that time.

The final sessions are family meetings. After a summary of the major family traumatic events, usually provided by the clinician, the child or children are invited to share their narrative materials. The parents then comment and contrast their experiences of the same events. Later sessions are dedicated to discussing significant differences among family members regarding their experiences, perceptions, attributions, and reactions. As appropriate, any misattributions or distortions identified during the sharing of narratives, especially those regarding issues of blame, guilt or shame, need to be addressed by the family. Structured activities are then used to help the family develop a consensual family narrative and "healing theory" about the traumatic events (Figley 1989). The last session is devoted to identifying, prioritizing, and engaging in family problem-solving for current difficulties and plans for upcoming and continuing family stressors.

Conclusion

The next step for family intervention in the wake of psychological trauma is the development of systematic and replicable treatment protocols that can be evaluated in a more rigorous and controlled fashion. The field appears poised to develop systematic family-based interventions for childhood and adolescent traumatic stress and the requisite assessment tools and methodology necessary to mount well-controlled studies. These efforts hold great promise, not only for our understanding of traumatic stress, but also for the many families that are confronted with overwhelming and potentially devastating experiences.

References

Barnes, M.F. (1998). Understanding the secondary traumatic stress of parents. In C.R. Figley (ed.), *Burnout in families: The systemic costs of caring* (pp. 75–90). Boca Raton, FL: CRC Press.

Beardslee, W.R., Gladstone, T.R.G., Wright, E.J., and Cooper, A.B. (2003). A family-based approach to the prevention of depressive symptoms in children at risk: Evidence of parental and child change. *Pediatrics, 112*, e119–e1310.

Boney-McCoy, S., and Finkelhor, D. (1996). Is youth victimization related to trauma symptoms and depression after controlling for prior symptoms and family relationships? A longitudinal, prospective study. *Journal of Consulting and Clinical*

Psychology, 64(6), 1406–1416. Retrieved January 5, 2007, from PsycARTICLES database.

Brent, D.A., Perper, J.A., Moritz, G., and Liotus, L. (1995). Posttraumatic stress disorder in peers of adolescent suicide victims: Predisposing factors and phenomenology. *Journal of the American Academy of Child and Adolescent Psychiatry, 34*(2), 209–215. Retrieved December 30, 2006, from PsycINFO database.

Brewin, C.R., Andrews, B., and Valentine, J.D. (2000). Meta-analysis of risk factors for posttraumatic stress disorder in trauma-exposed adults. *Journal of Consulting and Clinical Psychology, 68*(5), 748–766. Retrieved December 30, 2006, from PsycARTICLES database.

Bruce, M. (2006). A systematic and conceptual review of posttraumatic stress in childhood cancer survivors and their parents. *Clinical Psychology Review, 26*(3), 233–256. Retrieved January 22, 2007, from PsycINFO database.

Catherall, D.R. (1998). Treating traumatized families. In C.R. Figley (ed.), *Burnout in families: The systemic costs of caring* (pp. 187–215). Boca Raton, FL: CRC Press.

Catherall, D.R. (ed.) (2004). *Handbook of stress, trauma and the family.* New York: Brunner-Routledge.

Danieli, Y. (ed.) (1998). *International handbook of multigenerational legacies of trauma.* New York: Plenum.

Deblinger, E., Lippmann, J., and Steer, R. (1996). Sexually abused children suffering posttraumatic stress symptoms: Initial treatment outcome findings. *Child Maltreatment, 1*(4), 310–321.

Diamond, G., and Josephson, A. (2005). Family-based treatment research: A 10-year update. *Journal of the American Academy of Child and Adolescent Psychiatry, 44*(9), 872–887.

Figley, C.R. (1989). *Helping traumatized families.* San Francisco, CA: Jossey-Bass.

Goff, B.S.N., and Schwerdtfeger, K.L. (2004). The systemic impact of traumatized children. In D.R. Catherall (ed.), *Handbook of stress, trauma and the family* (pp. 179–202). New York: Brunner-Routledge.

Green, B.L., Korol, M., Grace, M.C., and Vary, M.G. (1991). Children and disaster: Age, gender, and parental effects on PTSD symptoms. *Journal of the American Academy of Child and Adolescent Psychiatry, 30*(6), 945–951. Retrieved January 11, 2007, from PsycINFO database.

Greenberg, H.S., and Keane, A. (2001). Risk factors for chronic posttraumatic stress symptoms and behavior problems in children and adolescents following a home fire. *Child and Adolescent Social Work Journal, 18*(3), 205–221. Retrieved January 10, 2007, from PsycINFO database.

Hawkins, S.S., and Manne, S.L. (2004). Family support in the aftermath of trauma. In D.R. Catherall (ed.), *Handbook of stress, trauma and the family* (pp. 231–260). New York: Brunner-Routledge.

Jordan, B.K., Marmar, C.R., Fairbank, J.A., Schlenger, W.E., Kulka, R.A., Hough, R.L., et al. (1992). Problems in families of male Vietnam veterans with posttraumatic stress disorder. *Journal of Consulting and Clinical Psychology, 60*, 916–926.

Jovanovic, A.A., Aleksandric, B.V., Dunjic, D., and Todorovic, V.S. (2004). Family hardiness and social support as predictors of posttraumatic stress disorder. *Psychiatry, Psychology and Law, 11*(2), 263–268. Retrieved January 14, 2007, from PsycINFO database.

Kazak, A.E., Alderfer, M.A., Streisand, R., Simms, S., Rourke, M.T., and Barakat, L.P., et al. (2004). Treatment of posttraumatic stress symptoms in adolescent survivors of childhood cancer and their families: A randomized clinical trial. *Journal of Family Psychology, 18*(3), 493–504. Retrieved January 14, 2007, from PsycINFO database.

Kazdin, A.E., and Weisz, J.R. (1998). Identifying and developing empirically supported child and adolescent treatments. *Journal of Consulting and Clinical Psychology, 66*(1), 19–36. Retrieved January 11, 2007, from PsycARTICLES database.

Kellerman, N.P.F. (2001a). Psychopathology in children of holocaust survivors: A review of the research literature [special issue]. *Israel Journal of Psychiatry and Related Sciences, 38*(1), 36–46. Retrieved January 14, 2007, from PsycINFO database.

Kellermann, N.P.F. (2001b). Transmission of holocaust trauma: An integrative view. *Psychiatry: Interpersonal and Biological Processes, 64*(3), 256–267. Retrieved January 14, 2007, from PsycINFO database.

Kessler, R.C., Sonnega, A., Bromet, E., Hughes, M., Nelson, C.B., and Breslau, N. (1999). Epidemiological risk factors for trauma and PTSD. In R. Yehuda (ed.), *Risk factors for posttraumatic stress disorder* (pp. 23–59). Washington, DC: American Psychiatric Association.

Kolko, D.J. (1996). Clinical monitoring of treatment course in child physical abuse: Psychometric characteristics and treatment comparisons. *Child Abuse and Neglect, 20*(1), 23–43. Retrieved January 5, 2007, from PsycINFO database.

Layne, C.M., Saltzman, W.R., Arslanagic, B., Savjak, N., Popovic, T., Durakovic, E., et al. (2001). Trauma/grief-focused group treatment for war-exposed Bosnian adolescents: Preliminary results from a school-based post-war program. *Group Dynamics: Theory, Research, and Practice, 5*(4), 277–290.

Layne, C.M., Saltzman, W.R., and Pynoos, R.S. (2002). *Component therapy for trauma and grief: Adolescent version.* Los Angeles, CA: University of California.

Lebow, J., and Rekart, K.N. (2004). Research assessing couple and family therapies for posttraumatic stress disorder. In D.R. Catherall (ed.), *Handbook of stress, trauma and the family* (pp. 261–279). New York: Brunner-Routledge.

Lester, P., Stein, J.A., and Bursch, B. (2003). Developmental risk for somatization in adolescents of parents with AIDS. *Journal of Developmental and Behavioral Pediatrics, 24*(4), 242–250.

Lieberman, A.F., Van Horn, P., and Ippen, C.G. (2005). Toward evidence-based treatment: Child–parent psychotherapy with preschoolers exposed to marital violence. *Journal of American Academy of Child and Adolescent Psychiatry, 44*(12), 1241–1248.

Meiser-Stedman, R.A., Yule, W., Dalgleish, T., Smith, P., and Glucksman, E. (2006). The role of the family in child and adolescent posttraumatic stress following attendance at an emergency department [special issue]. *Journal of Pediatric Psychology: Posttraumatic Stress Related to Pediatric Illness and Injury, 31*(4), 397–402. Retrieved January 25, 2007, from PsycINFO database.

Nader, K., Pynoos, R., Fairbanks, L., and Frederick, C. (1990). Children's PTSD reactions one year after a sniper attack at their school. *American Journal of Psychiatry, 147*(11), 1526–1530. Retrieved January 14, 2007, from PsycINFO database.

National Institute for Clinical Excellence (NICE) (2005). *Posttraumatic stress disorder: The management of PTSD in adults and children in primary and secondary care. National clinical care guideline number 26.* Retrieved on January 5, 2007 from www.nice.org.uk.

Ozer, E.J., Best, S.R., Lipsey, T.L., and Weiss, D.S. (2003). Predictors of posttraumatic stress disorder and symptoms in adults: A meta-analysis. *Psychological Bulletin, 129*(1), 52–73.

Patterson, C. (1992). Children of lesbian and gay parents. *Child Development, 63*, 1025–1042.

Perry, B.D., and Azad, I. (1999). Posttraumatic stress disorders in children and adolescents. *Current Opinion in Pediatrics, 11*(4), 310–316. Retrieved January 5, 2007, from PubMed database.

Pfefferbaum, B. (1997). Posttraumatic stress disorder in children: A review of the past 10 years. *Journal of the American Academy of Child and Adolescent Psychiatry, 36*(11), 1503–1511.

Pinsof, W.M., and Wynne, L.C. (2000). Towards progress research: Closing the gap between family therapy practice and research. *Journal of Marital and Family Therapy, 26*(1), 1–8.

Pynoos, R.S., Steinberg, A.M., and Piacentini, J.C. (1999). A developmental psychopathology model of childhood traumatic stress and intersection with anxiety disorders. *Biological Psychiatry, 46*(11), 1542–1554.

Rossman, B.B.R., Bingham, R.D., and Emde, R.N. (1997). Symptomatology and adaptive functioning for children exposed to normative stressors, dog attack, and parental violence. *Journal of the American Academy of Child and Adolescent Psychiatry, 36*(8), 1089–1097. Retrieved January 22, 2007, from PsycINFO database.

Rotheram-Borus, M.J., Lee, M.B., Gwadz, M., and Draimin, B. (2001). An intervention for parents with AIDS and their adolescent children. *American Journal of Public Health, 91*, 1294–1302.

Rotheram-Borus, M.J., Lee, M., and Lester, P. (2004). Six year intervention outcomes for adolescent children of parents with HIV. *Archives of Pediatrics and Adolescent Medicine, 158*, 742–748.

Ruscio, A.M., Weathers, F.W., King, L.A., and King, D.W. (2002). Male war-zone veterans' perceived relationships with their children: The importance of emotional numbing. *Journal of Traumatic Stress, 15*, 351–357.

Schumm, J.A., Vranceanu, A., and Hobfoll, S.E. (2004). The ties that bind: Resource caravans and losses among traumatized families. In D.R. Catherall (ed.), *Handbook of stress, trauma and the family* (pp. 33–50). New York: Brunner-Routledge.

Scheeringa, M.S., and Zeanah, C.H. (2001). A relational perspective on PTSD in early childhood. *Journal of Trauma and Stress, 14*(4), 799–815.

Stallard, P. (2006). Psychological interventions for posttraumatic reactions in children and young people: A review of randomised controlled trials. *Clinical Psychology Review* (special issue) *Anxiety of childhood and adolescence: Challenges and opportunities, 26*(7), 895–911. Retrieved January 14, 2007, from PsycINFO database.

Steinberg, A. (1998). Understanding the secondary traumatic stress of children. In C.R. Figley (ed.), *Burnout in families: The systemic costs of caring* (pp. 29–46). Boca Raton, FL: CRC Press.

Steinberg, A., Brymer, M., Decker, K., and Pynoos, R. (2004). The University of California at Los Angeles Posttraumatic Stress Disorder Reaction Index. *Current Psychiatry Reports, 6*, 96–100.

Taylor, T.K., and Biglan, A. (1998). Behavioral family interventions for improving child-rearing: A review of the literature for clinicians and policy makers. *Clinical Child and Family Psychology Review, 1*(1), 41–60.

Waller, M.A. (2001). Resilience in ecosystemic context: Evolution of the concept. *American Journal of Orthopsychiatry, 71*(3), 290–297. Retrieved January 24, 2007, from PsycINFO database.

Chapter 16

Transforming troubled children into tomorrow's heroes

Richard Kagan

Therapists can combine an understanding of resilience with the metaphor of the hero's journey (Campbell 1968) to counter hopelessness and help children and families begin trauma therapy. This approach will be illustrated with *Real life heroes* (Kagan 2007a), a treatment model developed to engage children and caring adults to work together to rebuild (or build) attachments and reduce traumatic stress.

Resilience framework

Many factors have been identified in resilience research, including individual, family, and extra-familial supports (Masten and Coatsworth 1998). Primary factors promoting resilience have been described (Luthar et al. 2000; Masten 2001; Wyman et al. 2000) as including:

- positive connections to caring and competent adults within a youth's family or community
- development of cognitive and self-regulation abilities
- positive beliefs about oneself
- motivation to act effectively in one's environment.

Waller (2001) challenged the notion of resilience as a static concept and instead described resilience as functioning as a multidetermined and ever-changing product of interacting forces within an individual's family, social groups, community, society, and world. From this perspective, therapists can focus on rebuilding resilience from the point when development became mired as a primary clue and focus initial assessments from the point of referral on locating sources of nurture and support from the past, in the present, and for the future. Thus, resilience-focused therapists would want to know: who was there to help when the child was born? Who fed the child? Who helped the child with homework? Who took care of the child when the child was sick? Who taught the child to ride a bike? Often these caregivers, mentors, and teachers are more than just providers of immediate assistance and support: they also are role models who show the child how to overcome adversity and accomplish important life goals. In that sense, caring and facilitative adults are heroes that children can look to as models for how they too can become heroes in their own lives.

Resilience-based approaches to psychotherapy for traumatized children add to other therapeutic approaches by engaging or searching for caring adult who can help a child rebuild the safety needed to recover and reintegrate after traumas. Understanding how the metaphor of the hero can guide both the caregiver and the child, and how therapists can enlist this metaphor to assist them in this important quest, this chapter provides a novel framework for conceptualizing and conducting resilience-based psychotherapy with traumatized children.

Engaging families after abuse or neglect

For trauma therapists, often the greatest challenge is to help children who have often been hurt badly by their parents or other relatives, the people children needed to trust in order to survive, creating a profound paradox for these children. Children who have experienced repeated incidents of abuse and neglect from a young age and have grown up with both severe traumatic stress and chaotic and disorganized attachments often show symptoms of complex trauma (Cook et al. 2005), including affective dysregulation, dissociation, impulsive behaviors, decreased cognitive abilities, and poor social skills. A large proportion of their families may be mandated into services after authorities become alarmed over behaviors by children or adults that have put someone inside or outside the family at risk of significant harm.

After repeated traumas and family violence, children (and adults) often present as fragile and quick to react in dangerous ways that may parallel a lack of safety in the child's home and the lack of a caring, non-offending guardian committed to raising the child to maturity. These children and their families may be especially difficult to engage in directive models of trauma therapies. An important first step is the initial assessment of:

- the child's social and emotional developmental age as a clue to how far nurture and attachments have progressed (or the extent to which they been disrupted)
- traumas the child experienced
- strengths, including individual talents and the family's cultural and spiritual heritage
- risk factors, including triggers to traumatic stress reactions and what has helped reduce stress reactions.

Implicit in these assessment foci is an often overlooked or undervalued additional assessment question: who are the caring adults who have been and continue to be committed to nurture, care for, guide, and protect the child, and who are the adults who can feasibly and effectively serve as caregivers, mentors, and role models for the child now and in the future? Often, these adults have found these roles to be extremely difficult, both because of the stressors in their own lives and as a result of the child's posttraumatic stress reactions. These adults need guidance and support if they are to persevere in the face of these obstacles.

Distrust and resistance often cover childrens' and families feelings of vulnerability and feelings of shame. One of the first tasks in trauma therapy is to reengage a sense of hope after what may have been years or even generations of crises and family and externally imposed violence. The hero metaphor can be used to provide a framework to show respect to families, instill renewed hope, accentuate caring shown by family members, and engage these families to utilize components of trauma therapies.

The hero metaphor

Stories and images of heroes can be used by trauma therapists in much the same way that mythology and literature have served over time to symbolize profound experiences and challenges and pass on crucial lessons in a form that has always engaged children (and adults) across time and cultures. Joseph Campbell (1968) wrote of mythic heroes' call to adventure and the hero's courage to enter unknown territory:

> The call to adventure signified that destiny has summoned the hero and transferred his spiritual center of gravity from within the pale of his society to a zone unknown. This fateful region of both treasure and danger may be variously represented ... but it is always a place of strangely fluid and polymorphous beings, unimaginable torments, superhuman deeds, and impossible delights.
>
> (cited by Cousineau 2003, p. 1)

> Once having traversed the threshold, the hero moves in a dream landscape of curiously fluid, ambiguous forms, where he must survive a succession of trials.
>
> (cited by Cousineau 2003, p. 18)

> the full round, the norm of the mono-myth requires that the hero shall now begin the labor of bringing the runes of wisdom, the Golden fleece, or his sleeping princess, back into the kingdom of humanity, where the boon may redound to the renewing of the community, the nation, the planet, or the ten thousand worlds.
>
> (cited by Cousineau 2003, p. 114)

In trauma therapy, caring, safe parents (birth, foster, or adoptive) can utilize their skills, experiences, and courage to overcome oppressive forces that have blocked their child's growth. In this respect, they are much like the heroes of mythology, religion, literature, and popular movies and books who embody the effort to move forward despite fear and suffering and to overcome adversity and realize one's full potential by making creative advances (Campbell 1968). Like mythic heroes, they also contest with the darkness of fears and the weighty and oppressive forces that maintain constriction and oppression, in the form of the experience of psychological trauma and the symptoms of traumatic stress.

Parents, grandparents, aunts, uncles, clergy, and cultural leaders carry with them stories of struggle and transformation that can be tapped to enrich the next generation and the community. Each family and community has heroes, although, like a bewitched castle hidden behind seemingly impenetrable thorns, the heroes and the family's heritage may be hidden by the dark cloud of dangerous behaviors that typically lead to therapy. Trauma therapists need to understand how the cloud works in order to bring out the caring, nurture, and strengths in a family. With a resilience perspective, therapists can appeal to caring adults to regain control as guardians, teachers, and caretakers, and symbolically to cut through the thorns of adversity and elicit the strengths of the child and the family's heritage. The lessons and wisdom that helped in the past can also help in the present; and the effort of reclaiming one's family and cultural pride can help make recommitment possible to the next generation.

The framework for this work is a quest in which caring adults are encouraged to become the heroes children need to help vanquish their fears. In this process, caring adults must go through the steps of the hero's challenge outlined by Campbell (1968). They can utilize components of evidence-supported trauma therapies as tools in this quest. Caring adults working to reclaim a child with traumatic stress will very likely experience "unimaginable torments, superhuman deeds, and impossible delights" (cited by Cousineau 2003, p. 1), like the heroes of myths and legends. They must weather a child's storms and face the monsters within a child's nightmares. Caring adults can help a child move beyond terror and rage, violations of the child's body, self-denigration, and the child's bodily dysregulation and coping strategies, including hypervigilence, impulsivity, and distrust.

Children who have been traumatized, especially children with complex traumatic stress disorders (Cook et al. 2005), will test adults, often with what was so unbearable in the child's own life. By facing these tests, caring adults become heroes for troubled (and troubling) children and their communities. This may seem like a daunting process, but it may not be so much the process of winning the battle as sticking with the child, doing everything possible, and simply refusing to abandon children who have learned to expect (or provoke) breakdowns in attachment. This is the hero's calling – not always to succeed but to persevere on a path that is just and true. Rebuilding attachments means mustering the courage and the allies to cope with a "succession of trials" over time. With each test, caring adults, practitioners, and children challenge the power of old traumas and strive to learn from the wisdom of each other's past experiences and the legacy of heroes, in order to reduce the power of their nightmares.

In trauma-informed psychotherapies, caring adults and youths learn to master traumas and traumatic stress much as mythic heroes learned to defeat the curses and monsters of the past. "Monsters" can be transformed into real bodies or objects with weaknesses and vulnerabilities that can be stopped before they hurt again. What therapists call "trauma psychoeducation" can be understood as a preparation for adults and children to take on the heroic quest of mastering and overcoming the fear and pain of past psychological trauma.

Trauma psychoeducation

In psychoeducation, the therapist serves as a mentor or coach, guiding and eliciting the family's own strengths during the therapeutic journey, and always recognizing that the journey needs to be owned by the child and those caring adults who are now or will become committed to caring for and raising the child into maturity. Psychoeducation can be particularly credible and motivating for adults and children if it is tied to a family's cultural background by inviting family members to share stories, beliefs, customs, and traditions which are then used to frame subsequent therapeutic interventions. In this process, the key message from trauma therapists is that everyone, even the greatest hero, needs the help of other caring persons.

In mythology, mentors are part wizards, part priests (holders of knowledge), and part substitute parent-figures, but over time these roles end and the hero must go on, carrying the "wisdom" of the mentor on to a new generation. In resilience-based therapy for traumatized children, the challenge is to reconnect the child with committed caring adults who will nurture, guide, and protect the child into maturity. That often means repairing a gap that has formed when parent–child bonds have broken down, relinking children with caring adults from their biological family, or if necessary, another family, who can step in to guide and protect the child to maturity. Building on principles of resilience from a strength-inducing perspective, trauma therapists can emphasize how children cannot heal alone, but can be strengthened by the commitment and support of adults who validate their experience (Farber and Egeland 1987), caring adults who show the child they can listen and accept even what may be painful to hear.

Traumatized children can be seen in many ways to be like wounded angels (Kagan 2003) lighting a pathway, or more often directly challenging adults, to face unspoken and unresolved traumas in a family and community through their behaviors. Therapists can join with the caring side of parents and guardians to take on this quest and show children that the horrors of the past no longer need remain as unspoken nightmares blocking their children's future.

Thinking of traumas operating like a curse may be helpful for parents from some cultural backgrounds. Strong, committed adults can break the curse, like a knight fighting a dragon, and free their child. Practitioners and family members can reopen the child's eyes and help the child begin developing again, moving past the point in time when social and emotional development appeared to have slowed or became mired after severe traumas or breakdowns of attachments. Caring adults can join with the child to become stronger than the traumatic "monsters" of the past.

Using crises

Families may come into therapy in the midst of a crisis or serial crises making effective work difficult with trauma protocols. The ancient Greek meaning of "crisis" referred to separation (Vogler 1998). In many stories and legends of heroes, crises marked both a time of loss or death of past relationships and an ordeal through which the hero becomes transformed and reborn (Campbell 1968; Vogler 1998). For caring adults and therapists, the challenge is to help children overcome crises and to reattach children to caring committed adults through the activities, practice, "trials" and "ordeals" of therapy.

Facing crises or "trials" means, in effect, transforming the child's troubled 'present' of repetitions of beliefs, feelings, and behaviors that leave the child mired in a traumatized past. The therapist working with caring adults can guide children to learn and practice new ways to cope with stressors, including learning to recognize and manage their feelings. The quest reopens possibilities for the child's future. By making this a shared quest, caring adults are simultaneously rebuilding family attachments across generations and time. Caring adults, practitioners and children can rewrite the meaning of traumas and, over time, change a child's life story from living *within* a state of traumatic stress to living *with* trauma in the past and *personal power* (M. Purdy, personal communication, 2003) in the present. Thus, as crises are dealt with in the current family or school setting, adults and children learn that not only are they able to escape dire dangers but moreover they are gaining knowledge and skills that give them the same kind of strength and hope that enables the mythic hero to not just survive but also triumph in the face of adversity. This can be a new and profoundly encouraging perspective for children (and adults) who have felt that they could never break free of the problems that have haunted and burdened them, and that they could never amount to anything because of the posttraumatic stress reactions that they suffer from.

Trauma therapies adapted from contemporary literature

Trauma therapies can be informed by present-day popular books, movies, and music. The mythic heroes in these works have the potential to engage children and adolescents in evidence-supported interventions. For instance, psychological trauma can be viewed as constricting and taking away a child's abilities and choices just like the "dementers" in the Harry Potter books (Rowling 1999).

For young children, Maurice Sendak's *Where the wild things are* (1963) provides a wonderful illustration that trauma therapists can use to help adults see how "wild" children can be reclaimed. The story of Max and the wild things can also help children see that it is okay to give up being "wild" in order to "be loved best of all". In the story, Max dresses up in a wolf suit and qualifies for placement in many communities by chasing his little doggie with a dangerous object, in this case a large fork. His mother calls him a wild thing and sends him off to bed with no supper (inviting neglect if this cycle were to get out of control). Instead, Max escapes to a fantasy land of monsters which would frighten most adults, but not Max. He tames the monsters with a trick of staring into their eyes, a trick that only resilient, well-loved children with a secure attachment can do, unlike the "monsters" of his fantasy land, who are really quite weak despite their massive heads, giant claws, and sharp teeth. However, Max is lonely. Being king, even of a gang of monsters, is not enough. Max wants to be somewhere where he is loved best of all. Sendak describes the rich sensory experiences that occur when Max, the "wild thing," is transformed back into Max, the ordinary little boy, returning him back into his family, with the warm smell of his mother's home-cooked meal wafting through the air in his own room. And so, "Max, the king of all wild things," and by analogy, potential qualifier for juvenile delinquent programs or placements, returned home where he was loved "best of all".

For latency children, the second book of the Harry Potter series (Rowling 1999) provides a dramatic illustration of how trauma therapies work. Trauma therapists can model skill-building on what could be called the Rowling Buggert therapy technique. Buggerts are classic shapeshifters in mythology, in this case taking on forms of what people fear. For the children in the story, this means that when the Buggert is released from its cage, it turns into a giant hissing snake or a menacing spider, representing fears shared by many people and likely built into basic human survival systems.

Consistent with the tenets of a number of trauma therapies, the children in Harry Potter's tale are carefully guided by their instructor, one at a time, to bring up a strong visual image of a comical image that is stronger than the feared image. In the movie version this appears to take place quickly, while in actuality therapists would likely need to provide a lot of practice to develop a powerful image, possibly including drawing the image, adding details to the image, adding color and richness, and memorizing the image so the child could bring it up quickly in a stressful situation, as when the Buggert, or a real-life trauma trigger, is approaching. This also affords therapists a chance to incorporate lessons that the children in the wizard class have presumably already learned, such as practice in vivid guided imagery, including transforming snakes into clowns.

A strong laugh is a key part of the Buggert technique. That means developing the capacity for deep breathing, a natural lead-in to self-soothing exercises. The child needs to learn how to stand strong and flexibly, like an athlete, ready to move left or right with knees slightly bent. The child raises an arm and simultaneously takes a deep breath while bringing up the funny image. The child then drives the wand down, pointing it directly at the Buggert while loudly laughing "Ridiculous!"

Harry Potter fans around the world, of course, know that this charm failed for their hero. Harry's Buggert takes the shape of a "dementer", far more menacing than a snake or a spider, which are common fears. Therapists can use Rowling's story about dementers as an illustration about why, perhaps, children and adults who have experienced traumas are more sensitive than others to reminders of pain. Dementers from this perspective could be described as sucking out all the hope and happiness in one's life, leaving you with just the negative, somewhat like burned-out zombies. Explicit verbal memories may be eaten away and the victim may respond to implicit memories with fast, impulsive responses, often freezing or dissociating.

In the story, the teacher intervenes to protect Harry as the dementer approaches, as therapists need to do in order to protect children from facing too many memories of traumatic experiences too soon. Earlier in the series, Harry had fainted when confronted by a dementer. The traumas in his life make him stronger, and wiser, but at the same time more vulnerable. So, his teacher has to teach him a stronger technique than "Buggert therapy". Harry has to go to individual sessions and learn what therapists use when they help patients imagine a safe place in order to reduce anxiety, and then he must practice this imagery over and over until he can bring it out at the tip of his wand and make it stronger than a dementer.

Harry's teacher guides him to develop one happy, powerful memory and then to allow this memory, to learn about and explore his past, add details to this beautiful memory and experience it filling up his body so that he can, in effect, lose himself within this memory. In trauma work this means developing the safety and support to let go of protective defenses. Using Rowling's imagery as inspiration for trauma skill building, a child can be guided to take a strong flexible stance, take a deep breath to fill the body with strength, raise up one's arm and command "expecto potronum", calling forth the rich moving image of the protective parent that all children need, especially after experiencing psychological traumas.

For Harry, the image becomes a strong white stag which flies out of his wand to absorb and defend against any dementers. Rowling's Potronus charm could be used as a model for developing the strong, safe, rich memory of being loved and cared for that is so strong that a child can call it forth and shoot it forward to fight off anyone who would rob children of their heritage, family, strengths or future.

Similarly, trauma therapists working with children who enjoyed *Star Wars* (Lucas 2004) can use the themes of the *Star Wars* stories of father–son struggles of good versus evil, weakness and redemption to evoke hope that heroes can rise again, even in the midst of seemingly overwhelming darkness and lead a better life. Some youths will identify with Darth Vader, others with Luke or Princess Lea. In any case, therapists can join with the child to explore how their favorite hero learned crucial skills, overcame weaknesses, and ultimately succeeded by overcoming the "dark side". This exploration serves as a natural way to teach elements of cognitive restructuring, as the therapist helps the child develop realistic but confident beliefs that are exemplified by the hero's quest.

Teaching affect regulation, concentration, and trust can be aided by the analogy of Obi Wan guiding Luke to battle the ultimate machine menace, the Death Star, which, like the empire, appears hollow on the inside and dependent on violence and power to achieve its means. Obi Wan, Luke's mentor, guides him in a soothing voice befitting a master hypnotist. He calls to Luke in a deep, slow, calming voice in the midst of the battle. Obi Wan calls to Luke, not the impulsive, reckless teenager, torn between his feelings of loyalty to his aunt and uncle and his drive to get away, but Luke, the young Jedi, and guides him as trauma therapists do, to trust again in a higher power with Obi Wan's support, reminding him of their repeated practice and training to "stretch out with your feelings", to "trust your feelings . . . trust me". Luke turns off his machine and listens to his mentor, the orphan reattuning to his mentor. Obi Wan's messages can be used to invoke courage and help youths see themselves as heroes who can succeed by utilizing strength and guidance from trustworthy mentors.

The *Star Wars* movies work well to engage youths who like science fiction and tap into core components of trauma therapy. The appeal is especially strong in child therapy as the orphaned hero, Luke, finds a mentor who teaches him that he is not alone. The "Force" connects and empowers them. The injunction to "Use the Force" reminds youths of the positive energy within and around them. "Stretch out your feelings" provides an antidote for the constriction of traumatic stress and opens up the possibility of new perceptions and solutions. "Let the Force guide you" invokes an image of using one's own past experience and knowledge and the guidance of mentors instead of attempting to overcome problems impulsively or in isolation. The "Force" is a metaphorical description of the strength that comes from interconnectedness, the invisible bonds of connection that link human to human.

Using the "Force" evokes gaining power, something every child who has had an insecure, shattered, or chaotic, or disorganized life and support system craves. The "Force" also connotes a quality of goodness that can be found in relationships and through positive values. When guided by the "Force", children can envision themselves doing good deeds and finding the quality of goodness within themselves. Thus, the metaphor of the "Force" connotes several qualities – trust, wisdom, and altruism – that are key components in many models of support and resilience.

Luke's mentors teach him to give up his assumptions, learn how hatred leads to the "dark side", acknowledge and own his fears, overcome his angry impulses, and develop the capacity to trust again. Yoda's instruction to "Do or do not. There is no *trying*" models the conviction and commitment the hero needs to prevail and a readiness to accept failures as part of life. They also challenge him to enter "the cave", one of the primary challenges in mythology where the hero must confront fears of the monsters who dwell in dark places like "the cave" and the unknown that is symbolized by the darkness of "the cave".

These selected examples illustrate how the mythic hero can be used to elucidate the qualities, beliefs, and actions that traumatized children can draw upon in order to experience themselves as real-life heroes rather than helpless victims, intractably ill patients, or bad persons. The hero is imperfect and feels distressing emotions such as fear or despair, but overcomes adversity by relying upon trustworthy guides and mentors in order to find the courage and wisdom needed to solve big problems. Thus, the hero represents a "coping" model, rather than an all-knowing and all-powerful "mastery" model, to which children can realistically aspire.

It is crucial that therapists recognize that the specific qualities and examples that are best applicable to helping each child develop a sense of what it means to be a real-life hero must be carefully individualized to the child, the family, and their community and culture. The hero for one child of one background may be an adversary for another child because of their different life experiences, family environment, and culture. Although certain qualities are almost universally espoused as positive (e.g. honesty, dedication, altruism, respect for self and others, productivity), the specific ways in which a hero embodies these skills and qualities differs substantially across communities and cultures.

Real life heroes

In *Real life heroes* (*RLH*; Kagan 2007a), children are encouraged to identify heroes from their favorite books and movies, from contemporary culture including those that can be found in popular music, sports, arts, politics, and from leaders in community, religious, and cultural life. The *Real life heroes practitioner's manual* (Kagan 2007b) includes a Heroes Library for children and adults. Therapists are guided to search especially for heroes that can help children rebuild links that may been broken to their family and ethnic heritage after violence, wars, natural disasters and other factors that led to separation and loss of protection, caring, and transmission of positive family and cultural values. For example, this might include encouraging children to learn about their community's historical role in important "heroic" challenges (e.g. ending slavery, curing diseases, winning championships, making great art or music) and that of real people who, currently or in the past, have played heroic roles in these achievements. Also, asking children about their favorite sports or music heroes can help them to regain a sense of pride by drawing on valuable lessons epitomized in the accomplishments of real-life heroes who have overcome adversity and made a positive difference in their world.

RLH builds on cognitive behavioral therapy models to reduce traumatic stress and utilizes nonverbal creative arts, narrative interventions, and gradual exposure to help process traumatic memories and bolster adaptive individual and interpersonal coping strategies. Techniques integrated into *RLH* were based on safety planning, life story work (e.g. Jewett 1978), TARGET (Ford and Russo 2006), affect regulation, skill-building, and problem-solving, cognitive restructuring, nonverbal processing of events, and enhanced social support. The intervention begins with a Pledge, and continues with nine lessons:

- A Little about Me
- Heroes and Heroines
- People in My Life
- Good Times
- Developing the Hero Inside
- The ABCs of Trauma and the Hero's Challenge
- Timelines and Moves
- Through the Tough Times
- Into the Future.

The Pledge is defined as the beginning of the adventure and a written contract to strengthen or find caring, committed adults who will validate and protect the child. "A Little about Me" provides activities for children to practice recognition and expression of feelings in a safe way. These include techniques for helping children calm themselves with breathing, muscle relaxation, imagery, "thought-stopping", and other emotional regulation skills. The child is helped to visualize a memory or a fantasy and then picture it with a drawing or a photograph. In order to draw upon somatosensory modalities, the child also is guided in tapping out how a visual image would sound in rhythm, adding musical notes on a two-octave xylophone or showing how it would look through movement as a dance or a movie. Over time, the therapist encourages the child to add more detail to the drawings, more differentiation to the rhythm, more notes or chords to the tonality, and more action to the movement. Questions are provided for the therapist to use in order to boost children's sense of being valued and competent in different situations. In this way, the children are encouraged to integrate or reintegrate important memories of their life experiences.

RLH sessions utilize a structure highlighting safety and magic adapted for different developmental levels with welcoming messages, safety assurances, self-ratings on thermometers of stress and self-control (Ford and Russo 2006), focusing (Ford and Russo 2006) and centering exercises, and a magical moment before drawing in response to workbook page instructions. At the end of sessions, children are asked to repeat self-ratings (Ford and Russo 2006), with safety planning and reassurances (as needed), as well as plans for the next session. Caring adults are encouraged to work separately with therapists and children share their drawings with caring adults, and may work in sessions with caring adults, who meet safety criteria.

In subsequent sessions, the hero metaphor is explained and children are encouraged to identify people from their families, ethnic group, community, and broader culture who have struggled to build strengths and overcome adversity, as a means of rekindling hope and modeling mastery over traumas. This can be done by drawing, acting out, or describing someone in their lives who has acted like a hero, remembering how they helped others, and to envision what they could do in the future. Hero exploration highlights the courage required to help others as an integral part of the making of a hero, and provides a framework for therapists to engage children in understanding the skills their heroes utilize to succeed. These skills include cultural attributes. The child also is helped to identify heroes who cared for them day by day, through sickness and health, even in small ways.

With the image of their distant and close-at-hand heroes in mind, children and caring adults are engaged to develop the emotion-regulation, problem-solving, and trauma resolution skills and beliefs needed to reduce the power of the traumas that have afflicted them and their families. Children and caring adults are helped to develop skills to make things better in their lives including calming and self-soothing skills and developing positive beliefs in their own capacity to cope and overcome adversity. They also work on integrating psychoeducation about psychological trauma with cognitive behavioral exercises designed to help them replace dysfunctional beliefs with positive self-statements. The therapist helps the child develop a timeline of good and bad events in their lives. The timeline helps accentuate positive events in children's lives and to help children learn lessons about who helped them succeed, how they helped themselves, and how they and important people in their lives overcame problems.

Ultimately, *RLH* helps each child utilize the skills and support that helped them in the past in order to learn from difficult times in their lives and desensitize a series of progressively more difficult "Tough Times". The child writes a short narrative about what helped children get through their "toughest time ever". *RLH* concludes by inviting children to enhance images of themselves becoming successful in the future and to plan ways they can actively "be a hero" by working toward achieving their goals.

Real Life Heroes pilot study

RLH was tested with forty-one children in a pilot study (Kagan et al. 2008) with children referred to child and family services, including intensive home-based family counseling, foster family care, residential treatment or an outpatient mental health program. Results at four months included significant levels ($p<0.05$) of improvement on child self-reports of trauma symptoms and fewer problem behaviors reported on caregiver checklists. At twelve months, significant levels of improvement were found, with correlations between a decrease in parent reports of child trauma symptoms and the number of workbook chapters completed and also for child perceptions of increased security with parents or guardians. While conclusions were limited by lack of a control group and the small sample, the activities in *RLH* appeared to enhance children's perception that they were not alone and enable them to gradually give up common beliefs that no one cares and instead recognize that they could count on guidance and protection from important people in their lives.

The boon

In the end of every hero's story, the hero must bring back a lesson or a gift, the "boon". *Real Life Heroes* was developed to help children and families strengthen skills and resources to overcome the "monsters" that afflicted their past. Caring adults are asked to take charge, providing leadership, nurture, permission, and protection so their children can grow past the point when traumas overwhelmed family members. Children can then incorporate new skills and resources, and by so doing, transform themselves from troubled children into tomorrow's heroes.

References

Campbell, J. (1968). *The hero with a thousand faces*. Princeton, NJ: Princeton University Press.

Cook, A., Spinazzola, J., Ford, J.D., Lanktree, C., Blaustein, M., Cloitre, M., et al. (2005). Complex trauma in children and adolescents. *Psychiatric Annals, 35*, 390–398.

Cousineau, P. (2003) *The hero's journey: Joseph Campbell on his life and work*. San Francisco, CA: Harper and Row.

Farber, E.A., and Egeland, B. (1987). Invulnerability among abused and neglected children. In E.J. Anthony and B.J. Choler (eds.), *The Invulnerable Child* (pp. 253–288). New York: Guilford.

Ford, J.D., and Russo, E. (2006). A trauma-focused, present-centered, emotional self-regulation approach to integrated treatment for posttraumatic stress and addiction: Trauma Adaptive Recovery Group Education and Therapy (TARGET). *American Journal of Psychotherapy, 60*, 335–355.

Jewett, C. (1978). *Adopting the older child.* Cambridge, MA: Harvard Common Press.

Kagan, R. (2003). *Wounded angels: Lessons of courage from children in crisis.* Washington, DC: Children's Press, Child Welfare League of America.

Kagan, R. (2007a). *Real life heroes: A life storybook for children*, 2nd edition. Binghamton, NY: Haworth Press.

Kagan, R. (2007b). *Real life heroes practitioner's manual.* Binghamton, NY: Haworth Press.

Kagan, R., Douglas, A., Hornik, J., and Kratz, S. (2008). *Real Life Heroes* pilot study: Evaluation of a treatment model for children with traumatic stress. *Journal of Child and Adolescent Trauma*, 5–22.

Lucas, G. (2004). *Star Wars Trilogy* [Motion Pictures]. United States: 20th Century Fox.

Luthar, S.S., Cicchetti, D., and Becker, B. (2000). The construct of resilience: a critical evaluation and guidelines for future work. *Child Development, 71*, 543–562.

Masten, A.S. (2001). Ordinary magic: Resilience processes in development. *American Psychologist, 56*(3), 227–238.

Masten, A.S., and Coatsworth, J.D. (1998). The development of competence in favorable and unfavorable environments, *American Psychologist, 53*(2), 205–220.

Rowling, J.K. (1999). *Harry Potter and the Prisoner of Azkaban.* New York: Scholastic Press.

Sendak, M. (1963). *Where the wild things are.* New York: Harper and Row.

Vogler, C. (1998). *The writer's journey: Mythic structure for writers.* Studio City, CA: Michael Weise Productions.

Waller, M.A. (2001). Resilience in ecosystemic context: Evolution of the concept. *American Journal of Orthopsychiatry, 71*(3), 290–297.

Wyman, P.A., Sandler, I., Wolchik, S., and Nelson, K. (2000). Resilience as cumulative competence promotion and stress protection: Theory and intervention. In D. Cicchetti, J. Rappaport, I. Sandler, and R.P. Weissberg (eds.), *The promotion of wellness in children and adolescents* (pp. 133–184). Washington, DC: Child Welfare League of America Press.

Chapter 17

Toward a developing science and practice of childhood traumatic stress

Concluding comments

Ruth Pat-Horenczyk, Julian D. Ford, and Danny Brom

This book, although divided into separate parts on risk factors, resilience and clinical interventions, is based on an integral view of the field, that is the idea that prevention and treatment for traumatized children are part of a conceptual continuum. Clinicians have focused too long on risk factors, pathology, and deficits rather than resilience, resources and potentialities, and prevention specialists often fall into that same trap. It is our contention that a major shift has occurred since the mid-1990s in both prevention programs and clinical work. In this book, a diverse international group of clinicians and researchers make a strong case for a systematic focus in the traumatic stress field on understanding and utilizing resilience to meet the needs of traumatized children and families.

In these concluding comments we will point to some issues we consider essential for the development of the field. Integration among different perspectives is an overarching theme we consider important. In addition we will touch upon the uneven development of theory and research in the resilience field. We will reiterate the importance of the role of parents in keeping children resilient and will discuss some aspects of posttraumatic growth in order to finish with some remarks on the development of interventions for traumatized children.

Why do clinicians need to know about resilience and how can the clinical perspective be useful for resilience research and prevention programs?

The evolving field is now heavily influenced by a new emphasis on resilience and adaptation as a counterbalance to the adverse impact of psychological trauma. We know now that, although traumatic stressors have an acute impact on every child and family, only a minority of traumatized children reach clinical levels of psychopathology. This has catalysed a paradigm shift in models of treatment and prevention for traumatized children with the aim of integrating a focus on strength and resilience with the traditional emphasis on distress. As a result, current interventions try first of all to strengthen resilience factors, such as regulation of cognitive, emotional and/or bodily arousal, thus building intra- and interpersonal resources and creating stabilization before attempting to process the traumatic experience (e.g. Ford et al. 2005).

To utilize concepts of resilience therapeutically the clinician needs to be familiar with the resilience literature, which can give information not only about the necessary conditions for strengthening resilience, but also about its multidimensional nature. Resilience cuts across and integrates many contrasting points of emphasis within the fields of traumatic stress, child development, and developmental psychopathology. For example, resilience involves the strengths of both the body and mind, the person and his or her social support system, the processing of emotions and cognitions, and faith as well as scientific fact. Resilience requires change and the acceptance of what cannot or should not be changed. Resilience involves the capacity to regain empowerment after having been powerless, to renew lost or damaged relationships, to learn from failure as well as success, and to persevere in the face of overwhelming obstacles. Resilience derives not only from the attributes of the person, but also from the social, political, physical, and technological environment. Resilience is at the core of child development, because to grow is to be buffeted by stressors and to learn, adapt, and become stronger and healthier as a result not of the stressor per se but of the ability to gain from the encounter.

The multidimensional nature of resilience provides the clinician with an understanding that even if there is psychopathology in one domain, other domains may remain intact and can even be utilized as a resource to leverage the process of change and recovery. Conversely, prevention of posttraumatic stress disorder and related psychopathology has been shown to be an elusive goal. When conceptualized in terms of promoting resilience, prevention is not limited to avoiding or overcoming an adverse outcome. Rather than merely minimizing risk and pathology, prevention can focus on facilitating adaptation and building strengths. The integration of resilience as well as treatment of psychopathology into prevention programs can create a more differentiated set of services that can facilitate the achievement of many different trajectories of adaptation for children and families in the wake of psychological trauma. In this book, we begin with a discussion of the risk factors that can undermine resilience and lead to psychopathology when psychological trauma occurs (Part I), to provide a foundation for considering how resilience can be understood and promoted in traumatized children (Parts II and III).

The clinical perspective can make several contributions to the resilience field. First of all, clinical theory has developed for over a hundred years and consists basically of theories of change. Resiliency-building activities can benefit from cumulative knowledge in the field of behavioral, cognitive and emotional change. Strengthening resilience works through strategies of implementing change in the fields of self-regulation, cognition, and behavior. Understanding and adopting some of the clinical knowledge can help build a more integrated body of information on how resilience can be strengthened.

In addition, the field of resilience is closely connected to research on the prevention of mental-health problems. We know by now that prevention programs are not strong enough to prevent all development of psychopathology. Therefore, people in the resilience field need to be aware of the different forms of psychopathology and integrate the detection of signs of pathology into their programs.

The discrepancy between conceptual and empirical development in the field of childhood traumatic stress and resilience

The recent advances in the young and developing field of childhood trauma and resilience differ in pace and maturity. Prompted by the knowledge that the majority of children exposed to traumatic events are resilient, research has begun to move from focusing solely on risk factors leading to PTSD and other posttraumatic sequelae to a broader perspective encompassing positive adaptation and growth in the wake of trauma. This new angle of resilience research includes the search for possible mitigating elements that moderate the effects of trauma exposure in childhood as well as the later development of posttraumatic distress and impairment.

Layne and colleagues (Chapter 2 in this volume) describe a comprehensive framework for understanding risk, vulnerability, resistance, and resilience, and describe how this body of research has led to the creation of lists of variables that can distinguish between resilient and non-resilient children. One of the major limitations of these lists of variables is the lack of consensus on how to define and classify these two types of children. Another limitation of these lists is that they do not shed light on the mechanisms responsible for posttraumatic distress or the processes that occur in resilient and non-resilient children. Although the lists reflect an accumulation of evidence pinpointing attributes of resilient children and youth, the lack of methodologically sophisticated studies designed to elucidate resilience-related mechanisms, processes, and developmental trajectories of influence weakens the contribution of these lists (Layne et al. 2007).

In addition, there is a further need to explore and differentiate between protective and compensatory factors and between the mediating and moderating role of these resilience factors. Protective processes, as described by Rutter (1985) and Garmezy (1985), involve an interactive relationship between the protective factor, the risk exposure, and the outcome. A moderated protective relationship is one in which exposure to the resilience factor (e.g. strong emotional support and validation by family members) is beneficial to those exposed to the risk factor, but of limited or no additional benefit for those not risk exposed.

Compensatory processes, in contrast, occur in situations where the resilience factor has an equally beneficial effect on those exposed and those not exposed to adversity (Fergusson and Horwood 2003). A mediated compensatory relationship involves a positive outcome due to the changes in a risk relationship when a protective factor is interposed between the risk factors and the stressors, on the one hand, and the child's ongoing functioning and development, on the other. For example, when a child who has experienced severe aggression from peers or older children (bullying) has the support of a mentor, this may enable the child to feel sufficiently confident to acquire skills for interpersonal or physical assertiveness so that he or she can not only withstand but actually alter the adverse peer behaviors and thereby gain an enduring sense of self-efficacy and positive peer relationships. Mentoring might benefit any child, but in this case it may enable the victimized child to change roles fundamentally to master this and other challenges. There is clearly a need for further research to elucidate the distinctive role of the various resilience factors, whether they operate as compensatory (mediating) or protective (moderating) factors.

As can be seen in this book, there are substantive achievements in the direction of more differentiated and refined definitions of resilience on the conceptual level, as well as more sophisticated taxonomies and methodologies for describing the various trajectories of adaptation to trauma (see Chapters 2, 3, 8, 9, 10 and 12 by Layne et al., Pat-Horenczyk et al., Brom and Kleber, Hobfoll et al., Tol et al., and Ford et al. in this volume). However, the evidence base is lagging behind and has not yet provided sufficient, broad-based support for the usefulness of these theoretical concepts. In this book we confront the challenge by presenting innovative chapters, including the sophisticated clinical research described by Van Horn and Lieberman (Chapter 13) on evidence-based psychotherapy for young children and by Bifulco (Chapter 7), who reports new findings from a prospective longitudinal study of patterns of posttraumatic risk and resilience in adolescence. In addition, the book presents comprehensive programs for the development of treatments by DeRosa and colleagues, Saltzman and colleagues, and Kagan (Chapters 14, 15, and 16). Thus, the translation of theory into research (T1 translational research) and clinical research into practice (T2 translational research) is nascent but growing in fertile ground within the child traumatic stress field.

The critical role of parents

It is apparent from this book that the role of the parents is seen as the most crucial risk or protective factor in the lives of children. As Chapter 5 by Keren and Tyano amply demonstrates, the younger the child, the more important the influence of parents on the development of the child. The profound neurobiological and psychosocial growth that takes place in the first days, months, and years of life requires the guidance of caregivers who are able to provide a living, real-time, 24/7 model of self-regulation as well as the more apparent contributions of food, safety, love, and play. When psychological trauma disrupts this delicate balance, the resilience and resources of both the caregiver and the child are sorely tested. Fortunately, parents as well as clinicians are increasingly learning about the early developmental processes that require protection and repair when trauma strikes the lives of young children and their families. An array of validated and promising therapeutic approaches now exist to help young children and their caregivers preserve or restore secure attachment and self-regulation (Van Horn and Lieberman, Chapter 13).

As children grow into the latency years and adolescence, parents and other adult caregivers, mentors, and role models continue to play a crucial although evolving role in fostering healthy development and resilience in the face of trauma. As Chapter 4 by Cohen lucidly describes, parents are constantly challenged to grow and develop along with their children, in order to provide empathic guidance as well as scaffolding to support autonomy and individuation. The impact of psychological trauma on the parent's psyche is profound and often overlooked in the rush to assist the traumatized child – as is the case for the entire family as well (Saltzman et al., Chapter 15). There is a crucial need to care for the caregivers at the same time as providing therapy and caring for the traumatized children, and this can be done only if clinicians can empathically respond to the pain as well as the determination and resilience of the parents and families of traumatized children. Dyadic (Van Horn and Lieberman, Chapter 13) and systemic (DeRosa et al., Chapter 14, and Saltzman et al., Chapter 15) psychotherapies address the needs and support the resilience of the caregiver as well as the traumatized child.

The centrality of the parents' role is the most striking factor that becomes apparent in different cultures and societies, and there is no competing factor of the same importance. From the desperate poverty and violence faced by countless children in Africa (Grant-Knight et al., Chapter 6) to the stigma and violence faced by too many children and youths in Western urban centers such as London (Bifulco, Chapter 7), chronic exposure to psychological trauma, discrimination, and marginalization place millions of children at risk for posttraumatic trajectories of anger, despair, and alienation. The parents of these children often are courageous survivors themselves, whether single mothers or stand-in grandparents or foster and adoptive parents from an entirely different culture or country. Much remains to be understood, and much more to be done, to provide these parents and children with the opportunity to experience not just risk but also resilience and renewal.

Is posttraumatic growth possible for children?

Another concept in the field gaining increased attention is the notion of childhood posttraumatic growth which expands beyond the functional conceptualization of "returning to adaptive functioning" ("bouncing back"). It includes such elements as acceptance of loss, positive adaptation to enduring or ongoing change, "reasonably good" survival (Layne and colleagues, Chapter 2), and the possibility of posttraumatic growth (PTG) in childhood (Tedeschi 1999).

PTG is defined as the subjective experience of favorable psychological change in an individual as result of the struggle with trauma (Zoellner and Maercker 2006). Milam et al. (2004) found a positive relationship between age and PTG among adolescents, positing that a specific level of cognitive maturity is necessary for finding meaning in trauma and generating profound changes or benefits as a result of it. Since the growth process appears to involve a cognitive sophistication that allows recognition of both losses and gains, it is unclear whether something akin to PTG is possible for children and how similar the process might be to that observed in adults. Parents, and the attachment relationship, may provide the appropriate setting for helping children revise their views and beliefs to take into account the trauma-related information (what Piaget called *accommodation*) and develop new worldviews. In contrast, when the trauma-related information is perceived in a way that is consistent with pre-existing beliefs, individuals are said to have *assimilated* their experiences. This process often involves denial or suppression of trauma-related information in order to avoid contending with the more complex, yet often more adaptive, accommodation process (Payne et al. 2007). Although very few studies have investigated PTG in children and little is known about the developmental aspects of PTG, we wish to mention one such study by Cryder et al. (2006). They found that, first, children's competency beliefs (positive appraisals of one's ability to cope and adjust in the face of stress or trauma) were significantly related to indicators of PTG in children following trauma exposure, and second, a supportive social environment appears to be related to the participant children's positive competency beliefs. In addition, the study found that "adults can help children understand the meaning of events and the appropriateness of their reactions" (Cryder et al. 2006, p. 67), once again emphasizing the important role of parents not only in posttraumatic functioning but also in posttraumatic growth. Research on PTG in childhood thus can provide valuable information for clinicians working with children who have experienced trauma, perhaps guiding aspects of their assessments and interventions – to help youngsters cope effectively, make sense of their experiences, and even grow in the aftermath of trauma.

Developing interventions to reduce risk, enhance resilience, and support growth in children in the wake of psychological trauma

The ultimate challenge to developers of preventions and treatments is posed by the most consistent theme that emerges from each chapter in this book. Across the generations, family constellations, languages, races, nationalities, and cultures that are the life settings for traumatized children, there is not one but a large number of pathways or trajectories that children and their families can take as they develop. Complex alterations in these already complicated trajectories occur as a result of the intrusion of trauma at any point (or points) along the course of psychosocial development. Therefore, the greatest challenge to developers of prevention and treatment may be to design interventions that are sufficiently structured to be learned and replicated with fidelity, but sufficiently flexible to suit a wide range of not just ages or developmental epochs but also trajectories of adaptation and growth.

The field is moving from a paradigm based on preventing or treating PTSD at different ages in childhood to a more sophisticated paradigm involving the identification and alteration of trajectories of psychological, sociocultural, and biological development that have been interrupted or disrupted by exposure to psychological trauma (Ford et al., Chapter 12). Describing, naming, deconstructing, and reconstructing children's trajectories of traumatic adaptation and posttraumatic resilience, resistance, and growth will require the efforts, skills, and insights of a wide range of scientific and professional disciplines, including molecular neurobiology and genetics, developmental psychology and psychopathology, social and information systems analysis, and the prevention and clinical professions. As Stein et al. (2007) have discussed, there is a need to address the resilience and even heroism of children (and their families and communities) who have survived psychological trauma, as well as the biopsychosocial impairment that some of these individuals and their social ecologies experience. This may take the form of post-traumatic stress disorder and/or other medical and psychiatric sequelae of victimization.

The observations of this book's authors could provide a base for beginning these investigations and innovations. Our hope is that readers will take the keen insights offered by these authors, and those of the many expert researchers and clinicians whose work they have drawn upon, to develop new and fruitful pathways to further our understanding and our ability to effectively protect and promote the healing and growth of traumatized children and their families.

References

Cryder, C.H., Kilmer, R.P., Tedeschi, R.G., and Calhoun, L.G. (2006). An exploratory study of posttraumatic growth in children following a natural disaster. *American Journal of Orthopsychiatry, 76*(1), 65–69.

Fergusson, D.M., and Horwood, L.J. (2003). Resilience to childhood adversity: Results of a 21-year study. In S.S. Luthar (ed.), *Resilience and vulnerability: Adaptation in the context of childhood adversities* (pp. 1–25). New York: Cambridge University Press.

Ford, J.D., Courtois, C., van der Hart, O., Nijenhuis, E., and Steele, K. (2005). Treatment of complex posttraumatic self-dysregulation. *Journal of Traumatic Stress, 18*, 437–447.

Garmezy, N. (1985). Stress-resistant children: The search for protective factors. In J.E. Stevenson (ed.), *Recent research in developmental psychopathology: Journal of child psychology and psychiatry book supplement no. 4* (pp. 213–233). Oxford: Pergamon.

Layne, C.M., Warren, J., Shalev, A., and Watson, P. (2007). Risk, vulnerability, resistance, and resilience: Towards an integrative conceptualization of posttraumatic adaptation. In M.J. Friedman, T.M. Keane, and P.A. Resick (eds.), *Handbook of PTSD: Science and Practice* (pp. 497–520). New York: Guilford.

Milam, J.E., Ritt-Olson, A., and Unger, J.B. (2004). Posttraumatic growth among adolescents. *Journal of Adolescent Research, 19*(2), 192–204.

Payne, A.J., Joseph, S., and Tudway, J. (2007). Assimilation and accommodation processes following traumatic experiences. *Journal of Loss and Trauma, 12*(1), 73–89.

Rutter, M. (1985). Resilience in the face of adversity: Protective factors and resistance to psychiatric disorder. *British Journal of Psychiatry, 147*, 598–611.

Stein, D.J., Seedat, S., Iversen, A., and Wessely, S. (2007). Posttraumatic stress disorder: Medicine and politics. *Lancet, 369*, 139–144.

Tedeschi, R.G. (1999). Violence transformed: Posttraumatic growth in survivors and their societies. *Aggression and Violent Behavior, 4*(3), 319–341.

Zoellner, T., and Maercker, A. (2006). Posttraumatic growth in clinical psychology: A critical review and introduction of a two component model. *Clinical Psychology Review, 26*(5), 626–653.

Index

Page numbers followed by the letters 'F' and 'T' refer to Figures and Tables respectively.